To John and Ruth
Let's shoot for another 50

The FLSA – A User's Manual (Third Edition).

Aitchison, William Bruce, 1951 –

ISBN 1-880607-19-0
The FLSA – A User's Manual (Third Edition)

1. Fair Labor Standards Act
2. Wages
3. Overtime

THE FLSA: A USER'S MANUAL

(THIRD EDITION)

By Will Aitchison

ACKNOWLEDGEMENTS

The drama of updating a book on the FLSA is a shared one, with many able contributors to the final product. This book is a particularly difficult one to produce, what with numerous tables, a ton of regulatory references, and case law that seems to keep changing right up until the last minute.

Words of appreciation are owed to many in the LRIS family. The formatting of the book was grittily performed by three: Debbie Frields, the heart and soul of LRIS, Anya Dahab King, she of the Ethiopian names and amazing Access acumen, and Kim Litchman, whose return to working with us after a many-year absence is hugely appreciated. Proofreading any book is a critical and laborious project. Carol Green, whose incredible work as my assistant for the last nine years has enabled me to practice law, write books, and juggle half a dozen other things at the same time, was aided in the proofreading by Hank Armstrong, whose steady eyes have worked on numerous LRIS books.

In between sampling port wine, prowling through bookstores, and managing the process of yanking LRIS into the 21st century through his programming prowess and vision, Marc Fuller tracked down the various Internet references found in the book. Scott Preston, our law clerk, more than ably performed the incredibly onerous task of checking every single citation in the book, both for substance and for style.

To my wife, Valerie Fanning, I owe a special word of thanks. Her support as well as her good humor in her willingness to read the manuscripts of my books, tearing them apart for style and content, could not be more appreciated.

Will Aitchison
February, 2002

ABOUT THE AUTHOR

Will Aitchison is a Portland, Oregon attorney who has, over the course of his career, represented over 100 firefighter and law enforcement labor organizations in five western states.

Aitchison graduated from the University of Oregon (Honors College) in 1973, and received his Doctor of Jurisprudence Degree from the Georgetown University Law Center in Washington, DC in 1976. After two years of clerking for the chief justice of the Oregon Court of Appeals, Aitchison entered private practice in Portland, Oregon, and has been representing public safety labor organizations since that time. In addition to his private practice, Aitchison has served as both an arbitrator and a pro-tem district court judge, has contributed numerous articles to various periodicals, and has trained thousands of firefighters, administrators, and attorneys in the rights of firefighters.

Aitchison is the author of *The Rights of Law Enforcement Officers (Fourth Edition)*, *The Rights of Firefighters (Third Edition)*, *Model Law Enforcement Contract: A Labor Perspective (Third Edition)*, *A Model Firefighters Contract: A Labor Perspective,* and *Interest Arbitration (Second Edition)*, all published by the Labor Relations Information System. He has lectured on numerous occasions to management and labor groups throughout the country on topics concerning public sector collective bargaining and public safety personnel issues, and has served as an expert witness and consultant on matters pertaining to the rights of public safety officers.

TABLE OF CONTENTS

CHAPTER ONE

THE HISTORY BEHIND THE FLSA

A. The Enactment Of The Fair Labor Standards Act.

The Fair Labor Standards Act (referred to in this book as the "FLSA" or "the Act"), generally known as the "minimum wage law," was initially a product of the Depression years following 1929. Congress passed the FLSA in 1938 in one of a number of "New Deal" legislative packages proposed by the administration of President Franklin Roosevelt.

As initially enacted, the FLSA applied only to private sector employers, and specifically excluded from coverage the United States government, state governments, and local political subdivisions of state governments such as cities and counties. There were three major elements of the FLSA: (1) A requirement that all private employers pay a specified minimum wage to employees; (2) a requirement that employers pay employees who worked beyond a specified maximum number of hours per week at the rate of time and one-half their regular rate of pay; and (3) a prohibition on child labor.[1]

The general intent of Congress in passing the FLSA was fourfold. First, Congress intended to equalize wages among the various states, which at the time of the enactment of the FLSA had widely varying prevailing wage rates. Secondly, there existed a "public welfare" element of the FLSA, an element which stands even today as a national legislative declaration that the payment of wages below certain minimum levels is contrary to public policy. Third, Congress designed the FLSA to spread employment among different employees by placing financial pressure on employers through the overtime pay requirements.[2] Lastly, as noted by Professor Seth Harris in his comprehensive history of the passage of the FLSA, the intent of Congress was "to limit unfair price competition in product markets through the regulation of wages and hours in labor markets.[3] Given these intents, courts have held that the FLSA should not only be liberally construed, but that the provisions of the FLSA impose absolute non-waivable obligations upon employers to pay overtime compensation where it is required by the FLSA.[4]

Congress described the policies behind the FLSA in Section 202, the preface to the Act:

"(a) The Congress finds that the existence, in industries engaged in commerce or in the production of goods for commerce, of labor conditions detrimental to the maintenance of the minimum standard of living necessary for health, efficiency, and general well-being of workers (1) causes commerce and the channels and instrumentalities of commerce to be used to spread and perpetuate such labor conditions among the workers of the several States; (2) burdens commerce and the free flow of goods in commerce; (3) constitutes an unfair method of competition in commerce; (4) leads to labor disputes burdening and obstructing commerce and the free flow of goods in commerce; and (5) interferes with the orderly and fair marketing of goods in commerce. The Congress further finds that the employment of persons in domestic service in households affects commerce.

"(b) It is declared to be the policy of this Act, through the exercise by Congress of its power to regulate commerce among the several States and with foreign nations, to correct and as rapidly as practicable to eliminate the conditions above referred to in such industries without substantially curtailing employment or earning power."[5]

B. The Amendments To The FLSA Which Are Pertinent To Public Sector Employers.

The FLSA has been amended by Congress many times since 1938, with the amendments usually focusing on adjusting the minimum wage. The first amendments pertinent to public sector employers occurred in 1961, when the scope of the FLSA was significantly broadened. Though the 1961 amendments to the FLSA did not specifically apply the FLSA to public employers, they did expand the FLSA to "cover all employees of any 'enterprise' engaged in commerce or production for commerce." Prior to 1961, the FLSA was limited to employers (and employees) who were actually "engaged in commerce or in the production of goods for commerce." The 1961 amendments thus added "enterprise liability" as a basis for an employer's coverage under the FLSA, which subjected employers to coverage by the FLSA even though the employer was not directly engaged in interstate commerce.

The 1961 "enterprise liability" amendments took on greater significance in 1966, when the FLSA was first expanded to cover certain public employers. In 1966, Congress amended the FLSA to specifically apply to schools and hospitals, whether those institutions were in the public or private sector.[6]

The 1966 amendments to the FLSA were quickly challenged, resulting in the first of three decisions by the United States Supreme Court on the constitutionality of the application of the FLSA to state and local governments. In *Maryland v. Wirtz*,[7] the Supreme Court held that under the so-called Interstate Commerce Clause of the United States Constitution — which gives Congress the power to regulate interstate commerce — Congress had the authority to extend the coverage of the FLSA to state and local governments even in spite of the Tenth Amendment's preservation to the states of all authority not reserved for Congress elsewhere in the constitution. The crux of the Supreme Court's decision, as stated by Justice John Harlan, was that "it is clear that the federal government, when acting within a delegated power, may override countervailing state interests whether these be described as 'governmental' or 'proprietary' in nature."

Subsequent to the *Maryland v. Wirtz* decision, Congress did not again amend the FLSA until 1974. The 1974 amendments dramatically expanded the scope of coverage of the FLSA by including public agencies within the FLSA's definition of employers covered by the law. The 1974 amendments also expanded the definition of "commerce" to specifically include "an activity of a public agency."[8] Congress defined a public agency as including not only the United States government, but also state and local governmental bodies.[9]

C. The *National League Of Cities* And *Garcia* Cases.

As was the case with the 1966 amendments to the FLSA, the 1974 amendments were immediately challenged, this time by the National League of Cities in a case which produced the second Supreme Court decision on the question of whether the FLSA could be constitutionally applied to the states and local governments. In *National League of Cities v. Usery*, the Supreme Court reversed the thrust of its holding in *Maryland v. Wirtz* and expressly held that the 1974 amendments to the FLSA were beyond the powers of Congress to enact under the Interstate Commerce Clause of the Constitution. The essence of the Court's opinion, as expressed by now-Chief Justice William Rehnquist, was that "this exercise of congressional authority does not comport with the federal system of government embodied in the Constitution. We hold that insofar as the challenged amendments operate to directly displace the States' freedom to structure * * * operations in areas of traditional governmental functions, they are not within the authority granted Congress by Article I, Section 8, Cl. 3."[10]

Immediately after *National League of Cities*, various federal agencies, including the Wage and Hour Division of the Department of Labor, were faced with the difficulty of determining what were not "traditional" governmental functions — which under the Supreme Court's holding in *National League of Cities* could not be regulated by the Federal Government — and what governmental functions were traditional. In 1979, the Department issued an opinion that the operation of a mass transit district by the San Antonio Metropolitan Transit Authority was not a "traditional" governmental function, and that thus the Transit Authority was subject to the strictures of the FLSA.

The Transit Authority followed by filing a petition for declaratory relief in Federal District Court, seeking to have the Department of Labor's efforts to apply the FLSA to it declared unconstitutional under the theories of *National League of Cities*. On the same day, several of the Transit Authority's employees, including Joe Garcia, filed *Garcia v. San Antonio Metropolitan Transit Authority*, a suit seeking the payment of overtime wages under the FLSA.

The *Garcia* case was initially resolved in favor of the Transit Authority at the trial court level. However, while an appeal to the Supreme Court was pending, the Supreme Court rendered a decision in *Transportation Union v. Long Island Rail Road Company*,[11] where the Court held that a commuter rail service provided by a state-owned company did not constitute a "traditional governmental function" and thus did not enjoy constitutional immunity from federal regulation under *National League of Cities*. The Supreme Court vacated the District Court's first decision in the *Garcia* case and remanded the case back to the District Court for reconsideration in light of the *Transportation Union* case.

On remand, the District Court adhered to its original holding that the Transit Authority was not subject to regulation under the FLSA, and an appeal to the Supreme Court followed. Initially, the focus of the case seemed narrow, directed solely at the question of whether providing a mass transit service was a "traditional" governmental function under the *National League of Cities* case. The Supreme Court was not through reversing itself on the FLSA, however. After the *Garcia* case had already been orally argued before the Court, the Court requested the parties in the case to submit briefs on the question of whether the whole of the *National League of Cities* case should be reconsidered. On February 19, 1985, the Supreme Court resolved the six-year dispute between the Transit District and its employees in favor of the positions taken by the Transit District's employees.

In *Garcia*, the Court reexamined and overruled its decision in *National League of Cities*, discarding the legal tests erected in *National League of Cities* as not containing a "proper understanding of congressional power under the Commerce Clause."[12] Once again, the FLSA was made applicable to state and local governmental bodies.

The *Garcia* decision, though it caught many in the public sector by surprise, was not entirely unexpected by court watchers. In its prior decisions, *Maryland v. Wirtz* and *National League of Cities v. Usery*, the Supreme Court was badly divided. *National League of Cities v. Usery* resulted in a 5-4 vote. Only two years prior to the *Garcia* decision, the Supreme Court held that federal age discrimination laws could be constitutionally applied to the states.[13] Furthermore, there was clear and constant grumbling from lower federal courts that, quite apart from the results reached in *National League of Cities*, the constitutional tests erected in *National League of Cities* were unworkable.[14]

Nonetheless, even though the *Garcia* decision was not applied retroactively,[15] the immediate application of the FLSA to state and local governments sent a shock wave through public sector employment relations throughout the country. As was succinctly put by one court, the application of the FLSA means that the FLSA's obligation to pay overtime compensation and liquidated damages is immediately read into and becomes part of every employment contract between an employer and its employees.[16] In the public sector, this meant that virtually every employee, with the exception of executive, administrative and professional employees, and other employees who were either elected officials or on the personal staff of elected officials,[17] fell under the coverage of the FLSA.

D. The 1985 Amendments To The FLSA.

Following the *Garcia* decision, Congress was literally besieged by representatives of public sector employers and labor organizations to enact some sort of amendments to the FLSA to cushion the shock of the application of the FLSA. In November 1985, Congress responded by legislating a number of amendments to the FLSA. The most significant of the changes liberalized the FLSA's treatment of compensatory time off and altered how the FLSA deals with individuals who serve as volunteers to public sector agencies. In addition to changing some provisions of the FLSA, Congress also delayed by one year, to April 15, 1986, the date on which the FLSA applied to public sector agencies.[18]

E. Post-*Garcia* FLSA Litigation In The Supreme Court.

Because of the controversial nature of the *Garcia* decision, many expected that the Supreme Court's decision that the FLSA could constitutionally be applied to the public sector would be short-lived. Three factors fed this belief. First, four of the five justices making up the majority vote in *Garcia* retired over the course of the next ten years. Second, William Rehnquist, the Court's most vituperative critic of *Garcia*, became the chief justice of the Supreme Court. Third, in several decisions, the Supreme Court began to side more and more with "states' rights" arguments, striking down or limiting the application of federal laws that applied to state and local governmental bodies.[19]

The most significant effort by public sector employers to convince the Supreme Court to reverse *Garcia* occurred in 1997 in the case of *Auer v. Robbins. Auer* involved a claim by St. Louis, Missouri police sergeants that they were entitled to receive overtime under the FLSA. Numerous "friend of the court" or "*amicus curiae*" briefs were filed in the case by employer groups such as the International Association of Chiefs of Police. Many of the briefs urged the Supreme Court in the strongest of terms to reverse *Garcia*. Nonetheless, in its unanimous decision in *Auer*, the Supreme Court brushed aside arguments that the FLSA should not be applied to states and local governmental bodies.[20]

The Supreme Court did subsequently restrict the applicability of the FLSA in *Alden v. State of Maine*, holding that the Tenth Amendment to the Constitution barred state employees from bringing private causes of action against their employers either in federal or state court, unless the state had waived its "sovereign immunity" from such a suit.[21] Most cases decided subsequent to *Alden* have held that states have not waived their sovereign immunity from suit under the FLSA, and that their employees must rely on the Department of Labor to bring FLSA actions on their behalf.[22]

F. General Principles Guiding The Interpretation Of The FLSA.

Courts have stated on many occasions that the FLSA constitutes humanitarian legislation which is designed to remedy specific social and economic difficulties.[23] As such, the FLSA is liberally construed by courts in order to apply the law to the furthest reaches possible consistent with the intent of Congress in passing the FLSA.[24] Courts have even termed that "breadth of coverage is vital to the Act's mission."[25] Along these lines, courts have held that exemptions from coverage under the FLSA are narrowly construed, with the burden resting on the employer to prove that an employee is in fact exempt from the FLSA's broad coverage.[26]

.

NOTES TO CHAPTER 1

[1] *See Generally*, Wayne Outten & Adam Klein, *The FLSA: Hot Topics*, VLR9913 ALI-ABA 123 (March 28, 2000).

[2] *See Walling v. Helmerich & Payne, Inc.*, 323 U.S. 37 (1944).

[3] Seth Harris, *Conceptions of Fairness and the Fair Labor Standards Act*, 18 Hofstra Lab. & Employment L.J. 19 (Fall 2000).

[4] *See D.A. Schulte, Inc. v. Gangi*, 328 U.S. 108 (1946); *Ackler v. Cowlitz County*, 248 F.3d 1169 (9th Cir. 2001); *Reich v. Stewart*, 121 F.3d 400 (8th Cir. 1997).

[5] 29 U.S.C. §202.

[6] 29 U.S.C. §203(d)(1970)(current version at 29 U.S.C. §203(d)(1988).

[7] *Maryland v. Wirtz*, 392 U.S. 183 (1968).

[8] 29 U.S.C. §203(s)(1)(c).

[9] 29 U.S.C. §203(x); *see Beebe v. United States*, 640 F.2d 1283 (Ct.Cl. 1981).

[10] *National League of Cities v. Usery*, 426 U.S. 833 (1976).

[11] *United Transp. Union v. Long Island Co.*, 455 U.S. 678 (1982); *see Garcia v. San Antonio Metro. Transit Auth.*, 469 U.S. 528 (1985).

[12] *Garcia v. San Antonio Metro. Transit Auth.*, 469 U.S. 528 (1985).

[13] *EEOC v. Wyoming*, 460 U.S. 226 (1983). *EEOC v. Wyoming* has been overruled by the Supreme Court in the combination of the Court's decisions in *Seminole Tribe of Florida v. State of Florida*, 517 U.S. 44 (1996)

and *Kimel v. Florida Board of Regents*, 528 U.S. 62 (2000).

[14] *See Bonnette v. California Health and Welfare Agency*, 704 F.2d 1465 (9th Cir. 1983); *Williams v. Eastside Mental Health Center, Inc.*, 669 F.2d 671 (11th Cir. 1982); *Amersbach v. City of Cleveland*, 598 F.2d 1033 (6th Cir. 1979).

[15] *Brooks v. Lincolnwood*, 620 F.Supp. 24 (N.D.Ill. 1985).

[16] *Northwestern Yeast Co. v. Broutin*, 133 F.2d 628 (6th Cir. 1943); *Local 2961, IAFF v. City of Jacksonville*, 685 F.Supp. 513 (E.D.N.C. 1987).

[17] The executive, administrative and professional employee exemptions are discussed in Chapter 8. Section 203(e)(2)(C) of the FLSA establishes the "elected official" and "personal staff" exemptions from FLSA coverage. In *Barfield v. Madison County, Miss.*, 984 F.Supp. 491 (S.D.Miss. 1997), the Court held that a sheriff was an "elected official" not covered by the FLSA. *See Biggs v. Logan Valley Board of Commissioners*, 211 F.3d 1277 (10th Cir. 2000)(undersheriff on "personal staff" of sheriff and not covered by FLSA); *Rodriguez v. Township of Holiday Lakes*, 866 F.Supp. 1012 (N.D.Tex. 1994)(police chief on "personal staff" of city council). Markedly less persuasively, in *Nichols v. Hurley*, 921 F.2d 1101 (10th Cir. 1990), the Court held that at-will deputy sheriffs, who served at the pleasure of the sheriff, were exempt from coverage under the FLSA on the grounds that they were on the personal staff of the sheriff. *Contra Baker v. Stone County, Mo.*, 41 F.Supp.2d 965 (W.D.Mo. 1999) (deputies not part of "personal staff" of sheriff and thus covered by FLSA); *Oliver v. Layrisson*, 3 WH Cases2d 316 (E.D.La. 1996)(deputy sheriff not part of "personal staff"); *Smith v. Upson County, Ga.*, 859 F.Supp. 1504 (M.D.Ga. 1994)(investigator not on "personal staff" of sheriff).

[18] *Hendrix v. City of Yazoo*, 911 F.2d 1102 (5th Cir. 1990).

[19] During this time period, lower courts continued to follow the *Garcia* decision, rejecting arguments that the application of the FLSA to state and local governmental bodies violated the Tenth Amendment. *Reich v. New York*, 3 F.3d 581 (2nd Cir. 1993); *Adams v. Department of Juvenile Justice*, 3 WH Cases2d 295 (S.D.N.Y. 1996); *Jackson v. Kentucky*, 892 F.Supp. 923 (E.D.Ky. 1995).

[20] *Auer v. Robbins*, 519 U.S. 452 (1997).

[21] *Alden v. Maine*, 527 U.S. 706 (1999). *See Seminole Tribe of Florida v. State of Florida*, 517 U.S. 44 (1996).

[22] *E.g. King v. State of Nebraska*, 614 N.W.2d 341 (Neb. 2000); *Allen v. Fauver*, 768 A.2d 1055 (N.J. 2001); *Whittington v. State Dept. of Public Safety*, 4 P.3d 668 (N.M. 2000); *Lawson v. University of Tennessee*, 2000 WL 116312 (Tenn. App. 2000); *Griffin v. Virginia Department of Transportation*, 2000 WL 621091 (Va. 2000). *Contra Hartman v. Regents of the University of Colorado*, 22 P.3d 524 (Colo.App. 2000).

[23] *Arnold v. Ben Kanowsky*, 361 U.S. 388 (1960); *A. H. Phillips, Inc. v. Walling*, 324 U.S. 490 (1945).

[24] *Klem v. County of Santa Clara, California*, 208 F.3d 1085 (9th Cir. 2000); *Wilson v. City of Charlotte*, 717 F.Supp. 408 (W.D.N.C. 1989).

[25] *Hodgson v. University Club Tower*, 466 F.2d 745 (10th Cir. 1972); *see Mitchell v. Lublin McGaughy & Associates*, 358 U.S. 207 (1959); *Powell v. United States Cartridge Co.*, 339 U.S. 497 (1950).

[26] *Corning Glass Works v. Brennan*, 417 U.S. 188 (1974)("the general rule [is] that the application of an exemption under the [FLSA] is a matter of affirmative defense on which the employer has the burden of proof"); *Clark v. J. M. Benson Co., Inc.*, 789 F.2d 282

(4th Cir. 1986)(employer bears full burden of persuasion for the facts requisite to an exemption).

CHAPTER TWO
THE FLSA'S OVERTIME PROVISIONS

A. The Text Of The FLSA.

Most of the operative overtime provisions of the FLSA are found in Section 7 of the law. Since the provisions of the FLSA are relatively short, they are set out in full below. For the reader's ease, a brief explanatory title has been added to each major section of the FLSA.

Section 7(a). Basic Overtime Requirements and Maximum Work Hours.

"(1) Except as otherwise provided in this section, no employer shall employ any of his employees who in any workweek is engaged in commerce or in the production of goods for commerce, or is employed in an enterprise engaged in commerce or in the production of goods for commerce, for a workweek longer than forty hours unless such employee receives compensation for his employment in excess of the hours above specified at a rate not less than one and one-half times the regular rate at which he is employed.

"(2) No employer shall employ any of his employees who in any workweek is engaged in commerce or in the production of goods for commerce, or is employed in an enterprise engaged in commerce or in the production of goods for commerce, and who in such workweek is brought within the purview of this subsection by the amendments made to this Act by the Fair Labor Standards Amendments of 1966 —

"(A) for a workweek longer than forty-four hours during the first year from the effective date of the Fair Labor Standards Amendments of 1966,

"(B) for a workweek longer than forty-two hours during the second year from such date, or

"(C) for a workweek longer than forty hours after the expiration of the second year from such date, unless such employee receives compensation for his employment in excess of the hours above specified at a rate not less than one and one-half times the regular rate at which he is employed."

Section 7(b). Agreements Certified by the NLRB.

"(b) No employer shall be deemed to have violated subsection (a) by employing any employee for a workweek in excess of that specified in such subsection without paying the compensation for overtime employment prescribed therein if such employee is so employed —

"(1) in pursuance of an agreement, made as a result of collective bargaining by representatives of employees certified as bona fide by the National Labor Relations Board, which provides that no employee shall be employed more than one thousand and forty hours during any period of twenty-six consecutive weeks; or

"(2) in pursuance of an agreement, made as a result of collective bargaining by representatives of employees certified as bona fide by the National Labor Relations Board, which provides that during a specified period of fifty-two consecutive weeks the employee shall be employed not more than two thousand two hundred and forty hours and shall be guaranteed not less than one thousand eight hundred and forty hours (or not less than forty-six weeks at the normal number of hours worked per week, but not less than thirty hours per week) and not more than two thousand and eighty hours of employment for which he shall receive compensation for all hours guaranteed or worked at rates not less than those applicable under the agreement to the work performed and for all hours in excess of the guaranty which are also in excess of the maximum workweek applicable to such employee under subsection (a) or two thousand and eighty in such period at rates not less than one and one-half times the regular rate at which he is employed; or

"(3) by an independently owned and controlled local enterprise (including an enterprise with more than one bulk storage establishment) engaged in the whole-sale or bulk distribution of petroleum products if —

"(A) the annual gross volume of sales of such enterprises is less than $1,000,000 exclusive of excise taxes,

"(B) more than 75 per centum of such enterprise's annual dollar volume of sales is made within the State in which such enterprise is located, and

"(C) not more than 25 per centum of the annual dollar volume of sales of such enterprise is to customers who are engaged in the bulk distribution of such products for resale,

"and such employee receives compensation for employment in excess of forty hours in any workweek at a rate not less than one and one-half times the minimum wage rate applicable to him under section 6, and if such employee receives compensation for employment in excess of twelve hours in any workday, or for employment in excess of fifty-six hours in any workweek, as the case may be, at a rate not less than one and one-half times the regular rate at which he is employed."

Sections 7(c) and (d) have been repealed.

Section 7(e). The Regular Rate of Pay.

"(e) As used in this section the 'regular rate' at which an employee is employed shall be deemed to include all remuneration for employment paid to, or on behalf of, the employee, but shall not be deemed to include —

"(1) sums paid as gifts; payments in the nature of gifts made at Christmas time or on other special occasions as a reward for service, the amounts of which are not measured by or dependent on hours worked, production, or efficiency;

"(2) payments made for special occasional periods when no work is performed due to vacation, holiday, illness, failure of the employer to provide sufficient work, or other similar cause, reasonable payments for traveling expenses, or other expenses, incurred by an employee in the furtherance of his employer's interests and properly reimbursable by the employer; and other similar payments to an employee which are not made as compensation for his hours of employment;

"(3) sums paid in recognition of services performed during a given period if either, (a) both the fact that payment is to be made and the amount of the payment are determined at the sole discretion of the employer at or near the end of the period and not pursuant to any prior contract, agreement, or promise causing the employee to expect such payments regularly; or (b) the payments are made pursuant to a bona fide profit-sharing plan or trust, or bona fide thrift or savings plan, meeting the requirements of the Secretary of Labor set forth in appropriate regulations which he shall issue, having due regard, among other relevant factors, to the extent to which the amounts paid to the employee are determined without regard to hours of work, production, or efficiency; or (c) the payments are talent fees (as such talent fees are defined and delimited by regulations of the Secretary) paid to performers, including announcers, on radio and television programs;

"(4) contributions irrevocably made by an employer to a trustee or third person pursuant to a bona fide plan for providing old-age, retirement, life, accident, or health insurance or similar benefits for employees;

"(5) extra compensation provided by a premium rate paid for certain hours worked by the employee in any day or workweek because such hours are hours worked in excess of eight in a day or in excess of the maximum workweek applicable to such employee under subsection (a) or in excess of the employee's normal working hours or regular working hours, as the case may be;

"(6) extra compensation provided by a premium rate paid for work by the employee on Saturdays, Sundays, holidays, or regular days of rest, or on the sixth or seventh day of the workweek, where such premium rate is not less than one and one-half times the rate established in good faith for like work performed in non-overtime hours on other days; or

"(7) extra compensation provided by a premium rate paid to the employee, in pursuance of an applicable employment contract or collective-bargaining agreement, for work outside of the hours established in good faith by the contract or agreement as the basic, normal, or regular workday (not exceeding eight hours) or workweek (not exceeding the maximum workweek applicable to such employee under subsection (a) of this section), where such premium rate is not less than one and one-half times the rate established in good faith by the contract or agreement for like work performed during such workday or workweek."

Section 7(f). Regular Rate Where Irregular Hours Necessary.

"(f) No employer shall be deemed to have violated subsection (a) by employing any employee for a workweek in excess of the maximum workweek applicable to such employee under subsection (a) if such employee is employed pursuant to a bona fide individual contract, or pursuant to an agreement made as a result of collective bargaining by representatives of employees, if the duties of such employee necessitate irregular hours of work, and the contract or agreement (1) specifies a regular rate of pay not less than the minimum hourly rate provided in subsection (a) or (b) or section 6 (whichever may be applicable) and compensation at not less than one and one-half times such rate for all hours worked in excess of such maximum workweek and (2) provides a weekly guaranty of pay for not more than sixty hours based on the rates so specified."

Section 7(g). Employees Working on a Piece Rate Basis.

"(g) No employer shall be deemed to have violated subsection (a) by employing any employee for a workweek in excess of the maximum workweek applicable to such employee under such subsection if, pursuant to an agreement or understanding arrived at between the employer and the employee before performance of the work, the amount paid to the employee for the number of hours worked by him in such workweek in excess of the maximum workweek applicable to such employee under such subsection —

"(1) in the case of an employee employed at piece rates, is computed at piece rates not less than one and one-half times the bona fide piece rates applicable to the same work when performed during non-overtime hours; or

"(2) in the case of an employee performing two or more kinds of work for which different hourly or piece rates have been established, is computed at rates not less than one and one-half times such bona fide rates applicable to the same work when performed during non-overtime hours; or

"(3) is computed at a rate not less than one and one-half times the rate established by such agreement or understanding as the basic rate to be used in computing overtime compensation thereunder: Provided, that the rate so established shall be authorized by regulation by the Administrator as being substantially equivalent to the average hourly earnings of the employee, exclusive of overtime premiums, in the particular work over a representative period of time;

"and if (1) the employee's average hourly earnings for the workweek exclusive of payments described in paragraphs (1) through (7) of subsection (e) are not less than the minimum hourly rate required by applicable law, and (2) extra overtime compensation is properly computed and paid on other forms of additional pay required to be included in computing in the regular rate."

Section 7(h). Extra Compensation.

"(h) Extra compensation paid as described in paragraphs (5), (6), and (7) of subsection (e) shall be creditable toward overtime compensation payable pursuant to this section."

Section 7(i). Employees Receiving Commissions.

"(i) No employer shall be deemed to have violated subsection (a) by employing any employee of a retail or service establishment for a workweek in excess of the applicable workweek specified therein, if (1) the regular rate of pay of such employee is in excess of one and one-half times the minimum hourly rate applicable to him under section 6, and (2) more than half his compensation for a representative period (not less than one month) represents commissions on goods or services. In determining the proportion of compensation representing commissions, all earnings resulting from the application of a bona fide commission rate shall be deemed commissions on goods or services without regard to whether the computed commissions exceed the draw or guaranty.

Section 7(j). Hospital Employees.

"(j) No employer engaged in the operation of a hospital or an establishment which is an institution primarily engaged in the care of the sick, the aged, or the mentally ill or defective who reside on the premises shall be deemed to have violated subsection (a) if, pursuant to an agreement or understanding arrived at between the employer and the employee before performance of the work, a work period of fourteen consecutive days is accepted in lieu of the workweek of seven consecutive days for purposes of overtime computation and if, for his employment in excess of eight hours in any workday and in excess of eighty hours in such fourteen-day period, the employee receives compensation at a rate not less than one and one-half times the regular rate at which he is employed."

Section 7(k). Law Enforcement and Fire Protection Employees.

"(k) No public agency shall be deemed to have violated subsection (a) with respect to the employment of any employee in fire protection activities or any employee in law enforcement activities (including security personnel in correctional institutions) if —

"(1) in a work period of 28 consecutive days the employee receives for tours of duty which in the aggregate exceed the lesser of (A) 216 hours, or (B) the average number of hours (as determined by the Secretary pursuant to section 6(c)(3) of the Fair Labor Standards Amendments of 1974) in tours of duty of employees engaged in such activities in work periods of 28 consecutive days in calendar year 1975 or

"(2) in the case of such an employee to whom a work period of at least 7 but less than 28 days applies, in his work period the employee receives for tours of duty which in the aggregate exceed a number of consecutive days in his work period as 216 hours (or if lower, the number of hours referred to in clause (B) of paragraph (1) bears to 28 days,

"compensation at a rate not less than one and one-half times the regular rate at which he is employed."

Section 7(l). Domestic Service Employees.

"(l) No employer shall employ any employee in domestic service in one or more households for a workweek longer than forty hours unless such employee receives compensation for such employment in accordance with subsection (a)."

Section 7(m). Tobacco Employees.

"(m) For a period or periods of not more than fourteen workweeks in the aggregate in any calendar year, any employer may employ any employee for a workweek in excess of that specified in subsection (a) without paying the compensation for overtime employment prescribed in such subsection, if such employee —

"(1) is employed by such employer —

"(A) to provide services (including stripping and grading) necessary and incidental to the sale at auction of green leaf tobacco of type 11, 12, 13, 14, 21, 22, 23, 24, 31, 35, 36, or 37 (as such types are defined by the Secretary of Agriculture), or in auction sale, buying, handling, stemming, redrying, packing, and storing of such tobacco,

"(B) in auction sale, buying, handling, sorting, grading, packing or storing green leaf tobacco or type 32 (as such type is defined by the Secretary of Agriculture), or

"(C) in auction sale, buying, handling, stripping, sorting, grading, sizing, packing or stemming prior to packing, of perishable cigar leaf tobacco of type 41, 42, 43, 44, 45, 46, 51, 52, 53, 54, 55, 61, or 62 (as such types are defined by the Secretary of Agriculture); and

"(2) receives for —

"(A) such employment by such employer which is in excess of ten hours in any workday, and

"(B) such employment by such employer which is in excess of forty-eight hours in any workweek, compensation at a rate not less than one and one-half times the regular rate at which he is employed.

"An employer who receives an exemption under this subsection shall not be eligible for any other exemption under this section."

Section 7(n). Streetcar and Bus Employees.

"(n) in the case of an employee of an employer engaged in the business of operating a street, suburban or interurban electric railway, or local trolley or motorbus carrier (regardless of whether or not such railway or carrier is public or private or operated for profit or not for profit), in determining the hours of employment of such an employee to which the rate prescribed by subsection (a) applies there shall be excluded the hours such employee was employed in charter activities by such employer if (1) the employee's employment in such activities was pursuant to an agreement or understanding with his employer arrived at before engaging in such employment, and (2) if employment in such activities is not part of such employee's regular employment."

Section 7(o). Compensatory Time Off.

"(o)(1) Employees of a public agency which is a State, a political subdivision of a State, or an interstate governmental agency may receive, in accordance with this subsection and in lieu of overtime compensation, compensatory time off at a rate not less than one and one-half hours for each hour of employment for which overtime compensation is required by this section.

"(2) A public agency may provide compensatory time under paragraph (1) only—

"(A) pursuant to—

"(i) applicable provisions of a collective bargaining agreement, memorandum of understanding, or any other agreement between the public agency and representatives of such employees; or

"(ii) in the case of employees not covered by subclause (i), an agreement or understanding arrived at between the employer and employee before the performance of the work; and

"(B) if the employee has not accrued compensatory time in excess of the limit applicable to the employee prescribed by paragraph (3).

"In the case of employees described in clause (A)(ii) hired prior to April 15, 1986, the regular practice in effect on April 15, 1986, with respect to compensatory time off for such employees in lieu of the receipt of overtime compensation shall constitute an agreement or understanding under such clause (A)(ii). Except as provided in the previous sentence, the provision of compensatory time off to such employees for hours worked after April 14 1986, shall be in accordance with this subsection.

"(3)(A) If the work of an employee for which compensatory time may be provided included work in a public safety activity, an emergency response activity, or a seasonal activity, the employee engaged in such work may accrue not more than 480 hours of compensatory time for hours worked after April 15, 1986. If such work was any other work, the employee engaged in such work may accrue not more than 240 hours of compensatory time for hours worked after April 15, 1986. Any such employee who, after April 15, 1986, has accrued 480 or 240 hours, as the case may be, of compensatory time off shall, for additional overtime hours of work, be paid overtime compensation.

"(B) If compensation is paid to an employee for accrued compensatory time off, such compensation shall be paid at the regular rate earned by the employee at the time the employee receives such payment.

"(4) An employee who has accrued compensatory time off authorized to be provided under paragraph (1) shall, upon termination of employment, be paid for the unused compensatory time at a rate of compensation not less than —

"(A) the average regular rate received by such employee during the last 3 years of the employee's employment, or

"(B) the final regular rate received by such employee, whichever is higher.

"(5) An employee of a public agency which is a State, political subdivision of a State, or an interstate governmental agency —

"(A) who has accrued compensatory time off authorized to be provided under paragraph (1), and

"(B) who has requested the use of such compensatory time, shall be permitted by the employee's employer to use such time within a reasonable period after making the request if the use of the compensatory time does not unduly disrupt the operations of the public agency.

"(6) For purposes of this subsection —

"(A) the term 'overtime compensation' means the compensation required by subsection (a), and

"(B) the terms 'compensatory time' and 'compensatory time off' mean hours during which an employee is not working, which are not counted as hours worked during the applicable workweek or other work period for purposes of overtime compensation, and for which the employee is compensated at the employee's regular rate."

Section 7(p). Public Employees and Volunteer and Off-Duty Work.

"(p)(1) If an individual who is employed by a State, political subdivision of a State, or an interstate governmental agency in fire protection or law enforcement activities (including activities of security personnel in correctional institutions) and who, solely at such individual's option, agrees to be employed on a special detail by a separate or independent employer in fire protection, law enforcement, or related activities, the hours such individual was employed by such separate and independent employer shall be excluded by the public agency employing such individual in the calculation of the hours for which the employee is entitled to overtime compensation under this section if the public agency —

"(A) requires that its employees engaged in fire protection, law enforcement, or security activities be hired by a separate and independent employer to perform the special detail,

"(B) facilitates the employment of such employees by a separate and independent employer, or

"(C) otherwise affects the condition of employment of such employees by a separate and independent employer.

"(2) If an employee of a public agency which is a State, political subdivision of a State, or an interstate governmental agency undertakes, on an occasional or sporadic basis and solely at the employee's option, part-time employment for the public agency which is in a different capacity from any capacity in which the employee is regularly employed with the public agency, the hours such employee was employed in performing the different employment shall be excluded by the public agency in the calculation of the hours for which the employee is entitled to overtime compensation under this section.

"(3) If an individual who is employed in any capacity by a public agency which is a State, political subdivision of a State, or an interstate governmental agency, agrees, with the approval of the public agency and solely at the option of such individual, to substitute during scheduled work hours for another individual who is employed by such agency in the same capacity, the hours such employee worked as a substitute shall be excluded by the public agency in the calculation of the hours for which the employee is entitled to overtime compensation under this section."

B. Exemptions From FLSA Coverage.

Section 213(a) of the FLSA contains the FLSA's basic exclusions from coverage, which deem ineligible for overtime those employees who meet the tests established by Congress for executive, administrative, and professional employees:

"(a) Minimum wage and maximum hour requirements. The provisions of sections 206 (except section 6(d) in the case of paragraph (1) of this subsection) and 7 [29 USCS §§ 206, 207] shall not apply with respect to:

"any employee employed in a bona fide executive, administrative, or professional capacity (including any employee employed in the capacity of academic administrative personnel or teacher in elementary or secondary schools), or in the capacity of outside salesman (as such terms are defined and delimited from time to time by regulations of the Secretary, subject to the provisions of the Administrative Procedure Act except than [that] an employee of a retail or service establishment shall not be excluded from the definition of employee employed in a bona fide executive or administrative capacity because of the number of hours in his workweek which he devotes to activities not directly or closely related to the performance of executive or administrative activities, if less than 40 per centum of his hours worked in the workweek are devoted to such activities) * * *

C. The Portal-To-Portal Act.

In 1947, Congress enacted the Portal-to-Portal Act, designed to reduce an employer's liability for an employee's activities occurring before and after the normal workday. The provisions of the Portal-to-Portal Act, found in 29 U.S.C. §254, *et seq.*, are as follows:

"(a) Except as provided in subsection (b), no employer shall be subject to any liability or punishment under the Fair Labor Standards Act of 1938, as amended, * * * on account of the failure of such employer to pay an employee minimum wages, or to pay an employee overtime compensation, for or on account of any of the following activities of such employee engaged in on or after the date of the enactment of this Act:

"(1) Walking, riding, or traveling to and from the actual place of performance of the principal activity or activities which such employee is employed to perform, and

"(2) Activities which are preliminary to or postliminary to said principal activity or activities which occur either prior to the time on any particular workday at which such employee commences, or subsequent to the time on any particular workday at which he ceases, such principal activity or activities. For purposes of this subsection, the use of an employer's vehicle for travel by an employee and activities performed by an employee which are incidental to the use of such vehicle for commuting shall not be considered part of the employee's principal activities if the use of such vehicle for travel is within the normal commuting area for the employer's business or establishment and the use of the employer's vehicle is subject to an agreement on the part of the employer and the employee or representative of such employee.

"(b) Notwithstanding the provisions of subsection (a) which relieve an employer from liability and punishment with respect to an activity, the employer shall not be so relieved if such activity is compensable by either:

"(1) An express provision of a written or non-written contract in effect, at the time of such activity, between such employee, his agent, or collective-bargaining representative and his employer; or

"(2) A custom or practice in effect, at the time of such activity, at the establishment or other place where such employee is employed, covering such activity, not inconsistent with a written or non-written contract, in effect at the time of such activity, between such employee, his agent, or collective-bargaining representative and his employer.

"(c) For the purpose of subsection (b), an activity shall be considered as compensable under such contract provision or such custom or practice only when it is engaged in during the portion of the day with respect to which it is so made compensable.

"(d) In the application of the minimum wage and overtime compensation provisions of the Fair Labor Standards Act of 1938, as amended, * * * in determining the time for which an employer employs an employee with respect to walking, riding, traveling, or other preliminary or postliminary activities described in subsection (a) of this section, there shall be counted all that time, but only that time, during which the employee engages in any such activity which is compensable within the meaning of subsections (b) and (c) of this section."

D. The Regulations Promulgated Under The FLSA.

The Wage and Hour Division of the Department of Labor (referred to in this book as the "DOL") is charged with the responsibility of enforcing and administering the FLSA. Most of the policies of the DOL are expressed through regulations which are contained in Volume 29 of the Code of Federal Regulations, though the DOL also issues opinion letters and policy statements from time to time. Generally speaking, while the rulings, interpretations and opinions of the DOL are not controlling on courts, they are given great weight in judicial opinions construing the provisions of the FLSA.[1] The views of the DOL are not always credited; on one occasion, even the Supreme Court refused to adhere to the DOL's regulations when it found the regulations to be "legally untenable."[2]

In its most recent ruling involving the FLSA, *Auer v. Robbins*, the Supreme Court accorded great deference to the DOL's interpretation of the FLSA. At issue in *Auer* was the interpretation of when a high-ranking employee is "salaried" as the term is used in the FLSA and thus is potentially exempt from FLSA coverage. The Supreme Court relied on the judgment of the DOL on matters involving the interpretation and application of the FLSA. The Secretary of Labor, in an *amicus* brief filed at the request of the Court, interprets the salary-basis test to deny exempt status when employees are covered by a policy that permits disciplining or other deductions in pay "as a practical matter * * * Because the salary-basis test is a creature of the Secretary's own regulations, his interpretation of it is, under our jurisprudence, controlling unless 'plainly erroneous or inconsistent with the regulation.'"[3]

In addition to formal regulations, the DOL has published a series of letters offering opinions to employers as to how the FLSA would likely apply to a given factual situation. The DOL's opinion letters carefully state that they respond only to the particular questions asked by an employer, do not establish the DOL's policy on the issue, and do not have status of law with penalties for non-compliance. For these reasons, while opinion letters may be of some assistance to a court in considering the interpretation of a particular provision of the FLSA, they do not have nearly the same force and effect as the DOL's formal regulations.[4]

E. What Public Sector Agencies Are Covered By The FLSA?

As a result of the 1974 amendments to the Act, the FLSA applies to states, cities, counties, fire districts, and other special districts. There are several narrow classes of exemptions to the FLSA's public sector coverage, with the law excluding from coverage any employee:

"(i) who is not subject to the civil service laws of the State, political subdivision, or agency which employs him; <u>and</u>

"(ii) who - (I) holds a public elective office of that State, political subdivision, or agency, (II) is selected by the holder of such an office to be a member of his personal staff, (III) is appointed by such an officeholder to serve on a policymaking level, (IV) is an immediate adviser to such an officeholder with respect to the constitutional or legal powers of his office, or (V) is an employee in the legislative branch or legislative body of that State, political subdivision, or agency and is not employed by the legislative library of such State, political subdivision, or agency."[5]

Several questions have arisen concerning whether the FLSA can be applied to county sheriffs' offices, which historically have a great deal of autonomy under state law, or whether deputy sheriffs are members of the "personal staff" of the sheriff who are exempt from FLSA coverage. To date, the courts considering the issue have held that the FLSA can legally be applied to county sheriff offices and deputy sheriffs.[6]

F. The Time For Payment of Overtime.

Under the FLSA, overtime must be paid in a timely fashion. As Section 778.106 of the DOL's regulations describes, an employer must pay overtime as soon as practicable:

"There is no requirement in the Act that overtime compensation be paid weekly. The general rule is that overtime compensation earned in a particular workweek must be paid on the regular payday for the period in which such workweek ends. When the correct amount of overtime compensation cannot be determined until some time after the regular pay period, however, the requirements of the Act will be satisfied if the employer pays the excess overtime compensation as soon after the regular pay period as is practicable. Payment may not be delayed over a period longer than is reasonably necessary for the employer to compute and arrange for payment of the amount due and in no event may payment be delayed beyond the next payday after such computation can be made."[7]

Courts have generally construed these requirements to mandate that overtime be paid on the regular payday following the pay period in which the overtime was worked.[8] In so ruling, courts have rejected explanations for the late payment of overtime that they have termed "bureaucratic inertia" preventing the setting up of an efficient accounting system.[9]

Section 778.106 does contain an exception to the general rule that overtime must be paid on the following payday, allowing the later payment of overtime where the correct amount of overtime "cannot be determined" until "sometime after the regular pay period," provided the employer "pays the excess overtime as soon after the regular pay period as is practicable." In one case, a city facing liability under the FLSA for extra-duty shifts worked by its police officers cited as a defense that some officers did not immediately submit reports of their hours worked to the City, which delayed the City's preparation of invoices for the outside vendors, and that the City was unable to confirm the actual number of hours worked by an officer until it was itself paid by the outside vendor. The delay between a vendor's payment to the City and the City's payment of the officers was typically between two to four weeks. In setting the stage for the trial of the case, a court observed that a jury would "have to evaluate evidence relevant to when the City was first able to compute and arrange for payment of the correct amount of extra-duty overtime compensation; the period of time reasonably necessary to do so; whether the City paid extra-duty officers by the next regular payday after such computation was made; and generally whether the delay in payment was due to neglect by the officers or by the City. An employer may not set up an inefficient accounting procedure and then claim it is not responsible for timely payment of wages due to its own incompetence. And the City's explanation that outside vendors often delay their payments to the City improperly attempts to shift the blame to such third parties and to turn attention away from the appropriate "reasonableness standard."[10]

NOTES TO CHAPTER 2

[1] *See Skidmore v. Swift & Co.*, 323 U.S. 134 (1944); *Reich v. Newspapers of New England, Inc.*, 44 F.3d 1060 (1st Cir. 1995).

[2] *See Jewell Ridge Coal Corp. v. United Mine Workers*, 325 U.S. 161 (1945).

[3] *Auer v. Robbins,* 519 U.S. 452 (1997).

[4] *Taylor-Callahan-Coleman Counties District Adult Probation Department v. Dole*, 948 F.2d 953 (5th Cir. 1991).

[5] 29 U.S.C. §203(e)(2)(c).

[6] *Oliver v. Layrisson*, 2 WH Cases2d 1246 (E.D.La. 1995); *see Brickey v. Smyth County, Virginia*, 944 F.Supp. 1310 (W.D.Va. 1996).

[7] 29 C.F.R. §778.106 (2001).

[8] *Brooks v. Village of Ridgefield Park*, 185 F.3d 130 (3rd Cir.1999); *Reich v. Interstate Brands Corporation*, 57 F.3d 574 (7th Cir.1995); *Mullins v. Howard County, Maryland*, 730 F.Supp. 667 (D.Md. 1990); *see Biggs v. Wilson*, 1 F.3d 1537 (9th Cir.1993)(holding that late payment of minimum wages is the equivalent of non-payment under FLSA).

[9] *Dominici v. Chicago Bd. of Education*, 881 F.Supp. 315 (N.D.Ill. 1995).

[10] *Cahill v. City of New Brunswick*, 99 F.Supp.2d 464 (D.N.J. 2000).

CHAPTER THREE

THE FLSA AND COLLECTIVE BARGAINING AGREEMENTS

A. The FLSA And Collective Bargaining Agreements.

A question that often arises concerns the relationship between the FLSA and collective bargaining agreements. It is possible for collective bargaining agreements to be either more or less generous than the overtime requirements of the FLSA, or to mirror those requirements. Where a collective bargaining agreement contains provisions that are equal to or more generous to employees than the provisions of the FLSA, the provisions of the collective bargaining agreement are enforceable.[1] For example, it is perfectly acceptable for a collective bargaining agreement to require minimum callback payments to employees recalled to work on their days off, or to call for the payment of overtime when an employee works more than eight hours in a workday, even though neither requirement exists in the FLSA.

Where the collective bargaining agreement calls for benefits that are less generous than the FLSA, the provisions of the collective bargaining agreement conflicting with the FLSA are invalid. In such cases, the provisions of the FLSA will take precedence over the conflicting provisions in the collective bargaining agreement.[2] For example, if a collective bargaining agreement contains an overtime clause that calls for the payment of overtime at time and one-half the hourly rate of pay rather than time and one-half the regular rate of pay, the clause would be unenforceable.

These principles were first established by the United States Supreme Court in *Martino v. Michigan Window Cleaning Co.*, a case in which a labor organization negotiated a contract that called for employees to be paid overtime only when they worked more than 44 hours in a workweek. The Supreme Court rejected the employer's defense relying on the contract, finding that collective bargaining agreements "cannot supercede the Act."[3] Subsequent to *Martino*, the Supreme Court has restated that "we have held that FLSA rights cannot be abridged by contract or otherwise waived because this would nullify the purposes of the statute and thwart the legislative policies it was designed to effectuate. Moreover, we have held that congressionally granted FLSA rights take precedence over conflicting provisions in a collectively bargained compensation arrangement."[4]

Since most public sector collective bargaining agreements contain overtime clauses, occasionally employees can choose to either assert their rights under the FLSA or under the grievance procedure in the collective bargaining agreement, or both. Where such a dual remedy exists, employers have contended from time to time that employees must exhaust the provisions of the grievance procedure before bringing an FLSA claim in court. Alternatively, employers have contended that the failure to exhaust a contract's grievance procedure "estops" or bars an employee from later filing a lawsuit. Courts have rejected such arguments, finding that the FLSA provides an independent cause of action which is not dependent on whether any other remedies exist, including remedies under a collective bargaining agreement.[5] A slight distinction from this general rule exists in cases where employees have filed a lawsuit for both FLSA and contract violations. In such cases, courts will defer the contract claims to the grievance procedure in the contract while proceeding to hear the FLSA claims.[6]

B. The Procedures Used To Renegotiate Provisions Of A Collective Bargaining Agreement Which Conflict With The FLSA.

As of the time of the *Garcia* decision, a significant number of public sector collective bargaining agreements contained at least one provision that was in conflict with the FLSA. The question immediately arose as to how to conform these contracts with the FLSA. Usually, employers came into compliance with the FLSA through the renegotiation of conflicting provisions of a collective bargaining agreement under savings clauses. A typical savings clause in a collective bargaining agreement provides as follows:

"If any section of this agreement becomes in violation of the laws of the United States, the parties shall immediately renegotiate the section to eliminate the violation. The aim of the parties shall be to return the parties to the benefit of the bargain reached in the initial negotiations process."

Where a collective bargaining agreement did not contain a savings clause, renegotiations took place under general state statutes requiring parties to renegotiate invalid sections of collective bargaining agreements.

Under savings clauses, whether they exist in a collective bargaining agreement or through the operation of state law, the rule generally is that only those sections of the contract which violate the FLSA need be negotiated. However, in some cases (particularly with firefighters' collective bargaining agreements), the financial application of the FLSA was so dramatic that many parties chose to reopen negotiations on other sections of the collective bargaining agreement in order to maintain the overall balance of the agreement.

C. Offsetting FLSA Liability By Overtime Paid Under A Collective Bargaining Agreement Or Local Practice.

Section 7(h) of the FLSA allows an employer to offset its FLSA liability by certain types of overtime payments made under a collective bargaining agreement or local employment practice. The types of payments that can be used to offset FLSA liability are found in Sections (5), (6) and (7) of Section 7(e) of the FLSA:

"(5) extra compensation provided by a premium rate paid for certain hours worked by the employee in any day or workweek because such hours are hours worked in excess of eight in a day or in excess of the maximum workweek applicable to such employee under subsection (a) of this section or in excess of the employee's normal working hours or regular working hours, as the case may be;

"(6) extra compensation provided by a premium rate paid for work by the employee on Saturdays, Sundays, holidays, or regular days of rest, or on the sixth or seventh day of the workweek, where such premium rate is not less than one and one-half times the rate established in good faith for like work performed in non-overtime hours on other days; or

"(7) extra compensation provided by a premium rate paid to the employee, in pursuance of an applicable employee contract or collective-bargaining agreement, for work outside of the hours established in good faith by the contract or agreement as the basic, normal, or regular workday (not exceeding eight hours) or workweek (not exceeding the maximum workweek applicable to such employee under subsection (a) of this section, where such premium rate is not less than one and one-half times the rate established in good faith by the contract or agreement for like work performed during such workday or workweek."[7]

In the public sector, the greatest opportunity for a Section 7(h) offset will occur with the type of "extra compensation" paid under Section 7(e)(5). As one court described, Section 7(e)(5) describes overtime payments for hours worked in excess of the employee's normal workshift where those hours do not cause the employee to work longer hours than the applicable FLSA overtime threshold.[8] Under Section 7(h), for example, if a law enforcement employer who has adopted a 28-day work period is liable to an employee for four hours of overtime worked during the work period (i.e., the employee works 175 hours in the work period), the employee is allowed to offset that liability if it has paid the employee overtime during the work period for hours worked in excess of the employee's normal workshift before it was required to do so under the FLSA.

A question often arising with respect to the Section 7(h) offset is whether an employer's offsets are limited to the "extra compensation" paid in the same pay period for which the overtime is owed, or whether an employer is allowed to offset FLSA liability in one pay period against "extra compensation" owed in a separate pay period. Though the matter is not without some debate, the majority rule is that the Section 7(h) offset can only be used by an employer in the same pay period for which overtime is owed. Courts following this general rule cite the rules of the DOL that overtime must be computed and paid on a pay period-by-pay period basis unless it is impractical to do so.[9]

NOTES TO CHAPTER 3

[1] *See Walling v. Emery Wholesale Corp.*, 138 F.2d 548 (5th Cir. 1943).

[2] *See Adams v. Department of Juvenile Justice*, 3 WH Cases2d 295 (S.D.N.Y. 1996); *Secrist v. Developmental Services Of Tulsa*, 819 P.2d 718 (Okla.App. 1991); *Mullins v. Howard County, Md.*, 730 F.Supp. 667 (D.Md. 1990); *Casserly v. State of Colorado*, 844 P.2d 1275 (Colo.App. 1992).

[3] *Martino v. Michigan Window Cleaning Co.*, 327 U.S. 173 (1946).

[4] *E.g. Barrentine v. Arkansas-Best Freight System, Inc.*, 450 U.S. 728 (1961).

[5] *Utility Workers v. S. Calif. Edison*, 83 F.3d 292 (9th Cir. 1996); *Treece v. City of Little Rock*, 923 F.Supp. 1122 (E.D.Ark. 1996).

[6] *Summers v. Howard University*, 127 F.Supp.2d 27 (D.D.C. 2000).

[7] The compensation described in subsection (7) is for "clock pattern" premium pay, extra pay for working undesirable hours. *See* 29 C.F.R. §778.204.

[8] *Nolan v. City of Chicago*, 125 F.Supp.2d 324 (N.D.Ill. 2000).

[9] *Howard v. City of Springfield, Illinois*, 274 F.3d 1141 (7th Cir. 2001); *Alexander v. United States*, 32 F.3d 1571 (Fed.Cir. 1994); *Roland Electrical Co. v. Black*, 163 F.2d 417 (4th Cir. 1947); *Nolan v. City of Chicago*, 125 F.Supp.2d 324 (N.D.Ill. 2000); *Reich v. Southern New England Telecommunications Corp.*, 892 F.Supp. 389 (D.Conn. 1995); *United States Department of Labor v. Shenandoah Baptist Church*, 707 F.Supp. 1450 (W.D.Va. 1989); *see Samson v. Apollo Resources,*

Inc., 242 F.3d 629 (5th Cir. 2001)(employer using fluctuating workweek cannot gain credit in one workweek to apply against overtime liability in subsequent workweek). *Contra Dunn v. City of Muskegon*, 1998 U.S. Dist. LEXIS 19032 (W.D.Mich. 1998); *Abbey v. City of Jackson*, 883 F.Supp. 181 (E.D.Mich. 1995). Some courts have discussed an employer's right to an offset, but have failed to address whether the offset is limited to the same pay period for which overtime is due. *See Kohlheim v. Glynn County*, 915 F.2d 1473 (11th Cir. 1990).

CHAPTER FOUR

COMPUTATION OF THE REGULAR
RATE UNDER THE FLSA

A. Introduction.

The FLSA contains two basic requirements:

1. Employees covered by the FLSA must be paid at the minimum wage specified by Congress; and

2. Employees covered by the FLSA who work more than specified maximum time periods must receive pay at a rate of at least time and one-half their regular rate of pay for the excess hours worked.[1]

When considering potential overtime liability under the FLSA, the first major issue to address is the identification of an employee's regular rate of pay. Many employers in the public sector have long considered an employee's regular rate as being the hourly rate assigned for the job classification in which the employee works – practices that have developed either through collective bargaining agreements, memoranda of understanding, or simply through historical payroll practices. The FLSA requires that a different approach be taken in determining an employee's regular rate.

B. The Workweek — The Basic Unit Of Measurement Under The FLSA.

The basic unit of measurement with respect to an employee's services under the FLSA is the workweek.[2] An employee's workweek has a dual importance under the FLSA: (1) It serves as the measurement tool defining when an employee is entitled to overtime; and (2) it figures prominently in the calculation of the employee's regular rate of pay. Section 778.105 of the DOL's regulations define a workweek as follows:

> "An employee's workweek is a fixed and regularly recurring period of 168 hours — seven consecutive 24-hour periods. It need not coincide with the calendar week but may begin on any day and at any hour of the day. For purposes of computing pay due under the Fair Labor Standards Act, a single workweek may be established for a plant or other establishment as a whole or different workweeks may be established for different employees or groups of employees. Once the beginning time of an employee's workweek is established, it remains fixed regardless of the schedule of hours worked by him."[3]

The start of the workweek may be changed by an employer so long as the change is permanent and is not intended to evade the obligation to pay overtime.[4]

The calculation of the employee's regular rate begins with a determination of the income received by the employee over a workweek. Section 778.113(a) of the DOL's regulations provides the calculation mechanism for employees earning a weekly salary:

> "If the employee is employed solely on a weekly salary basis, his regular hourly rate of pay, on which time and one-half must be paid, is computed by dividing the salary by the number of hours which the salary is intended to compensate. If an employee is hired at a salary of $182.70 and if it is understood that this salary is compensation for a regular workweek of 35 hours, the employee's regular rate of pay is $182.70 divided by 35 hours, or $5.22/hour, and when he works overtime he is entitled to receive $5.22 for each of the first 40 hours and $7.83 (one and one-half times $5.22) for each hour thereafter. If an employee is hired at a

salary of $220.80 for a 40-hour week, his regular rate is $5.52 an hour."[5]

Thus, the starting point for determining an employee's regular rate is to divide the employee's weekly salary by the number of hours worked by the employee per week.[6] As discussed in Section C of this chapter, the employee's weekly salary must include all remuneration for employment. In performing this calculation, paid leave such as vacation time, sick leave, and compensatory time off need not be included as hours worked by the employee.

Because the regular rate of pay is produced by dividing the employee's compensation by hours worked, an increase in hours worked for an employee receiving the same level of compensation will result in a lower regular rate of pay. Occasionally, employers will argue that more time should be included in hours worked as a way of reducing the regular rate of pay. For example, in one case, a fire department tried to lower the regular rate of pay by firefighters by including "Kelly days" and vacation time in the calculation of the regular rate. The Court rejected this argument, finding that no form of paid leave should be included as hours worked in the calculation of the regular rate.[7]

Table 1 contains sample calculations of conversions of weekly salaries to an hourly wage, showing the effect that actual hours worked have on the regular rate of pay.

TABLE 1

SAMPLE CALCULATIONS OF REGULAR RATE

Classification	Weekly Rate	Weekly Hours	Regular Rate
Maintenance Technician	$ 700	40.0	$17.50
Police Officer	$1000	40.0	$25.00
Landscape Engineer	$1000	35.0	$28.57
Nurse	$ 900	37.5	$24.00
Secretary	$ 800	40.0	$20.00

With very few exceptions, the FLSA treats each work-week as a single unit.[8] Thus, the FLSA generally does not permit the averaging of hours over two or more weeks, nor does it allow the crediting of excess overtime paid in one workweek to overtime earned in another workweek. If an employee works overtime in one week, the employee must be paid the overtime, even if the employee only works 20 hours in the subsequent week.

A question that frequently arises concerns employees who are regularly scheduled to work more than a 40-hour week, but who are nonetheless paid on a weekly basis. For example, a building inspector may be scheduled to work a regular 40-hour week, but also be required to attend mandatory unpaid shift briefings of 30 minutes on each day of the workweek, which would raise the number of hours in the employee's workweek to 42.5. The results of such an approach are to lower the overall overtime costs for an employer who regularly schedules employees to work longer than a 40-hour workweek, as can be seen from Table 2:

TABLE 2
CALCULATION OF REGULAR RATE FOR EMPLOYEES
WITH OR WITHOUT UNPAID BRIEFINGS

Calculation	Weekly Rate	Weekly Hours	Regular Rate
Excluding Unpaid Briefing	$1000	40.00	$25.00
Including Unpaid Briefing	$1000	42.50	$23.52
Difference			$ 1.48
Percentage Difference			*6%*

This set of facts gives rise to the following question: May a workweek which is longer than 40 hours be used to compute the employee's hourly wage under Section 778.113(a) of the DOL's rules? The answer would seem to be no, though there is no clear cut indication to the contrary in the FLSA itself or in the regulations promulgated by the DOL. One of the major purposes of the FLSA is to ensure that all covered employees working longer than 40 hours a workweek receive overtime pay of at least time and one-half their regular rate of pay. Since the net effect of using a longer than 40-hour workweek to calculate an employee's regular rate of pay would be to reduce the value of an employee's right to time and one-half pay for overtime, it would seem a likely result that such a calculation method would be viewed as a contravention of the FLSA.

As will be seen below, certain law enforcement officers and fire protection employees may be eligible for alternative "work periods" under Section 207(k) of the FLSA, which permits such employees to work more than 40 hours per workweek without the employer incurring overtime liability. For employees who are covered by the 7(k) exemption, may a longer than 40-hour workweek be used to calculate an hourly wage under the provisions of Section 778.113 of the DOL's rules? Again, the answer is not clear from either the FLSA itself or from the DOL's interpretative regulations. While the 7(k) exemption, and the regulations thereunder, make it clear that an employer is not obligated to pay time and one-half the employee's regular rate until the employee has worked more than the maximum hours allowable for the work period, the same provisions contain no direct or indirect reference to the effect of the 7(k) exemption on the calculation of an employee's regular rate. As Table 3 shows, the effect of not taking into consideration the longer work periods for employees covered by the 7(k) exemption is dramatic indeed:

TABLE 3

CALCULATION OF REGULAR RATES FOR FIRE PROTECTION EMPLOYEES UNDER DIFFERENT SCENARIOS

Scenario	Hours Worked	Work Period	Salary	Regular Rate
No 7(k) Exemption	56.00	7 days	$1000.00	$25.00
7(k) Exemption	56.00	7 days	$1000.00	$17.86
Percentage Difference				*40%*
No 7(k) Exemption	216.00	27 days	$3858.00	$25.00
7(k) Exemption	216.00	27 days	$3858.00	$17.86
Percentage Difference				*40%*

Given Congress' specific intent to allow longer work periods for certain law enforcement and firefighter employees, the most likely result would seem to be that the longer work period may be taken into consideration in determining the employee's regular rate.[9] Thus, if a law enforcement employer with a daily one-half hour unpaid briefing period (which results in a 42.5 hour workweek) opts for a 7(k) exemption, the employee's regular rate should be the employee's weekly salary divided by the total number of regularly-scheduled hours of work in the seven-day work period. For example, if a law enforcement employee who is regularly scheduled to work a 42.5-hour week received a weekly wage of $500, and a 7(k) exemption was elected, the calculation of the employee's regular rate would be as follows:

$$\frac{\$500.00}{42.5} \;=\; \$11.76$$

The FLSA allows an employer to compensate two employees who work in the same classification at different regular rates of pay, so long as the different wage rates are not based on the race or gender of the employee. For example, in one case a fire department paid 56-hour-a-week and 40-hour-a-week employees the same weekly wage. Because the 56-hour-a-week employees worked more hours, their regular rate of pay was substantially lower than that of the 40-hour-a-week employees. The Court found no violation in this compensation scheme, holding that even similarly-situated employees within the same job classification need not receive the same regular rate of pay.[10]

1. Employees Receiving Salary For Working Longer Than A Week.

The regular rate for employees who are paid on a monthly basis is computed in much the same fashion as is the case with weekly schedules. Section 778.113(b) of the DOL's regulations requires that monthly or other rates must be converted to their weekly equivalent, with the weekly wage then being reduced to a regular rate pursuant to Section 778.113(a):

> "Where the salary covers a period longer than a workweek, such as a month, it must be reduced to its workweek equivalent. A monthly salary is subject to translation to its equivalent weekly wage by multiplying by 12 (the number of months) and dividing by 52 (the number of weeks). A semimonthly salary is translated into its equivalent weekly wage by multiplying by 24 and dividing by 52. Once the weekly wage is arrived at, the regular hourly rate of pay will be calculated as indicated above."[11]

To be valid under the FLSA, the use of annual or monthly salaries must provide no lesser compensation to employees than the workweek calculations required in the computation of the regular rate of pay.[12] Samples of the types of calculations envisioned by the regulations are set forth in Table 4:

TABLE 4

SAMPLES OF CONVERSIONS OF LONGER SALARIES TO WEEKLY SALARIES

Salary Basis	Conversion Formula
Monthly	Multiply by 12, Divide by 52
Twice Monthly	Multiply by 24, Divide by 52
Bi-Weekly	Divide by 2
Annual	Divide by 52

2. Employees With Fluctuating Work Hours.

Though the practice is more prevalent in the private sector, some public employees may have fluctuating work hours. For example, an employee may be called upon to work 34 hours in one week and 43 hours in the next, though the employee is receiving the same weekly salary regardless of the actual number of hours worked. How does the FLSA compute such an employee's regular rate? The answer to this question is provided by Section 778.114 of the DOL's regulations, which allows for such fluctuating hours to be taken into account in limited circumstances:

> "An employee employed on a salary basis may have hours of work fluctuate from week to week and the salary may be paid him pursuant to an understanding with his employer that he will receive such fixed amount as straight-time pay for whatever hours he is called upon to work in a workweek, whether few or many. Where there is a clear mutual understanding of the parties that the fixed salary is

compensation (apart from overtime premiums) for the hours worked each workweek, whatever their number, rather than for working 40 hours or some other fixed weekly work period, such a salary arrangement is permitted by the FLSA if the amount of the salary is sufficient to provide compensation to the employee at a rate not less than the applicable minimum wage rate for every hour worked in those workweeks in which the numbers of hours he works is greatest, and if he receives extra compensation, in addition to such salary, for all overtime hours worked at a rate not less than one-half his regular rate of pay."[13]

In schematic form, the requirements of Section 778.114 are as follows:

1. The employee must be employed on a salary basis;[14]

2. The employee must have hours of work that fluctuate from week to week;

3. The weekly salary must be the product of a mutual understanding or agreement between the employer and the employee that the fixed salary is due regardless of the number of hours worked in a particular workweek;

4. The employee must receive at least the minimum wage for all hours worked in every workweek; and

5. The employee must receive extra compensation in addition to the hourly rate for all overtime hours worked.

Under such a system, the employee will inevitably have different hourly rates for each workweek in which the employee's hours of work vary. While the employer is still obligated to pay at the overtime rate for all hours worked in excess of 40 hours, the overtime rates themselves will differ, and will be lower in those workweeks in which more overtime hours are worked. This result is described in Section 778.114(b):

"The application of the principles above stated may be illustrated by the case of an employee whose hours of work do not customarily follow a regular schedule but vary from week to week, whose overtime work is never in excess of 50 hours in a workweek, and whose salary of $250 is paid with the understanding that it constitutes his compensation, except for overtime premiums, for whatever hours are worked in the workweek. If during the course of four weeks this employee works 40, 44, 50, and 48 hours, his regular hourly rate of pay in each of these weeks is approximately $6.25, $5.68, $5, and $5.21, respectively. Since the employee has already received straight-time compensation on a salary basis for all hours worked, only additional half time pay is due. For the first week the employee is entitled to be paid $250; for the second week $261.36 ($250 plus 4 hours at $2.84, or 40 hours at $5.68 plus 4 hours at $8.52); for the third week $275.99 ($250 plus 10 hours at $2.50, or 40 hours at $5 plus 10 hours at $7.50); for the fourth week approximately $270.88 ($250 plus 8 hours at $2.61, or 40 hours at $5.21 plus 8 hours at $7.82)."

A fluctuating workweek employee's salary is, by definition, straight time compensation for whatever hours the employee is called upon to work during the workweek, no matter whether great or few. Accordingly, fluctuating workweek employees are entitled only to "half-time" for any overtime rather than the time-and-a-half to which other employees are entitled. The essence of the fluctuating workweek method is not merely that employees work a fluctuating number of hours, but rather that their salary is designed to be straight time pay for all hours worked, no matter whether great or few.[15] An employer using a fluctuating workweek system is not entitled to make deductions from an employee's pay for sick leave, even if the employee is absent from work because of illness and has no accrued sick leave to use.[16] Though the FLSA itself contains no reference to fluctuating workweeks, the legality of the DOL's fluctuating workweek regulations has been upheld by the courts.[17] As always, the FLSA requires that employees receive the minimum wage over the entire workweek, no matter whether a fluctuating workweek is used.[18]

Much of the debate over whether an employer is using a fluctuating workweek revolves around whether there is the requisite advance "mutual understanding" that compensation is to be paid on the basis of a fluctuating workweek.[19] Public sector employers have had mixed results in claiming that their employees work fluctuating workweeks and gaining the benefits of Section 778.114 of the DOL's regulations, with virtually all cases involving the matter arising out of states in the South. For example, in *Burgess v. Catawba County*, the Court rejected the County's attempt to apply the fluctuating workweek overtime formula to an emergency medical service employee, finding there is no evidence that there was a clear mutual understanding that the employee's salary covered any and all hours worked.[20] Similarly, in *Heder v. City of Two Rivers*, the Court rejected a claim for a fluctuating workweek, finding that "contract provision that salaried workers will be paid time-and-a-half for overtime hours would seem per se to establish that the fluctuating workweek method is not being used."[21]

However, in *Anderson v. County of Kershaw*, the Court upheld the use of a fluctuating workweek where "a decade of invariable practice" by the County was found to establish the requisite "mutual understanding" that a fluctuating workweek was to be used.[22] Similarly, in *Griffin v. Wake County*, the Court found the necessary "mutual understanding" in the form of a written memorandum distributed to employees describing the fluctuating workweek system.[23]

3. Employees Working At More Than One Wage Rate.

On occasion, employees assigned to do more than one task may work at different wage rates. This is especially prevalent where two departments within a public employer may "share" an employee, who may have different job classifications in each department. The DOL has a specific regulation under the FLSA to cover such employees, which requires that the "weighted average" of the employee's different wage rates be used to establish the employee's regular rate for the purpose of overtime calculation:

> "Where an employee in a single workweek works at two or more different types of work for which different non-overtime rates of pay (of not less than the minimum wage) have been established, his regular rate for that week is the weighted average of such rates. That is, his total earnings (except statutory exclusions) are computed to include his compensation during the workweek from all such rates, and are then divided by the total number of hours worked at all jobs."[24]

If, for example, an employee works 15 hours in a workweek in Job Classification A, which has a weekly salary of $1000.00, and works the remaining 25 hours in the workweek in Job Classification B, which has a weekly salary of $800.00, the following computation, as in Table 5, must be made to compute the employee's regular rate:

TABLE 5

CALCULATION OF REGULAR RATE FOR EMPLOYEE WORKING AT TWO OR MORE RATES

Classification	Weekly Rate	Hours Worked	Weighted Value
Classification A	$1000	15.00	$15,000
Classification B	$ 800	25.00	$20,000
Total		40.00	$35,000
Weighted Average			$875.00
Regular Rate			$ 21.87

C. Additions To The Regular Rate.

The FLSA does not define regular rate as merely the employee's salary. Rather, Section 7(a) of the FLSA specifically provides that regular rate means "all remuneration for employment paid to, or on behalf of, the employee * * * " This definition gives rise to an issue that is occasionally referred to as "overtime pyramiding." In many public sector labor agreements or compensation plans, the overtime rate has been calculated on the basis of the employee's salary or hourly wage alone. Certain other payments to the employee, including incentive plan payments, shift differential, and premium payments, have been excluded from overtime calculations.

The FLSA requires that "all remuneration" (with certain listed exceptions, which will be discussed below) must be taken into account in making overtime calculations,[25] and places on employers the burden of proving that payments should not be included in the regular rate of pay.[26] The following is a list of some types of remuneration which have not been taken into account by some public employers in the past in computing overtime rates, but which must be taken into account in computing the regular rate under the FLSA:

• Shift Differentials.[27]

• Payments for Achieving Certain Levels of Certification (e.g., EMT Certification, or Police Standards and Training Certification).

• Education Incentives. [28]

• Longevity Premiums.[29]

• Hazardous Duty Pay.[30]

• Assignment or Working Out of Classification Pay.

• Specialty Assignment Pay (e.g., Engineer Premiums or Detective Premiums).[31]

• Payments designed to supplement workers' compensation benefits to allow the employee to receive the same net wage.[32]

Even though a collective bargaining agreement may specify an overtime rate, the overtime rate specified by the contract is not valid unless it includes these types of payments in the regular rate of pay.[33] The effect of including such payments in overtime calculations can be significant, depending upon the employer's compensation structure. Table 6 illustrates the level of change in overtime payments as a result of "pyramiding" overtime on the basis of base rates plus other types of remuneration paid by an employer to an employee:

TABLE 6
COMPUTATION OF OVERTIME RATE

Regular Rate of Pay:	$20.00
Shift Differential:	$ 2.00
Education Incentive:	$ 2.00
Longevity Incentive:	$ 1.00
Assignment Premium:	$ 1.00
Hazardous Duty Pay:	$ 1.00
Working Out-of-Class Pay:	$ 1.00
Adjusted Rate of Pay:	$28.00
FLSA Overtime Rate:	$42.00
Non-Pyramided Overtime Rate:	$30.00

Percentage Difference: ***40%***

The effect of including premium pays in an employee's regular rate of pay may require the constant readjustment of the employee's overtime rate. For example, if an employee with a Monday-Friday schedule receives a shift differential for working a graveyard shift on a Monday and later works an overtime day shift on Saturday, the employee's overtime rate on Saturday must reflect the fact that the employee received the shift differential on Monday, since the shift differential must be included in the "remuneration for employment" from which the regular rate of pay for the workweek is derived. Moreover, depending upon the employee's eligibility for premium pay and the hours an employee works, it is theoretically possible for an employee to have different regular rates of pay every workweek.

D. Exclusions From The Regular Rate.

While the FLSA does include in calculations of the regular rate some items of compensation which have not been historically included by employers and labor organizations in the calculation of an overtime rate, the FLSA also excludes certain forms of remuneration which have been historically thought to be included. The following is an abbreviated list of the exclusions from the regular rate which is contained in Section 7(e) of the FLSA:

1. Any gifts made by the employer to the employee, including Christmas bonuses. However, Christmas bonuses that are "measured by or dependent on" hours worked, production, or efficiency, must be included in the calculation of regular rate;[34]

2. Payments made for vacation time;

3. Payments made for holiday time;

4. Payments made to an employee when an employee is utilizing paid sick leave provided by the employer;

5. Any expenses, including travel expenses "incurred by the employee in the furtherance of his employer's interests and properly reimbursable by the employer";

6. Payments to retirement plans;

7. Payments of health and other insurance premiums;[35] and

8. Premium payments for hours worked on an overtime basis, on Saturdays, Sundays, holidays, or the employee's regular days of rest.[36]

The most significant of the exclusions insofar as public sector employees are concerned are the exclusions for payments for vacation, holidays, and sick time. However, there is no financial effect of this exclusion. Since hours taken off by an employee for vacation, holiday, and sick time are not counted in "hours worked" under the FLSA,[37] the net effect of the exclusions for vacation, holiday, and sick time is non-existent, a fact which is demonstrated by Table 7:

TABLE 7
CALCULATION OF REGULAR RATE INCLUDING SICK LEAVE, VACATION, AND HOLIDAY ADJUSTMENTS

Week 1

Scheduled Hours:	40 hours
Extra Time Worked:	8 hours
Sick Leave Taken:	0 hours
Vacation Taken:	0 hours
Holiday Time Off:	8 hours
FLSA Hours Worked:	**40 hours**

Week 2

Scheduled Hours:	40 hours
Extra Time Worked:	16 hours
Sick Leave Taken:	8 hours
Vacation Taken:	0 hours
Holiday Time Off:	0 hours
FLSA Hours Worked:	**48 hours**

Week 3

Scheduled Hours:	40 hours
Extra Time Worked:	8 hours
Sick Leave Taken:	8 hours
Vacation Taken:	8 hours
Holiday Time Off:	8 hours
FLSA Hours Worked:	**24 hours**

E. Frequently Occurring Problems Involving Exclusions From The Regular Rate.

The following issues concerning the appropriate calculation of the regular rate of pay frequently arise.

1. "Show-up," "Reporting," Or "Callback" Pay.

A common feature of many public sector collective bargaining agreements is a provision that calls for the payment of a specified minimum number of hours of pay to an employee who is called back to work outside the employee's regular shift. The minimum compensation imposed by a "callback" provision is paid to the employee regardless of the actual number of hours worked by the employee (except, of course, if the employee works longer than the minimum number of hours specified, in which case the employee receives the overtime rate for all hours worked).

Under the FLSA, only the compensation for the actual number of hours worked by the employee on a callback need be included in the employee's "regular rate." The callback "premium," or the difference between the minimum number of callback hours specified by the callback provisions and the actual number of hours worked, need not be included in the employee's "regular rate." These conclusions are stated in Section 778.220(a) of the DOL's regulations:

> "Under some employment agreements, an employee may be paid a minimum of a specified number of hours' pay at the applicable straight time or overtime rate on infrequent and sporadic occasions when, after reporting to work at his scheduled starting time on a regular workday or on another day on which he has been scheduled to work, he is not provided with the expected amount of work. The amounts that may be paid under such an agreement over and above what the employee would receive if paid at his customary rate only for the number of

hours worked are paid to compensate the employee for the time wasted by him in reporting for work and to prevent undue loss of pay resulting from the employer's failure to provide expected work during regular hours. One of the primary purposes of such an arrangement is to discourage employers from calling their employees in to work for only a fraction of a day when they might get full-time work elsewhere. Pay arrangements of this kind are commonly referred to as 'show-up' or 'reporting' pay * * * (T)hat portion of such payment which represents compensation at the applicable rates for the straight time or overtime hours actually worked, if any, during such periods may be credited as straight-time or overtime compensation, as the case may be, in computing overtime compensation due under the [FLSA]. The amount by which the specified number of hours' pay exceeds such compensation for the hours actually worked is considered as a payment that is not made for hours worked. As such, it may be excluded from the computation of the employee's regular rate and cannot be credited toward statutory overtime compensation due him."[38]

2. Retirement "Pickup" And Deferred Compensation Contributions.

As part of the collective bargaining process, employers have occasionally agreed to "pickup" or pay a portion of or all of the employee's retirement contribution to a retirement plan in lieu of all or part of a pay increase. For example, in a year when wage increases in general are averaging 6%, an employer and a labor organization may agree to no wage increase, but may also agree to have the employer pay or "pickup" the employees' regular 6% retirement contribution. Since retirement pickup has significant tax deferral advantages (the amount "picked up" by the employer is not usually taxable until the employee retires), it has been a commonly-used settlement tool in states which have statutes or retirement plans which allow such pickup.

More recently, employers have agreed to make contributions to an employee's deferred compensation account. On occasion, these contributions are direct contributions made by the employer without regard as to what contributions the employee has made; on other occasions, the employer's contributions are designed to match an employee's contributions.

Under the FLSA, an employer's normal contributions to an employee's retirement account need not be included in "the regular rate of pay."[39] The same can be said of retirement "pickup" and an employer's contribution to an employee's deferred compensation account since the FLSA does not differentiate in its treatment of retirement contributions on the basis of the purpose for which the retirement contribution is made. Under the FLSA, an employer who has always paid 100% of the costs of a retirement system would not be required to include any portion of the retirement contribution in the calculation of the employee's regular rate; the results are not different for an employer who has recently changed from a partial contribution to a full or greater contribution to the retirement plan or to a contribution to a deferred compensation account.

3. Wellness Plans And Sick Leave Incentives.

As noted above, an employer's contribution to insurance premiums are not calculated in the regular rate of the employee for whom the premiums are paid. However, in response to the rapidly increasing costs of providing health insurance, employers and labor organizations have made efforts at devising "wellness" or cost-containment plans, which encourage the more efficient use of health insurance benefits. A common feature of such wellness plans is the payment of remuneration to employees for certain actions or inaction on the part of the employee. For example, an employee may be rewarded with a cash bonus for utilizing only a certain level of sick leave during the year. Other wellness plans feature a cash reimbursement to employees based upon pro rata use of the health insurance plan over the course of the fiscal year. Yet other plans contain such features as "nonsmokers" and "fitness" bonuses.

Whether such payments must be included in an employee's regular rate is uncertain. On one hand, such payments to an employee would appear to fall under the general heading of "remuneration for employment" that must be included in the regular rate of pay. On the other hand, the only court to address the issue, albeit in the briefest of opinions, has held that "awards for nonuse of sick leave are similar to payments made when no work is performed due to illness, which may be excluded from the regular rate. Thus, bonuses for the absence of medical claims and nonuse of sick leave may be excluded from the regular rate."[40] It is clear, however, that if a wellness payment is of the nature of an incentive paid for physical fitness, and where the employee's job requires the employee to be physically fit, the incentive must be included in the regular rate.[41]

4. Clothing Allowances.

A common feature of law enforcement and fire protection collective bargaining agreements is the payment by the employer of certain clothing allowances, which are to be used for the purchase, maintenance, or cleaning of clothing which the employer requires the employee to wear. Section 778.217(b)(2) of the DOL's regulations excludes most payments made to an employee as clothing allowance from the calculations of the employee's regular rate:

> "Payment by way of reimbursement for the following types of expenses will not be regarded as part of the employee's regular rate: * * * The actual or reasonably approximate amount expended by an employee in purchasing, laundering, or repairing

uniforms or special clothing which his employer requires him to wear."[42]

Thus, the only difficulty with clothing allowances would arise if the value of the clothing allowance were not a "reasonably approximate amount" of the employee's actual expenditures on purchasing, maintaining, or cleaning his or her work clothes. It is advisable that if an employer pays employees a relatively high clothing allowance, some sort of documentation should exist to justify the level of the clothing allowance, lest the clothing allowance or a portion of the clothing allowance be included in a computation of the employee's regular rate. The best type of such documentation would be bids or estimates from local merchants for the purchase or cleaning of clothing.

5. Holiday Premiums.

Many collective bargaining agreements, especially in the law enforcement and fire protection fields, provide that if an employee works on a specifically designated holiday, the employee is entitled to receive a holiday premium or "bonus." On such days, the employee is entitled to receive the regular rate of pay, plus a premium of straight time, time and one-half, or some other multiplier of the employee's regular rate of pay for all hours worked on the holiday.

Under the FLSA, the amount of the holiday bonus need not be included in the employee's regular rate of pay, though, of course, the employee's straight-time pay for all hours worked on a holiday must be included. Section 778.219(b)(1) of the regulations gives an explanation of how the DOL treats holiday bonuses in the context of determining an employee's regular rate of pay:

> "The typical situation is one in which an employee is entitled by contract to eight hours' pay at his rate of $5/hour for certain named holidays when no work is performed. If, however, he is required to work on such days, he does not receive his idle holiday pay. Instead he receives a premium rate of

$7.50 (time and one-half) for each hour worked on the holiday. If he worked 9 hours on the holiday and a total of 50 hours for the week, he would be owed, under his contract, $67.50 (9 x $7.50) for holiday work and $205 for the other 41 hours worked in the week, a total of $272.50. Under the statute (which does not require premium pay for a holiday), he is owed $275 for a workweek of 50 hours at a rate of $5 an hour. Since the holiday premium is one and one-half times the established rate for non-holiday work, it does not increase the regular rate because it qualifies as an overtime premium * * *."[43]

Holiday bonuses can be excluded from the regular rate of pay only if they are paid to employees who actually work the holiday. If a compensation system calls for employees to receive a fixed payment for holidays without regard to whether they work on particular holidays, the amount of the holiday pay must be included in the regular rate of pay.[44]

6. Retroactive Pay Increases.

On occasion, an employer may grant or negotiate a pay increase for employees which is retroactive to a date sometime in the past. Under the FLSA, the employee's regular rate must be recomputed on the basis of the retroactively applicable wage rates, and all overtime calculations must be appropriately adjusted. Section 778.303 of the DOL's regulations specifically indicates that such retroactive pay increases must be taken into account in the calculation of an employee's regular rate:

"Where a retroactive pay increase is awarded to employees as a result of collective bargaining or otherwise, it operates to increase the regular rate of pay of the employees for the period of its retroactivity. Thus, if an employee is awarded a retroactive increase of 10 cents per hour, he is owed, under the [FLSA], a retroactive increase of 15 cents for each overtime hour he has worked during the period, no matter what the agreement of the parties may be."[45]

When recomputing wages after a retroactive wage increase has been implemented, care must be taken to retroactively compute all "percentage-based" premiums (e.g., 5.0% for working out of classification), since such premiums must be included in the employee's regular rate. As Table 8 shows, the failure to recalculate percentage-based premiums can result in errors in the calculation of an employee's regular rate, which in turn can subject the employer to liability under the FLSA.

TABLE 8

RECOMPUTATION OF PREMIUMS AFTER A RETROACTIVE 10.0% WAGE INCREASE HAS BEEN NEGOTIATED

Type of Premium	Weekly Salary	Weekly Premium	Hours	Calculation	Regular Rate
Fixed					
(Pre-Wage Increase)	$1000.00	$100.00	40.00	$\frac{(1000 + 100)}{40}$	$27.50
Percentage					
(Pre-Wage Increase)	$1000.00	10.0% ($100.00)	40.00	$\frac{(1000 + 100)}{40}$	$27.50
Fixed					
(Post-Wage Increase)	$1100.00	$100.00	40.00	$\frac{(1100 + 100)}{40}$	$30.00
Percentage					
(Post-Wage Increase)	$1100.00	($110.00)	40.00	$\frac{(1100 + 110)}{40}$	$30.26

Note: Because value of percentage-based premium changes when wage increase is implemented, all retroactive overtime calculations must use a regular rate based on new value of premium.

Section 778.303 also specifically provides that if a retroactive pay increase is awarded on the basis of a "lump sum," the lump sum must be pro-rated over the period for which it is applicable to determine the employee's "regular rate."

7. Union Dues, Taxes, Social Security Payments, And Garnishments.

Though union dues, taxes, Social Security payments, garnishments of wages, and other types of deductions are frequently made from an employee's check, they do not affect the calculation of the employee's "regular rate."[46] However, an employer must take care not to make an aggregate total of deductions which will bring the employee's net wage below the minimum wage established by the FLSA, a situation which normally would only occur when large garnishments are made against an employee's salary.

8. Disciplinary Deductions.

As is the case with union dues, deductions from an employee's paycheck made for disciplinary reasons are not excludable from the computation of the employee's regular rate under the FLSA.[47]

9. Overtime Averaging Provisions.

Occasionally, a collective bargaining agreement or memorandum of understanding will contain a feature known as an "overtime averaging" device. Under such a device, an employee assigned to specific duties (e.g., a drug and vice detail) is paid a fixed amount for all overtime hours worked regardless of the actual number of overtime hours worked. Such "overtime averaging" devices are strongly discouraged by the FLSA, which requires the inclusion of all fixed-sum averaged overtime in an employee's "regular rate."[48] The effect of the inclusion of "average overtime" in the employee's regular rate not only is to increase the employee's regular rate, but also provides a higher basis on which to calculate the overtime rate (which is still applicable to all overtime hours worked, regardless of the existence of an overtime averaging device).

The reason for the harsh treatment of overtime averaging devices by the FLSA is explained in detail in Section 778.310 of the DOL's regulations:

> "The reason for this is clear. If the rule were otherwise, an employer desiring to pay an employee a fixed salary regardless of the number of hours worked in excess of the applicable maximum hour standard could merely label as overtime pay a fixed portion of such salary sufficient to take care of compensation for the maximum number of hours that would be worked."[49]

10. Insurance.

As noted above, health insurance premiums are not included in the regular rate. On occasion, employers and employees have agreed to substitute the provision of insurance benefits for regular overtime pay, which would thereafter be waived by the employee. Such agreements are invalid under the FLSA.[50]

NOTES TO CHAPTER 4

[1] Another aspect of the FLSA known as the Equal Pay Act forbids discrimination between employees on the basis of sex by paying wages to one sex which are less than those paid to employees of the opposite sex who are performing work which requires equal skill, effort, and responsibility, and which are performed under similar working conditions. 29 U.S.C. §206(d)(1) (2001); *see AFSCME v. County of Nassau*, 799 F.Supp. 1370 (E.D.N.Y. 1992). In order for the Equal Pay Act to apply, the places where the work is performed must not be geographically and operationally distinct. *Winther v. City of Portland*, 66 FEP Cases 1358 (D.Or. 1992).

[2] *See Dove v. Coupe*, 759 F.2d 167 (D.C.Cir. 1985); *McDowell v. Purolator Courier Corp.*, 25 WH Cases 503 (E.D.Ky. 1982); *Shain v. Armour & Co.*, 50 F.Supp. 907 (D.Ky. 1943).

[3] 29 C.F.R. §778.105 (2001).

[4] *Rogers v. City of Troy, New York*, 949 F.Supp. 118 (N.D.N.Y. 1996) *vacated by Rogers v. City of Troy*, 148 F.3d 52 (2nd Cir. 1998); *Blasdell v. State of New York*, 1 WH Cases2d 378 (N.D.N.Y. 1992); *see* Opinion Letter, Department of Labor, 1997 WL 998019 (July 21, 1997).

[5] 29 C.F.R. §778.113(a) (2001).

[6] *See Bay Ridge Operating Co., Inc. v. Aaron*, 334 U.S. 446 (1948); *Shearer v. E. Brame Trucking Co.*, 245 N.W.2nd 84 (Mich.App. 1976).

[7] *Aaron v. City of Wichita, Kansas*, 797 F.Supp. 898 (D.Kan. 1992), *reversed on other grounds*, 54 F.3d 652 (10th Cir. 1995).

[8] *Alexander v. United States*, 32 F.3d 1571 (Fed.Cir. 1994); *Roland Electrical Co. v. Black*, 163 F.2d 417

(4th Cir. 1947); *Nolan v. City of Chicago*, 125 F.Supp.2d 324 (N.D.Ill. 2000); *Reich v. Southern New England Telecommunications Corp.*, 892 F.Supp. 389 (D.Conn. 1995); *United States Department of Labor v. Shenandoah Baptist Church*, 707 F.Supp. 1450 (W.D.Va. 1989). *Contra Dunn v. City of Muskegon*, 1998 U.S. Dist. LEXIS 19032 (W.D.Mich. 1998); *Abbey v. City of Jackson*, 883 F.Supp. 181 (E.D.Mich. 1995). Some courts have discussed an employer's right to an offset, but have failed to address whether the offset is limited to the same pay period for which overtime is due. *See Kohlheim v. Glynn County*, 915 F.2d 1473 (11th Cir. 1990).

[9] *Lee v. Coahoma County, Mississippi*, 937 F.2d 220 (5th Cir. 1991).

[10] *Aaron v. City of Wichita, Kansas*, 797 F.Supp. 898 (D.Kan. 1992), *reversed on other grounds*, 54 F.3d 652 (10th Cir. 1995); *see Schneider v. City of Springfield*, 2000 WL 988279 (S.D.Ohio 2000); *Rushing v. Shelby County Government*, 8 F.Supp.2d 737 (W.D.Tenn. 1997).

[11] 29 C.F.R. §778.113(b) (2001).

[12] *Adams v. Department of Juvenile Justice*, 143 F.3d 61 (2nd Cir. 1998); *Cash v. Conn Appliances*, 2 F.Supp.2d 884 (E.D.Tex. 1997).

[13] 29 C.F.R. §778.114(a) (2001).

[14] *Hardrick v. Airway Freight Systems, Inc.*, 63 F.Supp.2d 898 (N.D.Ill. 1999).

[15] *See, e.g., Flood v. New Hanover County*, 125 F.3d 249 (4th Cir. 1997); *Heder v. City of Two Rivers*, 2001 WL 673505 (E.D.Wis. 2001).

[16] Opinion Letter, Department of Labor, 1999 WL 1002415 (May 28, 1999).

[17] *Condo v. Sysco Corp.*, 1 F.3d 599 (7th Cir.1993).

[18] Opinion Letter, Department of Labor, 1999 WL 1788149 (September 1, 1999).

[19] *See Samson v. Apollo Resources, Inc.*, 242 F.3d 629 (5th Cir. 2001).

[20] *Burgess v. Catawba County*, 805 F.Supp. 341 (W.D.N.C. 1992). *But see Roy v. Lexington County, South Carolina*, 948 F.Supp. 529 (D.S.C. 1996)(EMS employees properly paid on fluctuating workweek basis).

[21] *Heder v. City of Two Rivers*, 2001 WL 673505 (E.D.Wis. 2001).

[22] *Anderson v. County of Kershaw*, 172 F.3d 862 (4th Cir. 1999).

[23] *Griffin v. Wake County*, 142 F.3d 712 (4th Cir. 1998).

[24] 29 C.F.R. §778.115 (2001); *see* Opinion Letter, Department of Labor, 1999 WL 1002412 (May 27, 1999).

[25] 29 U.S.C. §207(e); *Martin v. D. Gunnels Inc.*, 30 WH Cases 997 (C.D.Cal. 1991).

[26] See *Herman v. Anderson Floor Company, Inc.*, 11 F.Supp.2d 1038 (E.D.Wis. 1998); *Idaho Sheet Metal Works, Inc. v. Wirtz*, 383 U.S. 190 (1966).

[27] *Bay Ridge Operating Co. v. Aaron*, 334 U.S. 446 (1948); *Herman v. City of St. Petersburg, Florida*, 131 F.Supp.2d 1329 (M.D.Fla. 2001); *Schmitt v. State of Kansas*, 844 F.Supp. 1449 (D.Kan. 1994); *Thomas v. Howard University Hospital*, 39 F.3d 370 (D.C.Cir. 1994); *Featsent v. City of Youngstown*, 859 F.Supp. 1134 (N.D.Ohio 1993), *rev'd on other grounds,* 70 F.3d 900 (6th Cir. 1995); Opinion Letter, Department of Labor, 1999 WL 1002353 (January 8, 1999).

[28] *Wisnewski v. Champion Health Care System*, 141 Lab.Cas. ¶34,095 (D.N.D. 2000).

[29] *Theisen v. City of Maple Grove*, 41 F.Supp.2d 932 (D.Minn. 1999); *Parisi v. Township of Salem*, 3 WH Cases2d 1460 (D.N.H. 1997); *Schmitt v. State of Kansas*, 844 F.Supp. 1449 (D.Kan. 1994); *Local 359*

Gary Firefighters, AFL-CIO-CLC v. City of Gary, 1995 WL 934175 (N.D.Ind. 1995); *Featsent v. City of Youngstown*, 859 F.Supp. 1134 (N.D.Ohio 1993), *rev'd on other grounds*, 70 F.3d 900 (6th Cir. 1995). [*See generally* Admin. Ltr. Rul., Dept. of Labor, Opinion of the Wage-Hour Administrator, Op. Ltr. No. 1669 (August 26, 1986)]. *But see Moreau v. Klevenhagen*, 956 F.2d 516 (5th Cir. 1992), *aff'd on other grounds* 508 U.S. 22 (1993).

[30] *Featsent v. City of Youngstown*, 859 F.Supp. 1134 (N.D.Ohio 1993), *rev'd on other grounds,* 70 F.3d 900 (6th Cir. 1995).

[31] *Theisen v. City of Maple Grove*, 41 F.Supp.2d 932 (D.Minn. 1999)(canine pay); *Thomas v. Howard University Hospital*, 39 F.3d 370 (D.C.Cir. 1994). *But see Albanese v. Bergen County, N.J.*, 991 F.Supp. 410 (D.N.J. 1997)(canine pay).

[32] *Utility Workers v. S. Calif. Edison*, 83 F.3d 292 (9th Cir. 1996).

[33] *Walling v. Youngerman-Reynolds Hardwood Co., Inc.*, 325 U.S. 419 (1945); *Herman v. City of St. Petersburg, Florida*, 131 F.Supp.2d 1329 (M.D.Fla. 2001); *Featsent v. City of Youngstown*, 859 F.Supp. 1134 (N.D.Ohio 1993), *rev'd on other grounds,* 70 F.3d 900 (6th Cir. 1995).

[34] *Herman v. Anderson Floor Company, Inc.*, 11 F.Supp.2d 1038 (E.D.Wis. 1998). It is rare to find a court declare a payment made by a public sector agency to be a "bonus" excluded from the regular rate. *See Herman v. City of St. Petersburg, Florida*, 131 F.Supp.2d 1329 (M.D.Fla. 2001)(shift differential not a "bonus"); *Dunn v. County of Muskegon*, 1998 U.S. Dist. LEXIS 19032 (W.D.Mich. Nov. 5, 1998)(longevity not a "bonus"); *Parisi v. Township of Salem*, 3 WH Cases2d 1460 (D.N.H. 1997)(longevity not a "bonus").

[35] *Theisen v. City of Maple Grove*, 41 F.Supp.2d 932 (D.Minn. 1999).

[36] *Slugocki v. United States*, 816 F.2d 1572 (Fed.Cir. 1987)(premium payments for overtime hours worked need not be included in regular rate); *Pullano v. City of Bluefield*, 342 S.E.2d 164 (W.Va. 1986)(premium payments for holidays need not be included in regular rate).

[37] *Aaron v. City of Wichita, Kansas*, 797 F.Supp. 898 (D.Kan. 1992), *reversed on other grounds*, 54 F.3d 652 (10th Cir. 1995).

[38] 29 C.F.R. §778.220(a) (2001).

[39] 29 U.S.C. §207(e)(4).

[40] *Featsent v. City of Youngstown*, 70 F.3d 900 (6th Cir. 1995).

[41] *See Donovan v. Two "R" Drilling Co.*, 581 F.Supp. 526 (E.D.La. 1984) *rev'd by Brock v. Two "R" Drilling*, 772 F.2d 1199 (5th Cir. 1985).

[42] *See Nolan v. City of Chicago*, 125 F.Supp.2d 324 (N.D.Ill. 2000).

[43] 29 C.F.R. §778.219(b)(1) (2001).

[44] *Hoke v. City of Omaha*, 29 WH Cases 1142 (D.Neb. 1989).

[45] 29 C.F.R. §778.303 (2001); *see Laffey v. Northwest Airlines, Inc.*, 740 F.2d 1071 (D.C.Cir. 1984).

[46] 29 C.F.R. §778.304 (2001).

[47] 29 C.F.R. §778.304 (2001).

[48] Opinion Letter, Department of Labor, 1999 WL 1788148 (August 31, 1999).

[49] 29 C.F.R. §778.310 (2001).

[50] *See Dunlop v. Gray-Goto, Inc.*, 528 F.2d 792 (10th Cir. 1976).

CHAPTER FIVE
THE CALCULATION OF "HOURS WORKED" UNDER THE FLSA

A. The Importance Of Hours Worked.

The concept of hours worked under the FLSA is important in two particulars. First, the number of hours worked, as has been seen above, is used in the calculation of the employee's "regular rate," which in turn determines the employee's overtime rate. Secondly, the number of hours worked defines when employees must be paid at the overtime rate. As such, it is necessary to have a clear understanding of the term "hours worked" under the FLSA.

The FLSA requires overtime pay only when an employee works longer than the applicable overtime threshold. For most employees, overtime must be paid when the employee works longer than 40 hours in a workweek. For some fire protection and law enforcement personnel, overtime must be paid when the employee works more than the overtime threshold called for under Section 7(k) of the FLSA for the work period selected by the employer. The FLSA contains no obligation that an employee receive overtime for working lengthy hours on a particular workday; it is only when an employee works over the applicable workweek or work period threshold that overtime compensation is required.[1]

B. The Definition Of Hours Worked; "Suffering Or Permitting" Work.

While the FLSA itself is vague in terms of defining "hours worked," the DOL's regulations are not. In general, hours worked are considered to be all time spent in physical or mental exertion, whether burdensome or not, controlled or required by the employer. Such time includes not only work that an employee is assigned to perform, but also work that an employee is "suffered or permitted" by the employer to perform.[2] The obligation of the employer to control an employee's hours worked or to pay the employee overtime for any excess hours worked is made clear by Section 785.13 of the DOL's Regulations:

> "In all such cases it is the duty of the management to exercise its control and see that the work is not performed if it does not want it to be performed. It cannot sit back and accept the benefits without compensating for them. The mere promulgation of a rule against such work is not enough. Management has the power to enforce the rule and must make every effort to do so."

An example of the application of the "suffers or permits" rule in the public sector can be found in *Reich v. Department of Conservation & Natural Resources*. In the case, a law enforcement employer reacted to the *Garcia* decision by issuing a memorandum stating "it continues to be Departmental policy that law enforcement officers may only work 40 hours per week." The employer informed all law enforcement personnel of the restriction in writing and the employer instructed its supervisors to monitor their subordinates' hours closely to ensure compliance. District captains reiterated the policy often at monthly district meetings, and officers were never told that they could or should violate the 40-hour policy.

In spite of these admonitions, many of the Department's law enforcement officers continued to work in excess of 40 hours per week without documenting the additional hours on their weekly reports. Since the law enforcement officers in question enforced game laws, much of the excess work was done in busy hunting seasons. The employer became aware of allegations that officers continued to work unreported overtime hours, and the Department's captains could have received actual notice of worked overtime hours by comparing arrest reports with weekly reports. The only direct evidence of the employer's knowledge of the work was that in one geographic area, one district supervisor (who retired in 1987) "told his officers to get their work done but not to report over 40 hours a week." It was clear, however, that the employer's policy was not to allow employees to work uncompensated time, and that the employer's directives that employees work no more than 40 hours in a week continued in force.

The Court held that the employer was liable for the uncompensated time worked by the officers. Citing 29 C.F.R. §785.13, the Court held that "an employer's knowledge is measured in accordance with his duty to inquire into the conditions prevailing in his business," and noted that an employer "does not rid himself of that duty because the extent of the business may preclude his personal supervision, and compel reliance on subordinates.[3] The cases must be rare where prohibited work can be done and knowledge or the consequences of knowledge avoided." The Court concluded with the following analysis of whether an employer had an obligation to do more than simply promulgate a rule and reinforce the rule in periodic staff meetings:

> "There is no indication in the record that the Department did anything at any time relevant to this litigation to discourage the overtime required by the vast majority of its officers to properly perform their duties other than to promulgate its policy against such work and urge the officers to 'work their best 40.' For example, no officer was ever disciplined for violating the forty-hour rule * * * The fact that some officers were able to comply with the forty-hour rule did not relieve the Department of its responsibility to ensure that the remaining officers did not violate the rule. We therefore conclude that the District Court erred as a matter of law by finding that the promulgation of the forty-hour policy, coupled with the ability of some officers to comply, insulated the Department from liability."[4]

Another illustration of the "suffers or permits" rule can be found in *Crow v. City of Derby, Kansas,* which involved a claim by a city police officer for overtime compensation for work at various non-police jobs including building toys and working for an ironworks company. All of the work was performed while the officer was working undercover on a task force with other police departments. Even though it was the officer's option to accept the undercover assignment and even though the police department claimed it had no knowledge that the officer had performed the work in question, the Court found the city liable for the work, noting the fact that the police department could fire the officer from the police force for any improper behavior, retained the ability to determine his work schedule and had control over his employment, pay, and records.[5] Applying the same set of principles to different facts, another court found work performed by a city police officer on a federal task force not compensable where the city lost complete supervisory control over the officer after making the assignment and had no way of determining what hours the officer was working, particularly since the officer submitted time sheets which understated his time worked.[6]

Other cases demonstrate the different ways an employer may be held liable for work it suffers or permits to be performed. In one case, a Court ruled that a state correctional facility should not escape liability for missed meal periods which it "knew or should have known" employees were unable to take.[7] In another case, an employer was held liable to firefighters who performed work during interruptions in their otherwise non-compensable sleep time in spite of the employer's contention that the work could have been performed during the non-sleep part of the work shift.[8] Employers who have permitted employees to volunteer time[9] or whose supervisors have allowed employees to work "off-the-clock" have all been held liable under the FLSA for suffering or permitting the work to be performed.[10]

Since the different ways in which "hours worked" issues arise are many, the following discussion will focus on the issues that arise the most often with respect to public sector employees.

1. Pre-Shift And Post-Shift Activities Such As Briefing Periods.

In addition to the hours actually scheduled by the employer, certain preparatory activities to a work shift must be counted as hours worked. For example, under the DOL's regulations, pre-shift briefings in police and fire agencies are hours worked, as are post-shift activities related to the job:

> "Such time thus includes all pre-shift and post-shift activities which are an integral part of the employee's principal activity or which are closely related to the performance of the principal activity, such as attending roll call, writing up and completing tickets or reports, and washing and re-racking fire hoses."[11]

Courts have not hesitated to uphold the DOL's regulations that pre-shift briefing periods must be compensated.[12] Analogously, one court has held that the time spent by police officers writing reports after the conclusion of the shift while the next shift was attending a briefing period must also be compensated under the FLSA.[13]

2. Rest Periods Or Breaks.

Some collective bargaining agreements provide that rest periods or break periods are not compensable time. Under the FLSA, short rest periods from five to 20 minutes in length must be included in hours worked regardless of any contrary provisions in a collective bargaining agreement or memorandum of understanding.[14]

3. Meal Periods.

Meal periods, unlike rest periods, are generally not included in hours worked under the FLSA.[15] In order to be excluded from hours worked under the FLSA, a meal period must be of at least 30 minutes in duration.[16] In addition, employees who are not allowed to leave their work stations in order to eat meals will usually have meal periods counted as "hours worked." As noted by one court:

> "During meal times the firefighters were required to remain at the station and were subject to emergency calls. The record makes clear that the firefighters were subject to significant affirmative responsibilities during these periods. The mealtime restrictions benefit the county by ensuring mainte-nance of an available pool of competent firefighters for immediate response to emergency situations. The firefighters are subject to real limitations on their freedom during mealtime which inure to the benefit of the county; accordingly, the three meal-time periods are compensable under FLSA regulations for overtime purposes."[17]

Where the employer has elected the 7(k) exemption for law enforcement or fire protection personnel, slightly different rules exist with respect to meal periods. Where a fire protection employee's shift is 24 hours or less in length, the meal period cannot be excluded from hours worked. Where a fire protection employee's shift is longer than 24 hours, the meal period can be excluded from hours worked only pursuant to an agreement between the employer and the employees.[18]

What constitutes "agreement" by an employee to ex-clude sleeping or meal time from hours worked under the 7(k) exemption? Most courts have held that there must be some affirmative indication from employees of a willing-ness to exclude meal or sleeping time from hours worked. In *Beebe v. United States*,[19] the Court held that employees who merely continued to accept paychecks which exclude meal and sleeping time had not agreed to exclude such time from hours worked.[20]

The DOL's position on the compensability of meal periods for law enforcement officers has varied over time. Initially, the DOL's regulations provided that law enforcement officers for whom the 7(k) exemption was claimed would be considered as engaging in "hours worked" during their meal periods, regardless of the activities the officers engaged in during their meal periods. Over the years following the promulgation of those initial regulations, the DOL indicated through letter opinions that there were circumstances under which meal periods need not be counted as "hours worked" for law enforcement employees even if the 7(k) exemption had been elected for those employees. Finally, when it adopted Section 553.223(a) of its regulations, the DOL reversed its earlier regulations, and specifically allowed for meal periods that are not counted as hours worked even where the 7(k) exemption has been claimed for the law enforcement employees in question if the employees were "completely relieved of duty" during the meal period:

> "If a public agency elects to pay overtime compensation to firefighters and law enforcement personnel in accordance with section 7(d)(1) of the [FLSA], the public agency may exclude meal time from hours worked if all the tests in §785.19 of this title are met."[21]

Prior to the mid-1990s, there was considerable litigation over the question of whether public safety officers were completely relieved of duty during the meal period. Most courts held that restrictions on where an officer could eat meals, requirements that the officer be available for call to duty and take appropriate action during the meal period, and limitations on what types of activities in which the officer could engage during the meal period were significant enough to require the conclusion that the employee was not "completely relieved of duty" and was thus entitled to compensation during the meal period.[22]

Then, almost abruptly, courts began to assess the compensability of meal periods using a different standard. Rather than applying Section 553.223(a) of the DOL's regulations and inquiring as to whether an employee was "completely relieved of duty" during the meal period, courts instead rejected the test found in the regulation and asked whether the meal period could be said to be "predominantly for the benefit of the employer."[23] Where public safety officers won most meal period FLSA cases under the "completely relieved of duty standard," they were virtually without success in claiming that meal periods were "predominantly for the benefit of the employer," as court after court held that meal periods should not be considered to be hours worked under the FLSA.[24]

4. Sleeping Time.

Under the FLSA, virtually all time that an employee is allowed to sleep on duty must be considered compensable time. Under Section 785.22 of the regulations, employees who are allowed to sleep on duty and who have shifts of less than 24 hours in duration must have such sleep time included in their hours worked. If the employee is on duty for 24 hours or more, sleep time of not greater than eight hours may be excluded from hours worked, but only if there is an agreement between the employer and the employee to exclude such sleep time.[25]

A slight modification of these rules occurs with employers who have elected a 7(k) exemption. Where with general employees the rule is that sleep time is includable in a work shift of less than 24 hours, with employers who have elected a 7(k) exemption for law enforcement or firefighter personnel, such sleep time is includable in shifts of 24 hours or less. In both cases, even if the test setting forth the length of the shift is met, an agreement between the employer and the employee is necessary in order to exclude sleep time from hours worked. The necessary agreement usually cannot be implied either by the employee's continuing employment or the failure of the employee to object to an employer's change in practices. As noted by one court:

> "To uphold [the City's] argument would mean placing [the firefighters] in a 'Catch-22,' no-win situation. [The firefighters] would be forced to agree in order to keep their jobs or quit to show their objection. [T]hese facts are hardly indicative of a meeting of the minds or mutual consent necessary for finding an implied contract."[26]

Courts have generally been fairly rigorous in demanding an arms-length fair agreement supported by adequate consideration in order to exclude sleep time from hours worked.[27] For example, in *Baker v. City of Pomona*, the Court held that an express agreement between the local firefighters association and the City to exclude sleep time from hours of work failed for lack of consideration. In exchange for the firefighters agreeing to exclude sleep time from hours worked, the City promised to pay overtime to the department's captains and battalion chiefs. The Court reasoned that since the captains and battalion chiefs were not, as a matter of law, exempt under the FLSA, the City's promise was illusory and could not support the agreed-upon exclusion of sleep time from hours worked. As the Court put it, promising what one is already bound to do cannot be consideration for a promise.[28]

Often the question of the exclusion of sleep time from hours worked occurs in the context of a non-union environment. In such cases, if an employer enacts rules that clearly exclude sleep time from hours worked, and if employees accept or continue work under such circumstances without protest, a court will hold that an implied agreement to exclude sleep time exists.[29] However, if the employer's attempt to exclude sleep time is not at all clear,[30] or if employees protest the exclusion of sleep time from hours worked,[31] courts will refuse to hold that an implied agreement to exclude sleep time from hours worked has been reached.

The DOL has established a similar enforcement policy with respect to sleep time for employees who work in residential care facilities. The enforcement policy was described by a court as follows:

> "This policy provides relief employees must be compensated for sleep time unless (1) employees are provided private quarters in a home-like environment, (2) the employer and employee have agreed in advance that sleep time will be deducted from "hours worked," (3) the employees get at least five hours of sleep during the scheduled sleeping period, (4) employees are compensated for any interruptions in sleep, (5) no more than eight hours is deducted for each full 24-hour on-duty period, and (6) relief employees are relieving a "full-time" employee as described more specifically in the policy."[32]

If sleep time is excluded from the computation of hours worked, what happens if an employee's sleep is disrupted? Under Section 785.22 of the regulations, "if the sleeping duty is interrupted by a call to duty, the interruption must be counted as hours worked." The DOL has also decided that if the interruption is such that an employee cannot get a "reasonable" night's sleep, the entire sleep period must be counted as hours worked, not just the hours worked during the interruption.[33] For the purposes of such regulations, a "reasonable" night's sleep has been defined as five hours or more.[34] Consequently, if the interruption prevents the employee from getting at least five hours of sleep during the schedule, the entire sleep time must be counted as hours worked.[35]

The DOL's enforcement policy also requires that employees be provided private sleeping quarters in a "home-like environment" without defining precisely what such an environment might look like. Generally speaking, sleeping quarters are adequate if they provide a "favorable environment that would enable sleep to occur and provide reasonable assurance that the employee will be rested and alert when his duty time begins."[36] In one case, a court found that firefighters stated a cause of action for sleep time under the FLSA when they alleged that their sleeping quarters had uncomfortable mattresses, were infested with insects and vermin, had wet floors, were noisy, had inadequate ventilation, heating and cooling and had inadequate shower facilities.[37]

5. Standby Or On-Call Status.

Perhaps no question of "hours worked" is as vague or has prompted quite as much litigation under the FLSA as when standby or "on-call" time must be compensated under the FLSA. Section 785.17 of the DOL's regulations provides a generalized definition of when standby time is considered hours worked:

> "An employee who is required to remain on call on the employer's premises or so close thereto that he cannot use the time effectively for his own purposes is working while 'on call.' An employee who is not required to remain on the employer's premises but is merely required to leave word at his home or with company officials where he may be reached is not working while on call."[38]

These general definitions are fleshed out a bit in the DOL's regulations pertaining to employees eligible for a 7(k) exemption. Section 553.221 of the regulations provides as follows:

> "Time spent away from the employer's premises under conditions so circumscribed that they restrict the employee from effectively using the time for personal pursuits also constitutes compensable hours of work. For example, where a police station must be evacuated because of an electri-

cal failure and the employees are expected to remain in the vicinity and return to work after the emergency has passed, the entire time spent away from the premises is compensable. The employees in this example cannot use the time for their personal pursuits * * * [On the other hand, a] police officer, who has completed his or her tour of duty and who is given a patrol car to drive home and use on personal business, is not working during the travel time even where the radio must be left on so that the officer can respond to emergency calls * * * The fact that employees cannot return home after work does not necessarily mean that they continue on duty after their shift. Firefighters working on a forest fire may be transported to a camp after their shift in order to rest and eat a meal. As a practical matter, the firefighters may be precluded from going to their homes because of the distance of the fire from their residences."[39]

Virtually all courts applying these regulations have held that issuing a pager or beeper to an employee, requiring the employee to respond to any pages within a reasonable amount of time, and mandating that the employee refrain from consuming alcohol does not constitute enough of a restriction on the employee's ability to effectively use his or her off-duty time for personal pursuits so as to convert the standby time into hours worked.[40] For example, a court held that guards who were required to be on standby status during a strike were not engaged in hours worked where they were "free to sleep, eat, and otherwise amuse themselves" while on standby.[41] Similarly, in *Allen v. United States*,[42] one of the seminal standby cases under the FLSA, the Court held that employees who were provided pagers and were required to remain sober and stay within the City of Baltimore were not engaged in hours worked under the FLSA.[43] In one particularly striking case, a court found that a hospital technician who was on standby status on a year-round basis when he was not working, and who was required to respond to calls within 20 minutes, was not engaged in hours worked under the FLSA even though the job was "oppressive" and "confining."[44] In addition, the mere fact that an employer pays an employee some compensation for standby time is not, in and of itself, enough to require a conclusion that the standby time is compensable under the FLSA.[45]

A lengthy discussion of how the FLSA treats standby time can be found in *Berry v. County of Sonoma*, which involved the standby time of coroners. The employer issued the coroners pagers and required a 15-minute response time to any calls for service – a requirement which the Court concluded did not impose excessive geographical limitations on where the coroners could travel while on standby. The Court also found relevant the fact that the collective bargaining agreement covering the coroners provided that the coroners would receive compensation only for the actual work conducted on call and not for the time spent while on standby. In concluding that the standby time was not compensable under the FLSA, the Court found that the coroners were free to pursue personal activities while on call, and had actually engaged in personal activities while on call such as shopping, eating out, entertaining, enjoying hobbies, and holding secondary employment.[46]

There are limited exceptions to the general rule that standby or on-call time is not compensable under the FLSA For example, if the frequency of the callbacks from standby status is great, the time spent while on standby may become hours worked under the FLSA. Several cases indicate that courts weigh a number of factors in determining when the frequency of callback becomes so high as to render all of the on-call time compensable under the FLSA. In one case, the fact that firefighters were called back to work from standby status an average of four times per day led a court to conclude that all hours spent on standby status were compensable as hours worked.[47] In a private sector case, a court similarly found that three to five calls per on-call period weighed heavily in favor of the compensability of the entire on-call period.[48] Moreover, the fact that employees may be required to continuously monitor equipment while on standby or on-call status also weighs in favor of compensation for the on-call period.[49]

In the *Berry v. County of Sonoma* case described above, the Court found that coroners who received death reports approximately every 6.45 hours while on call need not be compensated under the FLSA even where they were required to respond by telephone within 15 minutes. The factors the Court found important in rejecting the claim for compensation under the FLSA included the fact that the coroners could easily trade shifts, the geographic restrictions on the coroners who were on on-call status were not excessive since the coroners were issued pagers, and the coroners engaged in a variety of personal activities while on on-call status.[50]

There exists some debate as to whether a rapid response time requirement can place significant enough geographic restrictions on the use of an employee's time so as to render the standby time compensable. In one case, a court found that a response time of 20 minutes to any of seven facilities in a 12-mile area placed a geographic restriction on employees which was severe enough to make the standby time compensable.[51] In another case, however, a court found that a five-minute response time in a small town was not so onerous as to require the conclusion that the standby time should be compensated under the FLSA.[52] Following the same approach, a third court held that where EMTs living in a rural area were required to arrive at hospital within seven minutes of receiving a page, and had less than a 50% chance of being called in any 14-16 hour shift, the on-call hours were not compensable.[53]

6. Training.

Under the FLSA, attendance at training sessions is not counted as time worked only if four distinct criteria are met:

• Attendance at the training session is outside of the employee's regular working hours;[54]

• Attendance at the session is truly voluntary;[55]

• The training session is not directly related to the employee's job; and

• The employee does not perform any productive work during the training session.[56]

Prior to the *Garcia* decision, many law enforcement and fire protection employers had conducted training sessions while employees were on off-duty status and did not compensate the employees for the training at the overtime rate. With the advent of the applicability of the FLSA, virtually all such training time was eliminated by employers. In response to protests from employers about the elimination of this training time, Section 553.226 of the DOL's regulations mildly relaxed the circumstances under which overtime compensation must be paid for training time.

In particular, Section 553.226(b)(1) made it clear that attendance at classes required for certification required by law need not be counted as hours worked:

> "Attendance outside of regular working hours at specialized or follow-up training, which is required by law for certification of public and private sector employees within a particular governmental jurisdiction (e.g., certification of public and private emergency rescue workers), does not constitute compensable hours of work for public employees within that jurisdiction and subordinate jurisdictions."[57]

The same rules concerning attendance outside of regular working hours at classes required for certification has been applied by the DOL where the certification requirements are imposed by a governmental jurisdiction at a "higher level of government." Further, the rules concerning the non-compensable nature of such training are not altered even if part or all of the costs of training is borne by the employer. Lastly, time spent preparing for promotions or taking promotional examinations is not compensable under the FLSA.[58]

Some question has arisen as to the circumstances under which time spent at a fire or police academy is compensable as hours worked under the FLSA. Section 553.226 of the DOL's regulations provide only a general indication that the DOL believes that training time in an academy must be compensated:

> "(c) Police officers or firefighters, who are in attendance at a police or fire academy or other training facility, are not considered to be on duty during those times when they are not in class or at a training session, if they are free to use such time for personal pursuits. Such free time is not compensable."[59]

In an unreported decision, a court in the State of Washington found that the time spent in a police academy by Washington State Patrol troopers was compensable as hours worked under the FLSA. The Court rejected the employer's argument that recruits in a police academy were the law enforcement equivalent of private-sector apprentices, who are generally exempt from the FLSA's requirements. In addition, the DOL has issued letter opinions indicating that there is no exception under the FLSA which would make the time spent in classes or remedial training in an academy not compensable as hours worked. However, if the individuals attending the academy are not yet employees in that the employer has not yet tendered a job offer, the time spent in the academy is not compensable even though the employer operates the academy and attendance at the academy is a prerequisite to being hired by the employer.[60]

Occasionally, questions will arise as to how each of the DOL's four criteria for non-compensable training time should be interpreted. One court, for example, has found that training is not *voluntary* if it is expected of all employees;[61] the DOL has emphasized that if an employer at all "stresses attendance," attendance is not voluntary.[62] The DOL has opined that training is *directly related* to an employee's job if it is "designed to make an employee handle his/her job more effectively, as distinguished from training for another job or a new or additional skill."[63] A court has found that a deputy sheriff performed *productive work* during his field training officer program by making arrests, issuing citations, and engaging in general patrol responsibilities.[64]

7. Other Training Issues: Incentive Plans And Training Reimbursement.

An occasional feature of incentive plans is a requirement that as an exchange in whole or in part for the payment of the given premium, an employee is required to work uncompensated training. The FLSA does not distinguish between the different types of training time, and would require such training time to be counted towards hours worked since the four criteria set forth above would not be satisfied. Since the payments under an incentive plan must be counted towards an employee's "regular rate," employers with incentive plans incorporating uncompensated training hours may be subjected to significant amounts of overtime liability.[65]

Some employers facing high turnover rates have instituted requirements that if an employee quits within a specified period of the hire date, the employee is obligated to repay the employer the costs it expended in training the employee. Such training reimbursement requirements are only legal if, after the reimbursement has been made, the employee still received at least the minimum wage during the entire employment period.[66] One court has put the matter in even stronger terms, holding that "it was thus a transparent violation of the FLSA for defendant to require any part of a firefighter's regular wages or overtime compensation to be repaid if he or she resigned within a specified time. Any provisions of a training repayment agreement that violate the FLSA are per se unreasonable and will not be enforced."[67]

8. Travel Time.

For many years, travel time from home to work has not been considered to be compensable as hours worked under the FLSA.[68] In 1996, Congress amended the Portal-to-Portal Act to specifically provide that commuting time and time spent performing activities incidental to commuting time are not compensable as hours worked if an employer supplies the vehicle used in the commute.[69] However, under the DOL's regulations, if an employee is called to work in an emergency situation to a location that is a "substantial distance" from his home, such travel time is counted as hours worked.[70]

One additional exception to the general rule that commuting time is non-compensable is described in Section 785.37 of the DOL's regulations, which provides that travel to short-term assignments in another city may be compensable:

> "A problem arises when an employee who regularly works at a fixed location in one city is given a special one-day work assignment in another city. For example, an employee who works in Washington, D.C., with regular working hours from 9 a.m. to 5 p.m. may be given a special assignment in New York City, with instructions to leave Washington at 8 a.m. He arrives in New York at 12 noon, ready for work. The special assignment is completed at 3 p.m., and the employee arrives back in Washington at 7 p.m. Such travel cannot be regarded as ordinary home-to-work travel occasioned

merely by the fact of employment. It was performed for the employer's benefit and at his special request to meet the needs of the particular and unusual assignment. It would thus qualify as an integral part of the 'principal' activity which the employee was hired to perform on the workday in question * * * All the time involved, however, need not be counted. Since, except for the special assignment, the employee would have had to report to his regular work site, the travel between his home and the railroad depot may be deducted; it being in the 'home-to-work' category."[71]

In one case, officers who commuted as much as an hour each way to training classes claimed that they fell within the "one-day work assignment" exception described in Section 785.37. A federal appeals court disagreed, concluding "the officers' mandatory POST-approved training cannot be characterized as either 'special' or 'unusual' because it is a normal, contemplated and indeed mandated incident of their employment as described in their collective bargaining agreement. Furthermore, while the officers' training benefits the City, it is at least equally beneficial to the officers, who must attend POST-approved training in order to meet and maintain state law enforcement certification requirements."[72]

The main questions concerning travel time under the FLSA occur with respect to overnight travel to another city on special assignments. If necessary travel takes an employee away from home overnight, the travel time is counted as time worked.[73] A possible exception to this rule is created by the following paragraph in Section 785.39 of the DOL's regulations, which implies that certain types of overnight travel may not be counted as time worked:

"As an enforcement policy, the Divisions will not consider as worktime that time spent in travel away from home outside of regular working hours as a passenger on an airplane, train, boat, bus, or automobile."[74]

If there exist alternative forms of travel, such as public transportation, but the employee opts to use his personal car instead, the employer is only obligated to count as hours worked the time the employer would have had to count had the employee elected to fly or use whatever other public conveyance was offered by the employer.

One peculiar aspect of the compensability of travel time concerns the Portal-to-Portal Act, which amended the FLSA in 1947. The Portal-to-Portal Act was adopted by Congress in part to reassure employers that work time would not begin until the employee actually arrived at the work site. Occasionally, the results of the Portal-to-Portal Act can seem quite harsh. For example, in *Vega v. Gasper*, a court ruled that travel time of at least four hours spent by farm workers in riding on a farm labor contractor's buses to the fields where they worked was not compensable under the FLSA.[75] However, if the employee is ordered to report for work at a particular site to pick up instructions, the employee's work time begins when the employee begins to receive the instructions.[76]

9. Adjusting Grievances and Disciplinary Hearings.

Where a labor union is not in existence, all time spent in adjusting grievances between an employer and employees or a group of employees "during the time the employees are required to be on the premises" must be counted as hours worked.[77] However, where a labor union represents the employees, the DOL has announced that whether such time constitutes hours worked will be left to the process of collective bargaining or to the custom or practice under the collective bargaining agreement.[78]

If an employee's attendance at a disciplinary hearing is mandatory, the employee is entitled to compensation for the time spent at the hearing. If, however, attendance at the hearing is voluntary, and if the employer does not draw any adverse inferences from the employee's failure to personally attend the hearing, then the time spent at the hearing need not be compensated.[79]

10. Voluntary Time.

On occasion, public employees have either been permitted or compelled to work time which has been termed "voluntary time" and have not been compensated at the overtime rate for such time. Under the FLSA, it is clear that all such time must be considered as "time worked," and as noted above, the obligation to control employees working "voluntary time" rests with the employer. Even if the employer specifically prohibits voluntary time, if the employer thereafter tacitly or implicitly permits an employee to work voluntary time, the employer will be held to be liable for overtime compensation.[80]

11. Trade Time Or Shift Trades.

Generally, all hours worked by an employee must be counted under the FLSA, whether those hours are worked after a shift trade with another employee or not. However, Congress created an exception in the case of public sector employees who are allowed to voluntarily trade shifts without having such trade time counted as hours worked.

Under Section 7(p)(3) of the FLSA, two individuals employed in any occupation by the same public agency may agree "solely at their option" and with the approval of the public agency, to substitute for one another during regularly-scheduled hours of work. The work performed by the substituting employee may be excluded by the employer in the calculation of hours worked for that employee. As Section 553.31 of the DOL's regulations provides, "[w]here one employee substitutes for another, each employee will be credited as if he or she had worked his or her normal work schedule for that shift."

Under Section 7(p)(3), shift trading must be voluntary, with the employees not subject to "coercion, direct or implied." As well, any public agency which allows shift trading is "not required to keep a record of the hours of the substitute work."[81] Additionally, the DOL has ruled that Section 7(p) is not violated if employees pay one another to work their shifts in lieu of actually trading shifts.[82]

12. Dressing Time.

Generally speaking, the time an employee uses to dress for work is not counted as hours worked under the FLSA. The exception noted by the DOL is that if the employee's dressing activities are an integral part of the employee's principal activity, the dressing time must be considered as hours worked. For example, Section 785.24 of the DOL's regulations provides as follows:

> "If an employee in a chemical plant, for exam-ple, cannot perform his principal activities without putting on certain clothes, changing clothes on the employer's premises at the beginning and end of the workday would be an integral part of the em-ployee's principal activity. On the other hand, if changing clothes is merely a convenience to the employee and not directly related to his principal activities, it would be considered as a 'preliminary' or 'postliminary' activity rather than a principal part of the activity."[83]

Under Section 3(o) of the FLSA, if there is a "custom" under a labor contract of non-compensation for clothes-changing time, the time spent changing clothes need not be included as hours worked.[84] For such a "custom" to exist, there must be an ongoing understanding that the changing time is not counted as hours worked. Such a custom or practice will usually only exist where there have been contract negotiations in which the involved labor organiza-tion understood and accepted the employer's position that such time was non-compensable.[85]

Some questions were raised as to whether or not the provisions of Section 785.24 of the DOL's regulations requires that time spent by law enforcement and fire protection employees changing clothes at work must be considered as time worked under the FLSA if changing facilities are provided by the employer. The emerging answer appears to be that such compensation is not required. In *Turner v. City of Philadelphia*, a court rejected an FLSA claim for clothes-changing time brought by corrections officers, finding that a policy of 30 years of acquiescence by a union to the practice clearly established the "custom" necessary to make the change time non-compensable.[86]

13. Moonlighting.

Quite frequently, public employees "moonlight" for private companies, performing such tasks as working as security guards for local business establishments or working at dances, athletic events and the like. Section 7(p) of the FLSA, enacted by Congress in 1985, considerably relaxed prior rules of the FLSA which made such moonlighting difficult.

The DOL's regulations contain an extensive interpretation of new Section 7(p)(1) produced by the 1985 amendments to the FLSA. As explained in Section 553.227 of the regulations, fire protection and law enforcement employees who, at their own option, perform work in fire protection, law enforcement, or related activities for a separate and independent employer during their off-duty hours do not have the hours worked for the secondary employer counted towards the overtime threshold with respect to their primary employer. The regulations also allow an employer considerable rights in controlling the terms and conditions of the off-duty employment without the resulting loss of the exemption, including the right to the following:

• The right to maintain a roster of employees who wish to perform the work.

• The right to select employees for the off-duty work.

• The right to negotiate the pay at the secondary job.

• The right to retain a fee for administrative expenses resulting from the selection of employees.

• The right to require that the secondary employer pay an administrative fee directly to the primary employer.

• The right to require that employees observe their normal standard of conduct during the secondary employment, and to take disciplinary actions against those who fail to do so.

• The right to insist, through the passage of local ordinances, that only law enforcement and fire protection employees of a public agency in the same jurisdiction perform the secondary work.[87]

Two significant cases have been decided involving the application of Section 7(p) to off-duty work programs. In *Nolan v. City of Chicago*, the Court considered off-duty work by police officers at a city housing authority and a city transportation authority. The Court concluded the work was not compensable, finding that the two authorities were separate and independent from the City from a funding standpoint.[88] In a case decided coincidentally on the same day, a court in Kansas reserved judgment on whether a housing authority for which city police officers moonlighted was separate and independent from the City itself, finding that the fact that the two entities were treated separately for payroll purposes and maintained separate personnel policies and benefits systems was not the end of the inquiry.[89]

14. Mutual Aid Pacts.

Many fire agencies have mutual aid pacts with surrounding fire agencies, such that a call for assistance from one agency will produce a response from the surrounding agencies with whom a mutual aid pact has been negotiated. It occasionally occurs that a firefighter who is employed in one agency will work as a volunteer firefighter in another agency. Section 553.105 of the DOL's regulations requires that if, while acting as a volunteer for a second agency, an employee is required to respond to a call as the result of the existence of a mutual aid pact with his/her primary employer, all time worked on the call need not be compensated by the primary employer. If such a response is not required by a mutual aid pact, then the primary employer is not responsible for compensating "time worked" as a volunteer with another agency.[90]

15. Court Time.

Law enforcement officers are frequently required to testify on criminal matters in court during their off-duty hours. The DOL has announced that the time spent testifying in court must be counted as hours worked if the testimony is a result of the performance of the officer's official duties and if the employer benefits from the testimony.[91] Such time is compensable even if the officer volunteers to testify in court.[92]

16. Volunteers.

Another area Congress addressed in the November 1985 amendments to the FLSA were the rules concerning under what circumstances an individual could "volunteer" to work for a public agency without compensation. Individuals who are not employed in any capacity by a state or local government agency may donate hours of service to a public agency without being subject to the requirements of the FLSA "if their hours of service are provided with no promise, expectation, or receipt of compensation for the services rendered, except for reimbursement for expenses, reasonable benefits, and nominal fees."[93] What constitutes the payment of "expenses, reasonable benefits, and nominal fees" is governed by Section 553.106 of the DOL's regulations, which provides as follows:

> "(a) Volunteers may be paid expenses, reasonable benefits, a nominal fee, or any combination

thereof, for their service without losing their status as volunteers.

"(b) An individual who performs hours of service as a volunteer for a public agency may receive payment for expenses without being deemed an employee for purposes of the FLSA. A school guard does not become an employee because he or she receives a uniform allowance, or reimbursement for reasonable cleaning expenses or for wear and tear on personal clothing worn while performing hours of volunteer service. (A uniform allowance must be reasonably limited to relieving the volunteer of the cost of providing or maintaining a required uniform from personal resources.) Such individuals would not lose their volunteer status because they are reimbursed for the approximate out-of-pocket expenses incurred incidental to providing volunteer services, for example, payment for the cost of meals and transportation expenses.

"(c) Individuals do not lose their status as volunteers because they are reimbursed for tuition, transportation, and meal costs involved in their attending classes intended to teach them to perform efficiently the services they provide or will provide as volunteers. Likewise, the volunteer status of such individuals is not lost if they are provided books, supplies, or other materials essential to their volunteer training or reimbursement for the cost thereof.

"(d) Individuals do not lose their volunteer status if they are provided reasonable benefits by a public agency for whom they perform volunteer services. Benefits would be considered reasonable, for example, when they involve inclusion of individual volunteers in group insurance plans (such as liability, health, life, disability, workers' compensation) or pension plans or "length of service" awards, commonly or traditionally provided to volunteers of state and local government agencies, which meet the additional test in (f) of this section.

"(e) Individuals do not lose their volunteer status if they receive a nominal fee from a public agency. A nominal fee is not a substitute for compensation and must not be tied to productivity. However, this does not preclude the payment of a nominal amount on a 'per call' or similar basis to volunteer firefighters. The following factors will be among those examined in determining whether a given amount is nominal: The distance traveled and the time and effort expended by the volunteer; whether the volunteer has agreed to be available around the clock or only during certain specified time periods; and whether the volunteer provides services as needed or throughout the year. An individual who volunteers to provide periodic services on a year-round basis may receive a nominal monthly or annual stipend or fee without losing volunteer status.

"(f) Whether the furnishing of expenses, benefits, or fees would result in individuals losing their status as volunteers under the FLSA can only be determined by examining the total amount of payments made (expenses, benefits, fees) in the context of the economic realities of the particular situation."[94]

Thus far, the DOL has opined that the payment of $50.00 per shift is a "nominal" fee that does not convert a volunteer firefighter into one subject to the FLSA's requirements.[95] In an earlier opinion letter, the DOL found that the receipt of $8 to $52 per assignment, the furnishing of a uniform, and coverage under the city's workers' compensation plan did not impair volunteer status.[96] In a separate opinion letter, the DOL found the following benefits were nominal in value for volunteer firefighters: (a) Minimum city water and sewage allotments valued at $9 and $5.50 per month; (b) membership at the city swimming pool valued at $20 per month for a single person and $30 per month for a family; and (c) a contribution to the retirement fund valued at $250 per year with an increase of $25 per year up to $500.[97] A court considering the same issue found the payment of $7.50 per shift did not impair a firefighter's volunteer status.[98]

Only one reported court case has considered whether reserve or "special" police officers are volunteers for purposes of the FLSA. In *Todaro v. Township of Union*, the Court found that special police officers intended to volunteer their services to the City in spite of their subsequent lawsuit for compensation. In particular, the Court cited the fact that the special police officers continued providing law enforcement services even after the police chief removed their eligibility to compete with full-time police officers for paid off-duty work.[99]

The 1985 amendments to the FLSA also made it clear that the rules concerning volunteers also apply to individuals who are employed by the same public agency for which they are volunteering so long as the work in question does not involve the "same type of services" the employee performs on a regular basis for the public agency. As was the case with employees who work in a part-time capacity for the same employer, the DOL has indicated in Section 553.103(a) of its regulations that the phrase "same type of services" will be judged according to the underlying *Dictionary of Occupational Titles*.[100] The DOL's examples of what would and what would not constitute volunteering are instructive:

> "(b) An example of an individual performing services which constitute the 'same type of services' is a nurse employed by a State hospital who proposes to volunteer to perform nursing services at a State-operated health clinic which does not qual-

ify as a separate public agency as discussed in [section] 553.102. Similarly, a firefighter cannot volunteer as a firefighter for the same public agency.

"(c) Examples of volunteer services which do not constitute the 'same type of services' include: A city police officer who volunteers as a part-time referee in a basketball league sponsored by the city; an employee of the city parks department who serves as a volunteer city firefighter; and an office employee of a city hospital or other health care institution who volunteers to spend time with a disabled or elderly person in the same institution during off-duty hours as an act of charity."

17. Employees Working Two Jobs For The Same Employer.

Prior to the November 1985 amendments to the FLSA, significant questions existed with respect to employees working two different jobs for the same employer. Particularly, the question was raised whether the hours worked by such employees in the secondary job (usually a part-time job) counted towards the overtime thresholds for hours worked by the employee at the primary job.

Section 7(p)(2) eliminated the confusion that existed in this area. Under Section 7(p)(2), where public sector employees work "solely at their option" on an "occasional or sporadic" basis in a "different capacity" for the same public employer, the hours worked in the secondary job will not count towards the overtime thresholds applicable to the employee's primary job. In order to qualify for the exemption from the counting of hours worked at a secondary job for the same public employer, the work in question must be "occasional or sporadic." As defined in Section 553.30(b) of the DOL's regulations, "occasional or sporadic" means "infrequent, irregular, or occurring in scattered instances." Section 553.30(b)(3) of the regulations gives illustrative examples of such work:

"Typically, public recreation and park facilities, and stadiums or auditoriums utilize employees in occasional or sporadic work. Some of these employment activities are the taking of tickets, providing security for special events * * * officiating at youth or other recreation and sports events, or engaging in food or beverage sales at special events, such as a county fair. Employment in such activity may be considered occasional or sporadic for regular employees of State or local governmental agencies even where the need can be anticipated because it recurs seasonally (e.g., a holiday concert at a city college, a program of scheduled sports events, or assistance by a city payroll clerk in processing returns at tax filing time). An activity does not fail to be occasional merely because it is recurring. In contrast, for example, if a parks department clerk, in addition to his or her regular job, also regularly works additional hours on a part-time basis (e.g., every week or every other week) at a public park food and beverage sale center operated by that agency, the additional work does not constitute intermittent and irregular employment and, therefore, the hours worked would be combined in computing any overtime compensation due."[101]

In addition to being "occasional or sporadic," the employee's second job must involve work which is of a "different capacity" before the hours worked at the second job do not count towards the overtime thresholds for the employee's primary job. For example, if deputy sheriffs are assigned by their county to work a security detail at a hospital owned by the county, the time spent on the assignment will be considered as hours worked because it is not in a "different capacity" from the primary work of the deputies.[102] In Section 553.30(c)(1-2) of its regulations, the DOL set forth some general indications of what work in a "different capacity" is:

"(1) In order for employment in these occasional or sporadic activities not to be considered subject to the overtime requirements of Section 7 of the FLSA, the regular government employment of the individual performing them must also be in a different capacity, i.e., it must not fall within the same general occupational category.

"(2) In general, the Administrator will consider the duties and other factors contained in the definition of the three-digit categories of occupations in the *Dictionary of Occupational Titles* (except in the case of public safety employees as discussed below in Section (3)), as well as all the facts and circumstances in a particular case, in determining whether employment in a second capacity is substantially different from the regular employment."[103]

The examples given by the DOL are probably most helpful in determining what "different capacity" means:

"(3) For example, if a public park employee primarily engaged in playground maintenance also from time to time cleans an evening recreation center operated by the same agency, the additional work would be considered hours worked for the same employer and subject to the Act's overtime requirements because it is not in a '*different capacity*.' This would be the case even though the work was '*occasional or sporadic*,' and, was not regularly scheduled. Public safety employees taking on any kind of security or safety function within the same local government are never considered to be employed in a '*different capacity*.'

"(4) However, if a bookkeeper for a municipal park agency or a city mail clerk occasionally referees for an adult evening basketball league sponsored by the city, the hours worked as a referee would be considered to be in a different general occupational category than the primary employment and would not be counted as hours worked for overtime purposes on the regular job. A person regularly employed as a bus driver may assist in crowd control, for example, at an event such as a winter festival, and in doing so, would be deemed to be serving in a different capacity.

"(5) In addition, any activity traditionally associated with teaching (e.g. coaching, career counseling, etc.) will not be considered as employment in a *'different capacity.'* However, where personnel other than teachers engage in such teaching-related activities, the work will be viewed as employment in a *'different capacity,'* provided that these activities are performed on an occasional and sporadic basis and all other requirements for this provision are met. For example, a school secretary could substitute as a coach for a basketball team or a maintenance engineer could provide instruction on auto repair on an occasional or sporadic basis."[104]

18. Compulsory Medical Or Psychological Examinations.

In general, the time spent by an employee during a medical or physical examination which the employer orders the employee to undergo is counted as compensable time. Even if the examination occurs outside the employee's regular working hours, the time will be considered hours worked if the employer specifically requires the employee to undergo the examination as a condition of employment.[105]

19. Canine Programs.

In the years following the *Garcia* decision, law enforcement agencies with canine programs ran into unexpected difficulties with the hours worked requirements of the FLSA. In most canine programs, the law enforcement officer is expected or permitted to board the dog at home, and to groom, feed, train, and otherwise care for the dog while off duty. Courts have regularly held that to the extent that the employer benefits from these activities, the time spent by the officer performing these activities while off duty must be counted as hours worked under the FLSA.[106]

For example, in *Treece v. City of Little Rock*, the Court found that a wide variety of off-duty activities engaged in by canine officers were compensable under the FLSA since the officers were, in effect, maintaining a "critical law enforcement tool" through their activities.[107] The off-duty activities normally held compensable in canine cases include training the dog, maintaining the dog's shelter, feeding the dog, cleaning up after the dog, grooming the dog, taking the dog to the veterinarian, and exercising the dog. As the table set forth below describes, well over a dozen other cases have addressed the compensability of home dog care, with each court deciding the issue concluding that home dog care activities are compensable under the FLSA.

The time spent by a canine officer driving the dog to and from work is viewed on another footing. The majority of courts have held that canine officers are not entitled to compensation for transporting the dog between work and the officer's house.[108] Such courts have held variously that most of the commuting time does not involve traditional FLSA "work," and that the time that the officer is actually engaged in work during the commute (by cleaning up after the dog or tending to the dog's barking) is non-compensable because it is *de minimis* work (discussed below) under the FLSA.[109] A minority of courts have held contrary, finding commuting time compensable. The rationale for the decisions holding commuting time compensable focuses on the benefits to the employer of having the officer commute with the dog in a marked car. The Court commented that if the dog was kenneled, the officer would be entitled to compensation for the time spent driving the dog to and from the kennel, and reasoned that the result should be no different if the dog was kenneled at the officer's house.[110]

Normally under the FLSA, employers and employees are not allowed to reach agreements which call for less compensation than should be reflected by the hours the employee actually works. One exception occurs when the work is performed at the employee's house, where the employer typically has less of an ability to verify how much work is being performed. Under a DOL regulation, where work at home is involved, a good-faith agreement reached by an employee and an employer as to how much work is anticipated to be performed on a daily basis will be up-held.[111]

For example, in *Rudolph v. Metropolitan Airports Commission*, canine officers reached an agreement with their employer that their home dog care activities were likely to consume one-half hour per day. Several years later, the officers found that their home dog care activities were taking much more time than reflected by the agreement, and brought a suit in federal Court seeking additional compensation. Though the Court found that the officers in fact were working one hour per day on home dog care activities, it nonetheless upheld the agreement, ruling that since the agreement was reached on an arms-length basis, it was enforceable. The Court commented "it is not enough for [the officers] to show that they worked more than agreed. They must show that the agreement provided an unreasonably short amount of time to perform the assigned tasks."[112] Similarly, in *Brock v. City of Cincinnati*, the Court upheld an agreement compensating canine officers for 17 minutes per day of home dog care activities, commenting that "these officers entered the all-volunteer Canine Unit with eyes wide open, and the City twice negotiated with their exclusive bargaining representative, who first neglected and then outright refused to press the compensation issue on the officers' behalf. They have failed to introduce evidence to satisfy their burden of showing that the agreement provided an unreasonably short amount of time to perform the assigned tasks that constitute FLSA work and an unreasonably small amount of non-monetary benefits to compensate them for any time deficiency."[113]

Since the DOL's regulations also allow different rates of compensation for different types of work,[114] some employers have attempted to minimize their liability for the home dog care activities of canine officers by compensating the officers at a lower rate for the work performed at home. Such different rates of compensation are only legal, however, if they are the product of a voluntary agreement between the employer and the employee.[115]

Other employers have attempted to minimize their liability for home dog care activities by claiming that canine officers are independent contractors and not employees during the time they are responsible for the dog at home. Since independent contractors need not be compensated at the overtime rate, such an argument, if valid, would almost completely negate an employer's canine-time liability. However, to date, no court has accepted such an argument, with every court considering the issue finding that the canine officer remains an employee for purposes of compensation for home dog care activities.[116]

Often, an employer facing liability for off-duty dog care activities has already paid canine officers premium pay for the canine assignment. Understandably, employers in such a situation may wish to ask the Court to credit the canine premium pay against the liability for home dog care activities. Though the courts are split on the issue, the better rule appears to be that not only will an employer not be allowed such a credit, but in addition the amount of the canine premium pay must be included in the regular rate of pay for purposes of calculating the amount of overtime due.[117]

What follows is a matrix summarizing several salient features of the reported decisions on canine program activities:

Case	Off-Duty Dog Care Hours Specified	Other Pertinent Information
Baker v. Stone County, 41 F.Supp.2d 965 (W.D.Mo. 1999)	45 minutes per day.	Estimate of time worked accepted uncritically by Court.
Theisen v. City of Maple Grove, 41 F.Supp.2d 932 (D. Minn. 1999)	No reference.	Canine handler pay required to be included in the regular rate of pay for overtime purposes, even though City believed pay was for home dog care.
		Court recites jury's conclusion that canine handler pay served as compensation for specialized training and increased responsibility of handling canines.
		Court concludes that jury's verdict that employer did not act willfully required a finding that liquidated damages should not be awarded. *(Note: This portion of the court's opinion represents a distinctly minority viewpoint, and seems to ignore the different burdens of proof and persuasion on the willfulness and liquidated damages issue).*
		Court awards pre-judgment interest in lieu of liquidated damages.

Case	Off-Duty Dog Care Hours Specified	Other Pertinent Information
DeBraska v. City of Milwaukee, 11 F.Supp.2d 1020 (E.D.Wis. 1998)	At least 30 minutes, and potentially as much as 90 minutes, per day.	Officers met their burden of establishing a jury question on whether they spent more than the 30 minutes on home dog care activities reflected in their work shifts, which were reduced from 8.0 to 7.5 hours.
		Canine travel time is not *per se* non-compensable. Important facts to be considered are whether officers could make stops for personal activities during the commute, whether they were required to provide a significant amount of care to the dogs while traveling, and whether the officer is required to perform any other professional duties that benefit the employer. Court denies summary judgment to both parties on the issue of the compensability of travel time.

Case	Off-Duty Dog Care Hours Specified	Other Pertinent Information
Holzapfel v. Town of Newburgh, 145 F.3d 516 (2nd Cir. 1998)	Plaintiff claimed 44-45 hours per week; police chief believed work could have amounted to one hour per day.	Jury verdict for defendant reversed because instruction wrongly indicated compensation should be limited to home dog care activities that were "reasonably required" by employer, rather than for the time actually worked which was "controlled or required," "necessarily and primarily," or "integral and indispensable."

Case	Off-Duty Dog Care Hours Specified	Other Pertinent Information
Jerzak v. City of South Bend, 996 F.Supp. 840 (N.D.Ind. 1998)	For each of the two full years covered by the claim, officer estimated approximately 600 hours per year, including travel time.	Court concludes that home dog care activities are compensable, but reserves judgment on amount of compensation due in light of dispute as to hours actually worked, and fact that officer already worked a seven as opposed to an eight-hour shift to allow him to perform dog care activities. Summary judgment granted to employer on compensability of travel time. Summary judgment granted to employer on willfulness and liquidated damages issue, with Court citing department's intent to comply with the law through the reduced seven-hour shift.
Mayhew v. Wells, 125 F.3d 216 (4th Cir. 1997)	2 hours per day.	Vague opinion by Court appears to accept as accurate estimate of two hours per day of home dog care activities.
Albanese v. Bergen County, N.J., 991 F.Supp. 410 (D.N.J. 1997)	No reference.	Canine handler pay not required to be included in regular rate of pay for overtime purposes since it would result in a windfall for canine officers.

119

Case	Off-Duty Dog Care Hours Specified	Other Pertinent Information
Karr v. City of Beaumont, Texas, 950 F.Supp. 1317 (E.D.Tex. 1997)	No reference.	Court grants summary judgment to officers on compensability of home dog care activities, including travel time.
		Lack of time records of actual hours worked not fatal to claim because "employer bears the risk of inadequate recordkeeping."
		Court refuses to grant summary judgment on willfulness issue, noting that failure of City to conduct a survey or solicit information from officers as to whether they were performing the off-duty activities could reasonably be concluded by a jury to be recklessness within the *Richland Shoe* standard. Court makes same ruling with regard to liquidated damages.

Case	Off-Duty Dog Care Hours Specified	Other Pertinent Information
Bobo v. United States, 37 Fed. Cl. 690 (Fed.Cl. 1997)	One hour per day.	Case limited to commuting time issue. Court finds that commuting time can be compensable if the work-related activities during the commute are not *de minimis*. On the facts of the case, Court finds the work during the commuting time to be *de minimis*. Officers already paid one hour per day for home dog care activities.
Bolick v. Brevard County, 937 F.Supp. 1560 (M.D.Fla. 1996)	No reference.	Court's opinion limited to travel time. Court finds that commuting time can be compensable if the work-related activities during the commute are not *de minimis*. On the facts of the case, Court finds the work during the commuting time to be *de minimis*.

Case	Off-Duty Dog Care Hours Specified	Other Pertinent Information
Rudolph v. Metropolitan Airports Commission, 103 F.3d 677 (8th Cir. 1996)	Jury concluded time spent was one hour per day.	Court approves of agreement between employer and canine officers (not their labor organization) that home dog care activities amounted to one-half hour per day. Agreement was initially based on documented time spent on home dog care activities. Court cites DOL's regulation, 29 C.F.R. §785.23, which allows agreements between an "employer" and an "employee" as to the amount of work performed at home, and allows "reasonable agreement of the parties" as to the amount of work performed.

One of the plaintiffs in the FLSA action was a lead negotiator for the union which subsequently tried to negotiate home dog care compensation.

Note: As noted in settlement conference, dogs in question were drug dogs, which require little if any training off duty. |

Case	Off-Duty Dog Care Hours Specified	Other Pertinent Information
Treece v. City of Little Rock, 923 F.Supp. 1122 (E.D.Ark. 1996)	No reference.	Court grants summary judgment for officers on the issue of the compensability of home dog care activities, reserving for trial the amount of compensation due.

Court also grants summary judgment for officers on employer's liability for the time spent cleaning and maintaining take-home vehicles used to transport the dogs.

Court refuses to grant summary judgment to City on willfulness and liquidated damages issues, finding factual disputes prevented grant of summary judgment. |
| *Reich v. New York City Transit Authority*, 45 F.3d 646 (2nd Cir. 1995) | No reference. | Travel time for canine officers is only compensable if the "actual duties" performed by canine officers during the commute are not *de minimis*. |

Case	Off-Duty Dog Care Hours Specified	Other Pertinent Information
Andrews v. DuBois, 888 F.Supp. 213 (D.Mass. 1995)	No determination; officers estimated home dog care and commuting time of 3-4 hours per *day*.	Court grants summary judgment on home dog care liability issue. Time spent actually working during commute "rarely adds even marginal amounts of time to the officers' regular commute," and is *de minimis*. Court grants summary judgment on willfulness to employer, citing First Circuit precedent that an employer's awareness of the requirements of the law, standing alone, does not constitute willfulness (*note: The First Circuit stands alone on this issue*). Court finds factual dispute exists on matter of liquidated damages.
Wagner v. City of Santa Clara, 1994 WL 621667 (N.D.Cal. 1994)	No reference.	Canine officers not required to exhaust administrative remedies before bringing suit in federal court.

Case	Off-Duty Dog Care Hours Specified	Other Pertinent Information
Levering v. District of Columbia, 869 F.Supp. 24 (D.D.C. 1994)	30 minutes per day.	Based on the single affidavit of one officer that he spent 30 minutes per day on home dog care activities, appropriate amount of compensation is for 30 minutes per day. No indication as to why other canine officers in case did not submit affidavits.
		Court disregards evidence that the practices of other police departments compensate canine handlers up to 90 minutes per day for canine care.
		On the travel time issue, again criticizing the "sparseness" of the record before it (noting that in the *Graham* case the judge "had the benefit of testimony from numerous officers") Court rejects officers' motion for summary judgment. Court concludes that whether travel time is compensable "turns largely on whether plaintiffs are required to provide a significant amount of care to the dogs while traveling."

Case	Off-Duty Dog Care Hours Specified	Other Pertinent Information
Truslow v. Spotsylvania County Sheriff, 993 F.2d 1539, 1 WH Cases2d (BNA) 744 (4th Cir. 1993)	One hour per day.	Court upholds trial court's judgment in favor of canine deputy.
Graham v. City of Chicago, 828 F.Supp. 576 (N.D.Ill. 1993)	No reference.	The transportation of dogs in a canine program is an "integral and indispensable part of the officers' principal duties as canine police officers."
Nichols v. City of Chicago, 789 F.Supp. 1438 (N.D. Ill. 1992)	No reference.	Court denies summary judgment to employer on issue of liability for home dog care time.
Truslow v. Spotsylvania County Sheriff, 783 F.Supp. 274 (E.D.Va. 1992)	No reference.	Court rules that home dog care activities are compensable, holding that the fact that the officer "may have received some incidental benefit from the companionship of the dogs as pets is insufficient" for the employer to escape liability. Court reserves judgment on issues of willfulness and liquidated damages.

20. Physical Fitness Programs.

Questions have arisen under the FLSA as to the circumstances under which the time spent training for physical fitness programs is compensable under the FLSA. Much of the litigation has centered on law enforcement special response teams such as "SWAT Teams," which are required to meet higher standards of physical fitness than is required of the rest of the members of the department. Thus far, the only nationally-reported cases have rejected such claims for compensation. The leading case is *Dade County, Florida v. Alvarez*, involving a claim for physical training time made by members of the Metro-Dade Police Department's Special Response Team. While the Department required SRT members to pass a physical fitness test as a condition of the assignment, it did not mandate any particular type of physical fitness training. The Court held "it is clear that the officers did not perform any productive work while conducting off-duty physical training. SRT officers are employed to respond to potentially life-threatening situations, and no such work was undertaken while they were exercising. The officers presented no evidence that they were required to spend a specific amount of time training or to perform certain exercise routines during their off-duty hours. Moreover, the officers did not suggest that their employment would be adversely affected if they did not participate in any particular off-duty activities, as long as they could pass the fitness tests. In conducting off-duty exercise, SRT officers were free to train at any location, at any time, and for any duration. Given the freedom the officers enjoyed in selecting their off-duty activities, we conclude that the actual off-duty physical training performed by individual officers was voluntary within the meaning of the regulations."[118]

In the earlier case of *Thomas v. City of Hudson*, canine officers sought compensation for off-duty time they spent maintaining the level of physical fitness they claimed was required of them as members of the department's Special Response Team. A court rejected the claim, finding that there was no evidence that the officers were in fact required to meet a particular standard of fitness.[119]

21. Uniform Cleaning, And Equipment And Vehicle Maintenance.

One court has held that under some circumstances, the time spent by law enforcement officers caring for and cleaning and servicing their vehicles, guns, uniforms and other police equipment was compensable if it was not *de minimis* (see discussion below). The Court rejected the argument that there should be no compensation for the time because officers derived a benefit since they wore uniforms and carried guns to off-duty jobs as security officers. The Court found that the benefit derived by the officers was irrelevant to the issue of compensability, and that the appropriate test for determining the compensability of the time was whether the employer derives a significant benefit from the activity.[120]

In 1996, Congress passed the Small Business Job Protection Act (SBJPA), which contains several amendments to the FLSA. Among the amendments was new language to be added to the Portal-to-Portal Act which provides that time spent commuting in an employer-furnished vehicle is ordinarily not compensable:

> "For purposes of this subsection, the use of an employer's vehicle for travel by an employee and activities performed by an employee which are incidental to the use of such vehicle for commuting shall not be considered part of the employee's principal activities if the use of such vehicle for travel is within the normal commuting area for the employer's business or establishment and the use of the employer's vehicle is subject to an agreement on the part of the employer and the employee or representative of such employee."[121]

The legislative history behind the SBJPA is unclear as to precisely what activities are "incidental" to the use of a vehicle for commuting. It would seem to be most in keeping with the purposes behind the FLSA to conclude that fueling and washing the vehicle would be considered incidental, while performing maintenance on the vehicle would remain compensable as a non-incidental activity.

22. Early Relief In Fire Agencies.

Occasionally, firefighters will agree to relieve employees on the previous shift prior to their scheduled starting times. If such a practice is not required by the employer, the practice of early relief will not work to increase the employee's hours worked under the FLSA.[122] If, however, the employer does require such early relief, the time worked must be added to the employee's hours worked and compensated pursuant to the FLSA.

23. Sick Leave Confinement.

Though it is rare to find employers with such rules, occasionally a public safety agency will be concerned enough about sick leave use that it will issue rules confining employees to their residences on days on which the employees use sick leave. Most such "sick leave confinement" policies apply only during the hours for which the employee is using sick leave. For example, if the employee uses eight hours of sick leave to account for a day's absence, the confinement rule would only apply during the eight-hour period for which the leave is used, not the entire 24-hour calendar day. However, some sick leave confinement policies apply to the entire 24-hour period, prompting litigation under the FLSA as to whether the time spent in confinement constitutes "hours worked" under the FLSA.

The four courts addressing the issue have all found that sick leave confinement policies do not generate "hours worked" under the FLSA. All four courts have reasoned that "sick and injured officers are not fit to work, are not 'engaged to wait' at home for work, and therefore are not working."[123]

24. Minor Or *"De Minimis"* Amounts Of Time.

One general exception to the rule that an employer is obligated to compensate employees for all work time is generally referred to as the *"de minimis"* rule. Under the *de minimis* rule, an employer need not compensate employees for small amounts of work which come up only irregularly in the employee's workweek. To qualify as *de minimis* and not be compensable, the work must meet the following tests: Factors relevant are (1) the amount of time involved and the size of the aggregate claim; (2) the practical administrative difficulty of recording the time; and (3) the regularity with which the work at issue was performed.[124] For example, in one case a court ruled that the time spent by canine officers actually working during the commute to and from home with their dogs was *de minimis* and not compensable. The Court noted that the time spent by the officers disciplining the dogs was insubstantial; the instances in which dogs vomited, soiled cars, or required a stop to be walked were few and far between; that stops so that the dog could drink water consumed only a few minutes; and it would be administratively difficult to monitor and record this time expended by the officers.[125]

While there is no rigid rule or mathematical formula for applying the *de minimis* rule, it seems clear from court decisions that ten-minute increments of time are not *de minimis* and must be compensated.[126] The DOL has also indicated by regulation that it believes that an employee must be compensated whenever the employee works the greater part of 15 minutes (i.e., more than 7.5 minutes),[127] though the DOL allows rounding to the nearest half-hour if the result "is more beneficial to the employee."[128] One court has even found that the *de minimis* doctrine did not apply to time spent by meatpacking plant employees cleaning equipment at the end of a shift for an average of three minutes. In upholding the claim for compensation, the Court found that the amount of time worked was neither uncertain nor indefinite, and that the employees were required to clean equipment every day as part of their assigned duties, and that systems existed "in this day of technology" to calculate the amount of time employees spent cleaning the equipment.[129]

NOTES TO CHAPTER 5

[1] *Briggs v. Payless Cashways*, 1 WH Cases2d 503 (W.D.Tenn. 1993).

[2] *See* 29 U.S.C. §203(g).

[3] *See Cunningham v. Gibson Electric Co.*, 43 F.Supp.2d 965 (N.D.Ill. 1999).

[4] *Reich v. Department of Conservations & Natural Resources*, 28 F.3d 1076 (11th Cir. 1994).

[5] *Crow v. City of Derby, Kansas*, 1 WH Cases2d 288 (D.Kan. 1992).

[6] *Newton v. City of Henderson*, 47 F.3d 746 (5th Cir. 1995).

[7] *Abel v. Kansas Dep't of Corrections*, 2 WH Cases2d 1550 (D.Kan. 1995); *see Schwertfeger v. Village of Sauk Village*, 143 Lab.Cases ¶34,247 (N.D.Ill. 2001).

[8] *Allen v. City of Greenville*, 6 WH Cases2d 1167 (N.D.Miss. 1999).

[9] *Knowlton v. Greenwood School District*, 957 F.2d 1172 (5th Cir. 1992).

[10] *Lyle v. Food Lion, Inc.*, 954 F.2d 984 (4th Cir. 1992).

[11] 29 C.F.R. §553.221(b). *See Dole v. Enduro Plumbing, Inc.*, 30 WH Cases 196 (C.D.Cal. 1990)(pre-shift meeting for plumbers compensable as hours worked). In an exception to the general rule that pre-shift activities benefiting the employer must be counted as hours worked, the time spent changing clothes prior to a work shift is not compensable. *See* Dep't of Labor Op., [6A WHM 99:5269] Lab.Rel.Rep. (BNA) (Apr. 6, 1992); Dep't of Labor Op., Roll Call/Travel Training, [6A WHM 99:5198] Lab. Rel. Rep. (BNA) (Oct. 22, 1987).

[12] *Brinkman v. Department of Corrections*, 21 F.3d 370 (10th Cir. 1994); *Schwertfeger v. Village of Sauk Village*, 143 Lab.Cases ¶34,247 (N.D.Ill. 2001); *Local 889, AFSCME v. State of Louisiana*, 145 F.3d 280 (5th Cir. 1998); *Eustice v. Federal Cartridge Corp.*, 66 F.Supp. 55 (D.Minn. 1946); *Ballard v. Consolidated Steel Corp.*, 61 F.Supp. 996 (S.D.Cal. 1945); *Baylor v. United States*, 198 Ct.Cl. 331 (1972); *Cannella v. Village of Bridgeview*, 673 N.E.2d 394 (Ill.App. 1996); *Elbright v. City of Whitehall*, 455 N.E.2d 1307 (OhioApp. 1982). *cf. Bennett v. City of Albuquerque*, 130 Lab.Cases ¶33,223 (10th Cir. 1995); *Henson v. Pulaski County Sheriff's Department*, 1993 WL 438769 (E.D.Ark. 1993), *rev'd on other grounds*, 6 F.3d 531 (8th Cir. 1993); *Reich v. IBP Inc.*, 820 F.Supp. 1315 (D.Kan. 1993). In an exceptional case, *Lamon v. City of Shawnee, Kansas*, 972 F.2d 1145 (10th Cir. 1992), a court upheld a jury's verdict that police sergeants were not entitled to compensation for 15 to 30 minutes they spent preparing before pre-shift briefings, even though sergeants testified that briefings required them to review paperwork, review the duty roster, and make car, patrol, and meal period assignments to the officers on their shift. According great deference to the jury's verdict, the Court found that the jury may have simply found that pre-shift activities were not properly characterized as work.

[13] *Birdwell v. City of Gadsden, Alabama*, 970 F.2d 802 (11th Cir. 1992).

[14] *See* 29 C.F.R. §785.18 (2001); *see Schwertfeger v. Village of Sauk Village*, 143 Lab.Cases ¶34,247 (N.D.Ill. 2001); Opinion Letter, Department of Labor, 1998 WL 852687 (February 19, 1998).

[15] *See Marshall v. Valhalla Inn*, 590 F.2d 306 (9th Cir. 1979).

[16] 29 C.F.R. §785.19 (2001).

[17] *Kohlheim v. Glynn County*, 915 F.2d 1473 (11th Cir. 1990).

[18] 29 C.F.R. §553.223(d), 785.22(a) (2001).

[19] *Beebe v. United States,* 640 F.2d 1283 (Ct.Cl. 1981).

[20] *Bodie v. City of Columbia*, 934 F.2d 561 (4th Cir. 1991).

[21] 29 U.S.C. §553.223(d).

[22] *Burgess v. Catawba County*, 805 F.Supp. 341 (W.D.N.C. 1992); *Lamon v. City of Shawnee*, 754 F.Supp. 1518 (D.Kan. 1991); *Wahl v. City of Wichita*, 707 F.Supp. 473 (D.Kan. 1989); *Nixon v. City of Junction City*, 707 F.Supp. 473 (D.Kan. 1988); *see Brinkman v. Kansas Dep't of Corrections,* 804 F.Supp. 1163 (D.Kan. 1992). *But see City of University Park v. University Park Police Association*, 766 S.W.2d 531 (Tex.App. 1989).

[23] *Reich v. Southern New England Telecommuniations Corp.*, 121 F.3d 58 (2nd Cir.1997); *Henson v. Pulaski County Sheriff Dept.*, 6 F.3d 531 (8th Cir. 1993); *Alexander v. City of Chicago*, 994 F.2d 333 (7th Cir. 1993); *Lamon v. City of Shawnee, Kansas*, 972 F.2d 1145 (10th Cir. 1992); *Summers v. Howard University*, 127 F.Supp.2d 27 (D.D.C. 2000); *Abel v. Kansas Dep't of Corrections*, 2 WH Cases2d 1550 (D.Kan. 1995).

[24] *Bates v. Kansas Dep't of Corrections*, 81 F.3d 1008 (10th Cir. 1996); *Barefield v. Village of Winnetka*, 81 F.3d 704 (7th Cir. 1996); *Henson v. Pulaski County Sheriff's Dep't*, 6 F.3d 531 (8th Cir. 1993); *Alexander v. City of Chicago*, 994 F.2d 333 (7th Cir. 1993); *Armitage v. City of Emporia, Kansas*, 982 F.2d 430 (10th Cir. 1992); *Lamon v. City of Shawnee, Kansas*, 972 F.2d 1145 (10th Cir. 1992); *Maus v. City of Towanda, Kansas*, 165 F.Supp.2d 1223 (D. Kan. 2001); *Roy v. Lexington County*, 928 F.Supp. 1406 (D.S.C. 1996), *modified on other grounds*, 948 F.Supp. 529 (D.S.C. 1996); *Burnison v. Memorial Hosp. Inc.*, 820

F.Supp. 549 (D.Kan. 1993); *Myracle v. General Electric Co.*, 2 WH Cases2d 1067 (W.D.Tenn. 1992).

[25] 29 C.F.R. §785.22 (2001); *see Salazar v. Life Ambulance Service, Inc.*, 2001 WL 685755 (W.D.Tex. 2001).

[26] *Jacksonville Professional Firefighters Association, Local 2961, IAFF v. City of Jacksonville*, 685 F.Supp. 513 (E.D.N.C. 1987). *See also Beebe v. United States*, 640 F.2d 1283 (Ct.Cl. 1981)(agreement to lengthened shift for firefighters cannot be implied from continuing to work for employer); *Hultgren v. County of Lancaster*, 753 F.Supp. 809 (D.Neb. 1989), *rev'd on other grounds*, 913 F.2d 498 (8th Cir. 1990)(agreement cannot be implied as continuing condition of employment for caregivers at residential treatment facility); *IAFF, Local 349 v. City of Rome*, 682 F.Supp. 522 (N.D.Ga. 1988)(implied agreement to lengthened shift cannot exist if firefighter has expressed opposition to employer's actions). Some courts have reached a contrary result. *Brock v. El Paso Natural Gas Co.*, 826 F.2d 369 (5th Cir. 1987)(continuance of employment can be evidence of an implied agreement to the terms of that employment).

[27] *Doden v. Plainfield Fire Dist.*, 3 WH Cases2d 199 (N.D.Ill. 1995)(lack of evidence of agreement concerning sleep time requires that sleep time be included in hours worked).

[28] *Baker v. City of Pomona*, 1 WH Cases2d 1446 (C.D.Cal. 1993).

[29] *Roy v. Lexington County*, 928 F.Supp. 1406 (D.S.C. 1996), *modified on other grounds*, 948 F.Supp. 529 (D.S.C. 1996).

[30] *Johnson v. City of Columbia, SC*, 949 F.2d 127 (4th Cir. 1991).

[31] *Burgess v. Catawba County*, 805 F.Supp. 341 (W.D.N.C. 1992).

[32] *Hultgren v. County of Lancaster*, 913 F.2d 498 (8th Cir. 1990).

[33] *See* 29 C.F.R. §785.22 (2001).

[34] *Gay v. Extended Family Concepts*, 102 F.Supp.2d 449 (N.D.Ohio 2000).

[35] *Central Missouri Tel. Co. v. Conwell*, 170 F.2d 641 (8th Cir. 1948)(telephone operators); *Burnison v. Memorial Hospital*, 1 WH Cases2d 145 (D.Kan 1992)(paramedics); *Hultgren v. County of Lancaster*, 753 F.Supp. 809 (D.Neb. 1990), *rev'd on other grounds,* 913 F.2d 498 (8th Cir. 1990)(residential care facility). *See generally Rokey v. Day & Zimmerman*, 157 F.2d 734 (8th Cir. 1946)(firefighters with uninterrupted sleep not entitled to be paid for sleep time).

[36] *Trocheck v. Pellin Emergency Medical Service*, 61 F.Supp.2d 685 (N.D.Ohio 1999).

[37] *Allen v. City of Greenville*, 6 WH Cases2d 1167 (N.D.Miss. 1999).

[38] 29 C.F.R. §785.17 (2001).

[39] 29 C.F.R. §553.221 (2001).

[40] *Andrews v. Town of Skiatook*, 123 F.3d 1327 (10th Cir. 1997); *SEIU Local 102 v. San Diego County*, 60 F.3d 1346 (9th Cir. 1994); *Gilligan v. City of Emporia*, 986 F.2d 410 (10th Cir. 1993); *May v. Arkansas Forestry Commission*, 993 F.2d 632 (8th Cir. 1993); *Birdwell v. City of Gadsden, Alabama*, 970 F.2d 802 (11th Cir. 1992); *Martin v. Ohio Turnpike Commission*, 968 F.2d 606 (6th Cir. 1992); *Sletten v. First Care Medical Services*, 2000 WL 1196199 (D.Minn. 2000); *Brekke v. City of Blackduck*, 984 F.Supp. 1209 (D.Minn. 1997) *Darrah v. Missouri Highway Comm'n*, 885 F.Supp. 1307 (W.D.Mo. 1995); *Jackson v. City Council of Augusta*, 841 F.Supp. 1214 (S.D.Ga. 1993); *McIntyre v. Youth Rehabilitation Services*, 795 F.Supp. 668 (D.Del. 1992); *Wellman v. MCI Telecommunications Corporation, Inc.*, 30 WH Cases 1154 (W.D.Wash. 1991).

[41] *See Allen v. Atlantic Richfield Co.*, 724 F.2d 1131 (5th Cir. 1984).

[42] *Allen v. United States*, 1 Cl.Ct. 649 (1983).

[43] *See also Moss v. United States*, 353 F.2d 746 (Ct.Cl. 1965); *Clay v. City of Winona, Miss.*, 753 F.Supp. 624 (N.D.Miss. 1990); *Brennan v. Williams Investment Co.*, 390 F.Supp. 981 (W.D.Tenn. 1975).

[44] *Bright v. Houston Northwest Medical Ctr.*, 934 F.2d 671 (5th Cir. 1991).

[45] *Paniagua v. City of Galveston, Texas*, 995 F.2d 1310 (5th Cir. 1993).

[46] *Berry v. County of Sonoma*, 30 F.3d 1174 (9th Cir. 1994).

[47] *Renfro v. City of Emporia*, 948 F.2d 1529 (10th Cir. 1991); *see Casserly v. State of Colorado*, 844 P.2d 1275 (Colo.App. 1992)(10-12 calls per standby shift sufficient to convert standby time into hours worked). In another case, callbacks which averaged less than one per day were not sufficient to convert the standby time into hours worked. *Clay v. City of Winona, Miss.*, 753 F.Supp. 624 (N.D.Miss. 1990).

[48] *Pabst v. Oklahoma Gas and Electric Company*, 228 F.3d 1128 (10th Cir. 2000).

[49] *Pabst v. Oklahoma Gas and Electric Company*, 228 F.3d 1128 (10th Cir. 2000); *see Bright v. Houston Northwest Med. Ctr. Survivor, Inc.*, 934 F.2d 671 (5th Cir. 1991); *Cross v. Arkansas Forestry Comm'n*, 938 F.2d 912 (8th Cir. 1991).

[50] *Berry v. County of Sonoma*, 30 F.3d 1174 (9th Cir. 1994); *see Armitage v. City of Emporia, Kansas*, 982 F.2d 430 (10th Cir. 1992)(two calls to service per one week of standby does not render standby time compensable); *Owens v. Local No. 169, Association of Western Pulp and Paper Workers*, 971 F.2d 347 (9th Cir. 1992)(six calls per year does not render standby time compensable); *Burnison v. Memorial Hosp. Inc.*,

820 F.Supp. 549 (D.Kan. 1993)(1.1 callbacks per day of standby does not render standby time compensable).

[51] *Casserly v. State of Colorado*, 844 P.2d 1275 (Colo.App. 1992); *see Cross v. Arkansas Forestry Comm'n*, 938 F.2d 912 (8th Cir. 1991)(travel restriction of 50 miles and response time of 30 minutes may be sufficient to render standby time compensable); *O'Brien v. Dekalb-Clinton Counties Ambulance District*, 131 Lab.Cases ¶33,320 (W.D.Mo. 1995)(five-minute response time could convert standby time into hours worked).

[52] *Burnison v. Memorial Hosp. Inc.*, 820 F.Supp. 549 (D.Kan. 1993); *see Kartchner v. Town of Kearny*, 3 WH Cases2d 1153 (D.Ariz. 1996)(response time of ten minutes does not convert standby time into hours worked); *Pfister v. City of New Orleans*, 1 WH Cases2d 559 (E.D.La. 1993)(30-minute response time not overly burdensome on employees).

[53] *Dinges v. Sacred Heart St. Mary's Hospitals*, 164 F.3d 1056 (7th Cir. 1999)

[54] *See Wirtz v. Healy*, 227 F.Supp. 123 (N.D.Ill. 1964). *See generally Annotation: Employee Training Time as Exempt From Minimum Wage and Overtime Requirements of FLSA*, 80 A.L.R. Fed. 246 (1986).

[55] *Herman v. Hogar Praderas De Amor, Inc.*, 130 F.Supp.2d 257 (D.P.R. 2001)(new employees' attendance at training not voluntary).

[56] 29 C.F.R. §785.27 (2001). *See* Wage and Hour Memorandum No. 90-58, March 29, 1990 (Wage and Hour Division, Department of Labor); Administration Opinion, April 21, 1986 (Wage and Hour Division, Department of Labor); *see Atkins v. General Motors Corp.*, 701 F.2d 1124 (5th Cir. 1983)(employees who actually performed work during training sessions entitled to compensation). *But see Ballou v. General Electric Co.*, 433 F.2d 109 (1st Cir. 1970)(training time

not an integral part of the workday and as such is not compensable).

[57] 29 C.F.R. §553.226(b)(1) (2001); *see* Administrative Opinion, August 2, 1989 (Wage and Hour Division, Department of Labor).

[58] Opinion Letter, Department of Labor, 1999 WL 1788162 (September 30, 1999).

[59] 29 C.F.R. §553.226(c) (2001).

[60] *O'Neill v. Washington State Patrol* (unreported decision; copies available from Labor Relations Information System).

[61] *Herman v. Hogar Praderas De Amor, Inc.*, 130 F.Supp.2d 257 (D.P.R. 2001).

[62] Opinion Letter, Department of Labor, 2000 WL 33126563 (September 14, 2000).

[63] Opinion Letter, Department of Labor, 2001 WL 58915 (January 17, 2001).

[64] *Farmer v. Ottawa County*, 211 F.3d 1268 (6th Cir. 2000).

[65] Dep't of Labor Op., (January 24, 1990)(hours worked by trooper recruits at highway patrol academy are compensable under the FLSA and not subject to any exemption); Dep't of Labor Op., [6A WHM 99:5008] (BNA) (September 12, 1985)(time spent in remedial training compensable as hours worked).

[66] Opinion Letter, Department of Labor, 1999 WL 1788162 (September 30, 1999); Opinion Letter, Department of Labor, 1999 WL 1788152 (September 3, 1999). *See generally* Anthony W. Kraus, *Repayment Agreements for Employee Training Costs*, 44 Lab. L.J. 49, 49-50 (1993).

[67] *Heder v. City of Two Rivers*, 2001 WL 673505 (E.D.Wis. 2001).

[68] *Ballou v. General Electric Co.*, 433 F.2d 109 (1st Cir. 1970); *Walling v. Jacksonville Terminal Co.*, 148 F.2d 768 (5th Cir. 1945).

[69] 29 U.S.C. §254(a).

[70] *See* 29 C.F.R. §785.36 (2001).

[71] 29 C.F.R. §785.37 (1997) (2001).

[72] *Imada v. City of Hercules*, 138 F.3d 1294 (9th Cir. 1999); *see Kavanaugh v. Grand Union Company, Inc.*, 192 F.3d 269 (2nd Cir. 1999)(mechanic not entitled to compensation for travel to and from various stores where he performed services); *United Transportation Union 1745 v. City of Albuquerque*, 178 F.3d 1109 (10th Cir. 1999)(bus drivers not entitled to compensation for travel from last location on run, even though the drivers might end day at a relief point where own vehicle unavailable); *Vega v. Gasper*, 36 F.3d 417 (5th Cir. 1994)(farm workers' travel time on bus, sometimes as long as two hours, not compensable).

[73] *See* 29 C.F.R. §785.39 (2001).

[74] 29 C.F.R. §785.39 (2001); s*ee* Administrative Opinion, May 4, 1989 (Wage and Hour Division, Department of Labor)(discusses travel to and from mandated training).

[75] *Vega v. Gasper*, 36 F.3d 417 (5th Cir. 1994).

[76] *Martin v. D. Gunnels Inc.*, 30 WH Cases 997 (C.D.Cal. 1991).

[77] 29 C.F.R. §785.42 (2001); *see Koontz v. USX Corporation*, 2001 WL 752656 (E.D.Pa. 2001)(FMLA case).

[78] The Department of Labor has addressed the issue of the compensability of time spent while adjusting grievances on two occasions in recent years. *See* Administrative Opinion, May 10, 1988 (Wage and Hour Division, Department of Labor); Administrative Opinion, August 2, 1989 (Wage and Hour Division, Department of Labor); *see* Opinion Letter, Department of Labor, 1987 WL 467862 (July 17, 1987).

[79] *Debraska v. City of Milwaukee*, 189 F.3d 650 (7th Cir. 1999).

[80] *See Johnson v. Dierks Lumber & Coal Co.*, 130 F.2d 115 (8th Cir. 1942); *Pinkley v. Allied Oil Corp.*, 60 N.E.2d 106 (Ill.App. 1945).

[81] 29 C.F.R. §553.31(c) (2001).

[82] Opinion Letter, Department of Labor, 1993 WL 901178 (December 13, 1993).

[83] 29 C.F.R. §785.24(c) (2001).

[84] 29 U.S.C. §203(o).

[85] *Arcadi v. Nestle Food Corp.*, 38 F.3d 672 (2nd Cir. 1994).

[86] *Turner v. City of Philadelphia*, 96 F.Supp.2d 460 (E.D.Pa. 2000); *see Hoover v. Wyandotte Chemicals Corp.*, 455 F.2d 387 (5th Cir. 1972)(acquiescence in practice for four years sufficient to establish a "custom").

[87] 29 C.F.R. §553.227 (2001).

[88] *Nolan v. City of Chicago*, 125 F.Supp.2d 324 (N.D.Ill. 2000).

[89] *Johnson v. United Government of Wyandotte County/Kansas City, Kansas*, 127 F.Supp.2d 1181 (D.Kan. 2000), *affirmed Johnson v. Unified Government of Wyandotte County/Kansas City, Kansas*, 2001 WL 1566717 (D. Kan. 2001).

[90] 29 C.F.R. §553.105 (2001).

[91] Opinion Letter, Department of Labor, 1997 WL 958214 (January 21, 1997).

[92] *See* Administrative Opinion, August 2, 1989 (Wage and Hour Division, Department of Labor).

[93] 29 C.F.R. §553.104 (2001).

[94] 29 C.F.R. §553.106 (2001).

[95] Opinion Letter, Department of Labor, 1999 WL 1002403 (May 17, 1999).

[96] Opinion Letter, Department of Labor (October 1, 1987).

[97] Opinion Letter, Department of Labor (November 19, 1986).

[98] *Harris v. Mecosta County*, 1996 WL 343336 (W.D. Mich. 1996).

[99] *Todaro v. Township of Union*, 40 F.Supp.2d 226 (D.N.J. 1999).

[100] 29 C.F.R. §553.103(a) (2001).

[101] 29 C.F.R. §553.30(b)(3) (2001).

[102] Administrative Opinion, April 14, 1988 (Wage and Hour Division, Department of Labor).

[103] 29 C.F.R. §553.30(c)(1-2) (2001).

[104] 29 C.F.R. §553.30(c)(3-5) (2001).

[105] Administrative Opinion, August 2, 1989 (Wage and Hour Division, Department of Labor).

[106] *Thomas v. City of Hudson*, 3 WH Cases2d 513 (N.D.N.Y. 1996); *Andrews v. Dubois*, 888 F.Supp. 213 (D.Mass. 1995); *Levering v. Dist. of Columbia*, 869 F.Supp. 24 (D.D.C. 1994); *Nichols v. City of Chicago*, 789 F.Supp. 1438 (N.D.Ill. 1992); *Truslow v. Spotsylvania County Sheriff*, 783 F.Supp. 274 (E.D.Va. 1992), *aff'd* 993 F.2d 1539 (4th Cir. 1993); *cf. Udvari v. United States*, 28 Fed.Cl. 137 (1993).

[107] *Treece v. City of Little Rock*, 923 F.Supp. 1122 (E.D.Ark. 1996).

[108] *Reich v. New York City Transit Authority*, 45 F.3d 646 (2nd Cir. 1995); *Hellmers v. Town of Vestal*, 969 F.Supp. 837 (N.D.N.Y. 1997); *Jerzak v. City of South Bend*, 996 F.Supp. 840 (N.D.Ind. 1998); *Bolick v. Brevard County Sheriff's Dept.*, 937 F.Supp. 1560 (M.D.Fla. 1996); *Andrews v. Dubois*, 888 F.Supp. 213 (D.Mass. 1995); *Aguilar v. United States*, 36 Fed.Cl. 560 (1996).

[109] *Reich v. New York City Transit Authority*, 45 F.3d 646 (2nd Cir. 1995).

[110] *Graham v. City of Chicago*, 828 F.Supp. 576 (N.D.Ill. 1993); *Karr v. City of Beaumont*, 950 F.Supp. 1317 (E.D.Tex. 1997).

[111] *See* 29 C.F.R. §785.23 (2001).

[112] *Rudolph v. Metropolitan Airports Comm'n*, 103 F.3d 677 (8th Cir. 1996).

[113] *Brock v. City of Cincinnati*, 236 F.3d 793 (6th Cir. 2001).

[114] *See* Administrative Opinion, June 13, 1989 (Wage and Hour Division, Department of Labor).

[115] *Treece v. City of Little Rock*, 923 F.Supp. 1122 (E.D.Ark. 1996).

[116] *Thomas v. City of Hudson*, 3 WH Cases2d 513 (N.D.N.Y. 1996).

[117] *Theisen v. City of Maple Grove*, 41 F.Supp.2d 932 (D.Minn. 1999)(canine pay). *But see Albanese v. Bergen County, N.J.*, 991 F.Supp. 410 (D.N.J. 1997)(canine pay).

[118] *Dade County, Florida v. Alvarez*, 124 F.3d 1380 (11th Cir. 1997); *see* Opinion Letter, Department of Labor, 1994 WL 1004833 (June 1, 1994)(SWAT Team members not entitled to compensation for physical training time).

[119] *Thomas v. City of Hudson*, 3 WH Cases2d 513 (N.D.N.Y. 1996).

[120] *Treece v. City of Little Rock*, 923 F.Supp. 1122 (E.D.Ark. 1996).

[121] 29 U.S.C. §254(a) (2001).

[122] 29 C.F.R. §553.225 (2001).

[123] *Aiken v. City of Memphis*, 190 F.3d 753 (6th Cir. 1999); *Debraska v. City of Milwaukee*, 189 F.3d 650 (7th Cir. 1999); *Monserrate v. City of New York*, 142 Lab.Cases ¶34,171 (S.D.N.Y. 2000); *Hickman v. United States*, 43 Fed. Cl. 424 (1999).

[124] *Lindow v. United States*, 738 F.2d 1057 (9th Cir. 1984).

[125] *Reich v. New York City Transit Authority*, 45 F.3d 646 (2nd Cir. 1995).

[126] *Reich v. Monfort*, 144 F.3d 1329 (10th Cir. 1998); *Addison v. Huron Stevedoring Corp.*, 204 F.2d 88 (2nd Cir. 1953)(to disregard workweeks for which less than a dollar is due will produce capricious and unfair results); *Glenn L. Martin Nebraska Co. v. Culkin*, 197 F.2d 981 (8th Cir. 1952)(working time amounting to $1.00 of additional compensation a week is "not a trivial matter to a workingman," and was not *de minimis*); *Reich v. IBP, Inc.*, 3 WH Cases2d 324 (D.Kan. 1996)(14 minutes a day is not *de minimis*); *Hawkins v. E.I. du Pont de Nemours & Co.*, 12 WH Cases 448 (E.D.Va. 1955)(10 minutes of work per day is not *de minimis*).

[127] *See* 29 C.F.R. §785.48 (2001); Opinion Letter, Department of Labor, 1992 WL 845092 (April 6, 1992).

[128] Opinion Letter, Department of Labor, 1994 WL 1004879 (November 7, 1994).

[129] *Saunders v. John Morrell & Co.*, 1 WH Cases2d 885 (N.D.Iowa 1992).

CHAPTER SIX

COMPENSATORY TIME OFF UNDER THE FLSA

One of the major areas of impact of the application of the FLSA to public employers has been in the area of compensatory time off. As of the time of the *Garcia* decision, many public sector collective bargaining agreements and compensation plans allowed an employee to take compensatory time off in lieu of payment for overtime hours worked. Such compensatory time off may have been accrued at either the straight-time rate or at the rate of time and one-half.

The difficulty with these practices was that courts had repeatedly held that under the FLSA, allowing compensatory time off for all employees except those covered by a 7(k) exemption was permitted under the FLSA only if the compensatory time off was taken in the same workweek in which it is earned.

This policy was reflected in a DOL opinion letter of 1968:

> "An employer may not credit an employee with compensatory time (even at a time and one-half rate) for overtime earned which is to be taken at some mutually agreed upon later date subsequent to the end of the pay period in which the overtime was earned, rather than pay cash for the overtime as it is earned."

Certainly the leading case in this area was *Brennan v. New Jersey*, where the Court squarely faced the question of whether the DOL's opinion letter was correct. Relying on Section 531.27 of the DOL's regulations, the Court held that the FLSA clearly required that overtime compensation is to be paid in cash. The Court upheld the DOL's opinion letter, and held that the only type of compensatory time off which would be permissible as payment for overtime would be compensatory time used later in the same pay period. [1]

The rationale behind the Court's rejection of traditional forms of compensatory time off was explained at some length in *Dunlop v. New Jersey*:

> "We conceive this restrictive endorsement of compensatory time off to be perfectly consistent with the language and goals of the FLSA as well as the regulations surrounding it. The restriction that time off for overtime be granted within the same pay period as earned mirrors the stricture placed upon monetary payments for overtime. In fact, this restriction ensures that compensatory time off achieves the main objective of the FLSA's overtime compensation provision: the broadening of employment. That goal could be easily defeated if the employer were allowed discretion to manipulate the scheduled time off so as to coincide with off-season or slack work periods. Moreover, a program of compensatory time off also attains the secondary objective of the * * * FLSA's overtime provision which is that the worker will be compensated for the burden of overtime work. Under such a program, the worker is assured of receiving his fixed salary, even though he has worked less than the total number of hours required at regular pay rates to earn that salary."[2]

A. Section 7(o)'s Lifting Of The Ban On Compensatory Time Off In The Public Sector.

The ban on the use of compensatory time off in the public sector ended with the enactment of a new Section 207(o) of the FLSA in 1985. By enacting Section 7(o), Congress not only specifically authorized the use of compensatory time off for public sector employers as a means of compensation for overtime hours worked, but also established specific procedures under which compensatory time off could be used. One commentator summarized the purposes behind Section 7(o) as follows:

> "First, [Congress] wanted to reduce the monetary impact of overruling *National League of Cities* that would result from the attendant imposition of the FLSA regulations on states and municipalities. Second, Congress recognized that many public employees regard compensatory time as a welcome substitute to overtime, and prefer the extra time off to cash payments."[3]

Under Section 7(o) of the FLSA, different maximum allowable accruals of compensatory time off are established depending upon the type of work the employee performs. For employees engaged in "public safety," "emergency response," and "seasonal" activities, the maximum accrual is 480 hours. For all other employees, the maximum accrual is 240 hours.

Two points are in order about the accrual limitations on FLSA compensatory time. First, the accrual limitations set the maximum accruals of compensatory time. Lesser accruals pursuant to a collective bargaining agreement or local practice are permitted. As well, simply because Section 7(o) sets maximum accrual levels of compensatory time off does not in any way force an employer to grant any compensatory time off. Second, the accrual limitations are expressed in the form of straight-time hours. Thus, the 480 hour maximum accumulation reflects 320 hours of actual overtime (multiplied by the overtime factor of 1.5).

1. Employees Qualifying As Engaged In "Emergency Response Activity."

Under Section 7(o), employees engaged in "emergency response" activities as well as law enforcement officers and firefighters are eligible for the higher maximum accruals of compensatory time off. The DOL's regulations have fleshed out the statutory language as to which employees qualify as being engaged in "emergency response activity." Under the DOL's interpretation, such activity "includes dispatching of emergency vehicles and personnel, rescue work and ambulance services." Thus, individuals employed as dispatchers in police or fire agencies qualify for the 480-hour maximum accrual of compensatory time.

2. The Definition Of "Seasonal Activity."

Under Section 7(o) of the FLSA, employees who engage in "seasonal activity" are also eligible for the higher maximum accrual of compensatory time off. Section 553.24(e) of the DOL's regulations define in great detail what type of employees qualify for the "seasonal activity" higher compensatory time accrual:

> "The term 'seasonal activity' includes work during periods of significantly increased demand, which are of a regular and recurring nature. In determining whether employees are considered engaged in a seasonal activity, the first consideration is whether the activity in which they are engaged is a regular and recurring aspect of the employee's work. The second consideration is whether the projected overtime hours during the period of significantly increased demand are likely to result in the accumulation during such period of more than 240 compensatory time hours * * * Such projections will normally be based on the employer's past experience with similar employment situations."[4]

The DOL's definition of "seasonal activities" appears to point primarily to work that is greatly influenced by such regular and recurring events as the weather. Section 553.24(e)(2) makes it clear, however, that it is not simply weather-related periods of intense work that will qualify an employee for the "seasonal activity" maximum compensatory time accumulation:

> "Seasonal activity is not limited strictly to those operations that are very susceptible to changes in

the weather. As an example, employees processing tax returns over an extended period of significantly increased demand whose overtime hours could be expected to result in the accumulation during such period of more than 240 compensatory time hours will typically qualify as engaged in a seasonal activity."[5]

B. Who Controls Whether Compensatory Time Is Granted In Lieu Of Cash Payment For Overtime, The Employer Or The Employee?

Even with the enactment of Section 7(o), the FLSA remains very biased in favor of cash compensation for overtime hours worked. Absent a collective bargaining agreement or local practice to the contrary, under no circumstances is an <u>employee</u> entitled to insist upon compensatory time off as compensation for overtime hours worked. Put another way, if the employer insists upon cash compensation for overtime, nothing in the FLSA restricts the employer from never offering a choice of compensatory time to its employees. A collective bargaining agreement or local practice, however, may <u>allow</u> the employee such a choice between compensatory time off or cash compensation for overtime hours worked.

Similarly, with the very limited exceptions discussed below, an <u>employer</u> cannot insist that an employee take compensatory time off in lieu of cash payment for overtime. Under Section 7(o)(2), the FLSA makes it quite clear that compensatory time off can be granted only pursuant either to applicable provisions of a collective bargaining agreement or other agreement between the public agency and representatives of the employees[6] or, where there is no representative for the employees, an agreement reached between the employer and the employee.[7] Section 553.23(a) of the DOL's regulations emphasizes that, as a condition for use of compensatory time in lieu of overtime payment in cash, the FLSA "requires an agreement or understanding reached prior to the performance of work."

Accordingly, it is clear under the FLSA that neither an employer nor an employee may unilaterally insist upon the use of compensatory time off as the substitute for overtime payment in cash. It is only with the agreement of both the employer and the employee (or the representative of the employee) that FLSA compensatory time off may be substituted for cash payment for overtime.

Owing chiefly to different discussions in the Senate and the House of Representatives on the subject, there has been a significant amount of litigation on what a "representative" is for the purpose of Section 7(o). The report from the House of Representatives describes a Section 7(o) representative as not needing to be a "formal or recognized collective bargaining agent":

> "Where employees have selected a representative, which need not be a formal or recognized collective bargaining agent as long as it is a representative designated by the employees, the agreement or understanding must be between the representative and the employer."[8]

The report from the Senate puts the matter differently, and speaks in terms of a "recognized" representative:

> "Where employees do not have a recognized representative, the agreement or understanding must be between the employer and the individual employee."[9]

Owing chiefly to this confusing history, courts initially split on the question of whether employees working in agencies without collective bargaining are entitled to designate a representative for the purposes of Section 7(o).[10] In 1993, in *Moreau v. Klevenhagen*, the Supreme Court resolved the dispute by ruling that an agreement with a "representative" was only necessary if the representative had collective bargaining rights with the employer. In

Moreau, the Supreme Court concluded that deputy sheriffs who had designated a union as their representative for purposes of an agreement concerning compensatory time off did not have the right to have a representative with authority to enter into agreement with the County, since state law prohibited the County from entering into a collective agreement with the union.[11] Thus, in jurisdictions without collective bargaining, the agreement to implement compensatory time off must be with individual employees even if the employees have joined a labor union or other organization that does not have the right to collectively bargain.[12]

Where employees have a collective bargaining representative, the employer may only implement a system of compensatory time off with the agreement of the representative. For example, in one case a court declared illegal a system of compensatory time off where the collective bargaining agreement covering the employees provided that overtime compensation was to be paid in cash.[13]

C. The "Grandfathering" Exception For Employees Hired Prior To April 15, 1986.

The only significant exception to the above rules is that employees who were both hired prior to April 15, 1986 and who have no representative can be compelled by an employer to take compensatory time off in lieu of cash payment for overtime if the employer "has had a regular practice of rewarding compensatory time off in lieu of overtime pay" prior to April 15, 1986. In the words of Section 553.23(c)(2), such an employer will be "deemed" to have reached an "agreement" with its employees:

> "Section 2(a) of the 1985 amendments provides that in the case of employees who have no representative and were employed prior to April 15, 1986, a public agency that has had a regular practice of awarding compensatory time off in lieu of overtime pay is deemed to have reached an agreement or un-

derstanding with these employees as of April 15, 1986. A public agency need not secure an agreement or understanding with each employee employed prior to that date. If, however, such a regular practice does not conform to the provisions of Section 7(o) of the Act, it must be modified to do so with regard to practices after April 14, 1986. With respect to employees hired after April 14, 1986, the public employer who elects to use compensatory time must follow the guidelines on agreements discussed in paragraph (c)(1) of this Section."[14]

One case has fleshed out the circumstances under which a past practice that existed prior to April 15, 1986 can substitute as the necessary agreement to use compensatory time off in a non-collective bargaining environment. In the case, the employer had a practice in effect on April 15, 1986 of awarding compensatory time in lieu of cash compensation for overtime. Even though the president of the local firefighters' association (which did not have the right to collectively bargain under the law) sent a letter to the fire chief expressing the firefighters' dissatisfaction with the practice, the Court held that the City could properly continue to provide compensatory time in lieu of cash overtime to firefighters because of the pre-existing practice.[15]

D. The "Condition Of Employment" Exception.

The second exception to the general rule requiring an agreement between an employer and an employee prior to the use of FLSA compensatory time can be found in Section 553.23(c)(1) of the DOL's regulations. As described in the regulation, the "agreement" reached between an employer and employees who are unrepresented "may take the form of an express condition of employment" provided two requirements are met: (1) The employee "knowingly and voluntarily agrees to it as a condition of employment"; and (2) the employee is "informed that the compensatory time received may be preserved, used or cashed out consistent with the other requirements of Section 7(o) of the Act."[16]

E. The Formality Required For An "Agreement" To Take Compensatory Time Off.

The DOL's regulations require very little formality with respect to an agreement to take compensatory time off in lieu of overtime compensation in cash. Under Section 553.23(c)(1), where there is no collective bargaining representative, the agreement "need not be in writing." However, the regulation does require that a "record of its existence (of the agreement) must be kept." The regulations envision that a memorandum commemorating an agreement reached between employees and their employer regarding the use of compensatory time will suffice to meet the formality requirements of Section 7(o).[17]

Where there is a representative of the employees, Section 553.23(b)(1) states that the agreement concerning the use of compensatory time off may be "either through a collective bargaining agreement or through a memorandum of understanding or other type of oral or written agreement."[18] While Section 553.23(b)(1) does not contain the requirement that an employer keep a "record" of an oral agreement in the same fashion that Section 553.23(c)(1) does, a prudent employer would be well advised to keep such a record of an oral agreement concerning the utilization of compensatory time off.[19]

F. The Conditions For The Use Of FLSA Compensatory Time.

Section 7(o) of the FLSA establishes very different criteria for the use of FLSA compensatory time off than had generally been the case with respect to compensatory time off prior to the *Garcia* decision, or with forms of compensatory time off granted under collective bargaining agreements. The significant differences are two. First, under

Section 7(o), an employee who has accrued compensatory time off "shall be permitted to use such time off" within a "reasonable period" after making the request unless granting the time off would "unduly disrupt" the operations of the employer. Second, under a Supreme Court decision, employers have the right to force employees to use FLSA compensatory time off with or without the employees' agreement. In summary, FLSA compensatory time off is different from traditional forms of compensatory time off because either the employer or the employee has the right to, within only modest limits, unilaterally demand the ability to force the use of compensatory time off. [20]

1. The Meaning Of "Reasonable Period."

The key phrases in Section 7(o) are "reasonable period" and "unduly disrupt." In Section 553.25(c) of its interpretative regulations, the DOL stated that the first of these terms – "reasonable period" – will be determined by considering "the customary work practices within the agency based on the facts and circumstances in each case." The types of circumstances the DOL has indicated it considers important in determining a "reasonable period" include the following:

- The normal schedule of work for the employer;

- Any anticipated peak work loads on the day or days when compensatory time off is requested. Anticipated work loads will be judged based upon the past experience of the employer;

- Whether there are any emergency requirements for staff and services during the time in question; and

- The availability of qualified substitute staff.

The DOL has also encouraged that whatever "agreement" exists which allows the use of FLSA compensatory time off in lieu of cash payment of overtime define what a "reasonable period" is, and has indicated that such agreements or understandings will "govern" the meaning of "reasonable period."

156

Somewhat surprisingly, the first two courts to consider the issue of what a "reasonable period" is disagreed as to how the term should be defined. In the first case, *Aiken v. City of Memphis*, the employer's policy, incorporated into a collective bargaining agreement, was to define the "reasonable period" for requesting the use of compensatory time as beginning 30-days prior to the date in question and ending when the number of officers requesting the use of compensatory time on the given date would bring the precinct's staffing levels to the minimum necessary for efficient operation – without regard to whether other employees were available for call in on an overtime basis to maintain staffing at an acceptable basis. In upholding the policy, a divided court (the Court split 2-1 on the issue) focused on the fact that the agreement as to compensatory time off use had been voluntarily negotiated between the employer and employees.[21]

The second decision to interpret "reasonable period" not only declared illegal an employer's policy virtually identical to that in *Aiken*, but also specifically rejected the holding in *Aiken* as being contrary to both Section 7(o) and the DOL's regulations. In the case, *Debraska v. City of Milwaukee*, the Court held that a policy defining "reasonable period" in terms of minimum staffing: "transparently disguises a substantive rule about when it will deny comp time requests – whenever it is necessary to avoid having another officer work overtime – as a rule about timing. This creative definition of 'reasonable period', like the City of Milwaukee's, writes the 'unduly disrupt' standard out of the statute."[22]

2. The Meaning Of "Unduly Disrupt."

When the DOL first issued its draft regulations on Section 7(o), it indicated that the phrase "unduly disrupt" is strictly construed, and that "[m]ere inconvenience to the employer is an insufficient basis for denial of a request for compensatory time off" – a position to which it has adhered to the present time. In expanding on this point, the DOL also noted the following:

> "For an agency to turn down a request from an employee for compensatory time off requires that it should reasonably and in good faith anticipate that it would impose an unreasonable burden on the agency's ability to provide services of acceptable quality and quantity for the public during the time requested without the use of the employee's services."[23]

When the DOL was considering the text of its prospective regulations on Section 7(o), a good deal of public debate erupted concerning the meaning of "unduly disrupt." In particular, the debate focused on whether or not the fact that an employer would be required to fill in for an absent employee using compensatory time off with another employee on an overtime basis would constitute the requisite "undue disruption" justifying denial of the request for compensatory time off.

The DOL firmly resolved the issue with the issuance of 29 C.F.R. §553.25 (a). As noted in its comments to the regulation, the DOL rejected the arguments of employers that the phrase "unduly disrupt" should be read broadly enough to allow employers to deny requests for compensatory time off when employers would be required to fill in for the absent employee with another employee on an overtime basis:

> "With regard to the term 'unduly disrupt,' many commentators, including the International Association of Fire Chiefs (IAFC), suggested that the term be defined to state that it would be unduly disruptive to grant compensatory time off any time granting such leave to an employee would require another employee to work overtime to perform the services. Also, the [National League of Cities] and others disagreed with the statement in this section

that 'mere inconvenience to the employer is an insufficient basis for denial of a request for compensatory time off.'

"The legislative history to the 1985 Amendment specifically clarifies that the term 'unduly disrupt' means something more than mere inconvenience (H.Rep., p. 23 and S.Rep., p. 12). The Reports provide an example that a request by a snow plow operator in Vermont or Maine to use compensatory time in February would probably be unduly disruptive even if the request were made well in advance. On the other hand, the same request by the same employee for compensatory time in June would not be unduly disruptive.

"As stated in the proposed rule, for an agency to refuse an employee's request for compensatory time off, it must be clear that the granting of such compensatory time off must result in an unreasonable burden on the agency's ability to provide services of acceptable quality and quantity. The Department recognizes that situations may arise in which overtime may be required of one employee to permit another employee to use compensatory time off. However, such a situation, in and of itself, would not be sufficient for an employer to claim that it is unduly disruptive."[24]

Thus, under Section 553.25(d) of the DOL's regulations, the mere fact that an employer will have to replace the employee requesting compensatory time off with another employee hired on an overtime basis probably does not constitute an "undue disruption" allowing the denial of the request for compensatory time off.

In *Canney v. Town of Brookline*, a court squarely addressed the issue of whether the DOL's "undue disruption" regulations were valid. In the case, the employer had a practice of denying compensatory time off requests on the grounds that it would be required to replace the absent employee with another employee on an overtime basis. The Court, in upholding the DOL's regulations, declared the employer's practice to be in conflict with the FLSA:

> "The payment of one officer overtime to allow another officer to use compensatory time does not constitute an 'undue disruption.' On the present record nothing indicates that having to pay one or more officers overtime in cash, to permit another officer to take compensatory time would affect the police department's ability to provide services of acceptable quality and quantity."[25]

Another court reached the same result in *Debraska v. City of Milwaukee.* In *Debraska*, the employer's policies allowed it to deny a compensatory time off request if granting the request would have required it to call in an employee on an overtime basis or call in replacements from another precinct. In holding the employer's practice illegal, the Court held that the DOL's "approach is well-reasoned and consistent with the applicable statute and regulations."[26]

3. An Employer's Ability To Compel Use Of Compensatory Time Off.

After a period during which lower courts split on the issue, the United States Supreme Court held in *Christensen v. Harris County* that nothing in Section 7(o) forbids an employer from compelling an employee to use FLSA compensatory time off at a time selected by the employer, not the employee. In a divided opinion, the Court ruled that Section 7(o) "is more properly read as a minimal guarantee that an employee will be able to make some use of compensatory time when he requests to use it. As such, the proper *expressio unius* inference is that an employer may not, at least in the absence of an agreement, deny an employee's request to use compensatory time for a reason other than that provided in Section 7(o). The canon's application simply does not prohibit an employer from telling an employee to take the benefits of compensatory time by scheduling time off work with full pay."[27] In so holding, the Court rejected a DOL opinion letter on the subject, finding that the opinion letter was not as persuasive as a formal regulation adopted by the DOL.

G. The Accrual Rate For Compensatory Time Off.

If compensatory time off is used to compensate employees for overtime earned under the FLSA, the compensatory time off must be accrued at the rate of not less than one and one-half hours for each hour of overtime earned. Applying these principles, in one case a court declared illegal a county's practice of compensating emergency medical service employees at the rate of one-half hour compensatory time for each hour of overtime worked.[28]

H. Payments For Unused FLSA Compensatory Time.

Upon termination of employment, an employee is entitled to receive compensation for all accrued but unused compensatory time off. Under Section 7(o) of the FLSA, as interpreted by Section 553.27(b) of the DOL's regulations, the payment must be paid at the higher of the employee's final regular rate of pay or the average regular rate of pay received by the employee during the last three years of the employee's employment.[29] The statute of limitations for an employee seeking to recover for unused compensatory time off does not begin to run until the employee actually terminates service with the employer and is not paid at the final rate of pay.[30]

I. Non-FLSA Compensatory Time Off.

An important concept in Section 7(o) of the FLSA is that there exists a distinction between "FLSA compensatory time" and "other compensatory time." "FLSA compensatory time" is earned in lieu of cash payments for work which is considered to be overtime under the FLSA. "Other" compensatory time is payment for work that may be considered to be overtime under a local practice or collective bargaining agreement, but is not overtime under the FLSA.

An example of this difference is instructive. If, in a law enforcement agency, the employer has adopted a 28-day work period under the 7(k) exemption, overtime need not be paid until an individual employee has worked more than 171 hours in the work period. However, under a collective bargaining agreement, the same employee may be entitled to receive overtime for working greater than eight hours a day, more than 40 hours a week, or more than 160 hours in a 28-day period. The time that the employee works that is not considered to be "FLSA overtime" may be compensated in cash, in compensatory time off, or in some other fashion, and is essentially unregulated by the FLSA. Such compensatory time off is "other" compensatory time off, and is not subject to the restrictions on compensatory time off set forth under Section 7(o).

In its regulations, the DOL has expressly recognized this distinction between "FLSA compensatory time" and "other compensatory time." In Section 553.28 of the regulations, the DOL discussed this distinction at some length:

"(a) Compensatory time which is earned and accrued by an employee for employment in excess of a nonstatutory employment (that is, non-FLSA) requirement is considered 'other' compensatory time. The term 'other' compensatory time off means hours during which an employee is not working and which are not counted as hours worked during the period when used. For example, a collective bargaining agreement may provide that compensatory time be granted to employees for hours worked in excess of eight in a day, or for working on a scheduled day off in a non-overtime workweek. The FLSA does not require compensatory time to be granted in such situations.

"(b) Compensatory time which is earned and accrued by an employee working hours which are 'overtime' hours under State or local law, ordinance, or other provisions, but which are not overtime hours under Section 7 of the FLSA is also considered 'other' compensatory time. For example, a local law or ordinance may provide that compensatory time be granted to employees for hours worked in excess of 35 in a workweek. Under section 7(a) of the FLSA, only hours worked in excess of 40 in a workweek are overtime hours which must be compensated at one and one-half times the regular rate of pay.

"(c) Similarly, compensatory time earned or accrued by an employee for employment in excess of a standard established by the personnel policy or practice of an employer, or by custom, which does not result from the FLSA provision, is another example of 'other' compensatory time.

"(d) The FLSA does not require that the rate at which 'other' compensatory time is earned has to be at a rate of one and one-half hours for each hour of employment. The rate at which 'other' compensatory time is earned may be some lesser or greater multiple of the rate or the straight-time rate itself.

"(e) The requirements of section 7(o) of the FLSA, including the limitations on accrued compensatory time, do not apply to 'other' compensatory time as described above."[31]

Thus, "other compensatory time" can be paid at the straight time rate, or at some other lesser or greater multiple of the straight time rate. Further, since the accrual and usage of such "other compensatory time" does not fall within the scope of Section 7(o), parties are free to agree to other standards for the accrual and usage of compensatory time off. For example, it is perfectly permissible to have a local rule or a collective bargaining agreement that provides that an employer cannot force employees to use compensatory time off, or that employees cannot demand the use of compensatory time off where to do so would cause the employer overtime liability.

J. Damages Where Compensatory Time Off Systems Have Been Ruled Illegal.

Neither Section 7(o) nor the DOL's regulations give even the slightest hint of what damages should accrue when an employer has used an illegal compensatory time off system. The only court opinion to squarely address the issue is *Kimpel v. Williams*, a case involving a challenge to the Los Angeles Police Department's compensatory time off system. In the case, the Court appears to conclude that unless a compensatory time off system complies with all of the requirements of Section 7(o), the overtime compensation due under the FLSA when an employee works overtime hours remains "unpaid," thus violating the timely-pay requirements of the FLSA. In essence, the *Kimpel* ruling treats an unlawful compensatory time off system as providing no benefit to employees, requiring that employees be compensated in cash for all overtime hours worked for which compensatory time off was initially paid.[32]

NOTES TO CHAPTER 6

[1] *Brennan v. New Jersey*, 364 F.Supp. 156 (D.N.J. 1973); *cf. Walling v. Youngerman-Reynolds Hardwood Co.*, 325 U.S. 419 (1945).

[2] *Dunlop v. New Jersey*, 522 F.2d 504 (3rd Cir. 1975).

[3] Note, *The Public Sector Compensatory Time Exception to the Fair Labor Standards Act: Trying to Compensate for Congress' Lack of Clarity*, 75 Minn.L.Rev. 1807 (1991).

[4] 29 C.F.R. §553.24(e) (2001).

[5] 29 C.F.R. §553.24(e)(2) (2001).

[6] *Bleakley v. City of Aurora*, 679 F.Supp. 1008 (D.Colo. 1988).

[7] *Wilson v. City of Charlotte*, 702 F.Supp. 1232 (W.D.N.C. 1988), *rev'd on other grounds*, 964 F.2d 1391 (4th Cir. 1992); *D'Camera v. District of Columbia*, 693 F.Supp. 1208 (D.D.C. 1988). Where there is collective bargaining for public employees which concludes with the decision of an interest arbitrator, the necessary agreement for compensatory time off purposes cannot be the product of an arbitrator's decision. *Brewer v. City of Waukesha, Wisconsin*, 691 F.Supp. 160 (E.D.Wis. 1988).

[8] H.R. Rep. No. 99-331, pt.1, at 20 (1985).

[9] S.Rep. No. 99-159, pt. 1, at 10, *reprinted in* U.S.C.C.A.N. 651, 658.

[10] The following decisions have dealt with the questions concerning who a "representative" may be, and which employees are entitled to have a "representative." *State of Nevada Employees' Association, Inc. v. Bryan*, 916 F.2d 1384 (9th Cir. 1990); *Dillard v. Harris*, 885 F.2d 1549 (11th Cir. 1989); *Abbott v. City*

of Virginia Beach, 879 F.2d 132 (4th Cir. 1989); *International Ass'n of Fire Fighters, Local 2203 v. West Adams County Fire Protection Dist.*, 877 F.2d 814 (10th Cir. 1989); *Benzler v. State of Nevada*, 804 F.Supp. 1303 (D.Nev. 1992); *Wilson v. City of Charlotte*, 702 F.Supp. 1232 (W.D.N.C. 1988); *Jacksonville Professional Fire Fighters Association, Local 2961, IAFF v. City of Jacksonville*, 685 F.Supp. 513 (E.D.N.C. 1987).

[11] *Moreau v. Klevenhagen*, 508 U.S. 22 (1993).

[12] Additionally, courts had a surprisingly difficult time resolving the question of whether the employer can play any role in the designation of who the representative might be in the absence of any collective bargaining relationship. Though the notion of the employer being able to designate who a "representative" might be would seem to be an anathema to the general thrust of the FLSA's intent to provide basic wage and hour protections to employees, one court has come close to holding that, in the absence of collective bargaining, a public employer may well have such a right. *Nevada Highway Patrol Association v. State of Nevada*, 899 F.2d 1549 (9th Cir. 1990), *rev'd*, 968 F.2d 1221 (9th Cir. 1992). The better rule would appear to be that stated by the court in *Jacksonville Professional Fire Fighters Association, Local 2961, IAFF v. City of Jacksonville*, 685 F.Supp. 513 (E.D.N.C. 1987): "It is the employees' designation, and not the employer's recognition or attitude toward that representative, that is vital."

[13] *Adams v. Department of Juvenile Justice*, 3 WH Cases2d 295 (S.D.N.Y. 1996).

[14] 29 C.F.R. §553.23(c)(2) (2001).

[15] *Wilson v. City of Charlotte, North Carolina*, 964 F.2d 1391 (4th Cir. 1992).

[16] 29 C.F.R. §553.23(c)(1) (2001).

[17] 29 C.F.R. §553.23(c)(1) (2001).

[18] *D'Camera v. District of Columbia*, 693 F.Supp. 1208 (D.D.C. 1988)(employer violated the FLSA by using compensatory time off absent a provision in a collective bargaining agreement allowing such use); *Bleakly v. City of Aurora*, 679 F.Supp. 1008 (D.Colo. 1988)(same).

[19] 29 C.F.R. §553.23(b)(1) (2001).

[20] *See Maldonado v. Admin. De Correccion*, 1 WH Cases2d 116 (D.P.R. 1992).

[21] *Aiken v. City of Memphis*, 190 F.3d 753 (6th Cir. 1999).

[22] *Debraska v. City of Milwaukee*, 131 F.Supp.2d 1032 (E.D.Wis. 2000).

[23] 29 C.F.R. §553.25(d) (2001).

[24] Application Of The FLSA To Employees of State And Local Governments, 52 Fed. Reg. 2012-01 (1987).

[25] *Canney v. Town of Brookline*, 142 Lab.Cases ¶34,169 (D.Mass. 2000).

[26] *Debraska v. City of Milwaukee*, 131 F.Supp.2d 1032 (E.D.Wis. 2000)(The Department of Labor has issued an opinion letter reemphasizing its interpretation of "undue disruption," (*see* DOL FLSA opinion letter, 1994 WL 1004861), and submitted an *amicus curiae* brief in the *Debraska* case to the same effect.

[27] *Christensen v. Harris County*, 529 U.S. 576 (2000).

[28] *Burgess v. Catawba County*, 805 F.Supp. 341 (W.D.N.C. 1992).

[29] 29 C.F.R. §553.27(b) (2001); *see* Dep't of Lab. Op., [6A WHM 99:5212] Lab. Rel. Rep. (BNA).

[30] *Oliver v. Layrisson*, 3 WH Cases2d 316 (E.D.La. 1996).

[31] 29 C.F.R. §553.28 (2001).

[32] *Kimpel v. Williams*, 1999 WL 638580 (C.D.Cal. 1999).

CHAPTER SEVEN
THE 7(k) EXEMPTION

A. The Nature And Purpose Of The Exemption.

A partial exemption from the overtime provisions of the FLSA exists for certain law enforcement and fire protection employees. This exemption, which has become colloquially known as the "7(k) exemption," is based on Section 207(k) of the FLSA, which provides as follows:

"(k) No public agency shall be deemed to have violated subsection (a) with respect to the employment of any employee in fire protection activities or any employee in law enforcement activities (including security personnel in correctional institutions) if

—

"(1) in a work period of 28 consecutive days the employee receives for tours of duty which in the aggregate exceed the lesser of (A) 216 hours, or (B) the average number of hours (as determined by the Secretary pursuant to section 6(c)(3) of the Fair Labor Standards Amendments of 1974) in tours of duty of employees engaged in such activities in work periods of 28 consecutive days in calendar year 1975 or

"(2) in the case of such an employee to whom a work period of at least seven but less than 28 days applies, in his work period the employee receives for tours of duty which in the aggregate exceed a number of hours which bears the same ratio to the number of consecutive days in his work period as 216 hours (or if lower, the number of hours referred to in clause (B) of paragraph (1) bears to 28 days, compensation at a rate not less than one and one-half times the regular rate at which he is employed."[1]

In plain language, fire protection and law enforcement employers may elect to set a higher threshold of hours worked before the FLSA overtime compensation requirements apply. The purpose behind the 7(k) exemption was explained by one court as follows:

"In extending the coverage of the FLSA to employees engaged in fire protection activities or law enforcement activities, Congress was aware that the work schedules of these employees vary from the work schedules of other employees, and clearly recognized that some adjustment would have to be made in the usual rules for determining hours of work in their case. Thus, Congress departed from the standard 'hours of work' concept and adopted an overtime standard keyed to the length of the 'tour of duty.' In addition, Congress also adopted a new work period concept which may be used instead of the usual workweek basis for determining overtime hours."[2]

Section 7(k) authorized the DOL to investigate the actual hours worked for employees in law enforcement and fire protection activities, and to establish different maximum allowable hours worked than those specified in the statutes based upon the findings of the investigation. In its notes to the February 1987 regulations, the DOL explained how it conducted its investigation and what the results of the investigation were:

"The 1974 amendments to the FLSA required that the Department conduct studies of the average hours in tours of duty of fire protection and law enforcement personnel in calendar year 1975. The Department conducted the studies using only data concerning Federal employees in light of the Supreme Court decision in *National League of Cities* *v. Usery*, 426 U.S. 833 (1976). The results of these studies were challenged on various grounds and the Court held that the Department had erred in failing to take into consideration the hours worked by State and local government fire protection and law enforcement employees (*Jones v. Donovan*, 25 WH Cases 380 (D.D.C. 1981)) * * * In accordance with this ruling, the Department recalculated the average hours by including data on State and local government employees. The final results of the studies were published in the Federal Register on September 8, 1983 (48 FR 40518)."

Section 553.230 of the DOL's new regulations incorporates the standards announced in 1983, and sets forth the following maximum work periods for law enforcement and fire protection employees:

TABLE 9

MAXIMUM NON-OVERTIME HOURS UNDER 7(k) EXEMPTION

<u>DAYS</u>	<u>FIRE</u>	<u>POLICE</u>
7	53	43
8	61	49
9	68	55
10	76	61
11	83	67
12	91	73
13	98	79
14	106	86
15	114	92
16	121	98
17	129	104
18	136	110
19	144	116
20	151	122
21	159	128
22	167	134
23	174	141
24	182	147
25	189	153
26	197	159
27	204	165
28	212	171

The Section 7(k) exemption has occasionally come under fairly strident attack from labor advocates. As put by one commentator:

"Any way one slices it, using the subsection 207(k) exemption is a government abuse. It is a financial golden goose for the government employer, an unfair advantage over the private sector employer, and ultimately a disservice to the taxpaying public because, in the end, the public loses. Whether through costs of litigation brought against the government employer, reductions in work output by government employees, or simply a detriment to one of the vital responsibilities of government – public safety, the cost is high."[3]

B. How Does An Employer Obtain A 7(k) Exemption?

There are no set procedures that must be followed by an employer desiring to obtain the benefit of a 7(k) exemption. However, as one commentator noted, the 7(k) exemption is not "self-executing."[4] While the DOL's regulations require an employer to "establish" a 7(k) exemption, the regulations do not contain any guidelines as to what steps the employer must follow to establish the exemption. Since the regulations do contain strict recordkeeping requirements mandating that an employer keep contemporaneous records of the starting and stopping times for the 7(k) work periods for each employee, by implication the regulations seem to require that the employer follow some sort of formal steps to establish the exemption. A prudent employer, therefore, would be wise to create documents showing when the exemption was elected, what work period was elected, and the classes of employees to whom the exemption applies. Such documents could be created through the passage of an ordinance, entering into a collective bargaining agreement or memorandum of understanding with the affected labor organization,[5] or through the enactment of personnel rules or regulations or the issuance of memoranda.[6]

Courts have been wildly inconsistent in their rulings as to what actions an employer must take to avail itself of the

Section 7(k) exemption. One line of cases holds that an employer is not automatically entitled to a Section 7(k) exemption, but must take affirmative steps to avail itself of the benefits of the exemption.[7] Following this theory, one court has held that before an employer is entitled to claim the Section 7(k) exemption, it must maintain the records mandated by the DOL's regulations.[8] In another case, a court held that while an employer was not automatically entitled to a Section 7(k) exemption, it had done enough to "establish" the exemption by adopting personnel rules setting forth a 28-day work period for law enforcement employees and mandating that overtime be paid if employees worked more than 171 hours in the 28-day period.[9]

The opposite line of cases holds that if an employer merely operates on a work schedule that repeats every seven to 28 days, it is entitled to the Section 7(k) exemption without taking any formal steps to establish the exemption.[10] Since virtually all employers operate under schedules that repeat or "roll over" in some multiple of days between seven and 28 in length, such courts in fact make the "establishment" of a Section 7(k) exemption automatic. For example, in one case a court allowed an employer to claim the Section 7(k) exemption for employees it had inappropriately claimed were exempt from overtime as executive employees. Even though the employer did nothing whatsoever to "establish" the Section 7(k) exemption, the Court ruled that to deprive the employer of the exemption under the circumstances would be unfair.[11]

Some employees have argued that unless the employer's work schedules repeat every seven to 28 days in length, the Section 7(k) exemption is unavailable to the employer. This argument is based on Section 553.224(a) of the DOL's regulations, which define a Section 7(k) work period as "any established and regularly recurring period of work which, under the terms of the Act and legislative history, cannot be less than seven consecutive days nor more than 28 consecutive days."[12] However, in spite of the fairly specific language of the regulation, one court brushed aside this argument. The Court allowed an employer to claim a 28-day work period even though its schedule rotated every 42 days, holding that "the purpose of the regularly recurring, 28 day maximum work period in Section 7(k) is to ensure that employers neither continually change the length or start of the work period in an attempt to avoid overtime pay, nor set such a long period that overtime hours are always cancelled out. The work period limitations are intended to regulate overtime compensation. Nothing in the statute or regulations indicates that duty cycles of officers need have any correlation to that work period."[13] Another court took the opposite approach, refusing to allow an employer to claim a Section 7(k) exemption when all vacation, sick leave, hours of work, and schedule calculations were performed on the basis of a calendar month.[14]

Employees have had more success contending that the Section 7(k) work periods are unavailable to an employer that uses an irregular schedule that is not "regularly recurring" as described in Section 553.224(a). For example, in one case the work schedules for police officers in a small town showed a variety of consecutive and non-consecutive days off throughout different 28-day periods. A court refused the employer's initial request that it be allowed to claim the benefits of the Section 207(k) exemption, holding that "the record does not establish that the officers have a regularly recurring work period of 28 days or any other duration."[15]

Occasionally, employees have argued that the second portion of Section 7(k) requires a conclusion that an employer who does not actually compensate employees at the overtime rate when they work longer than the overtime thresholds found in Section 7(k) is not entitled to claim the exemption. Under this theory, unless an employer has been rigorous in compensating employees the overtime they are due under the Section 7(k) exemption, the employer is completely deprived of any of the benefits of the exemption.

Courts have rejected this argument, finding that the mere fact that employees were not paid overtime when they crossed Section 7(k) thresholds does not eliminate the employer's ability to claim the exemption.[16] In addition, an employer does not lose the opportunity to claim a Section 7(k) exemption merely by paying overtime before employees reach Section 7(k)'s overtime threshold.[17]

The FLSA does not, in and of itself, impose any obligations on the part of an employer to even discuss the election of a 7(k) exemption with employees or a labor organization, much less an obligation to collectively bargain over the exemption.[18] Such an obligation, where it exists, exists as a result of local collective bargaining laws and the interpretation of those laws. Where collective bargaining laws are in place for law enforcement officers and firefighters, they generally impose upon the employer a duty to "bargain collectively in good faith" over "wages, hours, and working conditions." Since choosing a 7(k) exemption directly affects, at a minimum, "wages and hours," an employer is likely required to bargain with a labor organization over the election of a 7(k) exemption. Where a duty to bargain exists, it will culminate with the normal method of impasse resolution for bargaining disputes established under the local collective bargaining act (whether the method of impasse resolution be factfinding, interest arbitration, strike, or unilateral implementation by the employer).

C. The Effects Of Electing A 7(k) Exemption.

Electing a 7(k) exemption can have a dramatic effect on an employer's overtime liability. The 7(k) exemption allows for the longer work hours which are frequently required for law enforcement and fire protection employees. For example, fire protection employees historically have worked some variation of a "24-on 48-off" work cycle, a work cycle which produces a much longer workweek than the 40-hour week permitted under Section 7(a) of the FLSA. Similarly, law enforcement officers, while generally following similar schedules to those worked by general employees, are frequently required to attend unpaid briefing periods at the commencement of their shift, or may be required to donate certain uncompensated training hours to the employer over the course of a month or year.

Electing a 7(k) exemption goes a long way (though not entirely) to accommodating these traditionally longer work periods for law enforcement and fire protection personnel. Nonetheless, even with the 7(k) exemption, the application of the FLSA to law enforcement and, particularly, fire protection personnel resulted in significant overtime liabilities for employers.

D. The Operation Of The 7(k) Exemption.

Two basic principles underlying the FLSA are important in understanding the operation of the 7(k) exemption:

1. The FLSA only requires the payment of overtime for hours which are worked which are defined as overtime under the FLSA (hereinafter referred to as "FLSA overtime"); and

2. The FLSA only requires that time and one-half be paid for "hours worked" in excess of the designated work period.

FLSA overtime is not necessarily overtime under a collective bargaining agreement, memorandum of understanding, or local personnel practice. For example, if a law enforcement employer selects a 28-day work period under the 7(k) exemption, FLSA overtime will not occur until after the employee has worked more than 171 hours in the work period. However, the same employer may well have a collective bargaining agreement, memorandum of understanding, or personnel practice that requires that employees be paid time and one-half for all time worked in excess of 40 hours in a workweek, or eight hours in a workday. While such time might be contractual overtime, it is not "FLSA overtime" until the time worked is in excess of 171 hours in the work period.

Table 10 demonstrates the flexibility the 7(k) exemption provides a law enforcement employer who has elected the 28-day work period under the 7(k) exemption:

TABLE 10
LAW ENFORCEMENT AGENCY
28-DAY WORK PERIOD

	WEEK	WORK PERIOD
Regular Hours of Work	40.00	160.00
Permissible Under FLSA	N/A	171.00
FLSA Flexibility		*11.00*

As can be seen from Table 10, there exists 11 hours of "FLSA flexibility" in a 28-day work period for an employer. These 11 hours would be compensated on an overtime basis had the employer not elected the 7(k) exemption and remained instead on a workweek basis. How does the FLSA treat these 11 hours of flexibility? The first court to address the issue has held that if the employee works overtime in the work period, the 11 hours must be paid at the <u>straight time</u> rate, not the overtime rate.[19] These same principles would apply to whatever length of 7(k) exemption has been elected.

What follows are some examples of how the "FLSA flexibility" can work to reduce an employer's overtime costs under the FLSA.

TABLE 11
LAW ENFORCEMENT AGENCY
UNPAID 15-MINUTE BRIEFING
28-DAY WORK PERIOD

	WEEK	WORK PERIOD
Regular Hours of Work	40.00	160.00
15-Minute Unpaid Briefing	1.25	5.00
Total Hours of Work	41.25	165.00
Permissible Under Contract	41.25	165.00
Permissible Under FLSA	N/A	171.00
FLSA Flexibility		*6.00*

TABLE 12
LAW ENFORCEMENT AGENCY
NO UNPAID BRIEFING
28-DAY WORK PERIOD

	WEEK	WORK PERIOD
Regular Hours of Works	40.00	160.00
Total Hours	40.00	160.00
Permissible Under Contract	40.00	160.00
Permissible Under FLSA	N/A	171.00
FLSA Flexibility		*11.00*

TABLE 13
LAW ENFORCEMENT AGENCY
15-MINUTE UNPAID BRIEFING
14-DAY WORK PERIOD

	WEEK	WORK PERIOD
Regular Hours of Work	40.00	80.00
15-Minute Unpaid Briefing	1.25	2.50
Total Hours of Work	N/A	82.50
Permissible Under Contract		82.50
Permissible Under FLSA		86.00
FLSA Flexibility		***3.50***

TABLE 14
LAW ENFORCEMENT AGENCY
NO UNPAID 15-MINUTE BRIEFING
14-DAY WORK PERIOD

	<u>WEEK</u>	WORK <u>PERIOD</u>
Regular Hours of Work	40.00	80.00
Briefing	(In Shift)	0.00
Total Hours of Work	N/A	80.00
Permissible Under Contract		80.00
Permissible Under FLSA		86.00
FLSA Flexibility		*6.00*

E. The Best Work Periods For Law Enforcement Employees.

For law enforcement personnel who work five eight-hour days or four ten-hour days in a workweek, there is not a single "best" work period which may be used under the 7(k) exemption. The 28-day work period allows the employer the most flexibility, since it allows the accumulation of hours worked over a longer period of time. However, an employer (and a labor organization if one is involved) should select the alternative work cycle which is most efficient, given the personnel, record keeping and accounting policies of the employer.

1. What Are The Best Work Periods To Select For Law Enforcement Employees On Alternative Shifts?

Increasingly, many law enforcement agencies operate on the basis of work shifts other than the traditional 5/8 schedule. Indeed, a recent study has shown that the majority of large law enforcement agencies now assign patrol officers to work some form of a "compressed workweek." One of the increasingly common work schedules for law enforcement agencies consists of four 12-hour days worked followed by four days off. This work schedule produces a work year that is considerably longer than the standard work year of 2,088 hours.[20] Other alternative work shifts include the 5-2, 5-3 shift, the 6-2 shift, and the 5-9 shift.

A good rule of thumb in selecting alternative work periods is to select the work period which is the longest work period which may be evenly divided by the number of days in a work schedule. For example, a 4-12 schedule involves an eight-day work cycle (four days on followed by four days off). A 24-day work period thus is the best work period for employees on such an eight-day cycle. Table 15 illustrates how a 4-12 shift works with a 24-day work period.

TABLE 15
LAW ENFORCEMENT
4-12 SCHEDULE
24-DAY WORK PERIOD

1	2	3	4	5	6	7
X	X	X	X	D/O	D/O	D/O
8	**9**	**10**	**11**	**12**	**13**	**14**
D/O	X	X	X	X	D/O	D/O
15	**16**	**17**	**18**	**19**	**20**	**21**
D/O	D/O	X	X	X	X	D/O
22	**23**	**24**				
D/O	D/O	D/O				

Regular Hours of Work:	144.0
Permissible Under FLSA:	147.0

FLSA Flexibility: *3.0*

Another shift which occasionally occurs in law enforcement agencies consists of six eight-hour days on, followed by two days off, followed by six eight-hour days on, followed by three days off. Since a 6-2, 6-3 work schedule involves a cycle of 17 days, a 17-day alternative work period should be elected. Table 16 illustrates how a 17-day work period operates with the 6-2, 6-3 schedule.

TABLE 16
LAW ENFORCEMENT
6-2, 6-3 SCHEDULE
17-DAY WORK PERIOD

1	2	3	4	5	6	7
X	X	X	X	X	X	D/O
8	**9**	**10**	**11**	**12**	**13**	**14**
D/O	X	X	X	X	X	X
15	**16**	**17**				
D/O	D/O	D/O				

Regular Hours of Work:	96.0
Permissible Under FLSA:	104.0

FLSA Flexibility: ***8.0***

Another shift which occasionally occurs in law enforcement agencies is a 10-5 shift. Under a 10-5 shift, an employee works ten eight-hour days, followed by five days off. Since a 10-5 shift is based upon a 15-day work cycle, a 15-day work period is the best to use under the FLSA, as is shown by Table 17.

TABLE 17
LAW ENFORCEMENT
10-5 SCHEDULE
15-DAY WORK PERIOD

1	2	3	4	5	6	7
X	X	X	X	X	X	X
8	**9**	**10**	**11**	**12**	**13**	**14**
X	X	X	D/O	D/O	D/O	D/O
15						
D/O						

Regular Hours of Work:	80.0
Permissible Under FLSA:	92.0
FLSA Flexibility:	***12.0***

As noted above, one of the distinct advantages to a law enforcement employer of the 7(k) exemption is the ability to preserve unpaid briefing periods, where such unpaid briefing periods exist. This flexibility arises from the longer work hours allowed under the alternative work cycles permissible under Section 7(k). Table 18 shows how an unpaid briefing period for an employee on a 5-8 schedule will not result in overtime liability under the FLSA.

TABLE 18
LAW ENFORCEMENT
15-MINUTE UNPAID BRIEFING UNDER THE
7(K) EXEMPTION

Regular Hours of Work	40.00
Briefing	2.50
Total Hours	**42.50**
Permissible Under Contract	40.00
Permissible Under FLSA	43.00
FLSA Flexibility	*0.50*

F. Fire Protection Employees' Work Schedules.

It is very difficult to avoid FLSA overtime under a traditional 24-on/48-off schedule worked by fire protection employees. Following the general rule of thumb in selecting alternative work periods (select the largest work period which may be evenly divided by the work cycle), the best alternative work period to use under Section 7(k) for a 24-on/48-off work cycle is a 27-day work period.[21] As can be seen below, even this work period will result in some hours of "FLSA overtime" liability on the part of the employer.

TABLE 19
FIRE PROTECTION AGENCY
24-ON/48-OFF SCHEDULE
27-DAY WORK PERIOD

1	2	3	4	5	6	7
X	D/O	D/O	X	D/O	D/O	X
8	**9**	**10**	**11**	**12**	**13**	**14**
D/O	D/O	X	D/O	D/O	X	D/O
15	**16**	**17**	**18**	**19**	**20**	**21**
D/O	X	D/O	D/O	X	D/O	D/O
22	**23**	**24**	**25**	**26**	**27**	
X	D/O	D/O	X	D/O	D/O	

Regular Hours of Work:	216.0
Permissible Under FLSA:	204.0
FLSA Flexibility:	***(12.0)***

Though the 27-day work period does involve roughly 12 hours of overtime pay per month, it is vastly superior to the alternative situation which would arise if no 7(k) exemption were elected, as is illustrated by Table 20.

TABLE 20
FIRE PROTECTION AGENCY
24-ON/48-OFF SCHEDULE
NO 7(k) EXEMPTION

1	2	3	4	5	6	7
X	D/O	D/O	X	D/O	D/O	X
8	**9**	**10**	**11**	**12**	**13**	**14**
D/O	D/O	X	D/O	D/O	X	D/O
15	**16**	**17**	**18**	**19**	**20**	**21**
D/O	X	D/O	D/O	X	D/O	D/O
22	**23**	**24**	**25**	**26**	**27**	
X	D/O	D/O	X	D/O	D/O	

	Week 1	Week 2	Week 3	Week 4	Total
Regular Hours	72.0	48.0	8.0	72.0	240.0
FLSA Overtime	32.0	8.0	8.0	32.0	80.0

1. The Kelly Day Option.

One possible solution to the problem of how fire protection employees' work schedules can be made to comport with the FLSA may be through the use of "Kelly Days." A Kelly Day is an extra day off which is added into a 24-on/48-off schedule. Depending upon the collective bargaining agreement, memorandum of understanding, or local personnel practice, a Kelly Day can occur as frequently as every third 24-on/48-off work cycle, or on a more infrequent basis. Today, many fire protection agencies already operate on the basis of the Kelly Day system, though the concept is virtually unused in large regions of the country. Tables 21-27 illustrate how the addition of a Kelly Day eliminates FLSA overtime in most cases:

189

TABLE 21
FIRE PROTECTION AGENCY
KELLY DAY EVERY 3RD CYCLE
20-DAY WORK PERIOD

1	2	3	4	5	6	7
X	D/O	D/O	X	D/O	D/O	X
8	**9**	**10**	**11**	**12**	**13**	**14**
D/O	D/O	D/O	X	D/O	D/O	X
15	**16**	**17**	**18**	**19**	**20**	
D/O	D/O	X	D/O	D/O	D/O	

Regular Hours of Work: 144.0

Permissible Under FLSA: 151.0

FLSA Flexibility: *7.0*

TABLE 22
FIRE PROTECTION AGENCY
KELLY DAY EVERY 4TH CYCLE
26-DAY WORK PERIOD

1	2	3	4	5	6	7
X	D/O	D/O	X	D/O	D/O	X
8	**9**	**10**	**11**	**12**	**13**	**14**
D/O	D/O	X	D/O	D/O	D/O	X
15	**16**	**17**	**18**	**19**	**20**	**21**
D/O	D/O	X	D/O	D/O	X	D/O
22	**23**	**24**	**25**	**26**		
D/O	X	D/O	D/O	D/O		

Regular Hours of Work: 192.0
Permissible Under FLSA: 197.0

FLSA Flexibility: ***5.0***

TABLE 23
FIRE PROTECTION AGENCY
KELLY DAY EVERY 5TH CYCLE
16-DAY WORK PERIOD

1	2	3	4	5	6	7
X	D/O	D/O	X	D/O	D/O	X
8	**9**	**10**	**11**	**12**	**13**	**14**
D/O	D/O	X	D/O	D/O	X	D/O
15	**16**					
D/O	D/O					

Regular Hours of Work:	120.0
Permissible Under FLSA:	121.0
FLSA Flexibility:	***1.0***

TABLE 24
FIRE PROTECTION AGENCY
KELLY DAY EVERY 6TH CYCLE
19-DAY WORK PERIOD

1	2	3	4	5	6	7
X	D/O	D/O	X	D/O	D/O	X
8	9	10	11	12	13	14
D/O	D/O	X	D/O	D/O	X	D/O
15	16	17	18	19		
D/O	X	D/O	D/O	D/O		

Regular Hours of Work: 144.0
Permissible Under FLSA: 144.0

FLSA Flexibility: *0.0*

TABLE 25
FIRE PROTECTION AGENCY
KELLY DAY EVERY 7TH CYCLE
22-DAY WORK PERIOD

1	2	3	4	5	6	7
X	D/O	D/O	X	D/O	D/O	X
8	**9**	**10**	**11**	**12**	**13**	**14**
D/O	D/O	X	D/O	D/O	X	D/O
15	**16**	**17**	**18**	**19**	**20**	**21**
D/O	X	D/O	D/O	X	D/O	D/O
22						
D/O						

Regular Hours of Work:	168.0
Permissible Under FLSA:	167.0
FLSA Flexibility:	***(1.0)***

TABLE 26
FIRE PROTECTION AGENCY
KELLY DAY EVERY 8TH CYCLE
25-DAY WORK PERIOD

1	2	3	4	5	6	7
X	D/O	D/O	X	D/O	D/O	X
8	**9**	**10**	**11**	**12**	**13**	**14**
D/O	D/O	X	D/O	D/O	X	D/O
15	**16**	**17**	**18**	**19**	**20**	**21**
D/O	X	D/O	D/O	X	D/O	D/O
22	**23**	**24**	**25**			
X	D/O	D/O	D/O			

Regular Hours of Work:	192.0
Permissible Under FLSA:	189.0
FLSA Flexibility:	***(3.0)***

TABLE 27
FIRE PROTECTION AGENCY
KELLY DAY EVERY 9TH CYCLE
28-DAY WORK PERIOD

1	2	3	4	5	6	7
X	D/O	D/O	X	D/O	D/O	X
8	**9**	**10**	**11**	**12**	**13**	**14**
D/O	D/O	X	D/O	D/O	X	D/O
15	**16**	**17**	**18**	**19**	**20**	**21**
D/O	X	D/O	D/O	X	D/O	D/O
22	**23**	**24**	**25**	**26**	**27**	**28**
X	D/O	D/O	X	D/O	D/O	D/O

Regular Hours of Work: 216.0

Permissible Under FLSA: 212.0

FLSA Flexibility: *(4.0)*

TABLE 28
FIRE PROTECTION AGENCY
"CALIFORNIA PLAN"
27-DAY WORK PERIOD

1	2	3	4	5	6	7
X	D/O	X	D/O	X	D/O	D/O
8	**9**	**10**	**11**	**12**	**13**	**14**
D/O	D/O	X	D/O	X	D/O	X
15	**16**	**17**	**18**	**19**	**20**	**21**
D/O	D/O	D/O	D/O	X	D/O	X
22	**23**	**24**	**25**	**26**	**27**	
D/O	X	D/O	D/O	D/O	D/O	

Regular Hours of Work: 216.0

Permissible Under FLSA: 204.0

FLSA Flexibility: ***(12.0)***

2. The Work Period Wage Option.

Another way in which the problem of dealing with a 24-on/48-off work schedule under the FLSA can be addressed is by looking at a "work period wage." This option, like the Kelly Day option, is one which would be required to be the subject of collective bargaining, where applicable collective bargaining laws exist.

A hypothetical example best explains the concept of a work period wage. Assume that a fire protection agency employee working a 24-on/48-off shift earns $2,000 per month. Prior to the application of the FLSA, this rate translated to an hourly rate of $8.24, and an overtime rate of $12.36. Assuming that the work schedule is not changed and that a 7(k) 27-day work period is elected, the lowest possible increase in costs would be computed as follows:

Work Periods per Year: 13.53

Overtime per Work Period: 12.00 hours

Overtime per Year: 162.33 hours

Additional Overtime Cost:

($12.36 x 162.33) - ($8.24 x 162.33) = $668.82

Percent Cost of Overtime: 2.79%

If one assumes that all concerned wish to return to the status quo in terms of monthly remuneration before the application of the FLSA, one first needs to set the desired monthly wage — in this case, $2,000. Then, working backwards, one needs to determine the desired "work period wage" in the following manner:

Work Periods per Year: 13.53

Work Periods per Month: 1.13

Desired Monthly Wage: $2,000

Desired Work Period Wage ($2,000/1.13): $1,769.91

The next step in the process is to calculate the desired hourly rate which will produce the desired work period wage. The following algebraic formula will calculate the desired hourly wage, where the letter "h" stands for hourly wage:

$$(204 \times (h)) + (12 \times (1.5 \times h)) = \$1,775$$
$$204h + 18h = \$1,775$$
$$222\ h = \$1,775$$
$$h = \$7.99$$

In this fashion, the hourly wage of the fire protection employee is lowered, from $8.24 to $7.99. However, the monthly pay of the employee remains the same. The only difficulty with this approach occurs if the employee works what would have been overtime prior to the application of the FLSA. Since the employee would now be working at a lower hourly rate, the employee would receive a reduction in overtime earnings. To compensate for this effect, all that need be done is to provide by collective bargaining agreement, memorandum of understanding, or personnel rules that the overtime rate for time worked in excess of 24 hours per workday, or 56 hours per week, will be at the former overtime rate of $12.36 per hour instead of at the new overtime rate of $11.99 per hour (nothing in the FLSA requires that employees be compensated only at the rate of time and one-half for overtime).

While courts have approved of such work period wage adjustments (also called wage recharacterizations),[22] they have been reluctant to do so in the absence of some form of agreement on the part of employees.[23]

G. Who Is A Law Enforcement Officer For The Purposes Of The FLSA?

Section 553.211 of the DOL's regulations provides a fairly concise definition of an employee engaged in law enforcement activities, as those terms are used in Section 7(k) of the FLSA. Under Section 553.211, an employee qualifies as a law enforcement officer if the following three conditions are met:

1. The employee is a uniformed or plainclothes member of a "body of officers" who are empowered by state or local ordinance to enforce laws, and to prevent and detect crimes;

2. Who has the power of arrest; and

3. Who has either undergone, will undergo, or is undergoing on-the-job training pertinent to law enforcement duties. Such training would include but not necessarily be limited to physical training, self-defense instruction, firearm classes, instruction on the principles of civil and criminal law, instruction on investigative and law enforcement

techniques, classes on community relations, medical aid, and ethics.[24]

As can be seen from the above definition, the exact job title of an employee is irrelevant to the question of whether or not the employee will be considered to be engaged in law enforcement activities under the FLSA. As such, employees who are "probationary" or "trainees" may still be considered to be employees engaged in law enforcement functions even though they hold no permanent rank.

In *Mills v. State of Maine*, the Court considered whether state probation officers were engaged in law enforcement activities for purposes of Section 7(k). Finding that the officers were covered by the Section 7(k) exemption, the Court noted that the officers have arrest powers, were empowered to enforce laws to maintain public peace and order, protect life and property, and prevent and detect crimes, and had undergone training or instruction in law enforcement matters. The Court also found that the officers had the responsibility to investigate criminal cases and probation or parole violations, all of which played a part in preventing and detecting crimes and protecting life and property.[25]

In addition to the definitions provided by Section 553.211 of the regulations, the definition of employees engaged in law enforcement activities under Section 7(k) of the FLSA itself also specifically includes "security personnel in correctional institutions." In determining whether or not an employee qualifies as a security personnel in a correctional institution, again it is the case that the precise job title given to the employee is irrelevant. Rather, under Section 553.211(f) of the regulations, if an employee has the "responsibility for controlling and maintaining custody of inmates and of safeguarding them from other inmates or for supervising such functions," and performs such work in "any government facility maintained as part of a penal system for the incarceration or detention of persons suspected or convicted of having breached the peace or committed some other crime," the employee is considered to be a security personnel in a correctional institution regardless of the job classification the employee holds.[26]

Since it is relatively easy to determine when an employee is engaging in law enforcement activities, it is perhaps better to list those employees who the DOL has indicated are not engaging in law enforcement activities. Such a list of employees would include at least those holding the following job classifications:

- Dispatchers[27]
- Radio operators
- Janitors, clerks, and stenographers employed at a law enforcement institution
- Building inspectors
- Health inspectors
- Animal control personnel
- Sanitarians
- Civil traffic employees who direct vehicular and pedestrian traffic at specified intersections or other control points
- Civilian parking checkers
- Public housing safety officers without arrest powers[28]
- Wage and hour compliance officers
- Equal employment opportunity compliance officers
- Tax compliance officers
- Building guards, whose primary duty is to protect the lives and properties of persons within the limited area of a building
- College security guards[29]
- Cooks in a correctional facility
- Teaching personnel in a correctional facility
- Psychological, medical, or paramedical service providers in a correctional institution.

H. Who Is A Fire Protection Employee For Purposes Of The 7(k) Exemption?

As is the case with the definition of employees engaged in law enforcement activities, the definition under the FLSA of employees engaged in fire protection activities is relatively clear. Under Section 553.210(a) of the DOL's regulations, fire protection employees must meet these standards:

1. The employee must be employed by an organized fire department or fire protection district;

2. The employee must have been trained to the extent required by state statute or local ordinance;

3. The employee must have been trained and have the legal authority and responsibility to engage in the prevention, control, or extinguishment of a fire of any type; and

4. The employee must actually perform activities which directly concern the prevention, control, or extinguishment of fires.[30]

Under Section 553.210(a) of the regulations, activities directly concerned with the prevention, control or extinguishment of fires specifically include incidental non-firefighting functions such as housekeeping, equipment maintenance, lecturing, attending community fire drills, and inspecting homes and schools for fire hazards. As well, as was the case with the definitions under the FLSA of employees engaged in law enforcement services, the dispositive consideration will be the actual duties performed by the employee, rather than the employer's job title. The DOL has ruled that the term "any employee in fire protection activities" as used in Section 7(k) also specifically includes employees who work for public agencies charged with forest firefighting responsibilities, and who are engaged in fire spotting, lookout activities, fighting fires on a fireline, fighting fires from an aircraft, or operating tank trucks, bulldozers, and tractors for the purposes of clearing fire breaks.

As is the case with law enforcement employees, it is perhaps easier to list those job classifications which the DOL has indicated it does not believe are included among the definitions of employees engaged in fire protection activities. As indicated in Section 553.210(c) of the regulations, such classifications include but are not limited to the following:

- Dispatchers[31]

- Alarm operators

- Apparatus and equipment repair and maintenance workers

- Clerks and stenographers employed within a fire department

- Camp cooks

As noted above, for a firefighter to be covered by the Section 7(k) exemption, the firefighter must be employed by a fire department or fire protection agency. In one case, a court refused to extend the Section 7(k) exemption to cover firefighters who provided firefighting services exclusively at a mental health facility. Critical in the Court's evaluation of the case was the fact that the firefighters were actually employees of the city's Commission on Mental Health Services, not the city's fire department.[32]

I. Paramedics, Emergency Medical Service, And Rescue Employees.

By its terms, the Section 7(k) exemption does not apply to employees whose sole function is performing paramedic or emergency medical service (EMS) duties. Therefore, EMS personnel are owed overtime under the ordinary 40-hour workweek standard unless their employer can prove that the EMS personnel should be treated as falling within the exemption for employees engaged in "fire protection activities."[33]

While the FLSA itself does not define fire protection activities or the manner in which EMS personnel may be brought within the Section 7(k) exemption, the DOL's regulations extensively discuss the issue. As noted above, the regulations provide a four-part test to define fire protection activities, defining as a firefighter an employee: "(1) who is employed by an organized fire department or fire protection district; (2) who has been trained to the extent required by State statute or local ordinance; (3) who has the legal authority and responsibility to engage in the prevention, control or extinguishment of a fire of any type; and (4) who performs activities which are required for, and directly concerned with, the prevention, control or extinguishment of fires, including such incidental non-firefighting functions as housekeeping, equipment maintenance, lecturing, attending community fire drills and inspecting homes and schools for fire hazards."[34] Under this standard, employees who perform only EMS functions – that is, who have training and responsibilities for medical but not firefighting duties – do not meet this test and cannot be brought within the Section 7(k) exemption on the ground that they are firefighters.[35]

There are two provisions of the DOL's regulations under which EMS personnel may be included within the Section 7(k) exemption. First, EMS personnel may be covered by the exemption "if such personnel form an integral part of the public agency's fire protection activities."[36] Second, under Section 553.215 of the regulations, EMS personnel may be covered by the Section 7(k) exemption if they have received certain training and are "regularly dispatched" to fire, crime, and similar scenes:

> "Ambulance and rescue service employees of a public agency other than a fire protection agency may be treated as employees engaged in fire protection * * * activities * * * if their services are substantially related to firefighting * * * activities in that (1) the ambulance and rescue service employees have received training in the rescue of fire, crime, and accident victims or firefighters * * * in-

jured in the performance of their * * * duties, and (2) the ambulance and rescue service employees are regularly dispatched to fires, crime scenes, riots, natural disasters and accidents."[37]

Mere employment by the fire department alone is not sufficient to constitute employment in fire protection activities to bring EMS personnel under the Section 7(k) exemption – fire department employees performing only EMS functions must be an "integral part" of firefighting to be covered. Similarly, EMS personnel employed by an agency separate from the fire department cannot be paid like firefighters unless the two-part "substantially related" test is met.[38] Moreover, the DOL's regulations include a provision under which employers may lose the Section 7(k) exemption if the employee spends more than 20% of work hours on non-exempt activities:

> "Employees engaged in fire protection * * * activities * * * may also engage in some nonexempt work which is not performed as an incident to or in conjunction with their fire protection * * * activities. For example, firefighters who work for forest conservation agencies may, during slack times, plant trees and perform other conservation activities unrelated to their firefighting duties. The performance of such nonexempt work will not defeat * * * the Section 7(k) exemption unless it exceeds 20 percent of the total hours worked by that employee during the workweek or applicable work period. A person who spends more than 20 percent of his/her working time in nonexempt activities is not considered to be an employee engaged in fire protection * * * activities."[39]

Under the 80/20 rule, at least 80% of an employee's time must be spent either on fire protection activities themselves, or on activities related to or incidental to fire protection activities such as equipment maintenance, housekeeping duties in the station, and inspections.[40] To retain the exemption, the employer has the burden of proving that the employee did not exceed the 20% limitation on nonexempt activity.

In applying these tests, most courts have found that EMS personnel do not meet the tests for the Section 7(k) exemption. Typical of this trend are the following:

• The Court in *Alex v. City of Chicago* found that Chicago's paramedics did not meet the tests for the Section 7(k) exemption. The Court, holding that both the "training" and "regularly dispatched" prongs of the DOL's tests must be met, found that the paramedics in the Chicago Fire Department did not "perform and are not trained to perform 'rescue' activities beyond a medical nature," and were not "trained to free victims from 'imminent rescue or harm by the most expeditious means,'" and as such were not engaged in exempt fire protection or law enforcement activities under Section 7(k).[41]

· In *Vela v. City of Houston*, the Court rejected the employer's arguments that EMS personnel should be covered by the Section 7(k) exemption where only 17% of EMS dispatches were related to crimes, fires, and accidents.[42]

• In *Spires v. Ben Hill County*, the Court found the Section 7(k) exemption inapplicable where, at most, only 24% of EMS dispatches were sent to fire, police, or accident calls.[43]

• In *Christian v. City of Gladstone*, the Court rejected a claim for a Section 7(k) exemption where it found that the nonexempt time spent by EMS personnel responding to, returning from, or completing paperwork on medical calls or accidents other than car accidents, and time devoted to emergency medical training or study related to emergency medical services exceeded 20% of total work hours.[44]

• In *Doden v. Plainfield Fire District*, the Court denied an employer the opportunity to claim a Section 7(k) exemption where paramedics were subject to discipline if they performed suppression or rescue services, were not allowed to treat fire victims until the victims had been evacuated from the vicinity of the fire, did not extricate victims from hazardous situations, and were only sent to fire or crime scenes when there was a report of an injury or a substantial likelihood of injury.[45]

The law that eventually emerged was that, generally speaking, only "dual function" EMS personnel – those who also have firefighting duties – were eligible for the Section 7(k) exemption.[46] In 1999, Congress added new Section 203(y) to the FLSA, the vagueness of which is likely to spur yet another spate of litigation involving EMS personnel. The new statute provides:

> "'Employee in fire protection activities' means an employee, including a firefighter, paramedic, emergency medical technician, rescue worker, ambulance personnel, or hazardous materials worker, who--

> "(1) is trained in fire suppression, has the legal authority and responsibility to engage in fire suppression, and is employed by a fire department of a municipality, county, fire district, or State; and

> "(2) is engaged in the prevention, control, and extinguishment of fires or response to emergency situations where life, property, or the environment is at risk."[47]

Thus far, no cases have construed whether simply responding to medical assistance calls constitutes a "response to emergency situations where life . . . is at risk" as described in Section 203(y). Section 203(y) has not been applied retroactively to claims filed before the statute was enacted.[48]

Ambulance and rescue service employees who work for other than a fire protection or law enforcement agency do not fall under the neat definitions of either law enforcement or fire protection personnel used in the FLSA. Such employees are, however, specifically covered by Section 553.215 of the DOL's regulations. Under the regulation, employees engaged in ambulance and rescue service are eligible for the 7(k) exemption provided the following tests are met:

1. The employee's activities must be "substantially related to firefighting or law enforcement activities," in that

a. The ambulance and rescue service employees received special training in the rescue of fire and accident victims, including firefighters injured in the performance of their duties; and

b. The employees are regularly dispatched to the scenes of fires, riots, natural disasters, and accidents.[49]

J. Is The 7(k) Exemption Available For Employees Who Perform "Mixed" Duties?

Occasionally, employees will engage in either law enforcement or fire protection activities for only a part of their workday, with the remainder of their workday being devoted to other non-exempt activities. Under the "80/20 rule" found in Section 553.5 of the DOL's regulations, such non-exempt activities, provided they do not exceed 20% of the employee's total hours worked, will not work to defeat the 7(k) exemption.

As described in the preceding section, the 80/20 rule has most commonly been applied in cases involving paramedics, usually producing the result that paramedics are not eligible for the Section 7(k) exemption.[50] For example, in *Burgess v. Catawba County*, the Court ruled that a county emergency medical service could not claim the Section 7(k) exemption for EMS employees where the employees spent over 70 percent of their work time responding to calls which were straight medical calls to which neither firefighters nor police were dispatched.[51] Similarly, in *Christian v. Gladstone, Missouri*, the Court found that paramedics did not qualify for the Section 7(k) exemption where, when the time spent on paperwork which did not pertain to fire protection was combined with actual time spent on emergency medical calls, the paramedics spent at least five hours and nine minutes per 24-hour shift on nonexempt activities.[52]

K. Employees Engaged In Both Fire Protection And Law Enforcement Activities.

In some public agencies, police and fire departments have merged, with the employees in the merged service being required to perform both law enforcement and fire protection activities. With yet other public employers, some police personnel may be required to assist in the prevention of fires, with some fire personnel occasionally being assigned to police duties.

Under Section 553.6 of the DOL's regulations, such employees who engage in both law enforcement and fire protection activities remain eligible for the 7(k) exemption, provided that all of the activities of the employee (subject to the 80/20 non-exempt time provision described immediately above) meet the test for work performed in a law enforcement or fire protection activity. However, since at the time Section 553.6 of the regulations was promulgated, the alternative work periods allowable for law enforcement and firefighter personnel were identical, the regulation does not address under which alternative work periods employees engaged in a combination of law enforcement and fire protection would fall. The first court addressing the issue held that investigators for a city's fire department arson squad fell under the law enforcement 7(k) standards, not the fire protection standards, reasoning that even though the investigators worked in fire stations and responded to fire calls, they did not control or extinguish fires and their primary job was the investigation of the crime of arson.[53]

In one case, an appeals court eventually remanded the matter for trial, concluding that it could not determine either whether Section 7(k) applied at all to paramedics or, if

Section 7(k) applied, whether the law enforcement or fire protection exemption applied. The appeals court directed the trial court to determine the number of hours spent in law enforcement activities, fire protection activities, and activities unrelated to each. The appeals court noted that to defeat the paramedic's FLSA overtime suit, the employer was required to prove by clear evidence that it was entitled to a Section 7(k) exemption under either the law enforcement or firefighter provisions of the exemption, and also that the paramedics worked at least 80 percent of time in activities related to the particular exemption claimed.[54]

L. Multiple Work Periods Under The 7(k) Exemption.

On occasion, it may be advantageous for an employer to have more than one alternative work period under a 7(k) exemption. For example, in a large fire department, employees assigned to fire suppression duties may work a 24-on/48-off shift, while employees responsible for fire education duties may work a traditional 5-on/2-off, eight-hour shift. Under Section 553.224(b) of the DOL's regulations, specific authorization is given to an employer to have more than one alternative work period:

"An employer may have one work period applicable to all employees, or different work periods for different employees or groups of employees."

NOTES TO CHAPTER 7

[1] 29 U.S.C. §207(k).

[2] *Beebe v. United States*, 640 F.2d 1283 (Ct.Cl. 1981).

[3] Lawrence Henke, *Is The FLSA Really Fair?*, 52 SMU L. Rev. 1847 (Fall, 1999).

[4] Paul Campo, *Law Enforcement Issues and the FLSA*, 56 J. Mo. B. 336 (December, 2000).

[5] *See Adair v. City of Kirkland*, 185 F.3d 1055 (9th Cir. 1999)(exemption established, in part, through collective bargaining agreement).

[6] *Milner v. City of Hazelwood*, 165 F.3d 1222 (8th Cir. 1999)(exemption established through memorandum); *Local 889, AFSCME v. State of Louisiana*, 145 F.3d 280 (5th Cir. 1998)(same); *Jerzak v. City of South Bend*, 996 F.Supp. 840 (N.D.Ind. 1998)(same).

[7] *Spradling v. Tulsa, Oklahoma*, 95 F.3d 1492 (10th Cir. 1996); *Lamon v. City of Shawnee*, 972 F.2d 1145 (10th Cir. 1992); *Kermit C. Sanders Lodge No. 13 v. City of Smyrna*, 862 F.Supp. 351 (N.D.Ga. 1994); *Maldonado v. Admin. De Correccion*, 1 WH Cases2d 913 (D.P.R. 1993); *Clayton v. State of Oregon*, 114 Lab.Cases ¶35,306 (D.Or. 1990); *Nixon v. City of Junction City*, 707 F.Supp. 473 (D.Kan. 1988); *see Birdwell v. City of Gadsden*, 970 F.2d 802 (11th Cir. 1992).

[8] *Holmes v. State of Washington*, 30 WH Cases 1630 (W.D.Wash. 1992).

[9] *Lamon v. City of Shawnee,* 972 F.2d 1145 (10th Cir. 1992).

[10] *Freeman v. City of Mobile, Alabama*, 146 F.3d 1292 (11th Cir. 1998); *Barefield v. Village of Winnetka*, 81 F.3d 704 (7th Cir. 1996); *Birdwell v. City of Gads-*

den, Alabama, 970 F.2d 802 (11th Cir. 1992); *McGrath v. City of Philadelphia*, 864 F.Supp. 466 (E.D.Pa. 1994); *see Martin v. Coventry Fire District*, 981 F.2d 1358 (1st Cir. 1992).

[11] *Feaser v. City of New York*, 2 WH Cases2d 1324 (S.D.N.Y. 1995).

[12] 29 CFR §553.224(a) (2001).

[13] *Franklin v. City of Kettering, Ohio*, 246 F.3d 531 (6th Cir. 2001); *see Sanders Lodge No. 13, Fraternal Order of Police v. City of Smyrna*, 862 F.Supp. 351 (N.D.Ga. 1994)(allows Section 7(k) exemption even though schedule was six days in length).

[14] *Taylor v. County of Fluvanna, Virginia*, 70 F.Supp.2d 655 (W.D.Va. 1999).

[15] *Schwertfeger v. Village of Sauk Village*, 143 Lab.Cas. ¶34,247 (N.D.Ill. 2001).

[16] *Martin v. Coventry Fire District*, 981 F.2d 1358 (1st Cir. 1992).

[17] *Birdwell v. City of Gadsden, Alabama*, 970 F.2d 802 (11th Cir. 1992); *Lamon v. City of Shawnee*, 972 F.2d 1145 (10th Cir. 1992).

[18] *Bedford v. City of Del City, Oklahoma*, 2 WH Cases2d 602 (W.D.Okla. 1993).

[19] *Lamon v. City of Shawnee*, 754 F.Supp. 1518 (D.Kan. 1991). The Court's interpretation is bolstered by Section 778.315 of the Department of Labor's regulations, which provides that "[Overtime] cannot be said to have been paid to an employee unless all the straight-time compensation due * * * under contract has been paid." Additional support for the Court's interpretation is found in Section 778.317 of the regulations, which provides that an "agreement not to compensate employees for certain non-overtime hours stands on no better footing since it would have the effect of diminishing the employee's total overtime compensation."

[20] Typically, negotiated adjustments in compensatory time off under the 4-12 schedule reduce the total hours worked to 2,088 in a work year.

[21] It should be noted parenthetically that computer runs appear to demonstrate that the most economical alternative work period for a fire protection employee on a 24-on/48-off schedule is a 28-day work period, though the 28-day work period does not become economically more efficient until the employee works hundreds of shifts. Since the bookkeeping difficulties of a fire protection agency operating on the basis of a 28-day work period would seem to offset the fairly insubstantial cost savings of moving to the work period, the examples in this book are based on a 27-day work period.

[22] *See Ingram v. City of Charleston*, 376 S.E.2d 327 (W.Va. 1988).

[23] *Blanton v. City of Murfreesboro*, 856 F.2d 731 (6th Cir. 1988); *Craven v. City of Minot*, 730 F.Supp. 1511 (D.N.D. 1989); *Alexander v. City of Plainview*, 694 F.Supp. 221 (N.D.Tex. 1988) (2001).

[24] 29 C.F.R. §553.221 (2001).

[25] *Mills v. State of Maine*, 839 F.Supp. 3 (D.Me. 1993).

[26] *See McBride v. Cox*, 567 N.E.2d 130 (Ind.App. 1991)(county jailers covered by 7(k) exemption).

[27] Opinion Letter, Department of Labor, 1999 WL 1002392 (April 23, 1999); Opinion Letter, Department of Labor, 1997 WL 998043 (October 15, 1997).

[28] Opinion Letter, Department of Labor, 1999 WL 1788153 (September 3, 1999).

[29] Opinion Letter, Department of Labor, 2000 WL 33126573 (July 20, 2000).

[30] 29 C.F.R. §553.210(a) (2001).

[31] Firefighters who are normally covered by the 7(k) exemption who are transferred into a dispatch role as

part of a normal training rotation will not fall outside the 7(k) exemption during their temporary status as dispatchers, even if the rotational period is as long as one year. *Schmidt v. Prince William County*, 929 F.2d 986 (4th Cir. 1991).

[32] *Ball v. District of Columbia*, 795 F.Supp. 461 (D.D.C. 1992), *remanded without opinion*, 22 F.3d 1184 (D.C.Cir. 1994).

[33] *See O'Neal v. Barrow County Bd. of Comm'rs*, 980 F.2d 674 (11th Cir. 1993)(holding that employer bears burden of proof on applying fire protection activities exemption to EMS personnel).

[34] 29 C.F.R. §553.210(a) (2001).

[35] *Falken v. Glynn County, Georgia*, 197 F.3d 1341 (11th Cir. 1999).

[36] *See* 29 C.F.R. §553.210(a) (2001).

[37] 29 C.F.R. §553.215 (2001).

[38] *See Wouters v. Martin County*, 9 F.3d 924 (11th Cir. 1993).

[39] 29 C.F.R. §553.212(a) (2001).

[40] 29 C.F.R. §553.210(a)(4) (2001); *see Adams v. City of Norfolk, Virginia*, 274 F.3d 148 (4th Cir. 2001).

[41] *Alex v. City of Chicago*, 29 F.3d 1235 (7th Cir. 1994).

[42] *Vela v. City of Houston*, 2001 WL 1607199 (5th Cir. 2001).

[43] *Spires v. Ben Hill County*, 980 F.2d 683 (11th Cir. 1993).

[44] *Christian v. City of Gladstone*, 108 F.3d 929 (8th Cir. 1997).

[45] *Doden v. Plainfield Fire District*, 3 WH Cases2d 199 (N.D.Ill. 1995).

[46] *Falken v. Glynn County, Georgia*, 197 F.3d 1341 (11th Cir. 1999). Seemingly marching to the beat of its own drum (as it customarily does in FLSA cases), the

federal Eighth Circuit Court of Appeals has held that non-dual function EMS personnel can be included within the Section 7(k) exemption, counting as exempt work for purposes of the 80/20 rule even time spent on calls unrelated to law enforcement or fire protection functions. *Lang v. City of Omaha*, 186 F.3d 1035 (8th Cir. 1999).

[47] 29 U.S.C. §203(y).

[48] *Vela v. City of Houston*, 2001 WL 1607199 (5th Cir. 2001).

[49] *See Spires v. Ben Hill County*, 980 F.2d 683 (11th Cir. 1993)(regular dispatch requirement not met where no more than 17-35% of dispatches were to fire and police calls); *Horan v. King County, Div. of Emergency Medical Services*, 740 F.Supp. 1471 (W.D.Wash. 1990)(regular dispatch requirement not met when no more than 5.5% of dispatches were fire or law enforcement related).

[50] *Roy v. Lexington County*, 928 F.Supp. 1406 (D.S.C. 1996), *modified on other grounds* 948 F.Supp. 529 (D.S.C. 1996).

[51] *Burgess v. Catawba County*, 805 F.Supp. 341 (W.D.N.C. 1992).

[52] *Christian v. Gladstone, Missouri*, 3 WH Cases2d 277 (W.D.Mo. 1995), *rev'd* 108 F.3d 935 (8th Cir. 1997).

[53] *Carlson v. City of Minneapolis*, 30 WH Cases 249 (8th Cir. 1991).

[54] *Wouters v. Martin County, Florida*, 9 F.3d 924 (11th Cir. 1993).

CHAPTER EIGHT

EXECUTIVE, ADMINISTRATIVE, OR PROFESSIONAL EMPLOYEES UNDER THE FLSA

Under Section 13(a)(1) of the FLSA, employees who work in a bona fide executive, administrative, or professional capacity and who are salaried employees are exempt from the overtime provisions of the FLSA. The FLSA itself does not define the terms "executive," "administrative," or "professional"; instead the definitions of the terms can be found in the DOL's regulations.[1] That the DOL's regulations have essentially remained unchanged for decades has brought criticism from a variety of sources. Labor advocates find somewhat unrealistic the notion embodied in the regulations that an individual earning $250 a week is a "highly-paid executive" employee. Employer advocates chafe at hyper-technical rules concerning salary status, as well as an approach to analyzing job duties that seems firmly rooted in the 1950s.[2]

Nonetheless, the regulations remain on the books, and provide the framework for the analysis of whether certain individuals are exempt from the overtime provisions of the FLSA. The DOL and courts state that they "strictly construe" the executive, administrative, and professional exemptions so as not to deprive eligible employees of overtime.[3] The employer has the burden of proving any of the exemptions by clear evidence,[4] and must show that the exemption "plainly and unmistakenly" applies to the employee.[5] FLSA exemptions are designed to be narrowly construed against employers and "are to be withheld except as to persons plainly and unmistakenly within their terms and spirit."[6] In addition, the employer must raise the exemption as an affirmative defense when responding to the filing of the lawsuit.[7]

A. The Definition Of A "Salaried" Employee.

In order to qualify as an executive, administrative or professional employee, the employee must be "salaried." Unless the employee meets the FLSA's definition of a salaried employee, the exemption from the payment of overtime will usually not apply.[8]

These principles are explained at length in the DOL's regulation defining a salaried employee:

"(a) An employee will be considered to be paid 'on a salary basis' within the meaning of the regulations if under his employment agreement he regularly receives each pay period on a weekly, or less frequent basis, a predetermined amount constituting all or part of his compensation, which amount is not subject to reduction because of variations in the quality or quantity of the work performed. Subject to the exceptions provided below, the employee must receive his full salary for any week in which he performs any work without regard to the number of days or hours worked. This policy is also subject to the general rule that an employee need not be paid for any workweek in which he performs no work.

"(2) Deductions may be made, however, when the employee absents himself from work for a day or more for personal reasons, other than sickness or accident. Thus, if an employee is absent for a day or longer to handle personal affairs, his salaried status will not be affected if deductions are made from his salary for such absences.

"(3) Deductions may also be made for absences of a day or more occasioned by sickness or disability (including industrial accidents) if the deduction is made in accordance with a bona fide plan, policy or practice of providing compensation for loss of salary occasioned by both sickness and disability.

Thus, if the employer's particular plan, policy or practice provides compensation for such absences, deductions for absences of a day or longer because of sickness or disability may be made * * * after he has exhausted his leave allowance thereunder."[9]

The years following the *Garcia* decision saw two spates of litigation over the application of the DOL's salary test to the public sector. Under the DOL's regulations, an employee is only considered to be salaried if his or her compensation does not vary from week to week depending upon the actual hours the employee has worked.[10] As put by one court, salaried employees are compensated for the general value of the services they provide rather than for the number of hours that they work.[11]

The first spate of litigation concerned employers who maintained rules requiring that employees who were absent from work for a portion of a day account for the time off work through either reductions in accrued leave accounts or through a reduction in pay.[12] Under the DOL's regulations, since the employees' compensation for the week would depend upon whether they had been absent for a portion of the week, the employees were not considered to be salaried and thus were not exempt under the FLSA.[13]

After a period of time during which public sector employees had a great deal of success claiming that they were not salaried employees because their salaries were subject to deduction for part-day absences from work, some courts began to question whether the DOL's regulations could legitimately apply to the public sector, particularly given what courts referred to as the necessarily higher degree of accountability which could be demanded of public sector employees.[14] Responding to these courts as well as to significant criticism from public sector employers, on September 6, 1991, the DOL amended Section 541.5 of its rules to permit a public employer to dock an employee's pay for missing less than full day's work without defeating the employee's salaried status under FLSA. Since the change in the DOL's approach, an employer's policy calling for salary deductions for part-day absences from work does not deprive the employer of the ability to claim that the employee is exempt,[15] though some courts questioned whether the DOL's changed rule could be applied retroactively.[16]

The second spate of litigation under the salary test concerned employees who were subject to disciplinary suspensions without pay. Under the DOL's rules, if an employee is subject to disciplinary suspension without pay for less than a full workweek or work period for other than a rule violation of major safety significance, the employee is not considered to be salaried since the employee's compensation for the week will depend upon the actual hours the employee works. Since at the time of the *Garcia* decision most public sector agencies had disciplinary rules which subject all employees, regardless of position, to suspension without pay, many employers quickly found themselves facing ultimately successful lawsuits that their disciplinary rules allowed high-ranking employees to claim overtime.[17]

Employers responded to these lawsuits by contending that the DOL's salary rules were originally designed for the private sector and did not take into account principles of accountability which apply to all public sector employees. Employers contended that for the DOL's salary regulations to apply to the public sector, the DOL was required to reenact them subsequent to the *Garcia* decision. In 1997, in *Auer v. Robbins*, the Supreme Court rejected this argument, holding that the DOL's rules concerning disciplinary suspensions could validly be applied to public sector employers. The Supreme Court reasoned that, given the historical deference given by the courts to the DOL's regulations, employers' arguments concerning the DOL's disciplinary suspension rules should more appropriately be lodged with the DOL than with the courts. Under *Auer*, if an employee is covered by a policy that permits disciplinary or other deductions in pay "as a practical matter" – in the sense that there is either an actual practice of making such deductions or an employment policy that creates a "significant likelihood" of such deductions – then the employee is not salaried and consequently not exempt.[18]

If an employer does not have an express policy subjecting employees to disciplinary suspensions without pay, courts will reject arguments that all employees are necessarily subject to suspension under a generalized disciplinary policy.[19] An express policy can be established in one of two ways. First, if an employer has rules specifically applicable to potentially exempt employees that list short-term suspensions without pay as an available disciplinary sanction, courts will usually find that an express policy exists.[20] Second, if an employer has a well-established practice of suspending employees whom it claims to be exempt, courts will infer the existence of a policy of disciplinary suspensions.[21]

The decisions of courts are anything but consistent on what constitutes a "policy or pattern" of disciplinary suspensions. What follows is a summary of the diverse decisions of courts on the issue following the *Auer* case:

FINDING THAT POLICY OR PATTERN ESTABLISHED:

· Store operations manual detailed disciplinary procedures and listed suspensions as an available penalty. Seven members of management suspended in 18-month period.[22]

· Fifty-three suspensions among 5,300 exempt employees established a practice.[23]

· At least seven suspensions involving several employees in 1992 and 1995 constitute an actual practice.[24]

· Suspensions of 11 of 39 plaintiffs constitute an actual practice.[25]

· Actual practice of deducting from leave bank for

partial day absences thereby lowering amount received at termination through cash-out provision met *Auer* test.[26]

NO CONCLUSION AS TO WHETHER POLICY OR PATTERN ESTABLISHED:

· Employer's general disciplinary policy allowed short-term suspensions of any employees, but no rule specifically applied only to exempt personnel. Limiting inquiry to period covered by statute of limitations, trial court found 12 suspensions out of a workforce of 1,814 managers, roughly 0.7%, and found no policy or practice. Appeals court reversed, holding inquiry should not be limited to statute of limitations, and "the object of the inquiry is whether the employer's practices reflect an objective intention to pay its employees on a salaried basis. That question cannot be answered by simply dividing the number of impermissible pay deductions by the number of managerial employees, but necessarily involves consideration of additional factors such as the number of times that other forms of discipline are imposed, the number of employee infractions warranting discipline, the existence of policies favoring or disfavoring pay deductions, the process by which sanctions are determined, and the degree of discretion held by the disciplining authority."[27]

FINDING THAT NO POLICY OR PATTERN ESTABLISHED:

· Police department's policies allowed suspensions of any employee; however, no exempt employee had ever been suspended.[28]

· Employer's general disciplinary policy allowed short-term suspensions, but no rules were specifically applicable to exempt employees. One suspension over ten-year period.[29]

· Employer's policies "theoretically" allowed suspensions of any employee; only one exempt employee had ever been suspended.[30]

· Disciplinary deduction policy that was never actually enforced against managers, and applicable to non-managerial employees as well, does not show a significant likelihood of deductions under *Auer*.[31]

· Four suspensions over eight years does not meet the *Auer* test.[32]

· Two suspensions "under unusual circumstances" do not amount to a practice. [33]

· Five suspensions "under unusual circumstances" over five-year period not enough to establish practice.[34]

· Two suspensions insufficient to satisfy actual practice test. Case contains only brief description of facts.[35]

Some debate has ensued as to what constitutes a safety violation of major significance. In one case, a court held that leaving the scene of a suicide and engaging in excessive force were not safety violations of major significance.[36] In another case, a court held that the suspension of a patrol sergeant for failure to respond to a traffic accident involving an injury was an infraction of a safety rule of major significance and did not deprive the employer of the ability to claim that the employee was exempt.[37] The DOL's regulations provide little guidance in the area, offering only the example that an employee smoking in an oil refinery would be considered to have committed a safety violation of major significance.[38]

Often, public sector employers require even high-ranking employees to observe strict attendance requirements and to follow involved timekeeping procedures accounting for all of their time at work. Courts have held that such requirements, standing alone, do not deprive the employer of the ability to claim that the employee is a salaried employee who is exempt under the FLSA.[39] In addition, the courts are divided as to whether the fact that a high-ranking employee receives some form of compensation for overtime hours worked — whether the compensation be in the form of time off or additional pay — is enough to deprive the employer of the ability to claim that the employee is exempt. Most courts hold that the payment of such additional compensation does not deprive the employer of the ability to claim the exemption.[40] A minority of courts finds to the contrary, reasoning that the payment of some form of overtime compensation is more consistent with an employee's hourly status than with the conclusion that the employee is salaried.[41]

B. The "Window Of Correction."

The DOL's regulations provide some relief for employers who have intended to treat employees as exempt but who have violated the technical rules concerning an employee's salaried status. Such employers have a "window of correction" available to them to reimburse the employee for any inappropriate deductions made from their salary, thereby regaining the employee's salaried status. This "window of correction" is described in Section 541.118(d)(6) of the DOL's regulations:

> "(6) The effect of making a deduction which is not permitted under these interpretations will depend upon the facts in the particular case. Where deductions are generally made when there is no work available, it indicates that there was no intention to pay the employee on a salary basis. In such a case the exemption would not be applicable to him during the entire period when such deductions were being made. On the other hand, where a deduction not permitted by these interpretations is inadvertent, or is made for reasons other than lack of work, the exemption will not be considered to have been lost

if the employer reimburses the employee for such deductions and promises to comply in the future."[42]

There are numerous examples of courts applying the "window of correction" to allow employers to reimburse employees for deductions made from pay and thereby escape a conclusion that the employees are not salaried. The most prominent of these cases is *Auer v. Robbins* itself, where the Supreme Court approved of the City of St. Louis' reimbursement of money to a suspended police sergeant and refused to hold that the suspension negated the sergeant's salaried status. Other factual scenarios in which the "window of correction" has been applied include where a city made deductions from the salary of fire platoon supervisors if they missed less than one day of work and did not have accumulated leave to cover the absence. Once the city discovered that the deductions imperiled the salary status of the employees, it immediately reimbursed the platoon supervisors and all affected exempt employees.[43]

At present there exists some controversy, not explicitly resolved in the Supreme Court's *Auer* decision, as to whether the "window of correction" is available to an employer which has suspended employees without pay for other than major safety violations, where the suspensions were pursuant to an official policy of the employer. Some courts have interpreted the DOL's regulations as holding that even in such cases, the employer should be able to use the "window of correction" to reimburse the suspended employees for the lost wages and regain the salaried status of the employees.[44] A significant majority of courts, and in particular all courts that have considered the DOL's subsequent interpretation of its own regulations as expressed in *amicus curiae* or "friend of the court" briefs, have held instead that the "window of correction" is only available for inadvertent deductions from an employee's salary, and is not available to an employer with a policy of such suspensions.[45]

C. Executive Employees.

The definition of an executive employee under the FLSA is twofold. The first definition, contained in Section 541.1 of the DOL's regulations, is known as the "long test," and provides that an employee is an executive if six tests are met:

1. The employee's primary duty must consist of the management of the enterprise in which he is employed or of a customarily recognized department, subdivision, or agency thereof;

2. The employee must customarily and regularly direct the work of two or more other employees;

3. The employee must have the authority to hire or fire other employees, or whose recommendation concerning such decisions and as to promotional and other change of status decisions will be given "particular weight" by the decision-maker on such issues;

4. The employee must customarily and regularly exercise discretionary powers;

5. The employee must not devote more than 20% of "hours worked" to activities which are not included in numbers 1-4 above; and

6. The employee must be compensated at a rate not less than $155.00 per week, exclusive of board, lodging, or other facilities.

Section 541.1(f) of the regulations describes the FLSA's second definition of an executive employee, known as the "short test." The "short test" is used in virtually all cases where the employee makes at least $250.00 per week, which, in the current economy, means that the "short test" is virtually the only test used in FLSA cases today.[46] If the employee meets the requirements of the "short test," he or she is exempt from overtime under the FLSA even if the employee does not meet all of the "long test" factors.

1. The employee must be compensated at the rate of at least $250.00 per week;

2. The employee's primary duty must consist of the management of the enterprise in which the employee is employed or of a customarily recognized department, subdivision or agency thereof; and

3. The employee's work must involve the customary and regular direction of the work of two or more employees.[47]

Since most public employees who are arguably executives earn more than $250 per week ($13,000 per year), the long test is rarely utilized by courts in determining the status of supposed executives.

The various phrases used in the definitions of executive personnel are described in greater detail below.

1. What Constitutes The Management Of Other Employees?

A key element to both definitions of executive employees is involvement in the "management" of an employer's operations. Section 541.102(b) of the regulations lists activities which indicate participation in management:

- Interviewing, selecting and training of employees.

- Setting and adjusting the rates of pay and hours of work of employees.

- Directing and scheduling the employees' work.

- Maintaining the employees' production or sales records for use in supervision or control.

- Appraising the employees' productivity and efficiency for the purposes of recommending promotions or other changes in status.

- Handling employees' complaints and grievances and disciplining them when necessary.

- Planning the work of employees.

- Determining the techniques to be used in work.

- Apportioning the work among different employees.

- Determining the types of materials, supplies, machinery or tools to be used or merchandise to be bought, stocked, or sold.

- Controlling the flow and distribution of materials, merchandise and supplies.

- Providing for the safety of employees and the property of the employer.[48]

An employee is usually an executive if the employee's primary duty, defined as greater than 50% of the employee's time, is spent in the type of functions listed above.[49] Under some circumstances, an employee who spends less than 50% of his or her time on the above types of duties may still be considered to be an executive employee. Such a situation arises when the frequency of the management responsibilities is low, but the significance of the duties is high.[50] In addition, some courts have held that an employee need not necessarily be physically present at all times in order to supervise other employees.[51]

In order to qualify as an executive, the individual must supervise other "employees." Two cases have held that employees supervising inmates performing work in a correctional institution were not executives since the inmates did not qualify as "employees."[52]

2. The Definition Of Department Or Subdivision.

In order to qualify as an executive under the FLSA, an employee's managerial duties must be performed either with respect to the enterprise in which the employee works or with respect to a customarily recognized "department or subdivision thereof."[53] Section 541.104 of the regulations defines the phrase "department or subdivision":

"The phrase 'a customarily recognized department or subdivision' is intended to distinguish between a mere collection of men assigned from time to time to a specific job or series of jobs and a unit with permanent status and function. In order to properly classify an individual as an executive he must be more than merely a supervisor of two or more employees; nor is it sufficient that he merely participates in the management of the unit. He must be in charge of and have as his primary duty the management of a recognized unit which has a continuing function."

In one case, a court held that a fire station was a recognized "department or subdivision" of city government.[54]

3. The Authority To Hire Or Fire.

Another part of the definition of an executive employee is that the employee must have the right to hire or fire, or make effective recommendations on hiring and firing.[55] For years, the question of what constitutes the ability to make an "effective" recommendation on disciplinary decisions has been debated with conflicting results in determining which employees should be properly included in bargaining units under local collective bargaining laws. The regulation of the DOL explaining what constitutes the authority to hire or fire does not shed much light on the subject:

"Thus no employee, whether high or low in the hierarchy of management, can be considered as employed in a bona fide executive capacity unless he is directly concerned either with the hiring or firing or other change of status of the employees under his supervision, whether by direct action or by recommendation to those to whom the hiring and firing functions are delegated."[56]

The authority to hire and fire must be real and not merely theoretical. For example, in one case a court rejected a claim that an employee was an executive when the only evidence of the employee's hiring or firing activities were that on one occasion, the employee had recommended that an employee be given a raise to prevent the employee from quitting.[57] In other cases, courts have rejected claims of exemptions for employees whose disciplinary recommendations have not been given "particular weight" by an employer.[58]

If collective bargaining laws exist and exclude from coverage those who are employed in a "supervisory" capacity, it is likely that the definition of what constitutes "effective" recommendations on hiring and firing decisions under those bargaining laws will be co-extensive with how the DOL will view what constitutes a recommendation which is given "particular weight" by those with authority to hire and fire subordinates. If no collective bargaining laws exist, an employer should exercise caution in excluding employees from the coverage of the FLSA by virtue of their "executive" status, bearing in mind that the FLSA contains a bias against excluding employees from its coverage. As such, before employees are excluded on the basis of their "executive" status, there should be clear evidence that they have actually participated in personnel decisions in a significant way, and that their recommendations have been taken into account by those charged with making hiring and firing decisions.

4. Discretionary Powers.

Another component in the definition of executive is an employee who regularly and customarily exercises discretionary powers. Unfortunately, the regulations of the DOL relevant to executive employees are not particularly helpful in defining what discretionary powers are, noting only that "[a] person whose work is so completely routinized that he has no discretion does not qualify for the exemption."[59] However, in the regulations explaining the tests for administrative employees, the DOL offers the following more specific definition of "discretion":

"In general, the exercise of discretion and independent judgment involves the comparison and the evaluation of possible courses of conduct and acting or making a decision after various possibilities have been considered. The term as used in the regulations in sub part (A) of this part, moreover, implies that the person has the authority or power to make an independent choice, free from immediate direction or supervision and with respect to matters of significance."[60]

The regulations give a good guidepost with respect to the meaning of the phrase "customarily or regularly":

"The phrase 'customarily and regularly' signifies a frequency which must be greater than occasional but which, of course, may be less than constant. The requirement will be met by the employee who normally and recurrently is called upon to exercise and does exercise discretionary powers in the day-to-day performance of his duties. The requirement is not met by the occasional exercise of discretionary powers."[61]

5. The Definition Of "Directly And Closely Related."

Under the definition of an executive employee, the employee cannot devote more than 20 percent of hours worked to activities which are not "directly and closely related" to the performance of otherwise executive work.[62] The regulations define "directly and closely related" as follows:

"This phrase brings within the category of exempt work not only the actual management of the department and the supervision of the employees therein, but also activities which are closely associated with the performance of the duties involved in such managerial and supervisory functions or responsibilities. The supervision of employees and the management of a department include a great many directly and closely related tasks which are different from the work performed by subordinates and are commonly performed by supervisors because they are helpful in supervising employees or contribute to the smooth functioning of the department for which they are responsible. Frequently such exempt work is of a kind which in establishments that are organized differently or which are larger and have greater specialization of function, may be performed by a non-exempt employee hired especially for that purpose."[63]

6. The Status Of "Working Foremen."

The DOL's regulations spend a good deal of time dealing with the status of "working foremen." Though such a phrase applies more to a production line or other industrial environment, there are examples of "working foremen" in the public sector. In general, the intent of the FLSA is to include "working foremen" within the coverage of the FLSA. As noted by the regulations, this bias towards including "working foremen" within the scope of the FLSA was the purpose of the "20% limitation" used in the definition of an executive employee:

> "The primary purpose of the exclusionary language placing a limitation on the amount of non-exempt work is to distinguish between the bona fide executive and the 'working' foreman or 'working' supervisor who regularly performs 'production' work or other work which is unrelated or only remotely related to his supervisory activities."[64]

The most readily identifiable type of working foreman will be one who "works alongside his subordinates."[65] Though working foremen typically have some supervisory responsibilities, the majority of their work is usually of the same nature and type as their subordinates.[66] In addition, working foremen will rarely have the broad type of discretion typically possessed by high-ranking executive employees.[67]

7. The Application Of The Executive Rules To Public Sector Employees.

Since the *Garcia* decision, courts have struggled in applying the definitions of executive employees to public sector agencies. Most of the disputes have involved law enforcement and fire protection employees. In general, the courts have ruled that law enforcement sergeants are generally not executives and are entitled to overtime compensation,[68] with employees in higher ranks generally exempt as executives.[69] For example, in one case, a court found that sergeants employed by the United States Secret Service did not have the necessary authority to be considered exempt under the FLSA.[70] To the contrary, though the Supreme Court did not analyze the issue in *Auer v. Robbins*, the lower court's decision in the case found police sergeants who supervised discrete units of six-ten officers to be executives.[71]

In fire protection agencies, the dividing line appears to be at approximately the rank of captain, though the cases lack much in the way of consistency. While the DOL and courts hold fairly consistently that lieutenants and below are entitled to overtime and that employees with ranks higher than captain are executives,[72] the cases are decidedly split on the issue of whether captains should be treated as executives. For example, in *Amos v. City of Winston-Salem*, a court held that fire platoon supervisors were executive employees even though the supervisors had no authority to discharge employees and performed some of the same tasks as other firefighters. The Court stressed the fact that the supervisors were in charge of a station's operation, had responsibility to manage fire scenes and determine whether additional companies and equipment were needed, and evaluated the performance of platoons and effectively made recommendations to battalion chiefs on personnel issues.[73]

In a seemingly contrary decision, in *Martin v. City of Sapulpa, Oklahoma*, the Court held that fire captains were not executive employees where they did not have management as their primary duty. The Court concluded that the captains did not spend more than half their time in management functions, had no authority to call additional personnel to a fire scene, did not set work schedules, participated in all routine manual station duties, did not have responsibility for management of individual fire stations, and did not have the responsibility to direct two or more employees.[74]

Several cases have involved non-sworn employees in a law enforcement or fire protection agency. For example, in *Kavanaugh v. City of Phoenix, Arizona*, the Court found the head of the legal unit working for the Phoenix Police Department to be an executive employee, citing his responsibility to manage other employees in the unit.[75]

Each case involving a question as to whether an employee is exempt as an executive turns on its individual facts. The job title the employee holds is irrelevant; what is critical are the duties performed by the employee. In addition, the fact that a higher-ranking employee may be compensated at a fixed salary which approximates the hourly earnings (plus overtime) of subordinates is irrelevant in determining whether an employee qualifies for the executive exemption.[76]

D. Administrative Employees.

The second broad exemption from coverage of the FLSA is for "administrative" employees. In general, administrative employees perform relatively high-level work in an organizational structure, including "work performed by so-called white-collar employees engaged in servicing a business, including advising the management, planning, and negotiating."[77] In large measure, the definition of administrative employees under the FLSA parallels the structure of the definition of executive employees.[78] As with the executive exemption, employees meeting either a "long test" or a "short test" are exempt from overtime under the FLSA. The long test has six elements:

1. The employee must be engaged in the performance of office or non-manual work;

2. The employee's work must be directly related to management policies or general business operations of the employer or the employer's customers;

3. The employee must customarily or regularly exercise discretionary independent judgment;

4. The employee must regularly and directly assist an employee working in a bona fide executive or administrative capacity or must perform under only general supervision work along specialized or technical lines requiring training, experience, or knowledge or must execute special assignments and tasks under only general supervision;

5. The employee must not devote more than 20% of hours worked to activities which are not closely related to the performance of the work described in numbers 1-3 above; and

6. The employee must be compensated at not less than $155.00 per week, exclusive of board, lodging, or other facilities.[79]

If the employee does not meet the six aspects of the "long test," the employee can still qualify as an administrative employee if the following two aspects of the so-called "short test" are met: As with the executive exemption, the "short test," used in cases where the employee earns more than $250.00 per week, is virtually the only test employed in FLSA decisions today.

1. The employee must be compensated at the rate of not less than $250.00 per week, exclusive of board, lodging, or other facilities; and

2. The employee must perform office or non-manual work directly related to management policies or general

business operations of the employer, and such work must include the exercise of discretion and independent judgment.[80]

As these definitions show, administrative employees are usually high-ranking employees who are given a great deal of latitude in defining and executing their job duties.[81] In general, the primary duty of an administrative employee must be to perform administrative functions essential to the operation of the employer's business.[82] In the public sector, such responsibilities usually mean either the supervision of a subdivision within the employer or a job which entails policy and budgetary responsibilities.[83]

Courts applying these regulations to public sector employees have generally reached the same conclusions about the administrative exemption as are reached with respect to the executive exemption. In the law enforcement environment, the DOL and courts have generally ruled that sergeants are not administrative employees.[84] In the fire protection environment, the DOL and courts have ruled that lieutenants are not administrative employees.[85] Employees of higher rank in each case have been held to be administrative employees.[86] In a significant case involving Los Angeles County, a court held that deputy probation officers were not administrative employees, reasoning as follows:

> "[T]o the extent that probation activities can be analogized to a business, the work of the [probation officers] primarily involves the day-to-day carrying out of the business' affairs, rather than running the business itself or determining its overall course or policies."[87]

An example of the application of the administrative employee exception in the law enforcement context was the Court's decision in *Ahern v. The State of New York.*[88] In the case, the Court described the traditional distinction between production work — which is work that constitutes primary mission of enterprise — and administrative work — which is work performed by employees engaged in servicing the business. The Court found that in a police agency, law enforcement is the service that the enterprise exists to produce. Applying this test, the Court found that investigators for the New York State Police Bureau of Criminal Investigation were not administrative employees since their primary duty was the prevention, investigation, and detection of crime — the production work of a police agency as opposed to administering the business affairs of the agency.

In another case, a court found that a police "ethics and standards" lieutenant was an administrative employee. The lieutenant spent all of her time accumulating and analyzing data and making recommendations that influenced the department's disciplinary policies, investigating complaints against other officers, analyzing the facts of disciplinary cases, interpreting department policy, and making disciplinary recommendations which were followed about 90 percent of the time. The same court held that public information officers were not administrative employees, where half their time was spent answering the phone, taking crime tips, and passing information to correct divisions in the department. Though the officers developed a news broadcast called "Crime of the Week," the Court found that the officers lacked the necessary discretion to be termed administrative employees.[89]

E. Professional Employees.

Under Section 13(a) of the FLSA, "professional employees" are exempt from the overtime requirements of the Act. The regulations again provide the familiar "long test" and "short test" for the exemption. The "long test" requires the following:

1. The employee's primary duties must consist of "work requiring knowledge of an advanced type in a field of science or learning customarily acquired by a prolonged course of specialized intellectual instruction and study" (which the regulations distinguish from a general academic

education, or from apprenticeships, or from the performance of "routine" processes), <u>or</u> the employee's primary duty must consist of work that is "original and creative in character in a recognized field of artistic endeavor * * * and the result of which depends primarily on the intention, imagination and talent of the employee," <u>or</u> the employee's primary work must consist of the teaching, tutoring, instructing or lecturing in the activity of imparting knowledge;

2. The employee's work must require the consistent exercise of discretion in judgment;

3. The employee's work must be predominately intellectual and varied in character (as opposed to routine), and must be of such character that the output produced cannot be standardized in relation to a given period of time;

4. The employee must not devote more than 20% of his or her hours to activities which are not listed in numbers 1-3 above; and

5. The employee must be compensated for services on a salary or fee basis at a rate not less than $170.00 per week.[90]

The second definition of a professional employee provided by Section 541.3 of the DOL's regulations, referred to as the "short test," provides an alternate set of tests which can be used by an employer to claim the professional exemption for an employee:

1. The employee must be compensated at the rate of not less than $250.00 per week, exclusive of board, lodging, or other facilities; and

2. The employee's work must either involve the type of work listed in paragraph 1 in the first definition of professional employee provided by the regulations, or must consist of work requiring invention, imagination, or talent in a recognized field of artistic endeavor.[91]

Where the DOL's regulations seemingly give a very broad definition to administrative employees, the definition given to professional employees is quite narrow.[92] Virtually the only application of the professional exemption in the public sector apart from teachers would occur with employees whose work requires "knowledge of an advance type in a field of science or learning customarily acquired by a prolonged course of specialized intellectual instruction and study." This standard is fleshed out somewhat in the DOL's regulations, which give this explanatory reading to the definition of "professional employee":

> "The first element in the requirement is that the knowledge be of an advanced type. Thus, generally speaking, it must be knowledge which cannot be obtained at the high school level. Second, it must be knowledge in a field of science or learning. This serves to distinguish the professions from the mechanical arts where in some instances the knowledge is of a fairly advanced type, but not in a field of science or learning. The requisite knowledge, in the third place, must be customarily acquired in a prolonged course of specialization in intellectual instruction and study."[93]

In general, the types of job classifications likely meeting the requirements for the professional exemption for the Fair Labor Standards Act are as follows:

- Teachers[94]
- Lawyers[95]
- Doctors
- Nurses[96]
- Athletic trainers[97]
- Engineers
- Architects
- Coroners
- Technical work in a crime laboratory
- Pharmacists
- Pilots[98]

- Accountants

- Actuaries

Applying these tests, a court in *Dybach v. Florida Department of Corrections* held that the determinative factors in deciding if the professional exemption applies are the requirements of the job, not the education the employee in fact has earned.[99] In the case, the Court ruled that a probation officer was not a professional employee exempt from overtime where her position did not require a college or an advanced degree in any specialized field of knowledge.[100] Courts applying virtually identical reasoning have concluded that paramedics are not professional employees exempt from overtime under the FLSA.[101] However, one court has held that game wardens meet the tests for professional employees, ruling that the degree required for the job prepared the game wardens to accomplish tasks such as developing wildlife management plans, setting population goals, and serving as the sole representative of the state's game and fish department within a geographic area.[102]

NOTES TO CHAPTER 8

[1] *See Mark J. Ricciardi & Lisa G. Sherman, Exempt or Not Exempt Under the Administrative Exemption of the FLSA * * * That Is The Question*, 11 Lab. Law. 209 (1995).

[2] *See* generally *Michael Faillace, Automatic Exemption Of Highly-Paid Employees And Other Proposed Amendments To The White Collar Exemptions: Bringing The FLSA Into The 21st Century*, 15 Lab. Law. 357 (Winter/Spring 2000).

[3] *Avery v. City of Talladega*, 24 F.3d 1337 (11th Cir. 1994). From time to time, proposals circulate to change some aspect of the Section 13(a) exemptions. *See G. Krueger, Straight-Time Overtime and Salary Basis: Reform of the Fair Labor Standards Act*, 70 Wash. L.Rev. 1097 (1995); P. DeChiara, Rethinking the Managerial-Professional Exemption of the Fair Labor Standards Act, 43 Amer.U.L.Rev. 139 (1993). In spite of such proposals, Section 13(a) and the DOL's regulations interpreting Section 13(a) have remained virtually unchanged since they were first promulgated.

[4] *West v. Anne Arundel County*, 3 WH Cases2d 234 (D.Md. 1996).

[5] *Banks v. City of North Little Rock*, 708 F.Supp. 1023 (E.D.Ark. 1988).

[6] *Klem v. County of Santa Clara*, 208 F.3d 1085 (9th Cir. 2000).

[7] *Magana v. Comm. of the Northern Mariana Islands*, 107 F.3d 1436 (9th Cir. 1997); *Renfro v. City of Emporia*, 948 F.2d 1529 (10th Cir. 1991).

[8] The most prominent exception to the salary rule applicable to public sector employers is that doctors, attorneys, teachers and employees engaged in certain types of computer work need not be salaried in order to

be exempt under the FLSA. 29 C.F.R. §541.3(e) (2001). *Close v. New York State*, 3 WH Cases2d 225 (N.D.N.Y. 1996).

[9] 29 C.F.R. §§541.118(a), (a)(2), (a)(3) (2001).

[10] *Thomas v. Fairfax County, Virginia*, 803 F.Supp. 1142 (E.D.Va. 1992).

[11] *Abshire v. County of Kern*, 908 F.2d 483 (9th Cir. 1990).

[12] While the "part-day absence" rule was still in effect, a clear, unambiguous policy requiring salary deductions for part-day absences was necessary to deprive an employer of the ability to claim that the employee was exempt under the FLSA. *Michigan Association of Governmental Employees v. Michigan Department of Corrections*, 122 Lab. Cas. ¶35,673 (W.D.Mich. 1992).

[13] *Abshire v. County of Kern*, 908 F.2d 483 (9th Cir. 1990); *Whitmore v. Port Authority of New York and New Jersey*, 907 F.2d 20 (2nd Cir. 1990); *Thomas v. County of Fairfax*, 30 WH Cases 62 (E.D.Va. 1990); *Wilson v. City of Charlotte*, 717 F.Supp. 408 (W.D.N.C. 1989); *Banks v. City of North Little Rock*, 708 F.Supp. 1023 (D.Ark. 1988); *Hawks v. City of Newport News, Va.*, 707 F.Supp. 212 (E.D.Va. 1988); *Persons v. City of Gresham*, 704 F.Supp. 191 (D.Or. 1988); *Knecht v. City of Redwood City*, 683 F.Supp. 1307 (N.D.Cal. 1987). There exists some dispute as to whether an employee is salaried if the employer's personnel practices allow the docking of wages for short-term absences from work, but the employer has never actually implemented those practices to dock an employees' wages. *Atlanta Professional Firefighters Union v. City of Atlanta*, 920 F.2d 800 (11th Cir. 1991)(compare majority and dissenting opinions).

[14] *E.g. SEIU Local 102 v. San Diego County*, 60 F.3d 1346 (9th Cir. 1994); *Jackson v. Kentucky*, 892 F.Supp. 923 (E.D.Ky. 1995).

[15] *Aaron v. City of Wichita, Kansas*, 54 F.3d 652 (10th Cir. 1995); *Quirk v. Baltimore County, Md.*, 895 F.Supp. 773 (D.Md. 1995).

[16] *Michigan Association of Governmental Employees v. Michigan Department of Corrections*, 992 F.2d 82 (6th Cir. 1993); *Kuchinskas v. Broward County*, 840 F.Supp. 1548 (S.D.Fla. 1993).

[17] *McGuire v. City of Portland*, 91 F.3d 1293 (9th Cir. 1996), *vacated* 108 F.3d 1182 (9th Cir. 1997); *Balgowan v. New Jersey Dep't of Transportation*, 3 WH Cases2d 488 (3rd Cir. 1996); *Carpenter v. City of Denver*, 82 F.3d 353 (10th Cir. 1996); *Bankston v. State of Illinois*, 60 F.3d 1249 (7th Cir. 1995); *Mueller v. Reich*, 54 F.3d 438 (7th Cir. 1995); *Shockley v. City of Newport News*, 997 F.2d 18 (4th Cir. 1993); *Klem v. County of Santa Clara*, 3 WH Cases2d 474 (N.D.Cal. 1996); *Reich v. Malcolm Pirnie Inc.*, 821 F.Supp. 905 (S.D.N.Y. 1993), aff'd 84 F.3d 655 (2nd Cir. 1996); *Yourman v. Dinkins*, 826 F.Supp. 736 (S.D.N.Y. 1993); *see Bowman v. City of Indianapolis*, 892 F.Supp. 212 (S.D.Ind. 1995).

[18] *Auer v. Robbins*, 519 U.S. 452 (1997).

[19] *Hackett v. Lane County*, 91 F.3d 1289 (9th Cir. 1996).

[20] *Kinney v. District of Columbia*, 994 F.2d 6 (D.C. Cir. 1993). *But see Quirk v. Baltimore County, Md.*, 895 F.Supp. 773 (D.Md. 1995).

[21] *Spradling v. Tulsa, Oklahoma*, 95 F.3d 1492 (10th Cir. 1996); *Klein v. Rush-Presbyterian-St. Luke's Medical Center*, 990 F.2d 279 (7th Cir. 1993); *Abbey v. City of Jackson*, 883 F.Supp. 181 (E.D.Mich. 1995).

[22] *Takacs v. Hahn Automotive Corporation*, 246 F.3d 776 (6th Cir. 2001).

[23] *Klem v. County of Santa Clara*, 208 F.3d 1085 (9th Cir. 2000).

[24] *Rushing v. Shelby County Gov.*, 1997 WL 901901 (W.D.Tenn. 1997).

[25] *Arrington v. City of Macon*, 973 F.Supp. 1467 (M.D.Ga. 1997).

[26] *Graziano v. Society of the New York Hospital*, 1997 WL 400127 (S.D.N.Y. 1997).

[27] *Yourman v. Guiliani*, 229 F.3d 124 (2nd Cir. 2000).

[28] *Kelly v. City of Mount Vernon*, 162 F.3d 165 (2nd Cir. 1998).

[29] *Ahern v. County of Nassau*, 118 F.3d 118 (2nd Cir. 1997).

[30] *Lilenfeld v. Kieper*, 4 WH Cases2d 307 (S.D.N.Y. 1997).

[31] *Balgowan v. State of New Jersey*, 115 F.3d 214 (3rd Cir. 1997).

[32] *Davis v. City of Hollywood*, 120 F.3d 1178 (11th Cir. 1997).

[33] *Carpenter v. City and County of Denver, Colo.*, 115 F.3d 765 (10th Cir. 1997).

[34] *Digiore v. Ryan*, 172 F.3d 454 (7th Cir. 1999).

[35] *Kendall v. Davis*, 1999 WL 357851 (2nd Cir. 1999).

[36] *Avery v. City of Talladega, Alabama*, 24 F.3d 1337 (11th Cir. 1994).

[37] *Childers v. City of Eugene*, 922 F.Supp. 403 (D.Or. 1996).

[38] 29 C.F.R. §541.118 (a)(5) (2001).

[39] *Kuchinskas v. Broward County*, 840 F.Supp. 1548 (S.D.Fla. 1993); *Michigan Supervisors' Union v. State of Michigan*, 826 F.Supp. 1081 (W.D.Mich. 1993).

[40] *West v. Anne Arundel County, Maryland*, 137 F.3d 752 (4th Cir. 1998); *Boykin v. Boeing Company*, 128 F.3d 1279 (9th Cir. 1997); *Hilbert v. District of Columbia*, 23 F.3d 429 (D.C.App. 1994); *Michigan Assoc. of Gov. Employees v. Michigan Dep't of Corr.*, 992 F.2d 82 (6th Cir. 1993); *Wright v. Aargo Security Services,*

Inc., 2001 WL 91705 (S.D.N.Y. 2001); *West v. Anne Arundel County*, 3 WH Cases2d 234 (D.Md. 1996); *Abbey v. City of Jackson*, 883 F.Supp. 181 (E.D.Mich. 1995); *McGrath v. City of Philadelphia*, 864 F.Supp. 466 (E.D.Pa. 1994); *Simmons v. City of Fort Worth, Texas*, 805 F.Supp. 419 (N.D.Tex. 1992); *Keller v. City of Columbus, Indiana*, 778 F.Supp. 1480 (S.D.Ind. 1991); *White v. City of Dothan*, 643 So.2d 1005 (Ala.App. 1994). *But see Allen v. County of Fairfax*, 127 Lab. Cas. ¶33,049 (4th Cir. 1994)(payment for excess hours worked inconsistent with salary status); *Brock v. Claridge Hotel & Casino*, 846 F.2d 180 (3rd Cir. 1988); *Hodgson v. Baker*, 544 F.2d 429 (9th Cir. 1976); *Banks v. City of North Little Rock*, 708 F.Supp. 1023 (E.D.Ark. 1988).

[41] *Balgowan v. New Jersey Dep't of Transportation*, 3 WH Cases2d 488 (3rd Cir. 1996); *Klein v. Rush-Presbyterian-St. Luke's Medical Center*, 990 F.2d 279 (N.D.Ill. 1992); *Close v. New York State*, 3 WH Cases2d 225 (N.D.N.Y. 1996).

[42] 29 C.F.R. §541.118(a)(6) (2001).

[43] *Amos v. City of Winston-Salem*, 1 WH Cases2d 578 (M.D.N.C. 1993).

[44] *Paresi v. City of Portland*, 182 F.3d 665 (9th Cir. 1999); *Davis v. City of Hollywood*, 120 F.3d 1178 (11th Cir. 1997) *Balgowan v. New Jersey*, 115 F.3d 214 (3rd Cir. 1997). The Ninth Circuit, which decided the *Paresi* case, later changed its mind, and ruled that the window of corrections was not available to an employer with a pattern of suspensions. *Klem v. County of Santa Clara*, 208 F.3d 1085 (9th Cir. 2000).

[45] *Whetsel v. Network Property Services*, LLC, 246 F.3d 897 (7th Cir. 2001); *Takacs v. Hahn Automotive Corporation*, 246 F.3d 776 (6th Cir. 2001); *Yourman v. Guiliani*, 229 F.3d 124 (2nd Cir. 2000); *Kelly v. City of New York*, 144 Lab. Cas. ¶34,388 (S.D.N.Y. 2001).

[46] *Wright v. Aargo Security Services, Inc.*, 2001 WL 91705 (S.D.N.Y. 2001).

[47] *See* generally *Annotation, Who is Employed in Executive Capacity*, 131 ALR Fed. 1 (1996).

[48] *See* generally *Aly v. Butts County, Georgia*, 841 F.Supp. 1199 (M.D.Ga. 1994); *Russell v. Mini Mart, Inc.*, 711 F.Supp. 556 (D.Mont. 1988); *Joiner v. City of Macon*, 647 F.Supp. 718 (M.D.Ga. 1986).

[49] *Wilson v. City of Charlotte*, 717 F.Supp. 408 (W.D.N.C. 1989); *Di Gregorio v. Temple University*, 26 WH Cases 1184 (E.D.Pa. 1983).

[50] *Guthrie v. Lady Jane Collieries, Inc.*, 722 F.2d 1141 (3rd Cir. 1983); *Donovan v. Burger King Corporation*, 672 F.2d 221 (1st Cir. 1982); *Marshall v. Western Union Tel. Co.*, 621 F.2d 1246 (3rd Cir. 1980).

[51] *Sturm v. TOC Retail*, 864 F.Supp. 1346 (M.D.Ga. 1994).

[52] *Wilks v. District of Columbia*, 721 F.Supp. 1383 (D.D.C. 1989); *Amos v. United States*, 13 Cl.Ct. 442 (1987).

[53] *See Gilstrap v. Synalloy Corp., Industrial Piping Supply Co. Div.*, 409 F.Supp. 621 (M.D.La. 1976).

[54] *Masters v. City of Huntington*, 800 F.Supp. 363 (S.D.W.Va. 1992).

[55] *Horne v. Crown Cent. Petroleum, Inc.*, 775 F.Supp. 189 (D.S.C. 1991); *Kelly v. Adroit, Inc.*, 480 F.Supp. 392 (E.D.Tenn. 1979), *aff'd* 657 F.2d 267 (6th Cir. 1979).

[56] 29 C.F.R. §541.106 (2001).

[57] *Wright v. Zenner & Ritter, Inc.*, 27 WH Cases 1135 (W.D.N.Y. 1986).

[58] *Harris v. District of Columbia*, 741 F.Supp. 254 (D.D.C. 1990); *Distelhorst v. Day & Zimmerman, Inc.*, 58 F. Supp. 334 (D.Iowa 1944); *Baca v. United States*, 29 Fed.Cl. 354 (1993).

[59] 29 C.F.R. §541.107(a) (2001).

[60] 29 C.F.R. §541.207(a) (2001).

[61] 29 C.F.R. §541.107(b) (2001).

[62] *See Harris v. District of Columbia*, 741 F.Supp. 254 (D.D.C. 1990); *Rigney v. Wilson & Co.*, 61 F.Supp. 801 (S.D.W.Va. 1945).

[63] 29 C.F.R. §541.108 (2001).

[64] 29 C.F.R. §541.115 (2001).

[65] 29 C.F.R. §541.115(b) (2001).

[66] *Brock v. Norman's Country Market, Inc.*, 835 F.2d 823 (11th Cir. 1988); *Brock v. Tierra Vista, Inc.*, 108 Lab. Cas. ¶35,019 (N.D.Okla. 1988).

[67] *Dole v. Papa Gino's of America, Inc.*, 712 F.Supp. 1038 (C.D.Mass. 1989).

[68] *Clayton v. State of Oregon*, 114 Lab. Cas. ¶35,306 (D.Or. 1990); *D'Camera v. District of Columbia*, 693 F.Supp. 1208 (D.D.C. 1988); *Adams v. United States*, 6 WH Cases2d 1097 (Fed. Cl. 1999)(supervisory Border Patrol agents). *But see Shockley v. City of Newport News*, 997 F.2d 18 (4th Cir. 1993)(patrol sergeants qualify as executive employees).

[69] *Anderson v. City of Cleveland, Tennessee*, 90 F.Supp.2d 906 (E.D.Tenn. 2000)(lieutenants considered to be executives).

[70] *Amshey v. United States*, 26 Cl.Ct. 582 (1992), vacated on other grounds, 35 Fed.Cl. 358 (1996).

[71] *Auer v. Robbins*, 65 F.3d 702 (8th Cir.1995), *aff'd*, 519 U.S. 452 (1997).

[72] *Spradling v. City of Tulsa*, 198 F.3d 1219 (10th Cir. 2000)(district chiefs are executives); *Allen v. County of Fairfax*, 127 Lab. Cas. ¶33,049 (4th Cir. 1994)(lieutenants are not executives); *McDonnell v. City of Omaha*, 999 F.2d 293 (8th Cir. 1993)(assistant chiefs are executives); *Smith v. City of Jackson*, 954 F.2d 296 (5th Cir. 1992)(district and battalion chiefs

are executives); *Atlanta Professional Firefighters Union v. City of Atlanta*, 920 F.2d 800 (11th Cir. 1991); *Aaron v. Wichita, Kansas*, 3 WH Cases2d 249 (D.Kan. 1996)(fire captains, battalion chiefs, and division chiefs are executives); *Simmons v. City of Ft. Worth*, 805 F.Supp. 419 (N.D.Tex. 1992)(deputy chiefs and district chiefs are executives); *Masters v. City of Huntington*, 800 F.Supp. 363 (S.D.W.Va. 1992)(lieutenants are not executives); *IAFF, Alexandria Local 2141 v. City of Alexandria*, 720 F.Supp. 1230 (E.D.Va. 1989)(captains are executives); *Sarver v. City of Roanoke*, 29 WH Cases 1442 (W.D.Va. 1989)(captain with extensive supervisory duties is an executive); *Hawks v. City of Newport News*, 707 F.Supp. 212 (E.D.Va. 1988) (lieutenants are not executives).

In *York v. City of Wichita Falls, Tex.*, 727 F.Supp. 1076 (N.D.Tex. 1989), the Court held that fire captains were not executives. In the same case, the Court held that battalion chiefs were executives. *See Abbey v. City of Jackson*, 883 F.Supp. 181 (E.D.Mich. 1995)(captains are not executives); *Schuller v. City of Livermore*, 28 WH Cases 507 (N.D.Cal. 1987)(captains are not executives). In *Keller v. City of Columbus, Indiana*, 778 F.Supp. 1480 (S.D.Ind. 1991), the Court held that both fire captains and lieutenants were executive employees.

[73] *Amos v. City of Winston-Salem*, 1 WH Cases2d 578 (M.D.N.C. 1993); see *Hartman v. Arlington County*, 903 F.2d 290 (4th Cir. 1990); *West v. Anne Arundel County*, 3 WH Cases2d 234 (D.Md. 1996); *DiMiro v. Township of Montclair*, 3 WH Cases2d 565 (N.J.Super. 1996)(municipal court administrator exempt even though she performed some of the same duties as her subordinates, where she had substantial supervisory duties).

[74] *Martin v. City of Sapulpa, Oklahoma*, 30 WH Cases 1752 (N.D.Okla. 1992).

[75] *Kavanaugh v. City of Phoenix*, 87 F.Supp.2d 958 (D.Ariz. 2000).

[76] *Keller v. City of Columbus, Indiana*, 778 F.Supp. 1480 (S.D.Ind. 1991).

[77] *Webster v. Public School Employees of Washington, Inc.*, 247 F.3d 910 (9th Cir. 2001).

[78] It seems doubtful whether the courts will recognize a "combination administrative-executive" exemption for employees who meet some of the tests for each exemption, but do not clearly qualify for either exemption. *See Dalheim v. KDFW-TV*, 918 F.2d 1220 (5th Cir. 1990).

[79] 29 C.F.R. §541.2 (2001).

[80] 29 C.F.R. §541.2 (2001). *See Campbell v. United States Air Force*, 755 F.Supp. 893 (E.D.Cal. 1990)(federal air traffic controllers at Air Force base are administrative employees as they provide flight-pattern and operation-and-safety information to aircraft, perform non-manual work requiring special training and experience in computers, radar, and other technical equipment, and use discretion and independent judgment during sudden changes in weather or unexpected mechanical failures).

[81] *Dambreville v. Boston*, 945 F.Supp. 384 (D.Mass. 1996)(work as neighborhood coordinator and liaison for mayor was administrative employee). *See generally Annotation, Who Is Employed in "Administrative Capacity,"* 124 ALR Fed. 1 (1995).

[82] *Guthrie v. Lady Jane Collieries, Inc.*, 722 F.2d 1141 (3rd Cir. 1983); *Donovan v. Burger King Corp.*, 672 F.2d 221 (1st Cir. 1982).

[83] *Wineland v. County Comm'rs.*, 892 F.Supp. 719 (D.Md. 1995).

[84] *Shockley v. City of Newport News*, 997 F.2d 18 (4th Cir. 1993)(media relations sergeant); *D'Camera v. District of Columbia*, 693 F.Supp. 1208 (D.D.C. 1988)(patrol sergeants).

[85] *West v. Anne Arundel County*, 3 WH Cases2d 234 (D.Md. 1996)(EMS lieutenant).

[86] *Smith v. City of Jackson, Mississippi*, 954 F.2d 296 (5th Cir. 1992)(battalion chiefs are administrative employees); *Atlanta Professional Firefighters Union v. City of Atlanta*, 920 F.2d 800 (11th Cir. 1991)(same).

[87] *Bratt v. County of Los Angeles*, 912 F.2d 1066 (9th Cir. 1990). On two separate occasions, the Department of Labor has concluded that probation officers are not administrative employees exempt from FLSA coverage. Opinion Letters, Wage and Hour Division, February 16, 1988 and April 12, 1988.

[88] *Ahern v. The State of New York*, 807 F.Supp. 919 (C.D.N.Y. 1992). *See Reich v. State of New York*, 3 F.3d 581 (2nd Cir. 1993)(criminal investigators not exempt); *Mulverhill v. State of New York*, 1994 WL 263594 (N.D.N.Y. 1994)(same). *But see Adams v. United States*, 27 Fed.Cl. 5 (1992)(criminal investigators for the Internal Revenue Service, Bureau of Alcohol, Tobacco and Firearms, Drug Enforcement Agency, Secret Service, and Customs are exempt as administrative employees).

[89] *Shockley v. City of Newport News*, 997 F.2d 18 (4th Cir. 1993).

[90] 29 C.F.R. §541.3 (2001).

[91] 29 C.F.R. §541.3 (2001).

[92] *See generally Annotation, Who is Employed in "Professional Capacity,"* 77 ALR Fed. 681 (1986).

[93] 29 C.F.R. §541.301 (2001).

[94] *Wong-Opasi v. Tennessee State University*, 229 F.3d 1155 (6th Cir. 2000).

[95] *Kavanaugh v. City of Phoenix*, 87 F.Supp.2d 958 (D.Ariz. 2000).

[96] *Richardson v. Genessee County Community Mental Health Services*, 45 F.Supp.2d 610 (E.D.Mich. 1999).

[97] *Owsley v. San Antonio Independent School District*, 187 F.3d 521 (5th Cir. 1999). The *Owsley* case has come under quite a bit of criticism. *See Joseph White, Owsley v. San Antonio Independent School District: Athletic Trainers Lose to School District In Overtime*, 75 Tul. L. Rev. 837 (February, 2001).

[98] *Paul v. Petroleum Equipment Tools Co.*, 708 F.2d 168 (5th Cir. 1983).

[99] *See Reeves v. International Tel. & Tel. Corp.*, 357 F.Supp. 295 (W.D.La. 1973).

[100] *Dybach v. Florida Department of Corrections*, 942 F.2d 1562 (11th Cir. 1991). *See Mills v. State of Maine*, 839 F.Supp. 3 (D.Me. 1993)(probation officers are not professional employees under the FLSA).

[101] *West v. Anne Arundel County*, 3 WH Cases2d 234 (D.Md. 1996); *Quirk v. Baltimore County, Md.*, 895 F.Supp. 773 (D.Md. 1995).

[102] *Reich v. State of Wyoming*, 993 F.2d 739 (10th Cir. 1993).

CHAPTER NINE
RECORDKEEPING REQUIREMENTS UNDER THE FLSA

Section 211(c) of the FLSA contains a general requirement that employers keep records of work hours and compensation:

> "Every employer subject to any provision of this chapter or of any order issued under this chapter shall make, keep, and preserve such records of the persons employed by him and of the wages, hours, and other conditions and practices of employment maintained by him, and shall preserve such records for such periods of time, and shall make such reports therefrom to the Administrator as he shall prescribe by regulation or order as necessary or appropriate for the enforcement of the provisions of this chapter or the regulations or orders thereunder. The employer of an employee who performs substitute work described in section 207(p)(3) of this title may not be required under this subsection to keep a record of the hours of the substitute work."[1]

In implementing Section 211(c), the DOL has issued what is perhaps the most unintentionally tongue-in-cheek of its FLSA regulations, Section 516.1. The regulation provides that "no particular order or form of records is prescribed by the regulations in this part."[2] The balance of the "recordkeeping" regulations provide exactly to the contrary, and demand that very specific records must be maintained by covered employers. These records include the following information on every employee:

• Name, and any payroll identification numbers used for the employee.

• Home address.

- Date of birth (if the employee is under 19 years of age).

- Sex.

- Occupation in which employed.

- Time of day and day of week on which the work-week (or 7(k) work period) begins.

- Regular hourly rate, and basis on which wages are paid (e.g., weekly, monthly).

- Hours worked each workday.

- Hours worked each workweek (or 7(k) work period).

- Total daily or weekly straight-time earnings or wages.

- Total overtime compensation.

- All deductions from gross wages.

- All wages paid each pay period.

- Date of payment of wages.

Under Section 516.5 of the regulations, these records must be maintained for three years. In addition, the following records must be maintained for two years pursuant to Section 516.6 of the regulations:

- Time cards, or starting and stopping "work sheets."

- Wage rate tables used in computing straight-time wages.

- Schedules showing hours of work.

All records which are required to be maintained under the FLSA must be made available within 72 hours following notice from the DOL, and are required by Section 516.7 of the regulations to be always available for inspection by the DOL. The records must be kept in such a fashion that relevant wage and hour information will be readily apparent to the DOL.[3] The falsification of any records required to be kept under the FLSA constitutes an independent violation of the FLSA.[4]

In a recent opinion letter, the DOL has indicated that an internet-based recordkeeping system can comport with the FLSA provided enough safeguards are in place to protect the integrity of the data. In approving the recordkeeping system, the Court provided the following description of the system:

> "The company's internet-based system allows employees to enter starting and stopping times ('hours worked') information via computer on a computer displayed 'timecard,' and also to record vacation or sick leave usage. Both systems incorporate appropriate security measures that include authentication procedures. Under both systems, time reporting will be on an 'exception basis,' i.e., only deviations will be captured, for employees who work fixed schedules. All FLSA required data will be stored in the company's data processing system and no paper records will be maintained."[5]

An employer's failure to produce any of the records the FLSA requires it to maintain may result in a presumption against the employer — a presumption that the records, if produced, would support an employee's claim that moneys are owed under the FLSA. In addition, in the absence of records, testimony by employees estimating the time they spent working is admissible to establish how many hours the employee worked.[6] As explained by the Supreme Court, when an employer fails to keep adequate employment records, an employee makes a *prima facie* case under the FLSA if the employee produces "sufficient evidence to show the amount and extent of [his] work as a matter of just and reasonable inference." The burden "then shifts to the employer to come forward with evidence of the precise amount of work performed or with evidence to negate the reasonableness of the inference to be drawn from the employee's evidence. If the employer fails to produce such evidence, the Court may then award damages to the employee, even though the result be only approximate."[7]

In the absence of records, the testimony of employees can be quite general and still satisfy the requisite burden of proof. In one case, for example, a court found sufficient an employee's testimony that he "worked more than 40 hours a week."[8] In another case, a court awarded damages to an officer participating in an undercover operation where there were no records whatsoever of the overtime work, but where the employee's supervisors had first-hand knowledge of some of the excess work hours.[9] While employees need not "prove each hour of overtime work with unerring accuracy or certainty,"[10] enough evidence must be offered so that the Court as "a matter of just and reasonable inference" may estimate the unrecorded hours.[11]

Evidence of the time worked by an employee can be developed in a variety of other ways. In the absence of records, courts will accept evidence of the time worked by similarly-situated employees.[12] For instance, in one case a court upheld the use of a sample of 2.5% of all affected employees to determine back wages due the rest.[13] If "representative plaintiffs" are used to establish damages, the employees must prove that the nature, character, and frequency of their work is similar to that of others in their class.[14]

Put succinctly by a lower court, while an employer may delegate its FLSA recordkeeping requirements to lower-ranking employees, it may do so at its peril.[15] In one case, a sheriff's office did not maintain adequate records of the accrual and usage of compensatory time off. When a deputy suing for overtime submitted a crudely-prepared "K-Time Report" showing his compensatory time off activity and the county was unable to produce any documentation to the contrary, the Court found that the county failed to rebut the employee's *prima facie* case that the compensatory time off was earned and not used.[16]

NOTES TO CHAPTER 9

1 29 U.S.C.A. §211(c).

2 29 C.F.R. §516.1 (2001).

3 *Martin v. Tiller Helicopter Services, Inc.*, 778 F.Supp. 1395 (S.D.Tex. 1991).

4 *Martin v. D. Gunnels Inc.*, 30 WH Cases 997 (C.D.Cal. 1991).

5 Opinion Letter, Department of Labor, 1998 WL 852676 (February 6, 1998).

6 *Reich v. Waldbaum Inc.*, 833 F.Supp. 1037 (S.D.N.Y. 1993), *rev'd on other grounds,* 52 F.3d 35 (2nd Cir. 1995); *Mabee v. White Plains Publishing Co.*, 41 N.Y.S.2d 534 (N.Y.S. 1943).

7 *Anderson v. Mt. Clemens Pottery Co.*, 328 U.S. 680 (1946); *see Arias v. U.S. Service Industries*, 80 F.3d 509 (D.C. Cir. 1996); *Herman v. Harmelech*, 2000 WL 420839 (N.D.Ill. 2000).

8 *Santelices v. Wiring*, 147 F.Supp.2d 1313 (S.D.Fla. 2001); *see Tran v. Tran*, 6 WH Cases2d 507 (S.D.N.Y. 2000)(testimony that employee worked 13-14 hours per day sufficient to meet burden of proof).

9 *AFSCME, Council 17 v. State of Louisiana*, 142 Lab.Cas. ¶ 34,195 (E.D.La. 2001).

10 *Pforr v. Food Lion, Inc.*, 851 F.2d 106 (4th Cir. 1988).

11 *Lee v. Vance Executive Protection, Inc.*, 7 Fed. Appx. 160 (4th Cir. 2001).

12 *Martin v. Tony and Susan Alamo Foundation*, 952 F.2d 1050 (8th Cir. 1992); *Archie v. Grand-Central Partnership, Inc.*, 86 F.Supp.2d 262 (S.D.N.Y. 2000).

13 *Reich v. Southern New England Telecomm. Corp.*, 121 F.3d 58 (2nd Cir. 1997).

[14] *Herman v. Hogar Praderas De Amor*, 130 F.Supp.2d 257 (D.P.R. 2001).

[15] *Castillo v. Givens*, 704 F.2d 181 (5th Cir. 1983).

[16] *Oliver v. Layrisson*, 3 WH Cases2d 316 (E.D.La. 1996).

CHAPTER TEN
REMEDIES FOR VIOLATION OF THE FLSA

A. General Remedies

Enforcement of the FLSA is through one of two routes. The first route entails the DOL conducting an investigation into an employer's employment practices, and making a determination as to whether the employer has violated the FLSA. If the DOL so determines, it has the right to seek enforcement of the FLSA by filing suit. Among the remedies the DOL may recover are the employee's back wages, an equivalent amount in "liquidated damages," an injunction restraining any person from violating the FLSA, and in cases of willful violations of the FLSA, criminal sanctions against the employer, including fines and imprisonment.

The second method of enforcement contemplated by the FLSA involves employees filing suit themselves, without the intervention of the DOL. In such cases, employees are entitled to recover their past-due wages, an equivalent amount in liquidated damages, their court costs, and their attorney fees. The DOL is free to intervene in such proceedings. Employee-initiated lawsuits under the FLSA may be filed in either state or federal court.[1] The sole exception to this rule is that state employees cannot bring lawsuits against their employers in either state court or federal court; claims for violation of the FLSA by state employee must be brought by the DOL.[2] Generally speaking, only employees (and not their labor organizations) have standing to bring FLSA lawsuits,[3] though unions may have the standing to bring lawsuits alleging that the compensatory time off provisions of the FLSA have been violated.[4] Employee lawsuits can only seek damages for FLSA violations; only the Department of Labor has the authority to seek an injunction.[5]

Employees who consider bringing FLSA claims must weigh different concerns when deciding whether to pursue the claim themselves or to ask the DOL to bring the claim. On one hand, when the employee brings the claim, he or she is responsible for the costs of litigation and the potential liability for attorney fees if the employee is not successful in the lawsuit. On the other hand, when the DOL brings the claim, it – not the employee – has complete control over the course of the litigation, including the right to make decisions as to whether to settle a claim and for how much to settle the claim.

B. The Statutes Of Limitation For FLSA Violations.

The normal statute of limitations for FLSA violations is two years, meaning that claims for violations of the FLSA must be brought within two years after they occur.[6] If an employee is a member of an FLSA class action, the statute of limitation is tolled (i.e., stops running) on the day the employee affirmatively joins the class action by filing a consent to join the lawsuit or on the date that notice is sent by the Court to all potential class members. In general, every new paycheck issued by an employer that does not comply with the FLSA starts a new statute of limitations running for FLSA violations reflected in that paycheck.[7] A state statute does not have the ability to extend the FLSA's normal statute of limitations.[8]

Where the employer's violation of the FLSA is "willful," the statute of limitations is three years. In the case of *McLaughlin v. Richland Shoe Co.*, the United States Supreme Court ruled that the word "willful" is considered synonymous with such words as "voluntary," "deliberate" and "intentional," and refers to conduct which is not merely negligent.[9] In the case, the Supreme Court established that the standard for a willful violation of the FLSA is where the employer either knew or showed reckless disregard for the matter of whether its conduct was prohibited by statute.

Such willfulness can be established where the employer acknowledges that the employee is entitled to overtime compensation, but refuses to pay the employee overtime because of a philosophical belief that "supervisors" should not be entitled to overtime.[10]

It has proven extremely difficult for public employees to establish that an employer's conduct is willful and that the FLSA's three-year statute of limitations apply. Factors courts have considered in ruling that an employer did not act willfully have included the employer's reliance on the terms of a labor contract,[11] an employer's reliance on the advice of counsel[12] or an FLSA "consultant,"[13] and where an employer merely failed to properly anticipate how the law with respect to compensation for canine time would develop.[14] Merely negligent conduct by an employer will ordinarily not suffice to prove willfulness;[15] similarly, conduct that simply "lacks prudence" does not establish willfulness.[16]

An example of conduct which justified a finding of willfulness can be found in *Bankston v. State of Illinois*, where the employer received a memorandum, which it ignored, advising it that a wage and hour practice was illegal several years before a lawsuit was eventually filed challenging the practice.[17] In another case, a court applied a three-year statute of limitations to a county that adopted a "compressed workweek" schedule resulting in hours worked greater than those permitted under the FLSA. In rejecting the County's claim that its conduct was not willful, the Court held that the fact that the County "knew that employees were working overtime without additional pay and knew or at least recklessly disregarded the fact that a collective bargaining agreement's terms cannot waive the requirements of the FLSA," required a finding of willful-ness. Moreover, the Court discarded as having "no legal relevance" the fact that the County acted to satisfy the desires of employees for a certain schedule.[18] Similarly, in a case applying a three-year statute of limitations to a canine claim, a court reasoned as follows:

> "The FLSA imposes significant burdens on an employer to ensure that its treatment of, behavior towards, and policies regarding its employees complies with the FLSA. When an employer is informed that it may be violating the FLSA, it must investigate its potential violation and should consult an attorney for legal advice. Defendants failed to fulfill its obligations in this case. Initially, the stipend may have been a good faith effort to pay plaintiffs for the additional work they had to perform, but after defendants learned about the "Garcia" decision and [other canine claim] cases, they had a duty to conduct a more extensive inquiry than they did. Defendants' effort of meeting with plaintiffs and asking for a memorandum does not comport with the FLSA's extensive duties for employers."[19]

Most states have enacted "notice of claim" or "tort claim" statutes, which require that claims against governmental bodies be made within a specified period after their accrual. Often, such statutes require the filing of claims within 180 days, or some other time period lesser than the FLSA's two and three-year statutes of limitation. The courts have consistently held that the overriding public policy purposes behind the FLSA requires the result that non-compliance with a state notice of claim statute does not bar FLSA claims against governmental subdivisions.[20]

C. When Liquidated Damages May Be Recovered.

Ordinarily, a plaintiff under the FLSA will automatically be entitled to liquidated damages in addition to wages or overtime not paid.[21] Liquidated damages under the FLSA are an amount of damages equivalent to the wages owed as a result of the finding of non-compliance with the FLSA. As one court explained, liquidated damages "are considered compensatory rather than punitive in nature, and constitute compensation for the retention of a workman's pay which might result in damages too obscure and difficult of proof for estimate other than by liquidated damages."[22]

In general, liquidated damages are presumed under the FLSA. However, the Portal-to-Portal amendments to the FLSA provide that liquidated damages are not mandatory if the employer acted in "good faith":

> "In any action...to...recover unpaid minimum wages, unpaid overtime compensation, or liquidated damages, under the Fair Labor Standards Act of 1938, as amended, if the employer shows to the satisfaction of the Court that the act or omission giving rise to such action was in good faith and that he had reasonable grounds for believing that his act or omission was not a violation of the Fair Labor Standards Act of 1938, as amended, the Court may, in its sound discretion, award no liquidated damages or award any amount thereof not to exceed the amount specified in section 16 of this title."[23]

In order to avoid liquidated damages, the employer must sustain a burden of persuading the Court by proof that its actions were in subjective and objective good faith.[24] As the Court noted in *Hayes v. Bill Haley & His Comets*, the granting of liquidated damages is mandatory unless the employer can show the requisite good faith.[25] Most cases turn on whether the employer was acting as a reasonable employer would under all of the circumstances.[26] Deliberate acts of malfeasance need not be proven to support liquidated damages; it is sufficient to establish unreasonable conduct on the part of the employer by simply showing that the employer did little or nothing to either determine what the law was or to bring its practices into compliance with the law.[27] As one court put it, good faith "requires more than ignorance of the prevailing law or uncertainty about its development. It requires that an employer first take active steps to ascertain the dictates of the FLSA and then move to comply with them."[28]

Factors leading to a conclusion that an employer acted in good faith include reliance on opinion letters issued by the DOL and a bona-fide effort on the part of the employer to evaluate the job duties and hours of work of employees for whom an FLSA exemption is claimed.[29] Examples of good faith conduct by employers that resulted in the avoidance of liquidated damages have included the following:

• Reliance on DOL regulations or the regulations of other federal agencies;[30]

• Reliance on erroneous conclusions from "minor" officials of the DOL[31] or other governmental agencies;[32]

• Reliance on erroneous advice from attorneys;[33]

• The formation of a committee to review the proper way to calculate the overtime rate and contracting with outside counsel to review employment practices with FLSA compliance in mind;[34] and

• Adopting a compensation plan after consultation between its attorneys and the DOL, only to have the compensation plan not be implemented by another employee.[35]

A classic case of reasonable conduct by an employer can be found in the case of *Doden v. Plainfield Fire District*, which involved whether the Section 7(k) exemption could be claimed for paramedics. The fire district avoided liquidated damages by showing that it had reviewed FLSA handbooks and materials, engaged in discussions with other fire districts and departments about the FLSA, conferred with its attorneys about the issue, and promptly changed its practices when court decisions on the paramedic issue began to be decided against employers.[36]

Examples of conduct that has been held insufficient to avoid the award of liquidated damages have included the following:

- An employer which "blindly" relied on unclear DOL regulations;[37]

- A county that relied on the lack of complaints from employees for the conclusion that it was not violating the FLSA;[38]

- A county sheriff who knew he was violating the FLSA, but who failed to pay his deputies and used available funds for "public safety purposes;"[39]

- A city that failed to seek or obtain DOL approval for its compensation structure for police officers at a time when it was subject to an FLSA lawsuit by its firefighters;[40]

- A county that failed to vigilantly monitor the work hours of its sheriff's deputies;[41]

- Where an employer was "well aware" of the FLSA's requirements;[42]

- An employer that made no changes in its practices after it had previously been involved in litigation under the FLSA;[43]

- A state that wrongly claimed some of its employees were not covered by the FLSA when a memorandum from one of its attorneys indicated to the contrary;[44]

- An employer that simply "chose to remain ignorant of case law;"[45]

- A state that processed the overtime claims of its employees in a "negligent" manner;[46]

- A city that merely adhered to "industry practice" without trying to determine the legality of the practice;[47] and

- An employer whose supervisors instructed employees not to report the hours they had worked.[48]

An example of an employer which was unable to demonstrate reasonable conduct can be found in *Renfro v. City of Emporia, Kansas*, which involved the compensability of on-call time. The Court awarded the City's firefighters liquidated damages, where the only evidence the City could produce that it tried to determine and comply with the law – a phone call to the DOL about its policy – was undercut by the fact that the individual who made the call could not recall the job title or name of the DOL representative to whom she spoke, whether she described their policy in detail to the DOL representative, and by the fact that the City never requested a written opinion from the DOL on the subject.[49]

There is some question whether an employer may simply rely on the terms of a collective bargaining agreement in support of the argument that it should not be assessed liquidated damages. Based upon the long-standing rule that collective bargaining agreements may not waive the FLSA rights of employees, the better (and majority) rule would seem to be that reliance on a collective bargaining agreement will not avoid FLSA liability.[50] A minority of courts find to the contrary, though, holding that reliance on a collective bargaining agreement considered with other factors can establish the requisite good faith and reasonableness necessary to avoid liquidated damages.[51]

D. Pre-Judgment Interest.

If employees are not awarded liquidated damages, they generally are entitled to prejudgment interest on the unpaid overtime, which begins to accrue from the time the overtime should have been paid.[52] The purpose behind prejudgment interest is to make employees whole for the lost compensation, taking into account the fact that employees could have earned interest on the money had it been appropriately paid by the employer.[53] If a party recovers liquidated damages, they are not entitled to recover prejudgment interest as well.[54] In one case, a fire department contended that it should not be required to pay prejudgment interest, contending that the unpaid overtime did not create a "windfall" for the city because it was not a profit-making operation. The Court rejected this argument, commenting that the city had a "local monopoly" on employing firefighters and that the overtime that the firefighters would receive in the lawsuit would not be worth as much as when it was earned.[55]

E. When Attorney Fees May Be Recovered.

Under the FLSA, a plaintiff who prevails in an FLSA lawsuit is entitled to reasonable attorney fees and court costs.[56]

Courts have held that this requirement is mandatory at the trial level; that is, whenever a plaintiff prevails in an FLSA suit at trial, attorney fees must be awarded.[57] On appeal, however, the appellate court has the discretion to either award or deny the prevailing plaintiff attorney fees.[58] Unlike many statutes, the FLSA makes no provision for payment of the employer's attorney fees if it prevails.

One court explained the reasons for the mandatory nature of the attorney fee provisions of the FLSA as follows: "The purpose of the FLSA attorney's fees provision is to insure effective access to the judicial process by providing attorney fees for prevailing plaintiffs with wage and hour grievances. Courts should not place an undue emphasis on the amount of plaintiff's recovery because an award of attorney fees encourages the vindication of congressionally identified policies and rights within the discretion of the court."[59] In the words of another court, the attorney fee provisions of the FLSA are part of the "comprehensive remedy" provided by the FLSA.[60]

Occasionally, disputes arise as to the appropriate amount of attorney fees in an FLSA case. As a general rule, a successful plaintiff is entitled to reimbursement for 100% of the hourly rate normally charged by the attorney for the hours worked by the attorney on the case, so long as the hourly rate is in keeping with the normal rates charged for such services in the community. This amount – referred to by the courts as the "lodestar" amount – may be adjusted upwards or downwards depending upon the individual circumstances of the case.[61] If the plaintiff fails to recover on a significant portion of the claims raised in the case, a court may reduce the fees downward;[62] however, simply because a plaintiff has "set high sights" in claiming damages which are not completely recovered does not warrant a reduction in the amount of attorney fees.[63] If the case presents novel or difficult questions of law or fact, the amount of attorney fees may be enhanced by a court.[64] The fact that an employee may have retained a small or a large law firm to pursue the case is irrelevant in the amount of fees the employee is entitled; what is most important is the overall market rate for the type of services provided by the attorney.[65]

Many employees bringing FLSA lawsuits are represented by attorneys on a contingent fee basis, under which the attorney is entitled to a percentage of the total recovery made by the employee. If the amount of the contingent fee is greater than what the attorney fees would be if the attorney's normal hourly rate were used, the employer is only liable for the hourly equivalent of the attorney's time, not the full amount of the contingent fee.[66] Moreover, the fact that a contingent fee agreement was used is an appropriate factor for a court to consider in determining the amount of attorney fees.[67] No matter what the fee agreement with the attorney, the amount of fees which may be recovered by a successful FLSA plaintiff for the services of expert witnesses is limited to the federal court expert witness fee (currently $40 per day), since the FLSA does not contain any language mandating the full reimbursement of all expert witness fees and expenses.[68]

A trial court's ruling on the matter of attorney fees is extremely unlikely to be overturned on appeal. Appellate courts will only review an attorney fee judgment if the trial court has "abused its discretion" in awarding attorney fees or calculating the amount of attorney fees.[69]

F. The Good Faith Defense.

The FLSA provides that an employer may be insulated from liability under the FLSA if the employer is relying in good faith on the regulations, orders, or opinions of the Wage and Hour Division of the DOL:

> "(a) In any action or proceeding based on any act or omission on or after [May 14, 1947], no employer shall be subject to any liability or punishment for or on account of the failure of the employer to pay minimum wages or overtime compensation under the Fair Labor Standards Act of 1938, as amended * * * if he pleads and proves that the act or omission complained of was in good faith in conformity with and in reliance on any written administrative regulation, order, ruling, approval, or interpretation, of the agency of the United States specified in subsection (b) of this section, or any administrative practice or enforcement policy of such agency with respect to the class of employers to which he belonged. Such a defense, if established, shall be a bar to the action or proceeding, notwithstanding that after such act or omission, such administrative regulation, order, ruling, approval, interpretation, practice, or enforcement policy is modified or rescinded or is determined by judicial authority to be invalid or of no legal effect."[70]

The DOL has fleshed out these provisions in Section 790.15 of its regulations, which defines the term "good faith" at some length:

> "The legislative history of the Portal Act makes it clear that the employer's 'good faith' is not to be determined merely from the actual state of his mind. Statements made in the House and Senate indicate that 'good faith' also depends upon an objective test — whether the employer, in acting or omitting to act as he did, and in relying upon the regulation, order, ruling, approval, interpretation, administrative practice or enforcement policy, acted as a reasonably prudent man would have acted un-

der the same or similar circumstances. 'Good faith' requires that the employer have honesty of intention and no knowledge or circumstances which ought to put him upon inquiry."

In short, the good faith defense has several specific elements. First, the defense requires that the DOL have issued an interpretation of the FLSA that specifically applies to the particular situation facing the employer. The interpretation must be by the DOL itself, and not a lower-ranking individual within the DOL.[71] Second, the defense requires that the employer actually rely on the interpretation of the DOL.[72] Third, the defense requires that the reliance be in good faith, with the employer acting as a reasonably prudent person would under the circumstances.[73] Because of the need for the DOL's interpretation to be squarely on point, and to be specifically relied upon by the employer in adopting or following a wage or hour practice, it is not surprising that cases upholding the "good faith" defense are extreme rarities.

G. Class Actions Under The FLSA.

Under the FLSA, employees are entitled to bring lawsuits for violation of the FLSA "in behalf of * * * themselves and other employees similarly situated."[74] FLSA class actions are usually different from the normal sort of class action in that employees who are not individually named in the complaint are not parties to the lawsuit unless they affirmatively "opt in" or join the lawsuit by filing a written consent with the Court indicating a willingness to participate in the lawsuit and be bound by the outcome.[75] Under "opt in" rules, an employee who does not affirmatively join the class action will not benefit from the Court's decision.[76]

Employees bringing an FLSA claim can ask the assistance of the Court in notifying other potential claimants of the opportunity to join the class action. Though the Court has the discretion to deny such a request to notify potential claimants, the Supreme Court has referred to the "propriety, if not the necessity" of courts taking affirmative steps to give notice to potential claimants.[77] Courts deciding whether to facilitate notice to potential plaintiffs usually only examine the Court pleadings to determine whether there has been an allegation that a common employer practice has impacted numerous individuals.[78] If so, courts will "leniently" grant the right to facilitated notice,[79] either through direct mail contact or through postings at the worksite.[80]

Where a court gives notice to potential class members of an FLSA claim, the Court has the authority to set a reasonable cut-off date for employees to join the lawsuit.[81] Employees joining the class before the cut-off date will usually have their statutes of limitations set as of the date the Court authorizes the sending of notice to potential class members; employees not joining the lawsuit who seek to assert the same claim will not be allowed to participate in the litigation and will not gain the benefit of the adjusted statute of limitation.[82] After notice has been provided, and additional employees have joined the lawsuit, the employer has the right to seek "decertification" of the class action if the claims of the employees indicate that they are not "similarly situated" as required by the FLSA's class action provisions.[83]

H. The Ability Of Labor Organizations To Assert FLSA Claims On Behalf Of Their Members.

In 1947, Congress amended the FLSA to limit the parties who could bring suit under the FLSA in what were known as the Portal-to-Portal amendments to the FLSA.[84] The Portal-to-Portal amendments barred unions from bringing actions under the FLSA as representatives of their members. The hostility of Congress to such so-called "representative actions" was undisguised, as revealed by the following comments made by a senator during the debates on the Portal-to-Portal amendments:

> "But the second class of cases, namely, cases in which an outsider, perhaps someone who is desirous of stirring up litigation without being an employee at all, is permitted to be the plaintiff in the case, may result in very decidedly unwholesome champertous situations which we think should not be permitted under the law."[85]

Accordingly, an individual employee cannot become a party to an action under the FLSA unless he or she specifically files a consent form with the Court, even if the representative labor organization has purported to file a lawsuit on behalf of the employee.[86]

I. Discrimination Against Employees Asserting Claims Under The FLSA.

There are two "anti-discrimination" provisions of the FLSA that protect employees who have asserted their rights under the law. The broadest protection is found in Section 15(a) of the FLSA, and provides as follows:

> "[I]t shall be unlawful for any person * * * to discharge or in any other manner discriminate against any employee because such employee has filed any complaint or instituted or caused to be instituted any proceeding under or related to this chapter, or has testified or is about to testify in any such proceeding, or has served or is about to serve on an industry committee."[87]

In evaluating retaliatory discharge claims filed under Section 15 of the FLSA, courts apply a test that involves shifting burdens of proof. Under the test, the employee must first make a *prima facie* showing of retaliation, which consists of the following factors: (1) that the employee engaged in protected activity; (2) that an adverse employment action was taken against the employee subsequent to or contemporaneous with the protected activity, and (3) that there exists a causal connection between the protected activity and the adverse employment action.[88] If the employee meets this burden of proof, the employer must show a legitimate, non-retaliatory reason for the adverse employment action. If the employer shows a non-retaliatory reason for the employment action,[89] or if the employer shows that it had no reason to know of the protected activity,[90] the burden shifts back to the employee to show that the articulated reason was a mere pretext.

Applying this approach, one court held that a discharged employee failed to establish retaliation where the employee was unable to show that the employer's asserted grounds for discharge were pretextual. The employer proved that the non-discriminatory disciplinary policy existed and that at least one other employee was terminated under the policy.[91] Similarly, in *Blackie v. State of Maine*, a court ruled that a state did not retaliate against probation officers by ending a 16% premium the officers had previously received under a collective bargaining agreement. The Court concluded that the state would have terminated the officers' premium pay in any event under the terms of the collective bargaining agreement, which provided that the employer need no longer pay the premium if it was determined that the officers were not exempt from the FLSA's overtime provisions.[92]

Often retaliation cases under the FLSA involve "mixed motives," where the employer was motivated to discharge an employee both because the employee asserted rights under the FLSA and by other, non-discriminatory reasons. Though the legal tests used by the courts in "mixed motive" cases are still evolving, it appears the rule is that the employee must show that his protected activities were a substantial factor in the employer's discharge decision, and that the employer must prove that it would have discharged the employee if the legitimate, non-discriminatory reason for the disciplinary action existed alone.[93] Under such a test, the existence of permissible reasons for a discharge does not, in and of itself, mean that an employer has not illegally retaliated against the employee because of the employee's exercise of FLSA rights.[94]

While individual employees have the right to bring private lawsuits seeking damages for discrimination or retaliation for asserting FLSA rights, courts have fairly uniformly held that only the DOL has the legal authority to obtain injunctive relief to prohibit future discrimination.[95]There is considerable debate in the courts as to the scope of the protections found in Section 15. A minority of courts, citing the specific language in Section 15 making it unlawful to discharge or in any other manner discriminate against any employee because such employee "has filed any complaint or instituted or caused to be instituted any proceeding under or related to this chapter, or has testified or is about to testify in any such proceeding, or has served or is about to serve on an industry committee," have held that "the plain language of this provision limits the cause of action to retaliation for filing formal complaints, instituting a proceeding, or testifying."[96] The significant majority of courts have taken a broader view, holding that even informal complaints about an employer's wage and hour practices are protected by Section 15 from employer retaliation.[97]

A second "anti-discrimination" provision of the FLSA is found in Section 8 of the 1985 amendments to the FLSA, which was a transitional statute that specifically applied to claims filed by public employees immediately after the applicability of the FLSA to state and local governments, but before the effective date of the 1985 amendments:

> "A public agency which is a State, political subdivision of a State, or an interstate governmental agency and which discriminates or has discriminated against an employee with respect to the employee's wages or other terms or conditions of employment because on or after February 19, 1985, the

employee asserted coverage under section 7 of the Fair Labor Standards Act of 1938 shall be held to have violated section 15(a)(3) of such Act. The protection against discrimination afforded by the preceding sentence shall be available after August 1, 1986, only for an employee who takes an action described in section 15(a)(3) of such Act."[98]

These provisions of the FLSA make it unlawful for an employer to discriminate against an employee because the employee has asserted a claim under the FLSA, or to retaliate against the employee for filing an FLSA claim, regardless of whether other grounds for the employer's action exist.[99] While these provisions bar intentional discrimination related to assertion of FLSA claims, they may also prohibit an employer's actions which do not amount to traditional forms of intentional discrimination.[100]

For example, in one case a city responded to the fact that the *Garcia* decision required it to pay overtime for certain hours worked by firefighters during their regular schedule by quickly lowering the hourly rates paid to the firefighters, so that the combination of the straight time and overtime hours equaled the former regular salary of the firefighters prior to the *Garcia* decision. The Court held that since the City's recharacterization of the firefighters' wages was in direct response to the application of the FLSA to the City under the *Garcia* decision, the firefighters were not required to prove either discriminatory intent or a retaliatory motive on the part of the City in order to establish a violation of Section 8 of the 1985 amendments.[101]

Most other cases involving post-*Garcia* unilateral adjustments of wage rates or conditions of employment by employers produced similar results, with courts regularly holding that employers violated the non-discrimination provisions of the FLSA unless proof existed that the wage or benefit adjustments were unrelated to the extension of the FLSA to public sector agencies.[102] One case even establishes that an employer can be found to illegally discriminate against an individual who merely testifies in an FLSA cause of action, and is not an FLSA claimant.[103] These interpretations of the non-discrimination provisions of the FLSA are bolstered by the discussions of Section 8 in Congress in 1985. As a joint explanatory statement from Congress reveals:

> "The [antidiscrimination] provision is * * * meant to apply where an employer's response to the assertion of FLSA coverage is to reduce wages or other monetary benefits for an entire unit of employees * * * [T]he actual victims of discrimination must show that coverage was asserted and they also must show actual discrimination, i.e., that the employer's action constituted retaliation for the * * * employee's assertion of coverage and avoidance of the asserted protections of Federal law. If a court so finds, that conduct would be unlawful under section 8 * * *.

> "A unilateral reduction of regular pay or fringe benefits that is intended to nullify this legislative application of overtime compensation to State and local government employees is unlawful. Any other conclusion would in effect invite public employers to reduce regular rates of pay shortly after the date of enactment so as to negate the premium compensation mandated by this legislation."[104]

Courts have split on the issue of whether a wage adjustment made before the effective date of the anti-retaliation provisions of Section 8 violates the FLSA. In one case, a city lowered the hourly wage rate for its firefighters in response to the *Garcia* decision, but did so in the hiatus period between *Garcia* and the date the FLSA became applicable to state and local governmental bodies. A court rejected a claim by the city's firefighters that the adjustment to the hourly rate was impermissible retaliation under Section 8, concluding that since the adjustment occurred prior to the effective date of Section 8, it was permissible.[105] A contrary decision was issued by a court in *Drollinger v. State of Arizona*, where the Court held that the FLSA prohibited not only violations of the FLSA in response to assertions by employees of FLSA coverage, but also violations which were in anticipation of any employee actually asserting coverage. The Court concluded that Section 8 would be "meaningless" if an employer could reduce hourly wages in response to the *Garcia* opinion.[106]

One FLSA retaliation case with unusual facts was *Glover v. City of North Charleston, South Carolina*. The case involved two firefighters employed by a fire district who were lead plaintiffs in FLSA lawsuits against the district. When a nearby city began to provide fire protection services for the geographic area formerly covered by the district, the city hired a number of the district's firefighters, but not the two who had brought the FLSA claims. A court dismissed the firefighters' lawsuit against the City, holding that individuals may not bring retaliation action against other than their employer; since the firefighters were never employed by the City, they were thus barred from bringing a lawsuit.[107]

J. "Gap-Time" Damages.

Where the employer has elected the 7(k) exemption, the obligation to pay overtime does not begin until the employee has worked more than the overtime threshold for the particular 7(k) exemption. A question that occasionally arises is whether the FLSA contains any obligation on the part of the employer to pay the employee anything more than the minimum wage for hours worked up to the overtime threshold. Owing to the lack of any DOL regulation on point, there has been disagreement in the courts as to what is often referred to as the "gap time" issue.

The majority of courts hold that so long as employees are paid at the minimum wage over the entire workweek or work period, there is no obligation to compensate employees for "gap time." As one court following the majority view point observed:

> "Plaintiffs' salaries were intended to compensate them for all hours worked up to 171 in a 28-day period. That is, prior to mid-1995 when straight time was instituted for hours worked 'in the gap,' Plaintiffs were paid a salary and their salary was the same whether they worked 160 hours or as many as 171 hours in a 28-day period. As a matter of law, there is no requirement that an employer reimburse employees for 'gap' time."[108]

The contrary view was expressed in *Lamon v. City of Shawnee*, where the employer had elected the 28-day 7(k) exemption for its police officers, which obligated it to pay the officers time and one-half the regular rate of pay for hours worked above 171 hours in a 28-day period. The employer paid the employees at the straight time regular rate for up to 160 hours in the work period, but was unwilling to pay the employees anything for the hours worked between 160 and 171 in the work period. The Court rejected this argument, and held that the time between 160 and 171 hours must be paid at the regular rate of pay:

> "The Court notes in defendant's extensive briefing of its argument that there is no express requirement under the FLSA that plaintiffs be paid for the hours between 160 and 171 which are statutorily exempt from the normal requirement that these hours are compensable at an overtime rate. However, the Court finds defendant's argument to be unreasonable in view of the remedial purpose of the FLSA. The Court finds the requirement that plaintiffs be paid compensation at their regular hourly rate to be implicit in the framework of the FLSA."[109]

K. The Settlement Of FLSA Cases.

Because the FLSA is a remedial statute designed to benefit employees, courts have held that the settlement of an FLSA claim for less than the full amount of money to which the employee was entitled will not act as a bar to a later lawsuit by the employee to recover the balance of the back pay which is due.[110] As put by one court, "The Fair Labor Standards Act was carefully designed to trump contracts and to give employees rights that they could not waive or contract away."[111] This rule was established in *Brooklyn Savings Bank v. O'Neal*, in which the Supreme Court considered the claim of an employee who had accepted the amount of overtime wages then due him, and waived his right to liquidated damages. The employee subsequently brought suit to recover the liquidated damages. The Supreme Court held the employee's earlier release of his FLSA claims to be ineffective, reasoning that where a statutory right is conferred on an individual but affects the public interest, it cannot be waived or released where the waiver or release would contravene public policy.[112] In the following year, the Supreme Court held in *Schulte v. Gangi*, that even where a genuine issue existed as to whether the FLSA applied to a particular case, a settlement and release by employees could be voided.[113]

If an employer wishes to ensure that an FLSA settlement is valid, the safest means is to petition either a court or the DOL to review and approve of the settlement.[114] Since employees who are covered by collective bargaining agreement are not bound by the terms of FLSA settlements reached between their labor organizations and an employer, an employer involved with a labor organization in FLSA settlement discussions would be best advised to insist that each individual employee covered by the settlement agree to the settlement in writing.[115]

L. Lawsuits Against States For FLSA Violation.

The FLSA authorizes state employees to bring lawsuits against employers either in federal or state court. In a series of decisions beginning in 1996, the United States Supreme Court has ruled unconstitutional those provisions of the FLSA, leaving state employees with no right to bring FLSA lawsuits against their employers. Instead, FLSA claims on behalf of state employees can only be brought by the DOL.

These developments involve the interpretation of the 11th Amendment to the United States Constitution, which provides that a state can only be sued in federal court if either (1) it has consented to such a suit; or (2) there is explicit authority elsewhere in the Constitution which abrogates a state's immunity from suit in federal court. For years, the Supreme Court had held that laws enacted under the so-called "Interstate Commerce Clause" of the Constitution – which gives Congress the authority to pass laws regulating interstate commerce – could subject a state to suit in federal court, ruling that the Interstate Commerce Clause contained the necessary authority in the Constitution to override a state's 11th Amendment immunity from suit in federal court.[116] Since Congress enacted the FLSA under the Interstate Commerce Clause, courts had consistently rejected attempts by states to have FLSA lawsuits dismissed from federal court on 11th Amendment grounds.[117]

In 1996, the Supreme Court decided *Seminole Tribe of Florida v. Florida*, a case seemingly completely unrelated to the FLSA. At issue in *Seminole Tribe of Florida* was whether the "Indian Commerce Clause" of the Constitution – which gives Congress the authority to regulate commerce with Indian tribes – was sufficient to override a state's 11th Amendment immunity from lawsuit in federal court. In holding that the Indian Commerce Clause did not override a state's 11th Amendment immunity, the Supreme Court also took the opportunity to overrule its leading decision holding that the Interstate Commerce Clause overrode a state's 11th Amendment immunity from suit in federal court.[118]

Almost immediately, states began seeking dismissal of FLSA lawsuits filed against them in federal court. Without exception, every court to consider the issue has held that *Seminole Tribe of Florida* requires the dismissal of federal court FLSA lawsuits against states.[119] Some state employees took the opportunity to refile their suits in state court, under the long-accepted notion that the Supremacy Clause of the Constitution required state courts to enforce federal statutes such as the FLSA. However, in *Alden v. State of Maine*, the Supreme Court 11th reversed almost 200 years of its decisions, and held that Amendment immunity applied not just to federal courts, but to state courts as well, thus eliminating the right of state employees to file FLSA lawsuits in state courts.[120]

The 11th Amendment only applies to states, not to political subdivisions of states. Thus, cities, counties, and special districts can continue to be sued in federal court under the FLSA.[121]

NOTES TO CHAPTER 10

[1] *See* 29 USC §§ 207(a)(1) and 216(b); *Dick v. Merillat*, 745 N.E.2d 507 (Ohio App. 2000).

[2] *See Alden v. Maine*, 527 U.S. 706 (1999).

[3] *United Food & Commercial Workers Union, Local 1564 of New Mexico v. Albertson's Inc.*, 207 F.3d 1193 (10th Cir. 2000); *Nevada Employees' Ass'n, Inc. v. Bryan*, 916 F.2d 1384, (9th Cir. 1990); *DeBraska v. City of Milwaukee*, 11 F.Supp.2d 1020, (E.D.Wis. 1998), *rev'd on other grounds*, 189 F.3d 650 (7th Cir. 1999); *OTR Drivers v. Frito-Lay, Inc.*, 160 F.R.D. 146, (D.Kan.1995); *International Ass'n of Firefighters, Local 349 v. City of Rome*, 682 F.Supp. 522, (N.D.Ga. 1988); *Arrington v. National Broad. Co.*, 531 F.Supp. 498 (D.D.C. 1982).

[4] *American Fed. of State County & Mun. Employees, AFL-CIO Local 935 v. Colorado*, 2 WH Cases2d (BNA) 799, (D.Colo. 1994)(holding that a union may be a proper plaintiff under the compensatory time off sections of the FLSA); *International Ass'n of Fire Fighters, Local 2203 v. West Adams County Fire Protection Dist.*, 28 WH Cas. (BNA) 981 (D.Colo. 1988)(same).

[5] *Howard v. City of Springfield, Illinois*, 274 F.3d 1141 (7th Cir. 2001).

[6] 29 U.S.C. §255(a).

[7] *Nealon v. Stone*, 958 F.2d 584, (4th Cir. 1992); *Higgins v. Good Lion, Inc.*, 2001 WL 77696 (D.Md. 2001); *McIntyre v. Youth Rehabilitation Services*, 795 F.Supp. 668 (D.Del. 1992), *Aaron v. City of Wichita, Kansas*, 797 F.Supp. 898 (D.Kan. 1992), *rev'd on other grounds,* 54 F.3d 652. An exception to this general rule occurs when the employee is alleging that the employer retaliated against the employee for bringing an FLSA

claim by making a permanent adjustment in payroll practices. So long as the adjustment does not itself violate the FLSA, the statute of limitations will start running on the date of the adjustment, not with every subsequent paycheck reflecting the amount of the adjustment. *Anderson v. City of Bristol*, 6 F.3d 1168 (6th Cir. 1993); *Alldread v. City of Grenada*, 988 F.2d 1425 (5th Cir. 1993).

[8] *Johnson v. North Carolina Department of Transportation,* 418 S.E.2d 700 (N.C.App. 1992).

[9] *McLaughlin v. Richland Shoe Co.*, 486 U.S. 128 (1988).

[10] *Harris v. District of Columbia*, 749 F.Supp. 301 (D.D.C. 1990). *See also Wyland v. District of Columbia*, 728 F.Supp. 35 (D.D.C. 1990).

[11] *Abbey v. City Of Jackson*, 883 F.Supp. 181 (E.D.Mich. 1995).

[12] *Nelson v. Waste Management of Alameda County*, 142 Lab.Cases ¶34,149 (N.D.Cal. 2000).

[13] *Baker v. Stone County, Missouri*, 41 F.Supp.2d 965 (W.D.Mo. 1999).

[14] *Andrews v. DuBois*, 888 F.Supp. 213 (D.Mass. 1995).

[15] *Lockwood v. Prince George's County, Maryland*, 58 F.Supp.2d 651 (D.Md. 1999).

[16] *Schneider v. City of Springfield*, 102 F.Supp.2d 827 (S.D.Ohio 1999).

[17] *Bankston v. State of Illinois*, 60 F.3d 1249 (7th Cir. 1995); *see Dole v. Elliott Travel & Tours*, 942 F.2d 962 (6th Cir. 1991)(employer acted willfully where it had reason to know of law because of prior FLSA violations).

[18] *Ackler v. Cowlitz County, Washington*, 7 Fed. Appx. 543 (9th Cir. 2001).

[19] *Albanese v. Bergen County, New Jersey*, 991 F.Supp. 410 (D.N.J. 1998).

[20] *E.g. Heder v. City of Two Rivers*, 2001 WL 673505 (E.D.Wis. 2001); *Mitchell v. La Barge*, 684 N.Y.S.2d 10 (App.Div. 1999).

[21] The Supreme Court has upheld the constitutionality of the FLSA's liquidated damages provisions. *Beovich v. C.D. Gredvig, Inc.*, 2 WH Cases2d 539 (D.Or. 1994); *see Overnight Motor Transp. Co. v. Missel*, 316 U.S. 572 (1942).

[22] *Roy v. County of Lexington*, 141 F.3d 533 (4th Cir. 1998).

[23] 29 U.S.C. §260.

[24] *Block v. City of Los Angeles*, 2001 WL 609818 (9th Cir. 2001); *Joiner v. City of Macon*, 814 F.2d 1537 (11th Cir. 1987). *See generally McClanahan v. Matthews*, 440 F.2d 320 (6th Cir. 1971), *quoting Rothman v. Publicker Industries, Inc.*, 201 F.2d 618 (3rd Cir. 1953).

[25] *Hayes v. Bill Haley & His Comets*, 274 F.Supp. 34 (E.D.Pa. 1967).

[26] *Dybach v. Florida Department of Corrections*, 942 F.2d 1562 (11th Cir. 1991); *Westfall v. District of Columbia*, 30 WH Cases 921 (D.D.C. 1991).

[27] *Thomas v. Howard University Hospital*, 39 F.3d 370 (D.C.Cir. 1994).

[28] *Lockwood v. Prince George's County, Maryland*, 58 F.Supp.2d 651 (D.Md. 2000).

[29] *Atlanta Professional Firefighters Union v. City of Atlanta*, 920 F.2d 800 (11th Cir. 1991).

[30] *Cross v. Arkansas Forestry Commission*, 938 F.2d 912 (8th Cir. 1991).

[31] *Bauler v. Pressed Steel Car Co.*, 81 F.Supp. 172 (N.D.Ill. 1948), *aff'd* 182 F.2d 357 (7th Cir. 1948).

[32] *Reed v. Murphy*, 232 F.2d 668 (5th Cir. 1956).

[33] *Coleman v. Jiffy June Farms, Inc.*, 458 F.2d 1139 (5th Cir. 1972). The court only discussed whether the

FLSA violation was willful so as to trigger the three-year statute of limitations; the lower court, 324 F.Supp. 664 (1970), denied plaintiff's request for liquidated damages without really discussing the reliance upon erroneous advice from the attorney.

[34] *Aaron v. City Of Wichita, Kansas*, 1 WH Cases2d 550 (D.Kan. 1993).

[35] *Lee v. Coahoma County, Mississippi*, 937 F.2d 220 (5th Cir. 1991).

[36] *Doden v. Plainfield Fire District*, 3 WH Cases2d 199 (N.D.Ill. 1995).

[37] *Adams v. Pittsburgh State Univ.*, 832 F.Supp. 318 (D.Kan. 1993).

[38] *Ackler v. Cowlitz County*, 7 Fed. Appx. 543 (9th Cir. 2001).

[39] *Taylor v. County of Fluvanna, Virginia*, 70 F.Supp.2d 655 (W.D. Va. 1999).

[40] *Armitage v. City of Emporia, Kansas*, 782 F.Supp. 537 (D.Kan. 1992), *rev'd on other grounds*, 982 F.2d 430 (10th Cir. 1992).

[41] *Burgess v. Catawba County*, 805 F.Supp. 341 (W.D.N.C. 1992).

[42] *Farmer v. Ottawa County Sheriff's Dept.*, 142 Lab.Cas. ¶34,182 (W.D. Mich. 2000).

[43] *Tripp v. May*, 189 F.2d 198 (7th Cir. 1991).

[44] *Bankston v. State of Illinois*, 60 F.3d 1249 (7th Cir. 1995).

[45] *Williams v. Tri-County Growers, Inc.*, 747 F.2d 121 (3d Cir. 1984); *Barcellona v. Tiffany English Pub., Inc.*, 597 F.2d 464 (5th Cir. 1979).

[46] *AFSCME, Council 17 v. State of Louisiana*, 2001 WL 29999 (E.D.La. 2001).

[47] *Renfro v. City of Emporia*, 948 F.2d 1529 (10th Cir. 1991).

[48] *Pearson v. Ross G. Stephenson Assoc.*, 1 WH Cases2d 46 (D.Kan. 1992).

[49] *Renfro v. City of Emporia*, 948 F.2d 1529 (10th Cir. 1991).

[50] *Ackler v. Cowlitz County*, 7 Fed. Appx. 543 (9th Cir. 2001).

[51] *Foremost Dairies, Inc. v. Ivey*, 204 F.2d 186 (5th Cir. 1953).

[52] *Herman v. Hogar Praderas De Amor, Inc.*, 130 F.Supp.2d 257 (D.P.R. 2001); *Roy v. Lexington County*, 928 F.Supp. 1406 (D.S.C. 1996), *modified on other grounds,* 948 F.Supp. 529 (D.S.C. 1996); *West v. Anne Arundel County*, 3 WH Cases2d 234 (D.Md. 1996); *Ball v. District of Columbia*, 795 F.Supp. 461 (D.D.C. 1992); *Thomas v. County of Fairfax*, 758 F.Supp. 353 (E.D.Va. 1991). *But see Reich v. Waldbaum Inc.*, 833 F.Supp. 1037 (S.D.N.Y. 1993), *rev'd on other grounds,* 52 F.3d 35 (2nd Cir. 1995)(prejudgment interest cannot be awarded where liquidated damages are not awarded).

[53] *Aaron v. City of Wichita, Kansas*, 822 F.Supp. 683 (D.Kan. 1993), *rev'd on other grounds,* 54 F.3d 652 (10th Cir. 1995).

[54] *Shea v. Galaxie Lumber & Construction Co., Ltd.*, 152 F.3d 729 (7th Cir. 1998).

[55] *Aaron v. City of Wichita, Kansas*, 822 F.Supp. 683 (D.Kan. 1993), *rev'd on other grounds,* 54 F.3d 652 (10th Cir. 1995).

[56] 29 U.S.C. §216(b).

[57] *See Weisel v. Singapore Joint Venture, Inc.*, 602 F.2d 1185 (5th Cir. 1979); *Nitterright v. Claytor*, 454 F.Supp. 130 (D.D.C. 1978).

[58] *International Ass'n of Fire Fighters, Local 2203 v. West Adams County Fire Protection Dist.*, 877 F.2d 814 (10th Cir. 1989).

[59] *Farmer v. Ottawa County*, 211 F.3d 1268 (6th Cir. 2000); *quoting United Slate, Tile and Composition*

Roofers, Damp and Waterproof Workers Ass'n, Local 307 et al. v. G & M Roofing and Sheet Metal Co. Inc., 732 F.2d 495 (6th Cir. 1984) and *Fegley v. Higgins*, 19 F.3d 1126 (6th Cir. 1994).

[60] *Adams v. United States*, 48 Fed.Cl. 602 (2001).

[61] *See Hensley v. Eckerhart*, 461 U.S. 424 (1983); *Blackman v. District of Columbia*, 59 F.Supp.2d 37 (D.D.C. 1999).

[62] *Pearson v. Ross G. Stephenson Assoc.*, 1 WH Cases2d 46 (D.Kan. 1992).

[63] *Bankston v. State of Illinois*, 60 F.3d 1249 (7th Cir. 1995).

[64] *Lyle v. Food Lion, Inc.*, 954 F.2d 984 (4th Cir. 1992).

[65] *Bankston v. State of Illinois*, 60 F.3d 1249 (7th Cir. 1995).

[66] *Lyle v. Food Lion, Inc.*, 954 F.2d 984 (4th Cir. 1992).

[67] *Jarrett v. ERC Properties, Inc.*, 211 F.3d 1078 (8th Cir. 2000).

[68] *Bankston v. State of Illinois*, 60 F.3d 1249 (7th Cir. 1995).

[69] *Spegon v. Catholic Bishop of Chicago*, 175 F.3d 544 (7th Cir. 1999).

[70] 29 U.S.C. §259.

[71] *Fazekas v. Cleveland Clinic Foundation Health Care Ventures, Inc.*, 204 F.3d 673 (6th Cir. 2000).

[72] *Bouchard v. Regional Governing Board Of Region v. Mental Retardation Services*, 939 F.2d 1323 (8th Cir. 1991); *Close v. New York State*, 3 WH Cases2d 225 (N.D.N.Y. 1996), *vacated on other grounds*, 3 WH Cases2d 856 (N.D.N.Y. 1996).

[73] *Hultgren v. County of Lancaster*, 913 F.2d 498 (8th Cir. 1990).

[74] 29 U.S.C. §216(b).

[75] 29 U.S.C. §216(b). *See Partlow v. Jewish Orphans' Home of Southern California*, 645 F.2d 757 (9th Cir. 1981); *Kinney Shoe Corp. v. Vorhes*, 564 F.2d 859 (9th Cir. 1977); *Garza v. Chicago Transit Authority*, 2001 WL 503036 (N.D.Ill. 2001). In unusual cases, courts have treated FLSA lawsuits as traditional class actions filed under Rule 23 of the Federal Rules of Civil Procedure, essentially converting the action from an "opt-in" class action to an "opt-out" class action. *Ansoumana v. Gristede's Operating Corp.*, 2001 WL 563906 (S.D.N.Y. 2001).

[76] *Udvari v. United States*, 28 Fed.Cl. 137 (1993); *Beale v. District of Columbia*, 789 F.Supp. 1172 (D.D.C. 1992).

[77] *Hoffman-La Roche Inc. v. Sperling*, 493 U.S. 165 (1989). *See also Adams v. United States*, 21 Cl.Ct. 795 (1990). At one time, courts held that neither an FLSA plaintiff, the attorneys for an FLSA plaintiff, or the court have the power to provide notice to potential FLSA class members to allow the members to choose to "opt in" the class. *See Partlow v. Jewish Orphans' Home of Southern California*, 645 F.2d 757 (9th Cir. 1981); *Locascio v. Teletype Corp.*, 74 F.R.D. 108 (N.D.Ill. 1977); *Roshto v. Chrysler Corp.*, 67 F.R.D. 28 (E.D.La. 1975); *Contra Braunstein v. Eastern Photographic Laboratories, Inc.*, 600 F.2d 335 (2nd Cir. 1979). *See generally FLSA - Notice to Class of Opt-In*, 67 A.L.R. Fed. 282 (1984).

[78] *Kane v. Gage Merchandising Services, Inc.*, 138 F.Supp.2d 212 (D. Mass. 2001).

[79] *Reeves v. Alliant Techsystems, Inc.*, 77 F.Supp.2d 242 (D.R.I. 1999).

[80] *Garza v. Chicago Transit Authority*, 2001 WL 503036 (N.D.Ill. 2001).

[81] *Fuentes v. Chase Manhattan Bank*, 84 Lab. Cas. ¶33,701 (S.D.N.Y. 1978).

[82] *Myers v. Copper Cellar Corp.* 3 WH Cases2d 1081 (E.D.Tenn. 1996).

[83] *Mooney v. Aramco Servs. Co.*, 54 F.3d 1207 (5th Cir. 1995); *Asencio v. Tyson Foods, Inc.*, 130 F.Supp.2d 660 (E.D.Pa. 2001); *Morisky v Public Service Electric and Gas Company*, 111 F.Supp.2d 493 (D.N.J. 2000).

[84] 29 U.S.C.§§251-262.

[85] *Arrington v. Nat'l Broadcasting Co., Inc.*, 531 F.Supp. 498 (D.D.C. 1982), *quoting* 93 Cong. Rec. 2182 (Remarks of Senator Donnell).

[86] *United Food & Commercial Workers Union, Local 1564 of New Mexico v. Albertson's, Inc.*, 207 F.3d 1193 (10th Cir. 2000); *State of Nevada Employees' Association, Inc. v. Bryan*, 916 F.2d 1384 (9th Cir. 1990); *DeBraska v. City of Milwaukee*, 11 F.Supp.2d 1020 (E.D. Wisc. 1998); *AFSCME v. Virginia*, 1995 WL 913191 (W.D.Va. 1995); *AFSCME v. Moore*, 1992 WL 118742 (W.D.Mo. 1992); *Arrington v. National Broadcasting Co.*, 531 F.Supp. 498, (D.D.C. 1982). *See also Local 100, SEIU v. Integrated Health Services, Inc.*, 96 F.Supp.2d 537 (M.D.La. 2000)(union not proper party in FMLA action brought through FLSA's remedial provisions). In a position seemingly contrary to the specific provisions of the Portal-to-Portal amendments, several courts have uncritically accepted causes of action under the FLSA filed by public sector labor organizations without examining whether the labor organization has the standing or the right to bring the lawsuit. *Abbott v. City of Virginia Beach*, 879 F.2d 132 (4th Cir. 1989)(plaintiff was Virginia Beach Benevolent Police Association); *Jacksonville Professional Firefighters Ass'n, Local 2691 v. City of Jacksonville*, 685 F.Supp. 513 (E.D.N.C. 1988)(plaintiff was firefighters' association).

[87] 29 U.S.C. §215(a)(3).

[88] *Cheng v. IDE Associates, Inc.,* 6 WH Cases2d 654 (D.Mass. 2000); *Strickland v. MICA Information Systems,* 800 F.Supp. 1320 (M.D.N.C. 1992).

[89] *See McDonnell Douglas Corp. v. Green,* 411 U.S. 792 (1973); *Marx v. Schnuck Markets, Inc.,* 863 F.Supp. 1489 (D.Kan. 1994).

[90] *Marshall v. Mardels, Inc.,* 84 Lab. Cas. ¶33,706 (E.D.N.Y. 1978).

[91] *Conner v. Schnuck Markets,* 906 F.Supp. 606 (D.Kan. 1995).

[92] *Blackie v. State of Maine,* 888 F.Supp. 203 (D.Me. 1995).

[93] *Knickerbocker v. City of Stockton,* 81 F.3d 907 (9th Cir. 1996).

[94] *Loos v. City of Concord, North Carolina,* 1 WH Cases2d 1236 (M.D.N.C. 1993).

[95] *Powell v. State of Florida,* 132 F.3d 677 (11th Cir. 1998); *Morelock v. NCR Corp.,* 546 F.2d 682 (6th Cir. 1976), *rev'd on other grounds,* 435 U.S. 911 (1978); *Powell v. Washington Post Co.,* 267 F.2d 651 (D.C.Cir. 1959); *Roberg v. Henry Phipps Estate,* 156 F.2d 958 (2d Cir. 1946); *Bowe v. Judson C. Burns, Inc.,* 137 F.2d 37 (3d Cir. 1943); *Bailey v. Gulf Coast Transportation, Inc.,* 139 F.Supp.2d 1358 (M.D.Fla. 2001).

[96] *Lambert v. Genessee Hospital,* 10 F.3d 46 (2nd Cir. 1993).

[97] *Lambert v. Ackerly,* 180 F.3d 997 (9th Cir. 1999); *Valerio v. Putnam Assocs, Inc.,* 173 F.3d 35 (1st Cir. 1999); *Conner v. Schnuck Markets, Inc.,* 121 F.3d 1390 (10th Cir. 1997); *Romeo Community Sch.,* 976 F.2d 985 (6th Cir. 1992); *Crowley v. Pace Suburban Bus Div.,* 938 F.2d 797 (7th Cir. 1991); *EEOC v. White & Son Enters.,* 881 F.2d 1006 (11th Cir. 1989); *Love v. RE/MAX of America, Inc.,* 738 F.2d 383 (10th Cir. 1984); *Brennan v. Maxey's Yamaha, Inc.,* 513 F.2d 179 (8th Cir. 1975). *See generally* Jennifer Redmond, *Are*

You Breaking Some Sort of Law?: Protecting An Employee's Informal Complaints Under the FLSA's Anti-Retaliation Provision, 42 Wm & Mary L. Rev. 319 (October, 2000).

[98] Section 8 is now attached as a note to Section 15(a) of the FLSA. When it was applicable, Section 8 did not apply to retaliation claims based on discrimination which occurred before the effective date of the *Garcia* decision. *Ridings v. Lane County, Oregon*, 862 F.2d 231 (9th Cir. 1988).

[99] *Brennan v. Maxey's Yamaha*, 513 F.2d 179 (8th Cir. 1975); *Bomham v. Copper Cellar Corp.*, 476 F.Supp. 98 (E.D.Tenn. 1979).

[100] *See Alexander v. City of Plainview*, 694 F.Supp. 221 (N.D.Tex. 1988); *O'Quinn v. Chambers County, Texas*, 650 F.Supp. 25 (S.D.Tex. 1986).

[101] *York v. City of Wichita Falls*, 727 F.Supp. 1076 (N.D.Tex. 1989), *vacated* 944 F.2d 236 (5th Cir. 1991).

[102] *Blanton v. City of Murfreesboro*, 856 F.2d 731 (6th Cir. 1988); *Professional Firefighters v. Clayton*, 759 F.Supp. 1408 (E.D.Mo. 1991); *Craven v. City of Minot*, 730 F.Supp. 1511 (D.N.D. 1989); *Hill v. City of Greenville*, 696 F.Supp 1123 (N.D.Tex. 1988); *Alexander v. City of Plainview*, 694 F.Supp. 221 (N.D.Tex. 1988); *Sanchez v. City of New Orleans*, 538 So.2d 709 (La.App. 1989). *But see York v. City of Wichita Falls*, 2 WH Cases2d 1092 (5th Cir. 1995)(No violation of Section 8 to reduce hourly wages so that total annual compensation was unchanged). While the reduction of an employee's hourly rate may well constitute illegal discrimination under the FLSA, the reduction of an employee's hours of work is generally thought to be permissible. *Adams v. City of McMinnville*, 890 F.2d 836 (6th Cir. 1989).

[103] *Travis v. Gary Community Mental Health Center*, 921 F.2d 108 (7th Cir. 1990).

[104] H.R. Conf. Rep. No. 99-357, at 8-9 (1985), reported in U.S.C.C.A.N. 668, 669-670.

[105] *Anderson v. City of Bristol*, 6 F.3d 1168 (6th Cir. 1993).

[106] *Drollinger v. State of Arizona*, 962 F.2d 956 (9th Cir. 1992).

[107] *Glover v. City of North Charleston, South Carolina*, 942 F.Supp. 243 (D.S.C. 1996). Though there is some controversy over the subject, the majority rule appears to be that the spouse of an employee who brings an FLSA claim is also protected by Section 15 against discrimination by the employer (where the spouse also works for the same employer). *See Haines v. Knight-Ridder Broadcasting, Inc.*, 32 FEP Cases 1113 (D.R.I. 1980).

[108] *Robertson v. Board of County Commissioners*, 78 F.Supp.2d 1142 (D.Colo. 1999). *See also Balducci v. Chesterfield County*, 187 F.3d 628 (4th Cir. 1999); *Local 889, AFSCME v. Louisiana Department of Health and Hospitals*, 145 F.3d 280 (5th Cir. 1998); *Monahan v. County of Chesterfield*, 95 F.3d 1263 (4th Cir. 1996); *Martin v. Coventry Fire Dist.*, 981 F.2d 1358 (1st Cir. 1992); *Hensley v. MacMillan Bloedel Containers, Inc.*, 786 F.2d 353 (8th Cir. 1986); *Braddock v. Madison County*, 34 F.Supp.2d 1098 (S.D. Ind. 1998).

[109] *Lamon v. City of Shawnee*, 754 F.Supp. 1518 (D.Kan. 1991), *modified on other grounds,* 972 F.2d 1145 (10th Cir. 1992).

[110] *E.g. Stillwell v. Hertz Drivurself Stations, Inc.*, 174 F.2d 714 (3rd Cir. 1949); *Torres v. American R. Company*, 157 F.2d 255 (1st Cir. 1946); *Thomas v. State of Louisiana*, 1975 WL 1223 (W.D.La. 1975).

[111] *Braddock v. Madison County*, 34 F.Supp.2d 1098 (S.D.Ind. 1998).

[112] *Brooklyn Savings Bank v. O'Neal*, 324 US 697 (1945). *See Reich v. Stewart*, 121 F.3d 400 (8th Cir. 1997)(individual cannot waive entitlement to FLSA

benefits); *Castillo v. Case Farms of Ohio, Inc.*, 96 F.Supp.2d 578 (W.D.Tex. 1999)("It is beyond question that workers cannot waive their rights under the FLSA, even by agreement").

[113] *Schulte v. Gangi*, 328 US 108 (1946). The DOL subsequently adopted the holding in *Schulte* into 29 CFR §4.187(d).

[114] *Lynn's Food Stores, Inc. v. United States*, 679 F.2d 1350 (11th Cir. 1982).

[115] *See Barrentine v. Arkansas-Best Freight System, Inc.*, 450 U.S. 728 (1981); *Watkins v. Hudson Coal Co.*, 151 F.2d 311 (3rd Cir. 1945).

[116] *Pennsylvania v. Union Gas Co.*, 491 U.S. 1 (1989).

[117] *E.g. Reich v. New York*, 3 F.3d 581 (2nd Cir. 1993).

[118] *Seminole Tribe of Florida v. Florida*, 517 U.S. 44 (1996).

[119] *E.g. Mercado v. Commonwealth of Puerto Rico*, 214 F.3d 34 (1st Cir. 2000); *Abril v. Commonwealth of Virginia*, 145 F.3d 182 (4th Cir. 1998); *Wilson-Jones v. Caviness*, 99 F.3d 203 (6th Cir. 1996); *Kess v. State of Maryland*, 2001 WL 85179 (D.Md. 2001); *Rosario v. Police Department*, 126 F.Supp.2d 167 (D.P.R. 2000); *Bunt v. Texas General Land Office*, 72 F.Supp.2d 735 (S.D.Tex. 1999); *Bergemann v. State of Rhode Island*, 958 F.Supp. 61 (D.R.I. 1997); *Taylor v. State of Virginia*, 3 WH Cases2d 1196 (E.D.Va. 1996); *AFSCME v. State of Virginia*, 3 WH Cases2d 1191 (W.D.Va. 1996); *Rehberg v. Dep't of Public Safety*, 946 F.Supp. 741 (S.D.Iowa 1996); *Chauvin v. State of Louisiana*, 937 F.Supp. 567 (E.D.La. 1996); *Raper v. State of Iowa*, 940 F.Supp. 1421 (S.D.Iowa 1996); *Close v. State of New York*, 3 WH Cases2d 856 (N.D.N.Y. 1996); *Mills v. State of Maine*, 3 WH Cases2d 767 (D.Me. 1996); *Adams v. State of Kansas*, 934 F.Supp. 371

(D.Kan. 1996); *Blow v. State of Kansas*, 929 F.Supp. 1400 (D.Kan. 1996).

[120] *Alden v. Maine*, 527 U.S. 706 (1999).

[121] *Cash v. Granville County Board of Education*, 242 F.3d 219 (4th Cir. 2001)(school district); *Prickett v. DeKalb County*, 92 F.Supp.2d 1357 (N.D.Ga. 2000); *Alderman v. Baltimore City Police Department*, 952 F.Supp. 256 (D.Md. 1997)(city); *Brickey v. Smyth County, Virginia*, 944 F.Supp. 1310 (W.D.Va. 1996) (county). The notion that political subdivisions of states are not protected by the 11th Amendment began with the Supreme Court's decision in *Lincoln County v. Luning*, 133 U.S. 529 (1890), holding that counties are not protected by the Eleventh Amendment from suit in federal court. In recent years, the Supreme Court has noted in passing on several occasions that cities and counties are unprotected by the 11th Amendment. *See, Alden v. Maine*, 527 U.S. 706 (1999) ("The second important limit to the principle of sovereign immunity is that it bars suits against States but not lesser entities."); *Hess v. Port Auth. Trans-Hudson Corp.*, 513 U.S. 30 (1994) ("[P]olitical subdivisions exist solely at the whim and behest of their State, yet cities and counties do not enjoy Eleventh Amendment immunity."); *Mount Healthy City Bd. of Ed. v. Doyle*, 429 U.S. 274 (1977)("The bar of the Eleventh Amendment to suit in federal courts extends to States and state officials in appropriate circumstances, but does not extend to counties and similar municipal corporations.")

CHAPTER ELEVEN
FLSA RESOURCES ON THE INTERNET

With the recognition that some of the information set forth below may be out-of-date as soon as it is printed given the ever-changing nature of the Internet, what follows is a summary of some of the FLSA resources on the Internet:

Title of Internet Resource	Uniform Resource Locator (URL)	Brief Description of the Site Contents
Americans for Effective Law Enforcement	http://www.aele.org	The home page for the publisher of the *Fire and Police Personnel Reporter*, a monthly journal containing FLSA and other cases.
Bureau of National Affairs	http://www.bna.com	The home page for the publisher of the *Wage and Hour Reporter*, the most comprehensive collection of FLSA cases.
Chamberlain & Kaufman	http://www.flsa.com	Summaries of recent FLSA cases provided by the New York law firm representing employees in FLSA lawsuits.
Code of Federal Regulations	http://www.access.gpo.gov/nara/cfr	Searchable on-line version of the Code of Federal Regulations. Relevant FLSA provisions are in Title 29.
Commerce Clearing House	http://onlinestore.cch.com/	An on-line ordering system for CCH products, some of which have information on the FLSA and other employment laws.

Title of Internet Resource	**Uniform Resource Locator (URL)**	**Brief Description of the Site Contents**
County News	http://www.naco.org	Web page for the National Association of Counties. Newsletter occasionally contains articles and advice on the FLSA.
Davies, Roberts & Reid	http://www.webcom .com/jamesd/ flsa.html	A summary of the FLSA's requirements prepared by a union-side labor law firm in Seattle.
Federal Judiciary	http://www.uscourts .gov/	The home page for the United States court system. Following the links will take you the pages of the Supreme Court, and federal courts of appeals and trial courts.
Findlaw	http://www.findlaw. com/	A comprehensive collection of labor law links, including court decisions, statutes, regulations, and organiza- tions interested in the FLSA and other labor issues.
Hieros Gamos	http://www.hg.org/ newsstand.html	A comprehensive listing of legal and related sites, including links to many labor law publications and compilations.
Labor Relations Information System	http://www.lris.com	The home page for the publisher of *Public Safety Labor News,* a monthly newsletter with regular FLSA features, and the publisher of *The FLSA - A User's Manual(Third Edition)*, released in 2002.

Title of Internet Resource	Uniform Resource Locator (URL)	Brief Description of the Site Contents
LawMemo	http://www.lawmemo.com	Professor Ross Runkel's web page collecting a variety of articles on labor law issues, as well as sample editions of the *Employment Law Memo*.
Management Assistance Program for Nonprofits	http://www.mapnp.org/library/legal/emp_law/laws/flsa.htm	A basic summary of the FLSA and some of the requirements of the law.
Medical College of Ohio	http://www.mco.edu/depts/hr/flsa.html	An "exemption checklist" to determine if positions qualify for a Section 213(a) exemption.
National Public Employment Labor Relations Association	http://www.npelra.org	Home page of the largest public sector labor relations association for management representatives; newsletter contains articles on the FLSA.
Thompson Publishing Group	http://www.thompson.com/	Sample newsletters provided by publishing company which distributes materials relevant to the FLSA. Includes ordering information on "Employer's Guide to the FLSA."
United States Code	http://www.law.cornell.edu:80/uscode	Cornell Law School's online searchable United States Code. Relevant FLSA provisions are in Title 29.
United States Department of Labor	http://www.dol.gov/	The Department of Labor home page, with links to all DOL pages and publications.

Title of Internet Resource	Uniform Resource Locator (URL)	Brief Description of the Site Contents
United States Department of Labor	http://www.elaws. dol.gov/flsa/	The DOL's "FLSA Advisor," a basic description of the FLSA's requirements.
United States Department of Labor	http://www.dol.gov/ dol/esa/public/regs/ compliance/posters/ flsa.htm	The DOL's "FLSA Poster," which employers are required by law to display in a prominent location.
United States Office of Personnel Management	http://www.opm.gov /flsa	The federal Office of Personnel Management's guide to the FLSA.

CHAPTER TWELVE
EXCERPTS FROM REGULATIONS UNDER THE FLSA

What follows is the complete text of the Department of Labor's regulations covering the following topics:

Section 516: Recordkeeping Requirements.

Section 541: Executive, Administrative and Professional Employees.

Section 553: The Application of the FLSA to Employees of State and Local Governments.

Section 778: Overtime Compensation.

Section 785: Hours Worked.

Section 790: Regulations Under the Portal To Portal Act.

SECTION 516--RECORDS TO BE KEPT BY EMPLOYERS

Subpart A--General Requirements

Section 516.2

Employees subject to minimum wage or minimum wage and overtime provisions pursuant to section 6 or sections 6 and 7(a) of the Act.

(a) Items required. Every employer shall maintain and preserve payroll or other records containing the following information and data with respect to each employee to whom section 6 or both sections 6 and 7(a) of the Act apply:

(1) Name in full, as used for Social Security recordkeeping purposes, and on the same record, the employee's identifying symbol or number if such is used in place of name on any time, work, or payroll records,

(2) Home address, including zip code,

(3) Date of birth, if under 19,

(4) Sex and occupation in which employed (sex may be indicated by use of the prefixes Mr., Mrs., Miss., or Ms.) (Employee's sex identification is related to the equal pay provisions of the Act which are administered by the

Equal Employment Opportunity Commission. Other equal pay recordkeeping requirements are contained in 29 CFR part 1620.),

(5) Time of day and day of week on which the employee's workweek begins (or for employees employed under section 7(k) of the Act, the starting time and length of each employee's work period). If the employee is part of a workforce or employed in or by an establishment all of whose workers have a workweek beginning at the same time on the same day, a single notation of the time of the day and beginning day of the workweek for the whole workforce or establishment will suffice,

(6)(i) Regular hourly rate of pay for any workweek in which overtime compensation is due under section 7(a) of the Act, (ii) explain basis of pay by indicating the monetary amount paid on a per hour, per day, per week, per piece, commission on sales, or other basis, and (iii) the amount and nature of each payment which, pursuant to section 7(e) of the Act, is excluded from the "regular rate" (these records may be in the form of vouchers or other payment data),

(7) Hours worked each workday and total hours worked each workweek (for purposes of this section, a "workday" is any fixed period of 24 consecutive hours and a "workweek" is any fixed and regularly recurring period of 7 consecutive workdays),

(8) Total daily or weekly straight-time earnings or wages due for hours worked during the workday or workweek, exclusive of premium overtime compensation,

(9) Total premium pay for overtime hours. This amount excludes the straight-time earnings for overtime hours recorded under paragraph (a)(8) of this section,

(10) Total additions to or deductions from wages paid each pay period including employee purchase orders or wage assignments. Also, in individual employee records, the dates, amounts, and nature of the items which make up the total additions and deductions,

(11) Total wages paid each pay period,

(12) Date of payment and the pay period covered by payment.

(b) Records of retroactive payment of wages. Every employer who makes retroactive payment of wages or compensation under the supervision of the Administrator of the Wage and Hour Division pursuant to section 16(c) and/or section 17 of the Act, shall:

(1) Record and preserve, as an entry on the pay records, the amount of such payment to each employee, the period covered by such payment, and the date of payment.

(2) Prepare a report of each such payment on a receipt form provided by or authorized by the Wage and Hour Division, and (i) preserve a copy as part of the records, (ii) deliver a copy to the employee, and (iii) file the original, as evidence of payment by the employer and receipt by the employee, with the Administrator or an authorized representative within 10 days after payment is made.

(c) Employees working on fixed schedules. With respect to employees working on fixed schedules, an employer may maintain records showing instead of the hours worked each day and each workweek as required by paragraph (a)(7) of this section, the schedule of daily and weekly hours the employee normally works. Also,

(1) In weeks in which an employee adheres to this schedule, indicates by check mark, statement or other method that such hours were in fact actually worked by him, and

(2) In weeks in which more or less than the scheduled hours are worked, shows that exact number of hours worked each day and each week.

Section 516.3

Bona fide executive, administrative, and professional employees (including academic administrative personnel and teachers in elementary or secondary schools), and outside sales employees employed pursuant to section 13(a)(1) of the Act.

With respect to each employee in a bona fide executive, administrative, or professional capacity (including employees employed in the capacity of academic administrative personnel or teachers in elementary or secondary schools), or in outside sales, as defined in part 541 of this chapter (pertaining to so-called "white collar" employee exemptions), employers shall maintain and preserve records containing all the information and data required by Sec. 516.2(a) except paragraphs (a) (6) through (10) and, in addition, the basis on which wages are paid in sufficient detail to permit calculation for each pay period of the employee's total remuneration for employment including fringe benefits and prerequisites. (This may be shown as the dollar amount of earnings per month, per week, per month plus commissions, etc. with appropriate addenda such as "plus hospitalization and insurance plan A," "benefit package B," "2 weeks paid vacation," etc.)

Section 516.5 Records to be preserved 3 years.

Each employer shall preserve for at least 3 years:

(a) Payroll records. From the last date of entry, all payroll or other records containing the employee information and data required under any of the applicable sections of this part, and

(b) Certificates, agreements, plans, notices, etc. From their last effective date, all written:

(1) Collective bargaining agreements relied upon for the exclusion of certain costs under section 3(m) of the Act,

(2) Collective bargaining agreements, under section 7(b)(1) or 7(b)(2) of the Act, and any amendments or additions thereto,

(3) Plans, trusts, employment contracts, and collective bargaining agreements under section 7(e) of the Act,

(4) Individual contracts or collective bargaining agreements under section 7(f) of the Act. Where such contracts or agreements are not in writing, a

written memorandum summarizing the terms of each such contract or agreement,

(5) Written agreements or memoranda summarizing the terms of oral agreements or understandings under section 7(g) or 7(j) of the Act, and

(6) Certificates and notices listed or named in any applicable section of this part.

(c) Sales and purchase records. A record of (1) total dollar volume of sales or business, and (2) total volume of goods purchased or received during such periods (weekly, monthly, quarterly, etc.), in such form as the employer maintains records in the ordinary course of business.

Section 516.6 Records to be preserved 2 years.

(a) Supplementary basic records: Each employer required to maintain records under this part shall preserve for a period of at least 2 years.

(1) Basic employment and earnings records. From the date of last entry, all basic time and earning cards or sheets on which are entered the daily starting and stopping time of individual employees, or of separate work forces, or the amounts of work accomplished by individual employees on a daily, weekly, or pay period basis (for example, units produced) when those amounts determine in whole or in part the pay period earnings or wages of those employees.

(2) Wage rate tables. From their last effective date, all tables or schedules of the employer which provide the piece rates or other rates used in computing straight-time earnings, wages, or salary, or overtime pay computation.

(b) Order, shipping, and billing records: From the last date of entry, the originals or true copies of all customer orders or invoices received, incoming or outgoing shipping or delivery records, as well as all bills of lading and all billings to customers (not including individual sales slips, cash register tapes or the like) which the employer retains or makes in the usual course of business operations.

(c) Records of additions to or deductions from wages paid:

(1) Those records relating to individual employees referred to in Sec. 516.2(a)(10) and

(2) All records used by the employer in determining the original cost, operating and maintenance cost, and depreciation and interest charges, if such costs and charges are involved in the additions to or deductions from wages paid.

Subpart B--Records Pertaining to Employees Subject to Miscellaneous Exemptions Under the Act; Other Special Requirements

Section 516.11 Employees exempt from both minimum wage and overtime pay requirements under section 13(a) (2), (3), (4), (5), (8), (10), (12), or 13(d) of the Act.

With respect to each and every employee exempt from both the minimum wage and overtime pay requirements of the Act pursuant to the provisions of section 13(a) (2), (3), (4), (5), (8), (10), (12), or 13(d) of the Act, employers shall maintain and preserve records containing the information and data required by Sec. 516.2(a) (1) through (4).

Section 516.24 Employees employed under section 7(f) "Belo" contracts.

With respect to each employee to whom both sections 6 and 7(f) of the Act apply, the employer shall maintain and preserve payroll or other records containing all the information and data required by Sec. 516.2(a) except paragraphs (a) (8) and (9), and, in addition, the following:

(a) Total weekly guaranteed earnings,

(b) Total weekly compensation in excess of weekly guaranty,

(c) A copy of the bona fide individual contract or the agreement made as a result of collective bargaining by representatives of employees, or where such contract or agreement is not in writing, a written memorandum summarizing its terms.

SECTION 541--DEFINING AND DELIMITING THE TERMS ANY EMPLOYEE EMPLOYED IN A BONA FIDE EXECUTIVE, ADMINISTRATIVE, OR PROFESSIONAL CAPACITY (INCLUDING ANY EMPLOYEE)

Subpart A--General Regulations

Section 541.0 Terms used in regulations.

(a) Administrator means the Administrator of the Wage and Hour Division, U.S. Department of Labor. The Secretary of Labor has delegated to the Administrator the functions vested in him under section 13(a)(1) of the Fair Labor Standards Act.

(b) Act means the Fair Labor Standards Act of 1938, as amended.

Section 541.1 Executive.

The term employee employed in a bona fide executive * * * capacity in section 13(a) (1) of the Act shall mean any employee:

(a) Whose primary duty consists of the management of the enterprise in which he is employed or of a customarily recognized department of subdivision thereof; and

(b) Who customarily and regularly directs the work of two or more other employees therein; and

(c) Who has the authority to hire or fire other employees or whose suggestions and recommendations as to the hiring or firing and as to the advancement and promotion or any other change of status of other employees will be given particular weight; and

(d) Who customarily and regularly exercises discretionary powers; and

(e) Who does not devote more than 20 percent, or, in the case of an employee of a retail or service establishment who does not devote as much as 40 percent, of his hours of work in the workweek to activities which are not directly and closely related to the performance of the work described in paragraphs (a) through (d) of this section: Provided,

That this paragraph shall not apply in the case of an employee who is in sole charge of an independent establishment or a physically separated branch establishment, or who owns at least a 20-percent interest in the enterprise in which he is employed; and

(f) Who is compensated for his services on a salary basis at a rate of not less than $155 per week (or $130 per week, if employed by other than the Federal Government in Puerto Rico, the Virgin Islands, or American Samoa), exclusive of board, lodging, or other facilities: Provided,

That an employee who is compensated on a salary basis at a rate of not less than $250 per week (or $200 per week, if employed by other than the Federal Government in Puerto Rico, the Virgin Islands or American Samoa), exclusive of board, lodging, or other facilities, and whose primary duty consists of the management of the enterprise in which the employee is employed or of a customarily recognized department or subdivision thereof, and includes the customary and regular direction of the work of two or more other employees therein, shall be deemed to meet all the requirements of this section.

Section 541.2 Administrative.

The term employee employed in a bona fide * * * administrative * * * capacity in section 13(a)(1) of the Act shall mean any employee:

(a) Whose primary duty consists of either:

(1) The performance of office or nonmanual work directly related to management policies or general business operations of his employer or his employer's customers, or

(2) The performance of functions in the administration of a school system, or educational establishment or institution, or of a department or subdivision thereof, in work directly related to the academic instruction or training carried on therein; and

(b) Who customarily and regularly exercises discretion and independent judgment; and (c)(1) Who regularly and directly assists a proprietor, or an employee employed in a bona fide executive or administrative capacity (as such terms are defined in the regulations of this subpart), or

(2) Who performs under only general supervision work along specialized or technical lines requiring special training, experience, or knowledge, or

(3) Who executes under only general supervision special assignments and tasks; and

(d) Who does not devote more than 20 percent, or, in the case of an employee of a retail or service establishment who does not devote as much as 40 percent, of his hours worked in the workweek to activities which are not directly and closely related to the performance of the work described in paragraphs (a) through (c) of this section; and

(e)(1) Who is compensated for his services on a salary or fee basis at a rate of not less than $155 per week ($130 per week, if employed by other than the Federal Government in Puerto Rico, the Virgin Islands, or American Samoa), exclusive of board, lodging, or other facilities, or

(2) Who, in the case of academic administrative personnel, is compensated for services as required by paragraph (e)(1) of this section, or on a salary basis which is at least equal to the entrance salary for teachers in the school system, educational establishment, or institution by which employed: Provided,

That an employee who is compensated on a salary or fee basis at a rate of not less than $250 per week ($200 per week if employed by other than the Federal Government in Puerto Rico, the Virgin Islands, or American Samoa), exclusive of board, lodging, or other facilities, and whose primary duty consists of the performance of work described in paragraph (a) of this section, which includes work requiring the exercise of discretion and independent judgment, shall be deemed to meet all the requirements of this section.

Section 541.3 Professional.

The term employee employed in a bona fide * * * professional capacity in section 13(a)(1) of the Act shall mean any employee:

(a) Whose primary duty consists of the performance of:

(1) Work requiring knowledge of an advance type in a field of science or learning customarily acquired by a prolonged course of specialized intellectual instruction and study, as distinguished from a general academic education and from an apprenticeship, and from training in the performance of routine mental, manual, or physical processes, or

(2) Work that is original and creative in character in a recognized field of artistic endeavor (as opposed to work which can be produced by a person endowed with general manual or intellectual ability and training), and the result of which depends primarily on the invention, imagination, or talent of the employee, or

(3) Teaching, tutoring, instructing, or lecturing in the activity of imparting knowledge and who is employed and engaged in this activity as a teacher

in the school system or educational establishment or institution by which he is employed, or

(4) Work that requires theoretical and practical application of highly-specialized knowledge in computer systems analysis, programming, and software engineering, and who is employed and engaged in these activities as a computer systems analyst, computer programmer, software engineer, or other similarly skilled worker in the computer software field, as provided in Sec. 541.303; and

(b) Whose work requires the consistent exercise of discretion and judgment in its performance; and

(c) Whose work is predominantly intellectual and varied in character (as opposed to routine mental, manual, mechanical, or physical work) and is of such character that the output produced or the result accomplished cannot be standardized in relation to a given period of time; and

(d) Who does not devote more than 20 percent of his hours worked in the workweek to activities which are not an essential part of and necessarily incident to the work described in paragraphs (a) through (c) of this section; and

(e) Who is compensated for services on a salary or fee basis at a rate of not less than $250 per week beginning February 13, 1981 and $280 per week beginning February 13, 1983 ($225 per week beginning February 13, 1981 and $250 per week beginning February 13, 1983 if employed by other than the Federal Government in Puerto Rico, the Virgin Islands, or American Samoa), exclusive of board, lodging, or other facilities: Provided,

That this paragraph shall not apply in the case of an employee who is the holder of a valid license or certificate permitting the practice of law or medicine or any of their branches and who is actually engaged in the practice thereof, nor in the case of an employee who is the holder of the requisite academic degree for the general practice of medicine and is engaged in an internship or resident program pursuant to the practice of medicine or any of its branches, nor in the case of an employee employed and engaged as a teacher as provided in paragraph (a)(3) of this section: Provided further,

That an employee who is compensated on a salary or fee basis at a rate of not less than $320 per week beginning February 13, 1981 and $345 per week beginning February 13, 1983 (or $260 per week beginning February 13, 1981 and $285 per week beginning February 13, 1983 if employed by other than the Federal Government in Puerto Rico, the Virgin Islands, or American Samoa), exclusive of board, lodging, or other facilities, and whose primary duty consists of the performance either of work described in paragraph (a) (1) or (3) of this section, which includes work requiring the consistent exercise of discretion and judgment, or of work requiring invention, imagination, or talent in a recognized field of artistic endeavor, shall be deemed to meet all of the requirements of this section.

Section 541.5d Special provisions applicable to employees of public agencies.

(a) An employee of a public agency who otherwise meets the requirements of Sec. 541.118 shall not be disqualified from exemption under Secs. 541.1, 541.2, or 541.3 on the basis that such employee is paid according to a pay system established by statute, ordinance, or regulation, or by a policy or practice established pursuant to principles of public accountability, under which the employee accrues personal leave and sick leave and which requires the public agency employee's pay to be reduced or such employee to be placed on leave without pay for absences for personal reasons or because of illness or injury of less than one workday when accrued leave is not used by an employee because--

(1) permission for its use has not been sought or has been sought and denied;

(2) accrued leave has been exhausted; or

(3) the employee chooses to use leave without pay.

(b) Deductions from the pay of an employee of a public agency for absences due to a budget-required furlough shall not disqualify the employee from being paid "on a salary basis" except in the workweek in which the furlough occurs and for which the employee's pay is accordingly reduced.

Subpart B--Interpretations

Section 541.99 Introductory statement.

(a) Section 13(a)(1) of the Fair Labor Standards Act, as amended, exempts from the wage and hour provisions of the act "any employee employed in a bona fide executive, administrative, or professional capacity (including any employee employed in the capacity of academic administrative personnel or teacher in elementary or secondary schools), or in the capacity of outside salesman (as such terms are defined and delimited from time to time by regulations of the Secretary, subject to the provisions of the Administrative Procedure Act, except that an employee of a retail or service establishment shall not be excluded from the definition of employee employed in a bona fide executive or administrative capacity because of the number of hours in his workweek which he devotes to activities not directly or closely related to the performance of executive or administrative activities, if less than 40 percent of his hours worked in the workweek are devoted to such activities)." The requirements of the exemption under this section of the act are contained in subpart A of this part.

Employee Employed in a Bona Fide Executive Capacity

Section 541.101 General.

The duties and responsibilities of an exempt executive employee are described in paragraphs (a) through (d) of Sec. 541.1. Paragraph (e) of Sec. 541.1 contains among other things, percentage limitations on the amount of time which an employee may devote to activities "which are not directly and closely related to the performance of the work described in paragraphs (a) through (d)" of that section. For convenience in discussion, the work described in paragraphs (a) through (d) of Sec. 541.1 and the activities directly and closely related to such work will be referred to as "exempt" work, while other activities will be referred to as "nonexempt" work.

Section 541.102 Management.

(a) In the usual situation the determination of whether a particular kind of work is exempt or nonexempt in nature is not difficult. In the vast majority of cases the bona fide executive employee performs managerial and supervisory functions which are easily recognized as within the scope of the exemption.

(b) For example, it is generally clear that work such as the following is exempt work when it is performed by an employee in the management of his department or the supervision of the employees under him: Interviewing, selecting, and training of employees; setting and adjusting their rates of pay and hours of work; directing their work; maintaining their production or sales records for use in supervision or control; appraising their productivity and efficiency for the purpose of recommending promotions or other changes in their status; handling their complaints and grievances and disciplining them when necessary; planning the work; determining the techniques to be used; apportioning the work among the workers; determining the type of materials, supplies, machinery or tools to be used or merchandise to be bought, stocked and sold; controlling the flow and distribution of materials or merchandise and supplies; providing for the safety of the men and the property.

Section 541.103 Primary duty.

A determination of whether an employee has management as his primary duty must be based on all the facts in a particular case. The amount of time spent in the performance of the managerial duties is a useful guide in determining whether management is the primary duty of an employee. In the ordinary case it may be taken as a good rule of thumb that primary duty means the major part, or over 50 percent, of the employee's time.

Thus, an employee who spends over 50 percent of his time in management would have management as his primary duty. Time alone, however, is not the sole test, and in situations where the employee does not spend over 50 percent of his time in managerial duties, he might nevertheless have management as his primary duty if the other pertinent factors support such a conclusion. Some of these pertinent factors are the relative importance of the managerial duties as compared with other types of duties, the frequency with which the employee exercises discretionary powers, his relative freedom from supervision, and the relationship between his salary and the wages paid other employees for the kind of nonexempt work performed by the supervisor. For example, in some departments, or subdivisions of an establishment, an employee has broad responsibilities similar to those of the owner or manager of the establishment, but generally spends more than 50 percent of his time in production or sales work. While engaged in such work he supervises other employees, directs the work of warehouse and delivery men, approves advertising, orders merchandise, handles customer complaints, authorizes payment of bills, or performs other management duties as the day-to-day operations require. He will be considered to have management as his primary duty. In the data processing field an employee who directs the day-to-day activities of a single group of programmers and who performs the more complex or responsible jobs in programming will be considered to have management as his primary duty.

Section 541.104 Department or subdivision.

(a) In order to qualify under Sec. 541.1, the employee's managerial duties must be performed with respect to the enterprise in which he is employed or a customarily recognized department or subdivision thereof. The phrase "a customarily recognized department or subdivision" is intended to distinguish between a mere collection of men assigned from time to time to a specific job or series of jobs and a unit with permanent status and function. In order properly to classify an individual as an executive he must be more than merely a supervisor of two or more employees; nor is it sufficient that he merely participates in the management of the unit. He must be in charge of and have as his primary duty the management of a recognized unit which has a continuing function.

(b) In the vast majority of cases there is no difficulty in determining whether an individual is in charge of a customarily recognized department or subdivision of a department. For example, it is clear that where an enterprise comprises more than one establishment, the employee in charge of each establishment may be considered in charge of a subdivision of the enterprise. Questions arise principally in cases involving supervisors who work outside the employer's establishment, move from place to place, or have different subordinates at different times.

(c) In such instances, in determining whether the employee is in charge of a recognized unit with a continuing function, it is the division's position that the unit supervised need not be physically within the employer's establishment and may move from place to place, and that continuity of the same subordinate personnel is not absolutely essential to the existence of a recognized unit with a continuing function, although in the ordinary case a fixed location and continuity of personnel are both helpful in establishing the existence of such a unit. The following examples will illustrate these points.

(d) The projects on which an individual in charge of a certain type of construction work is employed may occur at different locations, and he may even hire most of his workforce at these locations. The mere fact that he moves his location would not invalidate his exemption if there are other factors which show that he is actually in charge of a recognized unit with a continuing function in the organization.

(e) Nor will an otherwise exempt employee lose the exemption merely because he draws the men under his supervision from a pool, if other factors are present which indicate that he is in charge of a recognized unit with a continuing function. For instance, if this employee is in charge of the unit which has the continuing responsibility for making all installations for his employer, or all installations in a particular city or a designated portion of a city, he would be in charge of a department or subdivision despite the fact that he draws his subordinates from a pool of available men.

(f) It cannot be said, however, that a supervisor drawn from a pool of supervisors who supervises employees assigned to him from a pool and who is assigned a job or series of jobs from day to day or week to week has the status of an executive. Such an employee is not in charge of a recognized unit with a continuing function.

Section 541.105 Two or more other employees.

(a) An employee will qualify as an "executive" under Sec. 541.1 only if he customarily and regularly supervises at least two full-time employees or the equivalent. For example, if the "executive" supervises one full-time and two part-time employees of whom one works morning and one, afternoons; or four part-time employees, two of whom work mornings and two afternoons, this requirement would be met.

(b) The employees supervised must be employed in the department which the "executive" is managing.

(c) It has been the experience of the divisions that a supervisor of as few as two employees usually performs nonexempt work in excess of the general 20-percent tolerance provided in Sec. 541.1.

(d) In a large machine shop there may be a machine-shop supervisor and two assistant machine-shop supervisors. Assuming that they meet all the other qualifications Sec. 541.1 and particularly that they are not working foremen, they should certainly qualify for the exemption. A small department in a plant or in an office is usually supervised by one person. Any attempt to classify one of the other workers in the department as an executive merely by giving him an honorific title such as assistant supervisor will almost inevitably fail as there will not be sufficient true supervisory or other managerial work to keep two persons occupied. On the other hand, it is incorrect to assume that in a large department, such as a large shoe department in a retail store which has separate sections for men's, women's, and children's shoes, for example, the supervision cannot be distributed among two or three employees, conceivably among more. In such instances, assuming that the other tests are met, especially the one concerning the performance of nonexempt work, each such employee "customarily and regularly directs the work of two or more other employees therein."

(e) An employee who merely assists the manager or buyer of a particular department and supervises two or more employees only in the actual manager's or buyer's absence, however, does not meet this requirement. For example, where a single unsegregated department, such as a women's sportswear department or a men's shirt department in a retail store, is managed by a buyer, with the assistance of one or more assistant buyers, only one employee, the buyer, can be considered an executive, even though the assistant buyers at times exercise some managerial and supervisory responsibilities. A shared responsibility for the supervision of the same two or more employees in the same department does not satisfy the requirement that the employee "customarily and regularly directs the work of two or more employees therein."

Section 541.107 Discretionary powers.

(a) Section 541.1(d) requires that an exempt executive employee customarily and regularly exercise discretionary powers. A person whose work is so completely routinized that he has no discretion does not qualify for exemption.

(b) The phrase "customarily and regularly" signifies a frequency which must be greater than occasional but which, of course, may be less than constant. The requirement will be met by the employee who normally and recurrently is called upon to exercise and does exercise discretionary powers in the day-to-day performance of his duties. The requirement is not met by the occasional exercise of discretionary powers.

Section 541.108 Work directly and closely related.

(a) This phrase brings within the category of exempt work not only the actual management of the department and the supervision of the employees therein, but also activities which are closely associated with the performance of the duties involved in such managerial and supervisory functions or responsibilities. The supervision of employees and the management of a department include a great many directly and closely related tasks which are different from the work performed by subordinates and are commonly performed by supervisors because they are helpful in supervising the employees or contribute to the smooth functioning of the department for which they are responsible. Frequently such exempt work is of a kind which in establishments that are organized differently or which are larger and have greater specialization of function, may be performed by a nonexempt employee hired especially for that purpose. Illustration will serve to make clear the meaning to be given the phrase "directly and closely related".

(b) Keeping basic records of working time, for example, is frequently performed by a timekeeper employed for that purpose. In such cases the work is clearly not exempt in nature. In other establishments which are not large enough to employ a timekeeper, or in which the timekeeping function has been decentralized, the supervisor of each department keeps the basic time records of his own subordinates. In these instances, as indicated above, the timekeeping is directly related to the function of managing the particular department and supervising its employees. However, the preparation of a payroll by a supervisor, even the payroll of the employees under his supervision, cannot be considered to be exempt work, since the preparation of a payroll does not aid in the supervision of the employees or the management of the department. Similarly, the keeping by a supervisor of production or sales records of his own subordinates for use in supervision or control would be exempt work, while the maintenance of production records of employees not under his direction would not be exempt work.

(c) Another example of work which may be directly and closely related to the performance of management duties is the distribution of materials or merchandise and supplies. Maintaining control of the flow of materials or merchandise and supplies in a department is ordinarily a responsibility of the managerial employee in charge. In many nonmercantile establishments the actual distribution of materials is performed by nonexempt employees under the supervisor's direction. In other establishments it is not uncommon to leave the actual distribution of materials and supplies in the hands of the supervisor. In such cases it is exempt work since it is directly and closely related to the managerial responsibility of maintaining the flow of materials. In a large retail establishment, however, where the replenishing of stocks of merchandise on the sales floor is customarily assigned to a nonexempt employee, the performance of such work by the manager or buyer of the department is nonexempt. The amount of time the manager or buyer spends in such work must be offset against the statutory tolerance for nonexempt work. The supervision and control of a flow of merchandise to the sales floor, of course, is directly and closely related to the managerial responsibility of the manager or buyer.

(d) Setup work is another illustration of work which may be exempt under certain circumstances if performed by a supervisor. The nature of setup work differs in various industries and for different operations. Some setup work is typically performed by the same employees who perform the "production" work; that is, the employee who operates the machine also "sets it up" or adjusts it for the particular job at hand. Such setup work is part of the production operation and is not exempt. In other instances the setting up of the work is a highly skilled operation which the ordinary production worker or machine tender typically does not perform. In some plants, particularly large ones, such setup work may be performed by employees whose duties are not supervisory in nature. In other plants, however, particularly small plants, such work is a regular duty of the executive and is directly and closely related to his responsibility for the work performance of his subordinates and for the adequacy of the final product. Under such circumstances it is exempt work. In the data processing field the work of a supervisor when he performs the more complex or more responsible work in a program utilizing several computer programmers or computer operators would be exempt activity.

(e) Similarly, a supervisor who spot checks and examines the work of his subordinates to determine whether they are performing their duties properly, and whether the product is satisfactory, is performing work which is directly and closely related to his managerial and supervisory functions. However, this kind of examining and checking must be distinguished from the kind which is normally performed by an "examiner," "checker," or "inspector," and which is really a production operation rather than a part of the supervisory function. Likewise, a department manager or buyer in a retail or service establishment who goes about the sales floor observing the work of sales personnel under his supervision to determine the effectiveness of their sales techniques, checking on the quality of customer service being given, or observing customer preferences and reactions to the lines, styles, types, colors, and quality of the merchandise offered, is performing work which is directly and closely related to his managerial and supervisory functions. His actual participation, except for supervisory training or demonstration purposes, in such activities as making sales to customers, replenishing stocks of merchandise on the sales floor, removing merchandise from fitting rooms and returning to stock or shelves, however, is not. The amount of time a manager or buyer spends in the performance of such activities must be included in computing the percentage limitation on nonexempt work.

(f) Watching machines is another duty which may be exempt when performed by a supervisor under proper circumstances. Obviously the mere watching of machines in operation cannot be considered exempt work where, as in certain industries in which the machinery is largely automatic, it is an ordinary production function. Thus, an employee who watches machines for the purpose of seeing that they operate properly or for the purpose of making repairs or adjustments is performing nonexempt work. On the other hand, a supervisor who watches the operation of the machinery in his department in the sense that he "keeps an eye out for trouble" is performing work which is directly and closely related to his managerial responsibilities. Making an occasional adjustment in the machinery under such circumstances is also exempt work.

(g) A word of caution is necessary in connection with these illustrations. The recordkeeping, material distributing, setup work, machine watching and adjusting, and inspecting, examining, observing and checking referred to in the examples of exempt work are presumably the kind which are supervisory and managerial functions rather than merely "production" work. Frequently it is difficult to distinguish the managerial type from the type which is a production operation. In deciding such difficult cases it should be borne in mind that it is one of the objectives of Sec. 541.1 to exclude from the definition foremen who hold "dual" or combination jobs. (See discussion of working foremen in Sec. 541.115.) Thus, if work of this kind takes up a large part of the employee's time it would be evidence that management of the department is not the primary duty of the employee, that such work is a production operation rather than a function directly and closely related to the supervisory or managerial duties, and that the employee is in reality a combination foreman-"setup" man, foreman-machine adjuster (or mechanic), or foreman-examiner, floorman-salesperson, etc., rather than a bona fide executive.

Section 541.109 Emergencies.

(a) Under certain occasional emergency conditions, work which is normally performed by nonexempt employees and is nonexempt in nature will be directly and closely related to the performance of the exempt functions of management and supervision and will therefore be exempt work. In effect, this means that a bona fide executive who performs work of a normally nonexempt nature on rare occasions because of the existence of a real emergency will not, because of the performance of such emergency work, lose the exemption. Bona fide executives include among their responsibilities the safety of the employees under their supervision, the preservation and protection of the merchandise, machinery or other property of the department or subdivision in their charge from damage due to unforeseen circumstances, and the prevention of widespread breakdown in production, sales, or service operations. Consequently, when conditions beyond control arise which threaten the safety of the employees, or a cessation of operations, or serious damage to the employer's property, any manual or other normally nonexempt work performed in an effort to prevent such results is considered exempt work and is not included in computing the percentage limitation on nonexempt work.

(b) The rule in paragraph (a) of this section is not applicable, however, to nonexempt work arising out of occurrences which are not beyond control or for which the employer can reasonably provide in the normal course of business.

(c) A few illustrations may be helpful in distinguishing routine work performed as a result of real emergencies of the kind for which no provision can practicably be made by the employer in advance of their occurrence and routine work which is not in this category. It is obvious that a mine superintendent who pitches in after an explosion and digs out the men who are trapped in the mine is still a bona fide executive during that week. On the other hand, the manager of a cleaning establishment who personally performs the cleaning operations on expensive garments because he fears damage to the fabrics if he allows his subordinates to handle them is not performing "emergency" work of the kind which can be considered exempt. Nor is the manager of a department in a retail store performing exempt work when he personally waits on a special or impatient customer because he fears the loss of the sale or the customer's goodwill if he allows a salesperson to serve him. The performance of nonexempt work by executives during inventory-taking, during other periods of heavy workload, or the handling of rush orders are the kinds of activities which the percentage tolerances are intended to cover. For example, pitching in on the production line in a canning plant during seasonal operations is not exempt "emergency" work even if the objective is to keep the food from spoiling. Similarly, pitching in behind the sales counter in a retail store during special sales or during Christmas or Easter or other peak sales periods is not "emergency" work, even if the objective is to improve customer service and the store's sales record. Maintenance work is not emergency work even if performed at night or during weekends. Relieving subordinates during rest or vacation periods cannot be considered in the nature of "emergency" work since the need for replacements can be anticipated. Whether replacing the subordinate at the workbench, or production line, or sales counter during the first day or partial day of an illness would be considered exempt emergency work would depend upon the circumstances in the particular case. Such factors as the size of the establishment and of the executive's department, the nature of the industry, the consequences that would flow from the failure to replace the ailing employee immediately, and the feasibility of filling the employee's place promptly would all have to be weighed.

(d) All the regular cleaning up around machinery, even when necessary to prevent fire or explosion, is not "emergency" work. However, the removal by an executive of dirt or obstructions constituting a hazard to life or property need not be included in computing the percentage limitation if it is not reasonably practicable for anyone but the supervisor to perform the work and it is the kind of "emergency" which has not been recurring. The occasional performance of repair work in case of a breakdown of machinery, or the collapse of a display rack, or damage to or exceptional disarray of merchandise caused by accident or a customer's carelessness may be considered exempt work if the breakdown is one which the employer cannot reasonably anticipate. However, recurring breakdowns or disarrays requiring frequent attention, such as that of an old belt or machine which breaks down repeatedly or merchandise displays constantly requiring re-sorting or straightening, are the kind for which provision could reasonably be made and repair of which must be considered as nonexempt.

Section 541.110 Occasional tasks.

(a) In addition to the type of work which by its very nature is readily identifiable as being directly and closely related to the performance of the supervisory and management duties, there is another type of work which may be considered directly and closely related to the performance of these duties. In many establishments the proper management of a department requires the performance of a variety of occasional, infrequently recurring tasks which cannot practicably be performed by the production workers and are usually performed by the executive. These small tasks when viewed separately without regard to their relationship to the executive's overall functions might appear to constitute nonexempt work. In reality they are the means of properly carrying out the employee's management functions and responsibilities in connection with men, materials, and production. The particular tasks are not specifically assigned to the "executive" but are performed by him in his discretion.

(b) It might be possible for the executive to take one of his subordinates away from his usual tasks, instruct and direct him in the work to be done, and wait for him to finish it. It would certainly not be practicable, however, to manage a department in this fashion. With respect to such occasional and relatively inconsequential tasks, it is the practice in industry generally for the executive to perform them rather than to delegate them to other persons. When any one of these tasks is done frequently, however, it takes on the character of a regular production function which could be performed by a nonexempt employee and must be counted as nonexempt work. In determining whether such work is directly and closely related to the performance of the management duties, consideration should be given to whether it is: (1) The same as the work performed by any of the subordinates of the executive; or (2) a specifically assigned task of the executive employees; or (3) practicably delegable to nonexempt employees in the establishment; or (4) repetitive and frequently recurring.

Section 541.111 Nonexempt work generally.

(a) As indicated in Sec. 541.101 the term "nonexempt work," as used in this subpart, includes all work other than that described in Sec. 541.1 (a) through (d) and the activities directly and closely related to such work.

(b) Nonexempt work is easily identifiable where, as in the usual case, it consists of work of the same nature as that performed by the nonexempt subordinates of the "executive." It is more difficult to identify in cases where supervisory employees spend a significant amount of time in activities not performed by any of their subordinates and not consisting of actual supervision and management. In such cases careful analysis of the employee's duties with reference to the phrase "directly and closely related to the performance of the work described in paragraphs (a) through (d) of this section" will usually be necessary in arriving at a determination.

Section 541.112 Percentage limitations on nonexempt work.

(a) An employee will not qualify for exemption as an executive if he devotes more than 20 percent, or in the case of an employee of a retail or service establishment if he devotes as much as 40 percent, of his hours worked in the workweek to nonexempt work. This test is applied on a workweek basis and the percentage of time spent on nonexempt work is computed on the time worked by the employee.

(b)(1) The maximum allowance of 20 percent for nonexempt work applies unless the establishment by which the employee is employed qualifies for the higher allowance as a retail or service establishment within the meaning of the Act. Such an establishment must be a distinct physical place of business, open to the general public, which is engaged on the premises in making sales of goods or services to which the concept of retail selling or servicing applies. As defined in section 13(a)(2) of the Act, such an establishment must make at least 75 percent of its annual dollar volume of sales of goods or services from sales that are both not for resale and recognized as retail in the particular industry. Types of establishments which may meet these tests include stores selling consumer goods to the public; hotels; motels; restaurants; some types of amusement or recreational establishments (but not those offering wagering or gambling facilities); hospitals, or institutions primarily engaged in the care of the sick, the aged, the mentally ill, or defective residing on the premises, if open to the general public; public parking lots and parking garages; auto repair shops; gasoline service stations (but not truck stops); funeral homes; cemeteries; etc. Further explanation and illustrations of the establishments included in the term "retail or service establishment" as used in the Act may be found in part 779 of this chapter.

(2) Public and private elementary and secondary schools and institutions of higher education are, as a rule, not retail or service establishments, because they are not engaged in sales of goods or services to which the retail concept applies. Under section 13(a)(2)(iii) of the Act prior to the 1966 amendments, it was possible for private schools for physically or mentally handicapped or gifted children to qualify as retail or service establishments if they met the statutory tests, because the special types of services provided to their students were considered by Congress to be of a kind that may be recognized as retail. Such schools, unless the nature of their operations has changed, may continue to qualify as retail or service establishments and, if they do, may utilize the greater tolerance for nonexempt work provided for executive and administrative employees of retail or service establishments under section 13(a)(1) of the Act.

(3) The legislative history of the Act makes it plain that an establishment engaged in laundering, cleaning, or repairing clothing or fabrics is not a retail or service establishment. When the Act was amended in 1949, Congress excluded such establishments from the exemption under section 13(a)(2) because of the lack of a retail concept in the services sold by such establishments, and provided a separate exemption for them which did not depend on status as a retailer. Again in 1966, when this exemption was repealed, Congress made it plain by exclusionary language that the exemption for retail or service establishments was not to be applied to laundries or dry cleaners.

(c) There are two special exceptions to the percentage limitations of paragraph (a) of this section:

(1) That relating to the employee in "sole charge" of an independent or branch establishment, and

(2) That relating to an employee owning a 20-percent interest in the enterprise in which he is employed. These except the employee only from the percentage limitations on nonexempt work. They do not except the employee from any of the other requirements of Sec. 541.1. Thus, while the percentage limitations on nonexempt work are not applicable, it is clear that an employee would not qualify for the exemption if he performs so much nonexempt work that he could no longer meet the requirement of Sec. 541.1(a) that his primary duty must consist of the management of the enterprise in which he is employed or of a customarily recognized department or subdivision thereof.

Section 541.113 Sole-charge exception.

(a) An exception from the percentage limitations on nonexempt work is provided in Sec. 541.1(e) for "an employee who is in sole charge of an independent establishment or a physically separated branch establishment * * *". Such an employee is considered to be employed in a bona fide executive capacity even though he exceeds the applicable percentage limitation on nonexempt work.

(b) The term "independent establishment" must be given full weight. The establishment must have a fixed location and must be geographically separated from other company property. The management of operations within one among several buildings located on a single or adjoining tracts of company property does not qualify for the exemption under this heading. In the case of a branch, there must be a true and complete physical separation from the main office.

(c)(1) A determination as to the status as "an independent establishment or a physically separated branch establishment" of any part of the business operations on the premises of a retail or other establishment, however, must be made on the basis of the physical and economic facts in the particular situation. (See 29 CFR 779.225, 779.305, 779.306.) A leased department cannot be considered to be a separate establishment where, for example, it and the retail store in which it is located operate under a common trade name and the store may determine, or have the power to determine, the leased department's space location, the type of merchandise it will sell its pricing policy, its hours of operation and some or all of its hiring, firing, and other personnel policies, and matters such as advertising, adjustment, and credit operations, insurance and taxes, are handled on a unified basis by the store.

(2) A leased department may qualify as a separate establishment, however, where, among other things, the facts show that the lessee maintains a separate entrance and operates under a separate name, with its own separate employees and records, and in other respects conducts his business independently of the lessor's. In such a case the leased department would enjoy the same status as a physically separated branch store.

(d) Since the employee must be in "sole charge, only one person in any establishment can qualify as an executive under this exception, and then only if he is the top person in charge at that location. (It is possible for other persons in the same establishment to qualify for exemption as executive employees, but not under the exception from the nonexempt work limitation.) Thus, it would not be applicable to an employee who is in charge of a branch establishment but whose superior makes his office on the premises. An example is a district manager who has overall supervisory functions in relation to a number of branch offices, but makes his office at one of the branches. The branch manager at the branch where the district manager's office is located is not in "sole charge" of the establishment and does not come within the exception. This does not mean that the "sole-charge" status of an employee will be considered lost because of an occasional visit to the branch office of the superior of the person in charge, or, in the case of an independent establishment by the visit for a short period on 1 or 2 days a week of the proprietor or principal corporate officer of the establishment. In these situations the sole-charge status of the employee in question will appear from the facts as to his functions, particularly in the intervals between visits. If, during these intervals, the decisions normally made by an executive in charge of a branch or an independent establishment are reserved for the superior, the employee is not in sole charge. If such decisions are not reserved for the superior, the sole-charge status will not be lost merely because of the superior's visits.

(e) In order to qualify for the exception the employee must ordinarily be in charge of all the company activities at the location where he is employed. If he is in charge of only a portion of the company's activities at his location, then he cannot be said to be in sole charge of an independent establishment or a physically separated branch establishment. In exceptional cases the divisions have found that an executive employee may be in sole charge of all activities at a branch office except that one independent function which is not integrated with those managed by the executive is also performed at the branch. This one function is not important to the activities managed by the executive and constitutes only an insignificant portion of the employer's activities at that branch. A typical example of this type of situation is one in which "desk space" in a warehouse otherwise devoted to the storage and shipment of parts is assigned a salesman who reports to the sales manager or other company official located at the home office. Normally only one employee (at most two or three, but in any event an insignificant number when compared with the total number of persons employed at the branch) is engaged in the nonintegrated function for which the executive whose sole-charge status is in question is not responsible. Under such circumstances the employee does not lose his "sole-charge" status merely because of the desk-space assignment.

Section 541.115 Working foremen.

(a) The primary purpose of the exclusionary language placing a limitation on the amount of nonexempt work is to distinguish between the bona fide executive and the "working" foreman or "working" supervisor who regularly performs "production" work or other work which is unrelated or only remotely related to his supervisory activities. (The term "working" foreman is used in this subpart in the sense indicated in the text and should not be construed to mean only one who performs work similar to that performed by his subordinates.)

(b) One type of working foreman or working supervisor most commonly found in industry works alongside his subordinates. Such employees, sometimes known as strawbosses, or gang or group leaders perform the same kind of work as that performed by their subordinates, and also carry on supervisory functions. Clearly, the work of the same nature as that performed by the employees' subordinates must be counted as nonexempt work and if the amount of such work performed is substantial the exemption does not apply. ("Substantial," as used in this section, means more than 20 percent. See discussion of the 20-percent limitation on nonexempt work in Sec. 541.112.) A foreman in a dress shop, for example, who operates a sewing machine to produce the product is performing clearly nonexempt work. However, this should not be confused with the operation of a sewing machine by a foreman to instruct his subordinates in the making of a new product, such as a garment, before it goes into production.

(c) Another type of working foreman or working supervisor who cannot be classed as a bona fide executive is one who spends a substantial amount of time in work which, although not performed by his own subordinates, consists of ordinary production work or other routine, recurrent, repetitive tasks which are a regular part of his duties. Such an employee is in effect holding a dual job. He may be, for example, a combination foreman-production worker, supervisor-clerk, or foreman combined with some other skilled or unskilled occupation. His nonsupervisory duties in such instances are unrelated to anything he must do to supervise the employees under him or to manage the department. They are in many instances mere "fill-in" tasks performed because the job does not involve sufficient executive duties to occupy an employee's full time. In other instances the nonsupervisory, nonmanagerial duties may be the principal ones and the supervisory or managerial duties are subordinate and are assigned to the particular employee because it is more convenient to rest the responsibility for the first line of supervision in the hands of the person who performs these other duties. Typical of employees in dual jobs which may involve a substantial amount of nonexempt work are:

(1) Foremen or supervisors who also perform one or more of the "production" or "operating" functions, though no other employees in the plant perform such work. An example of this kind of employee is the foreman in a

millinery or garment plant who is also the cutter, or the foreman in a garment factory who operates a multiple-needle machine not requiring a full-time operator;

(2) Foremen or supervisors who have as a regular part of their duties the adjustment, repair, or maintenance of machinery or equipment. Examples in this category are the foreman-fixer in the hosiery industry who devotes a considerable amount of time to making adjustments and repairs to the machines of his subordinates, or the planer-mill foreman who is also the "machine man" who repairs the machines and grinds the knives;

(3) Foremen or supervisors who perform clerical work other than the maintenance of the time and production records of their subordinates; for example, the foreman of the shipping room who makes out the bills of lading and other shipping records, the warehouse foreman who also acts as inventory clerk, the head shipper who also has charge of a finished goods stock room, assisting in placing goods on shelves and keeping perpetual inventory records, or the office manager, head bookkeeper, or chief clerk who performs routine bookkeeping. There is no doubt that the head bookkeeper, for example, who spends a substantial amount of his time keeping books of the same general nature as those kept by the other bookkeepers, even though his books are confidential in nature or cover different transactions from the books maintained by the under bookkeepers, is not primarily an executive employee and should not be so considered.

Section 541.116 Trainees, executive.

The exemption is applicable to an employee employed in a bona fide executive capacity and does not include employees training to become executives and not actually performing the duties of an executive.

Section 541.117 Amount of salary required.

(a) Except as otherwise noted in paragraph (b) of this section, compensation on a salary basis at a rate of not less than $155 per week, exclusive of board, lodging, or other facilities, is required for exemption as an executive. The $155 a week may be translated into equivalent amounts for periods longer than 1 week. The requirement will be met if the employee is compensated biweekly on a salary basis of $310, semimonthly on a salary basis of $335.84 or monthly on a salary basis of $671.67. However, the shortest period of payment which will meet the requirement of payment "on a salary basis" is a week.

(b) In Puerto Rico, the Virgin Islands, and American Samoa, the salary test for exemption as an "executive" is $130 per week for other than an employee of the Federal Government.

(c) The payment of the required salary must be exclusive of board, lodging, or other facilities; that is, free and clear. On the other hand, the regulations in subpart A of this part do not prohibit the sale of such facilities to executives on a cash basis if they are negotiated in the same manner as similar transactions with other persons.

(d) The validity of including a salary requirement in the regulations in subpart A of this part has been sustained in a number of appellate court decisions. *See*, for example, *Walling v. Yeakley*, 140 F. (2d) 830 (C.A. 10); *Helliwell v. Haberman*, 140 F. (2d) 833 (C.A. 2); and *Walling v. Morris*, 155 F. (2d) 832 (C.A. 6) (reversed on another point in 332 U.S. 442); *Wirtz v. Mississippi Publishers*, 364 F. (2d) 603 (C.A. 5); *Craig v. Far West Engineering Co.*, 265 F. (2d) 251 (C.A. 9) cert. den. 361 U.S. 816; *Hofer v. Federal Cartridge Corp.*, 71 F. Supp. 243 (D.C. Minn.).

Section 541.118 Salary basis.

(a) An employee will be considered to be paid "on a salary basis" within the meaning of the regulations if under his employment agreement he regularly receives each pay period on a weekly, or less frequent basis, a predetermined amount constituting all or part of his compensation, which amount is not subject to reduction because of variations in the quality or quantity of the work performed. Subject to the exceptions provided below, the employee must receive his full salary for any week in which he performs any work without regard to the number of days or hours worked. This policy is also subject to the general rule that an employee need not be paid for any workweek in which he performs no work.

(1) An employee will not be considered to be "on a salary basis" if deductions from his predetermined compensation are made for absences occasioned by the employer or by the operating requirements of the business. Accordingly, if the employee is ready, willing, and able to work, deductions may not be made for time when work is not available.

(2) Deductions may be made, however, when the employee absents himself from work for a day or more for personal reasons, other than sickness or accident. Thus, if an employee is absent for a day or longer to handle personal affairs, his salaried status will not be affected if deductions are made from his salary for such absences.

(3) Deductions may also be made for absences of a day or more occasioned by sickness or disability (including industrial accidents) if the deduction is made in accordance with a bona fide plan, policy or practice of providing compensation for loss of salary occasioned by both sickness and disability. Thus, if the employer's particular plan, policy or practice provides compensation for such absences, deductions for absences of a day or longer because of sickness or disability may be made before an employee has qualified under such plan, policy or practice, and after he has exhausted his leave allowance thereunder. It is not required that the employee be paid any portion of his salary for such days or days for which he receives compensation for leave under such plan, policy or practice. Similarly, if the employer operates under a State sickness and disability insurance law, or a private sickness and disability insurance plan, deductions may be made for absences of a working day or longer if benefits are provided in accordance with the particular law or plan. In the case of an industrial accident, the "salary basis" requirement will be met if the employee is compensated for loss of salary in accordance with the applicable compensation law or the plan adopted by the employer, provided the employer also has some plan, policy or practice of

providing compensation for sickness and disability other than that relating to industrial accidents.

(4) Deductions may not be made for absences of an employee caused by jury duty, attendance as a witness, or temporary military leave. The employer may, however, offset any amounts received by an employee as jury or witness fees or military pay for a particular week against the salary due for that particular week without loss of the exemption.

(5) Penalties imposed in good faith for infractions of safety rules of major significance will not affect the employee's salaried status. Safety rules of major significance include only those relating to the prevention of serious danger to the plant, or other employees, such as rules prohibiting smoking in explosive plants, oil refineries, and coal mines.

(6) The effect of making a deduction which is not permitted under these interpretations will depend upon the facts in the particular case. Where deductions are generally made when there is no work available, it indicates that there was no intention to pay the employee on a salary basis. In such a case the exemption would not be applicable to him during the entire period when such deductions were being made. On the other hand, where a deduction not permitted by these interpretations is inadvertent, or is made for reasons other than lack of work, the exemption will not be considered to have been lost if the employer reimburses the employee for such deductions and promises to comply in the future.

(b) *Minimum guarantee plus extras.* It should be noted that the salary may consist of a predetermined amount constituting all or part of the employee's compensation. In other words, additional compensation besides the salary is not inconsistent with the salary basis of payment. The requirement will be met, for example, by a branch manager who receives a salary of $155 or more a week and in addition, a commission of 1 percent of the branch sales. The requirement will also be met by a branch manager who receives a percentage of the sales or profits of the branch, if the employment arrangement also includes a guarantee of at least the minimum weekly salary (or the equivalent for a monthly or other period) required by the regulations. Another type of situation in which the requirement will be met is that of an employee paid on a daily or shift basis, if the employment arrangement includes a provision that the employee will receive not less than the amount specified in the regulations in any week in which the employee performs any work. Such arrangements are subject to the exceptions in paragraph (a) of this section. The test of payment on a salary basis will not be met, however, if the salary is divided into two parts for the purpose of circumventing the requirement of payment "on a salary basis". For example, a salary of $200 in each week in which any work is performed, and an additional $50 which is made subject to deductions which, are not permitted under paragraph (a) of this section.

(c) *Initial and terminal weeks.* Failure to pay the full salary in the initial or terminal week of employment is not considered inconsistent with the salary basis of payment. In such weeks the payment of a proportionate part of the employee's salary for the time actually worked will meet the requirement. However, this should not be construed to mean that an employee is on a salary basis within the meaning of the regulations if he is employed occasionally for a few days and is paid a proportionate part of the weekly salary when so employed. Moreover, even payment of the full weekly salary under such circumstances would not meet the requirement, since casual or occasional employment for a few days at a time is inconsistent with employment on a salary basis within the meaning of the regulations.

Section 541.119 Special proviso for high salaried executives.

(a) Except as otherwise noted in paragraph (b) of this section, Sec. 541.1 contains an upset or high salary proviso for managerial employees who are compensated on a salary basis at a rate of not less than $250 per week exclusive of board, lodging, or other facilities. Such a highly paid employee is deemed to meet all the requirements in paragraphs (a) through (f) of Sec. 541.1 if the employee's primary duty consists of the management of the enterprise in which employed or of a customarily recognized department or subdivision thereof and includes the customary and regular direction of the work of two or more other employees therein. If an employee qualifies for exemption under this proviso, it is not necessary to test that employee's qualifications in detail under paragraphs (a) through (f) of Sec. 541.1 of this part.

(b) In Puerto Rico, the Virgin Islands, and American Samoa the proviso of Sec. 541.1(f) applies to those managerial employees (other than employees of the Federal Government) who are paid on a salary basis at a rate of not less than $200 per week.

(c) Mechanics, carpenters, linotype operators, or craftsmen of other kinds are not exempt under the proviso no matter how highly paid they might be.

Employee Employed in a Bona Fide Administrative Capacity

Section 541.201 Types of administrative employees.

(a) Three types of employees are described in Sec. 541.2(c) who, if they meet the other tests in Sec. 541.2, qualify for exemption as "administrative" employees.

(1) Executive and administrative assistants. The first type is the assistant to a proprietor or to an executive or administrative employee. In modern industrial practice there has been a steady and increasing use of persons who assist an executive in the performance of his duties without themselves having executive authority. Typical titles of persons in this group are executive assistant to the president, confidential assistant, executive secretary, assistant to the general manager, administrative assistant and, in retail or service establishments, assistant manager and assistant buyer. Generally speaking, such assistants are found in large establishments where the official assisted has duties of such scope and which require so much attention that the work of personal scrutiny, correspondence, and interviews must be delegated.

(2) Staff employees.

(i) Employees included in the second alternative in the definition are those who can be described as staff rather than line employees, or as functional rather than departmental heads. They include among others employees who act as advisory specialists to the management. Typical examples of such advisory specialists are tax experts, insurance experts, sales research experts, wage-rate analysts, investment consultants, foreign exchange consultants, and statisticians.

(ii) Also included are persons who are in charge of a so-called functional department, which may frequently be a one-man department. Typical examples of such employees are credit managers, purchasing agents, buyers, safety directors, personnel directors, and labor relations directors.

(3) Those who perform special assignments.

(i) The third group consists of persons who perform special assignments. Among them are to be found a number of persons whose work is performed away from the employer's place of business. Typical titles of such persons are lease buyers, field representatives of utility companies, location managers of motion picture companies, and district gaugers for oil companies. It should be particularly noted that this is a field which is rife with honorific titles that do not adequately portray the nature of the employee's duties. The field representative of a utility company, for example, may be a "glorified serviceman."

(ii) This classification also includes employees whose special assignments are performed entirely or partly inside their employer's place of business. Examples are special organization planners, customers' brokers in stock exchange firms, so-called account executives in advertising firms and contact or promotion men of various types.

(b) Job titles insufficient as yardsticks. (1) The employees for whom exemption is sought under the term "administrative" have extremely diverse functions and a wide variety of titles. A title alone is of little or no assistance in determining the true importance of an employee to the employer or his exempt or nonexempt status under the regulations in subpart A of this part. Titles can be had cheaply and are of no determinative value. Thus, while there are supervisors of production control (whose decisions affect the welfare of large numbers of employees) who qualify for exemption under section 13(a)(1), it is not hard to call a rate setter (whose functions are limited to timing certain operations and jotting down times on a standardized form) a "methods engineer" or a "production-control supervisor."

(2) Many more examples could be cited to show that titles are insufficient as yardsticks. As has been indicated previously, the exempt or nonexempt status of any particular employee must be determined on the basis of whether his duties, responsibilities, and salary meet all the requirements of the appropriate section of the regulations in subpart A of this part.

(c) Individuals engaged in the overall academic administration of an elementary or secondary school system include the superintendent or other head of the system and those of his assistants whose duties are primarily concerned with administration of such matters as curriculum, quality and methods of instructing, measuring and testing the learning potential and achievement of students, establishing and maintaining academic and grading standards, and other aspects of the teaching program. In individual school establishments those engaged in overall academic administration include the principal and the vice principals who are responsible for the operation of the school. Other employees engaged in academic administration are such department heads as the heads of the mathematics department, the English department, the foreign language department, the manual crafts department, and the like. Institutions of higher education have similar organizational structure, although in many cases somewhat more complex.

Section 541.202 Categories of work.

(a) The work generally performed by employees who perform administrative tasks may be classified into the following general categories for purposes of the definition: (This classification is without regard to whether the work is manual or nonmanual. The problem of manual work as it affects the exemption of administrative employees is discussed in Sec. 541.203.) (1) The work specifically described in paragraphs (a), (b), and (c) of Sec. 541.2; (2) routine work which is directly and closely related to the performance of the work which is described in paragraphs (a), (b), and (c) of Sec. 541.2; and (3) routine work which is not related or is only remotely related to the administrative duties. (As used in this subpart the phrase "routine work" means work which does not require the exercise of discretion and independent judgment. It is not necessarily restricted to work which is repetitive in nature.)

(b) The work in category 1, that which is specifically described in Sec. 541.2 as requiring the exercise of discretion and independent judgment, is clearly exempt in nature.

(c) Category 2 consists of work which if separated from the work in category 1 would appear to be routine, or on a fairly low level, and which does not itself require the exercise of discretion and independent judgment, but which has a direct and close relationship to the performance of the more important duties. The directness and closeness of the relationship may vary depending upon the nature of the job and the size and organization of the establishment in which the work is performed. This "directly and closely related" work includes routine work which necessarily arises out of the administrative duties, and the routine work without which the employee's more important work cannot be performed properly. It also includes a variety of routine tasks which may not be essential to the proper performance of the more important duties but which are functionally related to them directly and closely. In this latter category are activities which an administrative employee may reasonably be expected to perform in connection with carrying out his administrative functions including duties which either facilitate or arise incidentally from the performance of such functions and are commonly performed in connection with them.

(d) These "directly and closely related" duties are distinguishable from the last group, category 3, those which are remotely related or completely unrelated to the more important tasks. The work in this last category is nonexempt and must not exceed the 20-percent limitation for nonexempt work (up to 40 percent or service establishment) if the exemption is to apply.

(e) Work performed by employees in the capacity of "academic administrative" personnel is a category of administrative work limited to a class of employees engaged in academic administration as contrasted with the general use of "administrative" in the act. The term "academic administrative" denotes administration relating to the academic operations and functions in a school rather than to administration along the lines of general business operations. Academic administrative personnel are performing operations directly in the field of education. Jobs relating to areas outside the educational field are not within the definition of academic administration. Examples of jobs in school systems, and educational establishments and institutions, which are outside the term academic administration are jobs relating to building management and maintenance, jobs relating to the health of the students and academic staff such as social workers, psychologist, lunch room manager, or dietitian. Employees in such work which is not considered academic administration may qualify for exemption under other provisions of Sec. 541.2 or under other sections of the regulations in subpart A of this part provided the requirements for such exemptions are met.

Section 541.203 Nonmanual work.

(a) The requirement that the work performed by an exempt administrative employee must be office work or nonmanual work restricts the exemption to "white-collar" employees who meet the tests. If the work performed is "office" work it is immaterial whether it is manual or nonmanual in nature. This is consistent with the intent to include within the term "administrative" only employees who are basically white-collar employees since the accepted usage of the term "white-collar" includes all office workers. Persons employed in the routine operation of office machines are engaged in office work within the meaning of Sec. 541.2 (although they would not qualify as administrative employees since they do not meet the other requirements of Sec. 541.2).

(b) Section 541.2 does not completely prohibit the performance of manual work by an "administrative" employee. The performance by an otherwise exempt administrative employee of some manual work which is directly and closely related to the work requiring the exercise of discretion and independent judgment is not inconsistent with the principle that the exemption is limited to "white-collar" employees. However, if the employee performs so much manual work (other than office work) that he cannot be said to be basically a "white-collar" employee he does not qualify for exemption as a bona fide administrative employee, even if the manual work he performs is directly and closely related to the work requiring the exercise of discretion and independent judgment. Thus, it is obvious that employees who spend most of their time in using tools, instruments, machinery, or other equipment, or in performing repetitive operations with their hands, no matter how much skill is required, would not be bona fide administrative employees within the meaning of Sec. 541.2. An office employee, on the other hand, is a "white-collar" worker, and would not lose the exemption on the grounds that he is not primarily engaged in "nonmanual" work, although he would lose the exemption if he failed to meet any of the other requirements.

Section 541.205 Directly related to management policies or general business operations.

(a) The phrase "directly related to management policies or general business operations of his employer or his employer's customers" describes those types of activities relating to the administrative operations of a business as distinguished from "production" or, in a retail or service establishment, "sales" work. In addition to describing the types of activities, the phrase limits the exemption to persons who perform work of substantial importance to the management or operation of the business of his employer or his employer's customers.

(b) The administrative operations of the business include the work performed by so-called white-collar employees engaged in "servicing" a business as, for, example, advising the management, planning, negotiating, representing the company, purchasing, promoting sales, and business research and control. An employee performing such work is engaged in activities relating to the administrative operations of the business notwithstanding that he is employed as an administrative assistant to an executive in the production department of the business.

(c) As used to describe work of substantial importance to the management or operation of the business, the phrase "directly related to management policies or general business operations" is not limited to persons who participate in the formulation of management policies or in the operation of the business as a whole. Employees whose work is "directly related" to management policies or to general business operations include those whose work affects policy or whose responsibility it is to execute or carry it out. The phrase also includes a wide variety of persons who either carry out major assignments in conducting the operations of the business, or whose work affects business operations to a substantial degree, even though their assignments are tasks related to the operation of a particular segment of the business.

(1) It is not possible to lay down specific rules that will indicate the precise point at which work becomes of substantial importance to the management or operation of a business. It should be clear that the cashier of a bank performs work at a responsible level and may therefore be said to be performing work directly related to management policies or general business operations. On the other hand, the bank teller does not. Likewise it is clear that bookkeepers, secretaries, and clerks of various kinds hold the run-of-the-mine positions in any ordinary business and are not performing work directly related to management policies or general business operations. On the other hand, a tax consultant employed either by an individual company or by a firm of consultants is ordinarily doing work of substantial importance to the management or operation of a business.

(2) An employee performing routine clerical duties obviously is not performing work of substantial importance to the management or operation of

the business even though he may exercise some measure of discretion and judgment as to the manner in which he performs his clerical tasks. A messenger boy who is entrusted with carrying large sums of money or securities cannot be said to be doing work of importance to the business even though serious consequences may flow from his neglect. An employee operating very expensive equipment may cause serious loss to his employer by the improper performance of his duties. An inspector, such as, for example, an inspector for an insurance company, may cause loss to his employer by the failure to perform his job properly. But such employees, obviously, are not performing work of such substantial importance to the management or operation of the business that it can be said to be "directly related to management policies or general business operations" as that phrase is used in Sec. 541.2.

(3) Some firms employ persons whom they describe as "statisticians." If all such a person does, in effect, is to tabulate data, he is clearly not exempt. However, if such an employee makes analyses of data and draws conclusions which are important to the determination of, or which, in fact, determine financial, merchandising, or other policy, clearly he is doing work directly related to management policies or general business operations. Similarly, a personnel employee may be a clerk at a hiring window of a plant, or he may be a man who determines or effects personnel policies affecting all the workers in the establishment. In the latter case, he is clearly doing work directly related to management policies or general business operations. These examples illustrate the two extremes. In each case, between these extreme types there are many employees whose work may be of substantial importance to the management or operation of the business, depending upon the particular facts.

(4) Another example of an employee whose work may be important to the welfare of the business is a buyer of a particular article or equipment in an industrial plant or personnel commonly called assistant buyers in retail or service establishments. Where such work is of substantial importance to the management or operation of the business, even though it may be limited to purchasing for a particular department of the business, it is directly related to management policies or general business operations.

(5) The test of "directly related to management policies or general business operations" is also met by many persons employed as advisory specialists and consultants of various kinds, credit managers, safety directors, claim agents and adjusters, wage-rate analysts, tax experts, account executives of advertising agencies, customers' brokers in stock exchange firms, promotion men, and many others.

(6) It should be noted in this connection that an employer's volume of activities may make it necessary to employ a number of employees in some of these categories. The fact that there are a number of other employees of the same employer carrying out assignments of the same relative importance or performing identical work does not affect the determination of whether they meet this test so long as the work of each such employee is of substantial importance to the management or operation of the business.

(7) In the data processing field some firms employ persons described as systems analysts and computer programmers. If such employees are concerned with the planning, scheduling, and coordination of activities which are required to develop systems for processing data to obtain solutions to complex business, scientific, or engineering problems of his employer or his employer's customers, he is clearly doing work directly related to management policies or general business operations.

(d) Under Sec. 541.2 the "management policies or general business operations" may be those of the employer or the employer's customers. For example, many bona fide administrative employees perform important functions as advisers and consultants but are employed by a concern engaged in furnishing such services for a fee. Typical instances are tax experts, labor relations consultants, financial consultants, systems analysts, or resident buyers. Such employees, if they meet the other requirements of Sec. 541.2, qualify for exemption regardless of whether the management policies or general business operations to which their work is directly related are those of their employer's clients or customers or those of their employer.

Section 541.206 Primary duty.

(a) The definition of "administrative" exempts only employees who are primarily engaged in the responsible work which is characteristic of employment in a bona fide administrative capacity. Thus, the employee must have as his primary duty office or nonmanual work directly related to management policies or general business operations of his employer or his employer's customers, or, in the case of "academic administrative personnel," the employee must have as his primary duty work that is directly related to academic administration or general academic operations of the school in whose operations he is employed.

(b) In determining whether an employee's exempt work meets the "primary duty" requirement, the principles explained in Sec. 541.103 in the discussion of "primary duty" under the definition of "executive" are applicable.

Section 541.207 Discretion and independent judgment.

(a) In general, the exercise of discretion and independent judgment involves the comparison and the evaluation of possible courses of conduct and acting or making a decision after the various possibilities have been considered. The term as used in the regulations in subpart A of this part, moreover, implies that the person has the authority or power to make an independent choice, free from immediate direction or supervision and with respect to matters of significance. (Without actually attempting to define the term, the courts have given it this meaning in applying it in particular cases. *See*, for example, *Walling v. Sterling Ice Co.*, 69 F. Supp. 655, reversed on other grounds, 165 F. (2d) 265 (CCA 10). *See* also *Connell v. Delaware Aircraft Industries*, 55 Atl. (2d) 637.)

(b) The term must be applied in the light of all the facts involved in the particular employment situation in which the question arises. It has been most frequently misunderstood and misapplied by employers and employees in cases involving the following: (1) Confusion between the exercise of discretion and independent judgment, and the use of skill in applying techniques, procedures, or specific standards; and (2) misapplication of the term to employees making decisions relating to matters of little consequence.

(c) Distinguished from skills and procedures:

(1) Perhaps the most frequent cause of misapplication of the term "discretion and independent judgment" is the failure to distinguish it from the use of skill in various respects. An employee who merely applies his knowledge in following prescribed procedures or determining which procedure to follow, or who determines whether specified standards are met or whether an object falls into one or another of a number of definite grades, classes, or other categories, with or without the use of testing or measuring devices, is not exercising discretion and independent judgment within the meaning of Sec. 541.2. This is true even if there is some leeway in reaching a conclusion, as when an acceptable standard includes a range or a tolerance above or below a specific standard.

(2) A typical example of the application of skills and procedures is ordinary inspection work of various kinds. Inspectors normally perform specialized work along standardized lines involving well-established techniques and procedures which may have been cataloged and described in manuals or other sources. Such inspectors rely on techniques and skills acquired by special training or experience. They may have some leeway in the performance of their work but only within closely prescribed limits. Employees of this type may make recommendations on the basis of the information they develop in the course of their inspections (as for example, to accept or reject an insurance risk or a product manufactured to specifications), but these recommendations are based on the development of the facts as to whether there is conformity with the prescribed standards. In such cases a decision to depart from the prescribed standards or the permitted tolerance is typically made by the inspector's superior. The inspector is engaged in exercising skill rather than discretion and independent judgment within the meaning of the regulations in Subpart A of this part.

(3) A related group of employees usually called examiners or graders perform similar work involving the comparison of products with established standards which are frequently cataloged. Often, after continued reference to the written standards, or through experience, the employee acquires sufficient knowledge so that reference to written standards is unnecessary. The substitution of the employee's memory for the manual of standards does not convert the character of the work performed to work requiring the exercise of discretion and independent judgment as required by the regulations in subpart A of this part. The mere fact that the employee uses his knowledge and experience does not change his decision, i.e., that the product does or does not conform with the established standard, into a real decision in a significant matter.

(4) For example, certain "graders" of lumber turn over each "stick" to see both sides, after which a crayon mark is made to indicate the grade. These lumber grades are well established and the employee's familiarity with them

stems from his experience and training. Skill rather than discretion and independent judgment is exercised in grading the lumber. This does not necessarily mean, however, that all employees who grade lumber or other commodities are not exercising discretion and independent judgment. Grading of commodities for which there are no recognized or established standards may require the exercise of discretion and independent judgment as contemplated by the regulations in subpart A of this part. In addition, in those situations in which an otherwise exempt buyer does grading, the grading even though routine work, may be considered exempt if it is directly and closely related to the exempt buying.

(5) Another type of situation where skill in the application of techniques and procedures is sometimes confused with discretion and independent judgment is the "screening" of applicants by a personnel clerk. Typically such an employee will interview applicants and obtain from them data regarding their qualifications and fitness for employment. These data may be entered on a form specially prepared for the purpose. The "screening" operation consists of rejecting all applicants who do not meet standards for the particular job or for employment by the company. The standards are usually set by the employee's superior or other company officials, and the decision to hire from the group of applicants who do meet the standards is similarly made by other company officials. It seems clear that such a personnel clerk does not exercise discretion and independent judgment as required by the regulations in subpart A of this part. On the other hand an exempt personnel manager will often perform similar functions; that is, he will interview applicants to obtain the necessary data and eliminate applicants who are not qualified. The personnel manager will then hire one of the qualified applicants. Thus, when the interviewing and screening are performed by the personnel manager who does the hiring they constitute exempt work, even though routine, because this work is directly and closely related to the employee's exempt functions.

(6) Similarly, comparison shopping performed by an employee of a retail store who merely reports to the buyer his findings as to the prices at which a competitor's store is offering merchandise of the same or comparable quality does not involve the exercise of discretion and judgment as required in the regulations. Discretion and judgment are exercised, however, by the buyer who evaluates the assistants' reports and on the basis of their findings directs that certain items be re-priced. When performed by the buyer who actually makes the decisions which affect the buying or pricing policies of the department he manages, the comparison shopping, although in itself a comparatively routine operation, is directly and closely related to his managerial responsibility.

(7) In the data processing field a systems analyst is exercising discretion and independent judgment when he develops methods to process, for example, accounting, inventory, sales, and other business information by using electronic computers. He also exercises discretion and independent judgment when he determines the exact nature of the data processing problem, and structures the problem in a logical manner so that a system to solve the problem and obtain the desired results can be developed. Whether a computer programmer is exercising discretion and independent judgment

depends on the facts in each particular case. Every problem processed in a computer first must be carefully analyzed so that exact and logical steps for its solution can be worked out. When this preliminary work is done by a computer programmer he is exercising discretion and independent judgment. A computer programmer would also be using discretion and independent judgment when he determines exactly what information must be used to prepare the necessary documents and by ascertaining the exact form in which the information is to be presented. Examples of work not requiring the level of discretion and judgment contemplated by the regulations are highly technical and mechanical operations such as the preparation of a flow chart or diagram showing the order in which the computer must perform each operation, the preparation of instructions to the console operator who runs the computer or the actual running of the computer by the programmer, and the debugging of a program. It is clear that the duties of data processing employees such as tape librarians, keypunch operators, computer operators, junior programmers and programmer trainees are so closely supervised as to preclude the use of the required discretion and independent judgment.

(d) Decisions in significant matters.

(1) The second type of situation in which some difficulty with this phrase has been experienced relates to the level or importance of the matters with respect to which the employee may make decisions. In one sense almost every employee is required to use some discretion and independent judgment. Thus, it is frequently left to a truckdriver to decide which route to follow in going from one place to another; the shipping clerk is normally permitted to decide the method of packing and the mode of shipment of small orders; and the bookkeeper may usually decide whether he will post first to one ledger rather than another. Yet it is obvious that these decisions do not constitute the exercise of discretion and independent judgment of the level contemplated by the regulations in subpart A of this part. The divisions have consistently taken the position that decisions of this nature concerning relatively unimportant matters are not those intended by the regulations in subpart A of this part, but that the discretion and independent judgment exercised must be real and substantial, that is, they must be exercised with respect to matters of consequence. This interpretation has also been followed by courts in decisions involving the application of the regulations in this part, to particular cases.

(2) It is not possible to state a general rule which will distinguish in each of the many thousands of possible factual situations between the making of real decisions in significant matters and the making of choices involving matters of little or no consequence. It should be clear, however, that the term "discretion and independent judgment," within the meaning of the regulations in subpart A of this part, does not apply to the kinds of decisions normally made by clerical and similar types of employees. The term does apply to the kinds of decisions normally made by persons who formulate or participate in the formulation of policy within their spheres of responsibility or who exercise authority within a wide range to commit their employer in substantial respects financially or otherwise. The regulations in subpart A of this part, however, do not require the exercise of discretion and independent judgment

at so high a level. The regulations in subpart A of this part also contemplate the kind of discretion and independent judgment exercised by an administrative assistant to an executive, who without specific instructions or prescribed procedures, arranges interviews and meetings, and handles callers and meetings himself where the executive's personal attention is not required. It includes the kind of discretion and independent judgment exercised by a customer's man in a brokerage house in deciding what recommendations to make to a customer for the purchase of securities. It may include the kind of discretion and judgment exercised by buyers, certain wholesale salesmen, representatives, and other contact persons who are given reasonable latitude in carrying on negotiation on behalf of their employers.

(e) *Final decisions not necessary.* (1) The term "discretion and independent judgment" as used in the regulations in subpart A of this part does not necessarily imply that the decisions made by the employee must have a finality that goes with unlimited authority and a complete absence of review. The decisions made as a result of the exercise of discretion and independent judgment may consist of recommendations for action rather than the actual taking of action. The fact that an employee's decision may be subject to review and that upon occasion the decisions are revised or reversed after review does not mean that the employee is not exercising discretion and independent judgment within the meaning of the regulations in subpart A of this part. For example, the assistant to the president of a large corporation may regularly reply to correspondence addressed to the president. Typically, such an assistant will submit the more important replies to the president for review before they are sent out. Upon occasion, after review, the president may alter or discard the prepared reply and direct that another be sent instead. This section by the president would not, however, destroy the exempt character of the assistant's function, and does not mean that he does not exercise discretion and independent judgment in answering correspondence and in deciding which replies may be sent out without review by the president.

(2) The policies formulated by the credit manager of a large corporation may be subject to review by higher company officials who may approve or disapprove these policies. The management consultant who has made a study of the operations of a business and who has drawn a proposed change in organization, may have the plan reviewed or revised by his superiors before it is submitted to the client. The purchasing agent may be required to consult with top management officials before making a purchase commitment for raw materials in excess of the contemplated plant needs for a stated period, say 6 months. These employees exercise discretion and independent judgment within the meaning of the regulations despite the fact that their decisions or recommendations are reviewed at a higher level.

(f) *Distinguished from loss through neglect.* A distinction must also be made between the exercise of discretion and independent judgment with respect to matters of consequence and the cases where serious consequences may result from the negligence of an employee, the failure to follow instruction or procedures, the improper application of skills, or the choice of the wrong techniques. The operator of a very intricate piece of machinery, for example, may cause a complete stoppage of production or a breakdown of his very expensive machine merely by pressing the wrong button. A bank teller who is engaged in receipt and disbursement of money at a teller's window and in related routine bookkeeping duties may, by crediting the wrong account with a deposit, cause his employer to suffer a large financial loss. An inspector charged with responsibility for loading oil onto a ship may, by not applying correct techniques fail to notice the presence of foreign ingredients in the tank with resulting contamination of the cargo and serious loss to his employer. In these cases, the work of the employee does not require the exercise of discretion and independent judgment within the meaning of the regulations in subpart A of this part.

(g) Customarily and regularly. The work of an exempt administrative employee must require the exercise of discretion and independent judgment customarily and regularly. The phrase "customarily and regularly" signifies a frequency which must be greater than occasional but which, of course, may be less than constant. The requirement will be met by the employee who normally and recurrently is called upon to exercise and does exercise discretion and independent judgment in the day-to-day performance of his duties. The requirement is not met by the occasional exercise of discretion and independent judgment.

Section 541.208 Directly and closely related.

(a) As indicated in Sec. 541.202, work which is directly and closely related to the performance of the work described in Sec. 541.2 is considered exempt work. Some illustrations may be helpful in clarifying the differences between such work and work which is unrelated or only remotely related to the work described in Sec. 541.2.(b)(1) For purposes of illustration, the case of a high-salaried management consultant about whose exempt status as an administrative employee there is no doubt will be assumed. The particular employee is employed by a firm of consultants and performs work in which he customarily and regularly exercises discretion and independent judgment. The work consists primarily of analyzing, and recommending changes in, the business operations of his employer's client. This work falls in the category of exempt work described in Sec. 541.2.

(2) In the course of performing that work, the consultant makes extensive notes recording the flow of work and materials through the office and plant of the client. Standing alone or separated from the primary duty such notemaking would be routine in nature. However, this is work without which the more important work cannot be performed properly. It is "directly and closely related" to the administrative work and is therefore exempt work. Upon his return to the office of his employer the consultant personally types his report and draws, first in rough and then in final form, a proposed table of organization to be submitted with it. Although all this work may not be essential to the performance of his more important work, it is all directly and closely related to that work and should be considered exempt.

While it is possible to assign the typing and final drafting to nonexempt employees and in fact it is frequently the practice to do so, it is not required as a condition of exemption that it be so delegated.

(3) Finally, if because this particular employee has a special skill in such work, he also drafts tables or organization proposed by other consultants, he would then be performing routine work wholly unrelated, or at best only remotely related, to his more important work. Under such conditions, the drafting is nonexempt.

(c) Another illustration is the credit manager who makes and administers the credit policy of his employer. Establishing credit limits for customers and authorizing the shipment of orders on credit, including the decisions to exceed or otherwise vary these limits in the case of particular customers, would be exempt work of the kind specifically described in Sec. 541.2. Work which is directly and closely related to these exempt duties may include such activities as checking the status of accounts to determine whether the credit limit would be exceeded by the shipment of a new order, removing credit reports from the files for analysis and writing letters giving credit data and experience to other employers or credit agencies. On the other hand, any general office or bookkeeping work is nonexempt work. For instance, posting to the accounts receivable ledger would be only remotely related to his administrative work and must be considered nonexempt.

(d) One phase of the work of an administrative assistant to a bona fide executive or administrative employee provides another illustration. The work of determining whether to answer correspondence personally, call it to his superior's attention, or route it to someone else for reply requires the exercise of discretion and independent judgment and is exempt work of the kind described in Sec. 541.2. Opening the mail for the purpose of reading it to make the decisions indicated will be directly and closely related to the administrative work described. However, merely opening mail and placing it unread before his superior or some other person would be related only remotely, if at all, to any work requiring the exercise of discretion and independent judgment.

(e) The following additional examples may also be of value in applying these principles. A traffic manager is employed to handle the company's transportation problems. The exempt work performed by such an employee would include planning the most economical and quickest routes for shipping merchandise to and from the plant, contracting for common-carrier and other transportation facilities, negotiating with carriers for adjustments for damages to merchandise in transit and making the necessary rearrangements resulting from delays, damages, or irregularities in transit. This employee may also spend part of his time taking city orders (for local deliveries) over the telephone. The order-taking is a routine function not directly and closely related to the exempt work and must be considered nonexempt.

(f) An office manager who does not supervise two or more employees would not meet the requirements for exemption as an executive employee but may possibly qualify for exemption as an administrative employee. Such an employee may perform administrative duties, such as the executive of the employer's credit policy, the management of the company's traffic, purchasing, and other responsible office work requiring the customary and regular exercise of discretion and judgment, which are clearly exempt. On the other hand, this office manager may perform all the bookkeeping, prepare the confidential or regular payrolls, and send out monthly statements of account. These latter activities are not directly and closely related to the exempt functions and are not exempt.

Section 541.209 Percentage limitations on nonexempt work.

(a) Under Sec. 541.2(d), an employee will not qualify for exemption as an administrative employee if he devotes more than 20 percent, or, in the case of an employee of a retail or service establishment if he devotes as much as 40 percent, of his hours worked in the workweek to nonexempt work; that is, to activities which are not directly and closely related to the performance of the work described in Sec. 541.2 (a) through (c).

(b) This test is applied on a workweek basis and the percentage of time spent on nonexempt work is computed on the time worked by the employee.

(c) The tolerance for nonexempt work allows the performance of nonexempt manual or nonmanual work within the percentages allowed for all types of nonexempt work.

(d) Refer to Sec. 541.112(b) for the definition of a retail or service establishment as this term is used in paragraph (a) of this section.

Section 541.210 Trainees, administrative.

The exemption is applicable to an employee employed in a bona fide administrative capacity and does not include employees training for employment in an administrative capacity who are not actually performing the duties of an administrative employee.

Section 541.211 Amount of salary or fees required.

(a) Except as otherwise noted in paragraphs (b) and (c) of this section, compensation on a salary or fee basis at a rate of not less than $155 a week, exclusive of board, lodging or other facilities, is required for exemption as an administrative employee. The requirement will be met if the employee is compensated biweekly on a salary basis of $310, semimonthly on a salary basis of $335.84, or monthly on a salary basis of $671.67.

(b) In Puerto Rico, the Virgin Islands, and American Samoa, the salary test for exemption as an administrative employee is $125 per week for other than an employee of the Federal Government.

(c) In the case of academic administrative personnel, the compensation requirement for exemption as an administrative employee may be met either by the payment described in paragraph (a) or (b) of this section, whichever is applicable, or alternatively by compensation on a salary basis in an amount which is at least equal to the entrance salary for teachers in the school system, or educational establishment or institution by which the employee is employed.

(d) The payment of the required salary must be exclusive of board, lodging, or other facilities; that is, free and clear. On the other hand, the regulations in subpart A of this part do not prohibit the sale of such facilities to administrative employees on a cash basis if they are negotiated in the same manner as similar transactions with other persons.

Section 541.212 Salary basis.

The explanation of the salary basis of payment made in Sec. 541.118 in connection with the definition of "executive" is also applicable in the definition of "administrative."

Section 541.213 Fee basis.

The requirements for exemption as an administrative employee may be met by an employee who is compensated on a fee basis as well as by one who is paid on a salary basis. For a discussion of payment of a fee basis, see Sec. 541.313.

Section 541.214 Special proviso for high salaried administrative employees.

(a) Except as otherwise noted in paragraph (b) of this section, Sec. 541.2 contains a special proviso including within the definition of "administrative" an employee who is compensated on a salary or fee basis at a rate of not less than $250 per week exclusive of board, lodging, or other facilities, and whose primary duty consists of either the performance of office or nonmanual work directly related to management policies or general business operations of the employer or the employer's customers, or the performance of functions in the administration of a school system, or educational establishment or institution, or of a department or subdivision thereof, in work directly related to the academic instruction or training carried on therein, where the performance of such primary duty includes work requiring the exercise of discretion and independent judgment. Such a highly paid employee having such work as his or her primary duty is deemed to meet all the requirements in Sec. 541.2 (a) through (e). If an employee qualifies for exemption under this provision, it is not necessary to test the employee's qualifications in detail under Sec. 541.2 (a) through (e).

(b) In Puerto Rico, the Virgin Islands, and American Samoa, the proviso of Sec. 541.2(e) applies to those administrative employees other than an employee of the Federal Government who are compensated on a salary or fee basis or not less than $200 per week.

Employee Employed in a Bona Fide Professional Capacity

Section 541.300 General.

The term "professional" is not restricted to the traditional professions of law, medicine, and theology. It includes those professions which have a recognized status and which are based on the acquirement of professional knowledge through prolonged study. It also includes the artistic professions, such as acting or music. Since the test of the bona fide professional capacity of such employment is different in character from the test for persons in the learned professions, an alternative test for such employees is contained in the regulations, in addition to the requirements common to both groups.

Section 541.301 Learned professions.

(a) The "learned" professions are described in Sec. 541.3(a)(1) as those requiring knowledge of an advanced type in a field of science or learning customarily acquired by a prolonged course of specialized intellectual instruction and study as distinguished from a general academic education and from an apprenticeship and from training in the performance of routine mental, manual, or physical processes.

(b) The first element in the requirement is that the knowledge be of an advanced type. Thus, generally speaking, it must be knowledge which cannot be attained at the high school level.

(c) Second, it must be knowledge in a field of science or learning. This serves to distinguish the professions from the mechanical arts where in some instances the knowledge is of a fairly advanced type, but not in a field of science or learning.

(d) The requisite knowledge, in the third place, must be customarily acquired by a prolonged course of specialized intellectual instruction and study. Here it should be noted that the word "customarily" has been used to meet a specific problem occurring in many industries. As is well known, even in the classical profession of law, there are still a few practitioners who have gained their knowledge by home study and experience. Characteristically, the members of the profession are graduates of law schools, but some few of their fellow professionals whose status is equal to theirs, whose attainments are the same, and whose word is the same did not enjoy that opportunity. Such persons are not barred from the exemption. The word "customarily" implies that in the vast majority of cases the specific academic training is a prerequisite for entrance into the profession. It makes the exemption available to the occasional lawyer who has not gone to law school, or the occasional chemist who is not the possessor of a degree in chemistry, etc., but it does not include the members of such quasi-professions as journalism in which the bulk of the employees have acquired their skill by experience rather than by any formal specialized training. It should be noted also that many employees in these quasi-professions may qualify for exemption under other sections of the regulations in subpart A of this part or under the alternative paragraph of the "professional" definition applicable to the artistic fields.

(e)(1) Generally speaking the professions which meet the requirement for a prolonged course of specialized intellectual instruction and study include law, medicine, nursing, accounting, actuarial computation, engineering, architecture, teaching, various types of physical, chemical, and biological sciences, including pharmacy and registered or certified medical technology and so forth. The typical symbol of the professional training and the best prima facie evidence of its possession is, of course, the appropriate academic degree, and in these professions an advanced academic degree is a standard (if not universal) perquisite. In the case of registered (or certified) medical technologists, successful completion of 3 academic years of preprofessional study in an accredited college or university plus a fourth year of professional course work in a school of medical technology approved by the Council of Medical Education of the American Medical Association will be recognized as a prolonged course of specialized intellectual instruction and study. Registered nurses have traditionally been recognized as professional employees by the Division in its enforcement of the act. Although, in some cases, the course of study has become shortened (but more concentrated), nurses who are registered by the appropriate State examining board will continue to be recognized as having met the requirement of Sec. 541.3(a)(1) of the regulations.

(2) The areas in which professional exemptions may be available are expanding. As knowledge is developed, academic training is broadened, degrees are offered in new and diverse fields, specialties are created and the true specialist, so trained, who is given new and greater responsibilities, comes closer to meeting the tests. However, just as an excellent legal stenographer is not a lawyer, these technical specialists must be more than highly skilled technicians. Many employees in industry rise to executive or administrative positions by their natural ability and good commonsense, combined with long experience with a company, without the aid of a college education or degree in any area. A college education would perhaps give an executive or administrator a more cultured and polished approach but the necessary know-how for doing the executive job would depend upon the person's own inherent talent. The professional person, on the other hand, attains his status after a prolonged course of specialized intellectual instruction and study.

(f) Many accountants are exempt as professional employees (regardless of whether they are employed by public accounting firms or by other types of enterprises). (Some accountants may qualify for exemption as bona fide administrative employees.) However, exemption of accountants, as in the case of other occupational groups (see Sec. 541.308), must be determined on the basis of the individual employee's duties and the other criteria in the regulations. It has been the Divisions' experience that certified public accountants who meet the salary requirement of the regulations will, except in unusual cases, meet the requirements of the professional exemption since they meet the tests contained in Sec. 541.3. Similarly, accountants who are not certified public accountants may also be exempt as professional employees if they actually perform work which requires the consistent exercise of discretion and judgment and otherwise meet the tests prescribed in the definition of "professional" employee. Accounting clerks, junior accountants, and other accountants, on the other hand, normally perform a great deal of routine work which is not an essential part of and necessarily incident to any professional work which they may do. Where these facts are found such accountants are not exempt. The title "Junior Accountant," however, is not determinative of failure to qualify for exemption any more than the title "Senior Accountant" would necessarily imply that the employee is exempt.

(g)(1) A requisite for exemption as a teacher is the condition that the employee is "employed and engaged" in this activity as a teacher in the school system, or educational establishment or institution by which he is employed.

(2) "Employed and engaged as a teacher" denotes employment and engagement in the named specific occupational category as a requisite for

exemption. Teaching consists of the activities of teaching, tutoring, instructing, lecturing, and the like in the activity of imparting knowledge. Teaching personnel may include the following (although not necessarily limited to): Regular academic teachers; teachers of kindergarten or nursery school pupils or of gifted or handicapped children; teachers of skilled and semiskilled trades and occupations; teachers engaged in automobile driving instruction; aircraft flight instructors; home economics teachers; and vocal or instrumental music instructors. Those faculty members who are engaged as teachers but also spend a considerable amount of their time in extracurricular activities such as coaching athletic teams or acting as moderators or advisers in such areas as drama, forensics, or journalism are engaged in teaching. Such activities are a recognized part of the school's responsibility in contributing to the educational development of the student.

(3) Within the public schools of all the States, certificates, whether conditional or unconditional, have become a uniform requirement for employment as a teacher at the elementary and secondary levels. The possession of an elementary or secondary teacher's certificate provide a uniform means of identifying the individuals contemplated as being within the scope of the exemption provided by the statutory language and defined in Sec. 541.3(a)(3) with respect to all teachers employed in public schools and those private schools who possess State certificates. However, the private schools of all the States are not uniform in requiring a certificate for employment as an elementary or secondary school teacher and teacher's certificates are not generally necessary for employment as a teacher in institutions of higher education or other educational establishments which rely on other qualification standards. Therefore, a teacher who is not certified but is engaged in teaching in such a school may be considered for exemption provided that such teacher is employed as a teacher by the employing school or school system and satisfies the other requirements of Sec. 541.3.

(4) Whether certification is conditional or unconditional will not affect the determination as to employment within the scope of the exemption contemplated by this section. There is no standard terminology within the States referring to the different kinds of certificates. The meanings of such labels as permanent, standard, provisional, temporary, emergency, professional, highest standard, limited, and unlimited vary widely. For the purpose of this section, the terminology affixed by the particular State in designating the certificates does not affect the determination of the exempt status of the individual.

Section 541.302 Artistic professions.

(a) The requirements concerning the character of the artistic type of professional work are contained in Sec. 541.3(a)(2). Work of this type is original and creative in character in a recognized field of artistic endeavor (as opposed to work which can be produced by a person endowed with general manual or intellectual ability and training), and the result of which depends primarily on the invention, imagination, or talent of the employee.

(b) The work must be "in a recognized field of artistic endeavor." This includes such fields as music, writing, the theater, and the plastic and graphic arts.

(c)(1) The work must be original and creative in character, as opposed to work which can be produced by a person endowed with general manual or intellectual ability and training. In the field of music there should be little difficulty in ascertaining the application of the requirement. Musicians, composers, conductors, soloists, all are engaged in original and creative work within the sense of this definition. In the plastic and graphic arts the requirement is, generally speaking, met by painters who at most are given the subject matter of their painting. It is similarly met by cartoonists who are merely told the title or underlying concept of a cartoon and then must rely on their own creative powers to express the concept. It would not normally be met by a person who is employed as a copyist, or as an "animator" of motion-picture cartoons, or as a retoucher of photographs since it is not believed that such work is properly described as creative in character.

(2) In the field of writing the distinction is perhaps more difficult to draw. Obviously the requirement is met by essayists or novelists or scenario writers who choose their own subjects and hand in a finished piece of work to their employers (the majority of such persons are, of course, not employees but self-employed). The requirement would also be met, generally speaking, by persons holding the more responsible writing positions in advertising agencies.

(d) Another requirement is that the employee be engaged in work "the result of which depends primarily on the invention, imagination, or talent of the employee." This requirement is easily met by a person employed as an actor, or a singer, or a violinist, or a short-story writer. In the case of newspaper employees the distinction here is similar to the distinction observed above in connection with the requirement that the work be "original and creative in character." Obviously the majority of reporters do work which depends primarily on intelligence, diligence, and accuracy. It is the minority whose work depends primarily on "invention, imaging, or talent." On the other hand, this requirement will normally be met by actors, musicians, painters, and other artists.

(e)(1) The determination of the exempt or nonexempt status of radio and television announcers as professional employees has been relatively difficult because of the merging of the artistic aspects of the job with the commercial. There is considerable variation in the type of work performed by various announcers, ranging from predominantly routine to predominantly exempt work. The wide variation in earnings as between individual announcers, from the highly paid "name" announcer on a national network who is greatly in demand by sponsors to the staff announcer paid a comparatively small salary in a small station, indicates not only great differences in personality, voice and manner, but also in some inherent special ability or talent which, while extremely difficult to define, is nevertheless real.

(2) The duties which many announcers are called upon to perform include: Functioning as a master of ceremonies; playing dramatic, comedy, or

straight parts in a program; interviewing; conducting farm, fashion, and home economics programs; covering public events, such as sports programs, in which the announcer may be required to ad lib and describe current changing events; and acting as narrator and commentator. Such work is generally exempt. Work such as giving station identification and time signals, announcing the names of programs, and similar routine work is nonexempt work. In the field of radio entertainment as in other fields of artistic endeavor, the status of an employee as a bona fide professional under Sec. 541.3 is in large part dependent upon whether his duties are original and creative in character, and whether they require invention, imagination or talent. The determination of whether a particular announcer is exempt as a professional employee must be based upon his individual duties and the amount of exempt and nonexempt work performed, as well as his compensation.

(f) The field of journalism also employs many exempt as well as many nonexempt employees under the same or similar job titles. Newspaper writers and reporters are the principal categories of employment in which this is found.

(1) Newspaper writers, with possible rare exceptions in certain highly technical fields, do not meet the requirements of Sec. 541.3(a)(1) for exemption as professional employees of the "learned" type. Exemption for newspaper writers as professional employees is normally available only under the provisions for professional employees of the "artistic" type. Newspaper writing of the exempt type must, therefore, be "predominantly original and creative in character." Only writing which is analytical, interpretative or highly individualized is considered to be creative in nature. (The writing of fiction to the extent that it may be found on a newspaper would also be considered as exempt work.) Newspaper writers commonly performing work which is original and creative within the meaning of Sec. 541.3 are editorial writers, columnists, critics, and "top-flight" writers of analytical and interpretative articles.

(2) The reporting of news, the rewriting of stories received from various sources, or the routine editorial work of a newspaper is not predominantly original and creative in character within the meaning of Sec. 541.3 and must be considered as nonexempt work. Thus, a reporter or news writer ordinarily collects facts about news events by investigation, interview, or personal observation and writes stories reporting these events for publication, or submits the facts to a rewrite man or other editorial employees for story preparation. Such work is nonexempt work. The leg man, the reporter covering a police beat, the reporter sent out under specific instructions to cover a murder, fire, accident, ship arrival, convention, sport event, etc., are normally performing duties which are not professional in nature within the meaning of the act and Sec. 541.3.

(3) Incidental interviewing or investigation, when it is performed as an essential part of and is necessarily incident to an employee's professional work, however, need not be counted as nonexempt work. Thus, if a dramatic critic interviews an actor and writes a story around the interview, the work of interviewing him and writing the story would not be considered as nonexempt work. However, a dramatic critic who is assigned to cover a routine news

event such as a fire or a convention would be doing nonexempt work since covering the fire or the convention would not be necessary and incident to his work as a dramatic critic.

Section 541.303 Computer related occupations under Public Law 101-583.

(a) Pursuant to Public Law 101-583, enacted November 15, 1990, Sec. 541.3(a)(4) provides that computer systems analysts, computer programmers, software engineers, or other similarly skilled workers in the computer software field are eligible for exemption as professionals under section 13(a)(1) of the Act. Employees who qualify for this exemption are highly-skilled in computer systems analysis, programming, or related work in software functions. Employees who perform these types of work have varied job titles. Included among the more common job titles are computer programmer, systems analyst, computer systems analyst, computer programmer analyst, applications programmer, applications systems analyst, applications systems analyst/programmer, software engineer, software specialist, systems engineer, and systems specialist. These job titles are illustrative only and the list is not intended to be all-inclusive. Further, because of the wide variety of job titles applied to computer systems analysis and programming work, job titles alone are not determinative of the applicability of this exemption.

(b) To be considered for exemption under Sec. 541.3(a)(4), an employee's primary duty must consist of one or more of the following:

(1) The application of systems analysis techniques and procedures, including consulting with users, to determine hardware, software, or system functional specifications;

(2) The design, development, documentation, analysis, creation, testing, or modification of computer systems or programs, including prototypes, based on and related to user or system design specifications;

(3) The design, documentation, testing, creation or modification of computer programs related to machine operating systems; or

(4) a combination of the aforementioned duties, the performance of which requires the same level of skills.

(c) The exemption provided by Sec. 541.3(a)(4) applies only to highly-skilled employees who have achieved a level of proficiency in the theoretical and practical application of a body of highly-specialized knowledge in computer systems analysis, programming, and software engineering, and does not include trainees or employees in entry level positions learning to become proficient in such areas or to employees in these computer-related occupations who have not attained a level of skill and expertise which allows them to work independently and generally without close supervision. The level of expertise and skill required to qualify for this exemption is generally attained through combinations of education and experience in the field. While such employees commonly have a bachelor's or higher degree, no particular academic degree is required for this exemption, nor are there any requirements for licensure or certification, as is required for the exemption for the learned professions.

(d) The exemption does not include employees engaged in the operation of computers or in the manufacture, repair, or maintenance of computer hardware and related equipment. Employees whose work is highly dependent upon, or facilitated by, the use of computers and computer software programs, e.g., engineers, drafters, and others skilled in computer-aided design software like CAD/CAM, but who are not in computer systems analysis and programming occupations, are also excluded from this exemption.

(e) Employees in computer software occupations within the scope of this exemption, as well as those employees not within its scope, may also have managerial and administrative duties which may qualify the employees for exemption under Sec. 541.1 or Sec. 541.2 (see Secs. 541.205(c)(7) and 541.207(c)(7) of this subpart).

Section 541.304 Primary duty.

(a) For a general explanation of the term "primary duty" see the discussion of this term under "executive" in Sec. 541.103. See also the discussion under "administrative" in Sec. 541.206.

(b) The "primary duty" of an employee as a teacher must be that of activity in the field of teaching. Mere certification by the State, or employment in a school will not suffice to qualify an individual for exemption within the scope of Sec. 541.3(a)(3) if the individual is not in fact both employed and engaged as a teacher (see Sec. 541.302(g)(2)). The words "primary duty" have the effect of placing major emphasis on the character of the employee's job as a whole. Therefore, employment and engagement in the activity of imparting knowledge as a primary duty shall be determinative with respect to employment within the meaning of the exemption as "teacher" in conjunction with the other requirements of Sec. 541.3.

Section 541.305 Discretion and judgment.

(a) Under Sec. 541.3 a professional employee must perform work which requires the consistent exercise of discretion and judgment in its performance.

(b) A prime characteristic of professional work is the fact that the employee does apply his special knowledge or talents with discretion and judgment. Purely mechanical or routine work is not professional.

Section 541.306 Predominantly intellectual and varied.

(a) Section 541.3 requires that the employee be engaged in work predominantly intellectual and varied in character as opposed to routine mental, manual, mechanical, or physical work. This test applies to the type of thinking which must be performed by the employee in question. While a doctor may make 20 physical examinations in the morning and perform in the course of his examinations essentially similar tests. It requires not only judgment and discretion on his part but a continual variety of interpretation of the tests to perform satisfactory work. Likewise, although a professional chemist may make a series of similar tests, the problems presented will vary as will the deductions to be made therefrom. The work of the true professional is inherently varied even though similar outward actions may be performed.

(b) Another example of this is the professional medical technologist who performs complicated chemical, microscopic, and bacteriological tests and procedures. In a large medical laboratory or clinic, the technologist usually specializes in making several kinds of related tests in areas such as microbiology, parasitology, biochemistry, hematology, histology, cytology, and nuclear medical technology. The technologist also does the blood banking. He will also conduct tests related to the examination and treatment of patients, or do research on new drugs, or on the improvement of laboratory techniques, or teach and perform administrative duties. The simple, routine, and preliminary tests are generally performed by laboratory assistants or technicians. However, technologists who work in small laboratories may perform tasks that are performed by nonexempt employees in larger establishments. This type of activity will not necessarily be considered nonexempt (see Sec. 541.307).

(c) On the other hand, X-ray technicians have only limited opportunity for the exercise of independent discretion and judgment, usually performing their duties under the supervision of a more highly qualified employee. The more complex duties of interpretation and judgment in this field are performed by obviously exempt professional employees.

Section 541.307 Essential part of and necessarily incident to.

(a) Section 541.3(d), it will be noted, has the effect of including within the exempt work activities which are an essential part of and necessarily incident to the professional work described in Sec. 541.3 (a) through (c). This provision recognizes the fact that there are professional employees whose work necessarily involves some of the actual routine physical tasks also performed by obviously nonexempt employees. For example, a chemist performing important and original experiments frequently finds it necessary to perform himself some of the most menial tasks in connection with the operation of his experiments, even though at times these menial tasks can be conveniently or properly assigned to laboratory assistants. See also the example of incidental interviewing or investigation in Sec. 541.303(a)(3).

(b) It should be noted that the test of whether routine work is exempt work is different in the definition of "professional" from that in the definition of "executive" and "administrative." Thus, while routine work will be exempt if it is "directly and closely related" to the performance of executive or administrative duties, work which is directly and closely related to the performance of the professional duties will not be exempt unless it is also "an essential part of and necessarily incident to" the professional work.

(c) Section 541.3(d) takes into consideration the fact that there are teaching employees whose work necessarily involves some of the actual routine duties and physical tasks also performed by nonexempt employees. For example, a teacher may conduct his pupils on a field trip related to the classroom work of his pupils and in connection with the field trip engage in activities such as driving a school bus and monitoring the behavior of his pupils in public restaurants. These duties are an essential part of and necessarily incident to his job as teacher. However, driving a school bus each day at the beginning and end of the schools day to pick up and deliver pupils would not be exempt type work.

Section 541.308 Nonexempt work generally.

(a) It has been the Divisions' experience that some employers erroneously believe that anyone employed in the field of accountancy, engineering, or other professional fields, will qualify for exemption as a professional employee by virtue of such employment. While there are many exempt employees in these fields, the exemption of individual depends upon his duties and other qualifications.

(b) It is necessary to emphasize the fact that section 13(a)(1) exempts "any employee employed in a bona fide * * * professional capacity." It does not exempt all employees of professional employers, or all employees in industries having large numbers of professional members, or all employees in any particular occupation. Nor does it exempt, as such those learning a profession. Moreover, it does not exempt persons with professional training, who are working in professional fields, but performing subprofessional or routine work. For example, in the field of library science there are large numbers of employees who are trained librarians but who, nevertheless, do not perform professional work or receive salaries commensurate with recognized professional status. The field of "engineering" has many persons with "engineer" titles, who are not professional engineers, as well as many who are trained in the engineering profession, but are actually working as trainees, junior engineers, or draftsmen.

Section 541.309 20 percent nonexempt work limitation.

Time spent in nonexempt work, that is, work which is not an essential part of and necessarily incident to the exempt work, is limited to 20 percent of the time worked by the employee in the workweek.

Section 541.310 Trainees, professional.

The exemption applies to an employee employed in a bona fide professional capacity and does not include trainees who are not actually performing the duties of a professional employee.

Section 541.311 Amount of salary or fees required.

(a) Except as otherwise noted in paragraphs (b) and (c) of this section, compensation on a salary or fee basis at a rate of not less than $170 per week, exclusive of board, lodging or other facilities, is required for exemption as a "professional employee." An employee will meet this requirement if paid a biweekly salary of $340, a semi monthly salary of $368.33 or a monthly salary of $736.67.

(b) In Puerto Rico, the Virgin Islands, and American Samoa the salary test for exemption as a "professional" for other than employees of the Federal Government is $150 per week.

(c) The payment of the compensation specified in paragraph (a) or (b) of this section is not a requisite for exemption in the case of employees exempted from this requirement by the proviso to Sec. 541.3(e), as explained in Sec. 541.314.

(d) The payment of the required salary must be exclusive of board, lodging, or other facilities; that is, free and clear. On the other hand, the regulations in subpart A of this part do not prohibit the sale of such facilities to professional employees on a cash basis if they are negotiated in the same manner as similar transactions with other persons.

Section 541.312 Salary basis.

The salary basis of payment is explained in Sec. 541.118 in connection with the definition of "executive." Pursuant to Public Law 101-583, enacted November 15, 1990, payment "on a salary basis" is not a requirement for exemption in the case of those employees in computer-related occupations, as defined in Sec. 541.3(a)(4) and Sec. 541.303, who otherwise meet the requirements of Sec. 541.3 and who are paid on an hourly basis if their hourly rate of pay exceeds 6\1/2\ times the minimum wage provided by section 6 of the Act.

Section 541.313 Fee basis.

(a) The requirements for exemption as a professional (or administrative) employee may be met by an employee who is compensated on a fee basis as well as by one who is paid on a salary basis.

(b) Little or no difficulty arises in determining whether a particular employment arrangement involves payment on a fee basis. Such arrangements are characterized by the payment of an agreed sum for a single job regardless of the time required for its completion. These payments in a sense resemble piecework payments with the important distinction that generally speaking a fee payment is made for the kind of job which is unique rather than for a series of jobs which are repeated an indefinite number of times and for which payment on an identical basis is made over and over again. Payments based on the number of hours or days worked and not on the accomplishment of a given single task are not considered payments on a fee basis. The type of payment contemplated in the regulations in subpart A of this part is thus readily recognized.

(c) The adequacy of a fee payment. Whether it amounts of payment at a rate of not less than $170 per week to a professional employee or at a rate of not less than $155 per week to an administrative employee can ordinarily be determined only after the time worked on the job has been determined. In determining whether payment is at the rate specified in the regulations in subpart A of this part the amount paid to the employee will be tested by reference to a standard workweek of 40 hours. Thus compliance will be tested in each case of a fee payment by determining whether the payment is at a rate which would amount to at least $170 per week to a professional employee or at a rate of not less than $155 per week to an administrative employee if 40 hours were worked.

(d) The following examples will illustrate the principle stated above:

(1) A singer receives $50 for a song on a 15-minute program (no rehearsal time is involved). Obviously the requirement will be met since the employee would earn $170 at this rate of pay in far less than 40 hours.

(2) An artist is paid $100 for a picture. Upon completion of the assignment, it is determined that the artist worked 20 hours. Since earnings at this rate would yield the artist $200 if 40 hours were worked, the requirement is met.

(3) An illustrator is assigned the illustration of a pamphlet at a fee of $150. When the job is completed, it is determined that the employee worked 60 hours. If the employee worked 40 hours at this rate, the employee would have earned only $100. The fee payment of $150 for work which required 60 hours to complete therefore does not meet the requirement of payment at a rate of $170 per week and the employee must be considered nonexempt. It follows that if in the performance of this assignment the illustrator worked in excess of 40 hours in any week, overtime rates must be paid. Whether or not the employee worked in excess of 40 hours in any week, records for such an employee would have to be kept in accordance with the regulations covering records for nonexempt employees (part 516 of this chapter).

Section 541.314 Exception for physicians, lawyers, and teachers.

(a) A holder of a valid license or certificate permitting the practice of law or medicine or any of their branches, who is actually engaged in practicing the profession, or a holder of the requisite academic degree for the general practice of medicine who is engaged in an internship or resident program pursuant to the practice of his profession, or an employee employed and engaged as a teacher in the activity of imparting knowledge, is excepted from the salary or fee requirement. This exception applies only to the traditional professions of law, medicine, and teaching and not to employees in related professions which merely serve these professions.

(b) In the case of medicine:

(1) The exception applies to physicians and other practitioners licensed and practicing in the field of medical science and healing or any of the medical specialties practiced by physicians or practitioners. The term physicians means medical doctors including general practitioners and specialists, and osteopathic physicians (doctors of osteopathy). Other practitioners in the field of medical science and healing may include podiatrists (sometimes called chiropodists), dentists (doctors of dental medicine), optometrists (doctors of optometry or bachelors of science in optometry).

(2) Physicians and other practitioners included in paragraph (b)(1) of this section, whether or not licensed to practice prior to commencement of an internship or resident program, are excepted from the salary or fee requirement during their internship or resident program, where such a training program is entered upon after the earning of the appropriate degree required for the general practice of their profession.

(c) In the case of medical occupations, the exception from the salary or fee requirement does not apply to pharmacists, nurses, therapists, technologists, sanitarians, dietitians, social workers, psychologists, psychometrists, or other professions which service the medical profession.

SECTION 553—THE APPLICATION OF THE FAIR LABOR STANDARDS ACT TO EMPLOYEES OF STATE AND LOCAL GOVERNMENTS

Subpart A--General
Introduction

Section 553.1 Definitions.

(a) Act or FLSA means the Fair Labor Standards Act of 1938, as amended (52 Stat. 1060, as amended; 29 U.S.C. 201-219).

(b) 1985 Amendments means the Fair Labor Standards Amendments of 1985 (Pub. L. 99-150).

(c) Public agency means a State, a political subdivision of a State or an interstate governmental agency.

(d) State means a State of the United States, the District of Columbia, Puerto Rico, the Virgin Islands, or any other Territory or possession of the United States (29 U.S.C. 203(c) and 213(f)).

Section 553.2 Purpose and scope.

(a) The 1985 Amendments to the Fair Labor Standards Act (FLSA) changed certain provisions of the Act as they apply to employees of State and local public agencies. The purpose of part 553 is to set forth the regulations to carry out the provisions of these Amendments, as well as other FLSA provisions previously in existence relating to such public agency employees.

(b) The regulations in this part are divided into three subparts. Subpart A interprets and applies the special FLSA provisions that are generally applicable to all covered and nonexempt employees of State and local governments. Subpart A also contains provisions concerning certain individuals (i.e., elected officials, their appointees, and legislative branch employees) who are excluded from the definition of "employee" and thus from FLSA coverage. This subpart also interprets and applies sections 7(o), and 7(p)(2), 7(p)(3), and 11(c) of the Act regarding compensatory time off, occasional or sporadic part-time employment, and the performance of substitute work by public agency employees, respectively.

(c) Subpart B of this part deals with "volunteer" services performed by individuals for public agencies. Subpart C applies various FLSA provisions as they relate to fire protection and law enforcement employees of public agencies.

Section 553.3 Coverage--general.

(a)(1) In 1966, Congress amended the FLSA to extend coverage to State and local government employees engaged in the operation of hospitals, nursing homes, schools, and mass transit systems.

(2) In 1972, the Education Amendments further extended coverage to employees of public preschools.

(3) In 1974, the FLSA Amendments extended coverage to virtually all of the remaining State and local government employees who were not covered as a result of the 1966 and 1972 legislation.

(b) Certain definitions already in the Act were modified by the 1974 Amendments. The definition of the term "employer" was changed to include public agencies and that of "employee" was amended to include individuals employed by public agencies. The definition of "enterprise" contained in section 3(r) of the Act was modified to provide that activities of a public agency are performed for a "business purpose." The term "enterprise engaged in commerce or in the production of goods for commerce" defined in section 3(s) of the Act was expanded to include public agencies.

Section 3(e)(2)(C) — Exclusions

Section 553.10 General.

Section 3(e)(2)(C) of the Act excludes from the definition of "employee", and thus from coverage, certain individuals employed by public agencies. This exclusion applies to elected public officials, their immediate advisors, and certain individuals whom they appoint or select to serve in various capacities. In addition, the 1985 Amendments exclude employees of legislative branches of State and local governments. A condition for exclusion is that the employee must not be subject to the civil service laws of the employing State or local agency.

Section 553.11 Exclusion for elected officials and their appointees.

(a) Section 3(e)(2)(C) provides an exclusion from the Act's coverage for officials elected by the voters of their jurisdictions. Also excluded under this provision are personal staff members and officials in policymaking positions who are selected or appointed by the elected public officials and certain advisers to such officials.

(b) The statutory term "member of personal staff" generally includes only persons who are under the direct supervision of the selecting elected official and have regular contact with such official. The term typically does not include individuals who are directly supervised by someone other than the elected official even though they may have been selected by the official. For example, the term might include the elected official's personal secretary, but would not include the secretary to an assistant.

(c) In order to qualify as personal staff members or officials in policymaking positions, the individuals in question must not be subject to the civil service laws of their employing agencies. The term "civil service laws" refers to a personnel system established by law which is designed to protect employees from arbitrary action, personal favoritism, and political coercion, and which uses a competitive or merit examination process for selection and placement. Continued tenure of employment of employees under civil service, except for cause, is provided. In addition, such personal staff members must be appointed by, and serve solely at the pleasure or discretion of, the elected official.

(d) The exclusion for "immediate adviser" to elected officials is limited to staff who serve as advisers on constitutional or legal matters, and who are not subject to the civil service rules of their employing agency.

Section 553.12 Exclusion for employees of legislative branches.

(a) Section 3(e)(2)(C) of the Act provides an exclusion from the definition of the term "employee for individuals who are not subject to the civil service laws of their employing agencies and are employed by legislative branches or bodies of States, their political subdivisions or interstate governmental agencies.

(b) Employees of State or local legislative libraries do not come within this statutory exclusion. Also, employees of school boards, other than elected officials and their appointees (as discussed in Sec. 553.11), do not come within this exclusion.

Section 7(o) – Compensatory Time And Compensatory Time Off

Section 553.20 Introduction.

Section 7 of the FLSA requires that covered, nonexempt employees receive not less than one and one-half times their regular rates of pay for hours worked in excess of the applicable maximum hours standards. However, section 7(o) of the Act provides an element of flexibility to State and local government employers and an element of choice to their employees or the representatives of their employees regarding compensation for statutory overtime hours. The exemption provided by this subsection authorizes a public agency which is a State, a political subdivision of a State, or an interstate governmental agency, to provide compensatory time off (with certain limitations, as provided in Sec. 553.21) in lieu of monetary overtime compensation that would otherwise be required under section 7. Compensatory time received by an employee in lieu of cash must be at the rate of not less than one and one-half hours of compensatory time for each hour of overtime work, just as the monetary rate for overtime is calculated at the rate of not less than one and one-half times the regular rate of pay.

Section 553.21 Statutory provisions.

Section 7(o) provides as follows:

(o)(1) Employees of a public agency which is a State, a political subdivision of a State, or an interstate governmental agency may receive, in accordance with this subsection and in lieu of overtime compensation, compensatory time off at a rate not less than one and one-half hours for each hour of employment for which overtime compensation is required by this section.

(2) A public agency may provide compensatory time under paragraph (1) only--

(A) Pursuant to--

(i) Applicable provisions of a collective bargaining agreement, memorandum of understanding, or any other agreement between the public agency and representatives of such employees; or

(ii) In the case of employees not covered by subclause (i), an agreement or understanding arrived at between the employer and employee before the performance of the work; and

(B) If the employee has not accrued compensatory time in excess of the limit applicable to the employee prescribed by paragraph (3).

In the case of employees described in clause (A)(ii) hired prior to April 15, 1986, the regular practice in effect on April 15, 1986, with respect to compensatory time off for such employees in lieu of the receipt of overtime compensation, shall constitute an agreement or understanding under such clause (A)(ii). Except as provided in the previous sentence, the provision of compensatory time off to such employees for hours worked after April 14, 1986, shall be in accordance with this subsection.

(3)(A) If the work of an employee for which compensatory time may be provided included work in a public safety activity, an emergency response activity, or a seasonal activity, the employee engaged in such work may accrue not more than 480 hours of compensatory time for hours worked after April 15, 1986. If such work was any other work, the employee engaged in such work may accrue not more than 240 hours of compensatory time for hours worked after April 15, 1986. Any such employee who, after April 15, 1986, has accrued 480 or 240 hours, as the case may be, of compensatory time off shall, for additional overtime hours of work, be paid overtime compensation.

(B) If compensation is paid to an employee for accrued compensatory time off, such compensation shall be paid at the regular rate earned by the employee at the time the employee receives such payment.

(4) An employee who has accrued compensatory time off authorized to be provided under paragraph (1) shall, upon termination of employment, be paid for the unused compensatory time at a rate of compensation not less than--

(A) The average regular rate received by such employee during the last 3 years of the employee's employment, or

(B) The final regular rate received by such employee, whichever is higher.

(5) An employee of a public agency which is a State, political subdivision of a State, or an interstate governmental agency--

(A) Who has accrued compensatory time off authorized to be provided under paragraph (1), and

(B) Who has requested the use of such compensatory time, shall be permitted by the employee's employer to use such time within a reasonable period after making the request if the use of the compensatory time does not unduly disrupt the operations of the public agency.

(6) For purposes of this subsection--

(A) The term overtime compensation means the compensation required by subsection (a), and

(B) The terms compensatory time and compensatory time off means hours during which an employee is not working, which are not counted as hours worked during the applicable workweek or other work period for purposes of overtime compensation, and for which the employee is compensated at the employee's regular rate.

Section 553.22 "FLSA compensatory time" and "FLSA compensatory time off".

(a) Compensatory time and compensatory time off are interchangeable terms under the FLSA. Compensatory time off is paid time off the job which is earned and accrued by an employee in lieu of immediate cash payment for employment in excess of the statutory hours for which overtime compensation is required by section 7 of the FLSA.

(b) The Act requires that compensatory time under section 7(o) be earned at a rate not less than one and one-half hours for each hour of employment for which overtime compensation is required by section 7 of the FLSA. Thus, the 480-hour limit on accrued compensatory time represents not more than 320 hours of actual overtime worked, and the 240-hour limit represents not more than 160 hours of actual overtime worked.

(c) The 480- and 240-hour limits on accrued compensatory time only apply to overtime hours worked after April 15, 1986. Compensatory time which an employee has accrued prior to April 15, 1986, is not subject to the overtime requirements of the FLSA and need not be aggregated with compensatory time accrued after that date.

Section 553.23 Agreement or understanding prior to performance of work.

(a) General. (1) As a condition for use of compensatory time in lieu of overtime payment in cash, section 7(o)(2)(A) of the Act requires an agreement or understanding reached prior to the performance of work. This can be accomplished pursuant to a collective bargaining agreement, a memorandum of understanding or any other agreement between the public agency and representatives of the employees. If the employees do not have a representative, compensatory time may be used in lieu of cash overtime compensation only if such an agreement or understanding has been arrived at between the public agency and the individual employee before the performance of work. No agreement or understanding is required with respect to employees hired prior to April 15, 1986, who do not have a representative, if the employer had a regular practice in effect on April 15, 1986, of granting compensatory time off in lieu of overtime pay.

(2) Agreements or understandings may provide that compensatory time off in lieu of overtime payment in cash may be restricted to certain hours of work only. In addition, agreements or understandings may provide for any combination of compensatory time off and overtime payment in cash (e.g., one hour compensatory time credit plus one-half the employee's regular hourly rate of pay in cash for each hour of overtime worked) so long as the premium pay principle of at least "time and one-half" is maintained. The agreement or understanding may include other provisions governing the preservation, use, or cashing out of compensatory time so long as these provisions are consistent with section 7(o) of the Act. To the extent that any provision of an agreement or understanding is in violation of section 7(o) of the Act, the provision is superseded by the requirements of section 7(o).

(b) Agreement or understanding between the public agency and a representative of the employees. (1) Where employees have a representative, the agreement or understanding concerning the use of compensatory time must be between the representative and the public agency either through a collective bargaining agreement or through a memorandum of understanding or other type of oral or written agreement. In the absence of a collective bargaining agreement applicable to the employees, the representative need not be a formal or recognized bargaining agent as long as the representative is designated by the employees. Any agreement must be consistent with the provisions of section 7(o) of the Act.

(2) Section 2(b) of the 1985 Amendments provides that a collective bargaining agreement in effect on April 15, 1986, which permits compensatory time off in lieu of overtime compensation, will remain in effect until the expiration date of the collective bargaining agreement unless otherwise modified. However, the terms and conditions of such agreement under which compensatory time off is provided after April 14, 1986, must not violate the requirements of section 7(o) of the Act and these regulations.

(c) Agreement or understanding between the public agency and individual employees. (1) Where employees of a public agency do not have a recognized or otherwise designated representative, the agreement or understanding concerning compensatory time off must be between the public agency and the individual employee and must be reached prior to the performance of work. This agreement or understanding with individual employees need not be in writing, but a record of its existence must be kept. (See Sec. 553.50.) An employer need not adopt the same agreement or understanding with different employees and need not provide compensatory time to all employees. The agreement or understanding to provide compensatory time off in lieu of cash overtime compensation may take the form of an express condition of employment, provided (i) the employee knowingly and voluntarily agrees to it as a condition of employment and (ii) the employee is informed that the compensatory time received may be preserved, used or cashed out consistent with the provisions of section 7(o) of the Act. An agreement or understanding may be evidenced by a notice to the employee that compensatory time off will be given in lieu of overtime pay. In such a case, an agreement or understanding would be presumed to exist for purposes of section 7(o) with respect to any employee who fails to express to the employer an unwillingness to accept compensatory time off in lieu of overtime pay. However, the employee's decision to accept compensatory time off in lieu of cash overtime payments must be made freely and without coercion or pressure.

(2) Section 2(a) of the 1985 Amendments provides that in the case of employees who have no representative and were employed prior to April 15, 1986, a public agency that has had a regular practice of awarding compensatory time off in lieu of overtime pay is deemed to have reached an agreement or understanding with these employees as of April 15, 1986. A public agency need not secure an agreement or understanding with each employee employed prior to that date. If, however, such a regular practice does not conform to the provisions of section 7(o) of the Act, it must be modified to do so with regard to practices after April 14, 1986. With respect to employees hired after April 14, 1986, the public employer who elects to use compensatory time must follow the guidelines on agreements discussed in paragraph (c)(1) of this section.

Section 553.24 "Public safety", "emergency response", and "seasonal" activities.

(a) Section 7(o)(3)(A) of the FLSA provides that an employee of a public agency which is a State, a political subdivision of a State, or an interstate governmental agency, may accumulate not more than 480 hours of compensatory time for FLSA overtime hours which are worked after April 15, 1986, if the employee is engaged in "public safety", "emergency response", or "seasonal" activity. Employees whose work includes "seasonal", "emergency response", or "public safety" activities, as well as other work, will not be subject to both limits of accrual for compensatory time. If the employee's work regularly involves the activities included in the 480-hour limit, the employee will be covered by that limit. A public agency cannot utilize the higher cap by simple classification or designation of an employee. The work performed is controlling. Assignment of occasional duties within the scope of the higher cap will not entitle the employer to use the higher cap. Employees whose work does not regularly involve "seasonal", "emergency response", or "public safety" activities are subject to a 240-hour compensatory time accrual limit for FLSA overtime hours which are worked after April 15, 1986.

(b) Employees engaged in "public safety", "emergency response", or "seasonal" activities, who transfer to positions subject to the 240-hour limit, may carry over to the new position any accrued compensatory time. The employer will not be required to cash out the accrued compensatory time which is in excess of the lower limit. However, the employee must be compensated in cash wages for any subsequent overtime hours worked until the number of accrued hours of compensatory time falls below the 240-hour limit.

(c) "Public safety activities": The term "public safety activities" as used in section 7(o)(3)(A) of the Act includes law enforcement, fire fighting or related activities as described in Secs. 553.210 (a) and (b) and 553.211 (a)-(c), and (f). An employee whose work regularly involves such activities will qualify for the 480-hour accrual limit. However, the 480-hour accrual limit will not apply to office personnel or other civilian employees who may perform public safety activities only in emergency situations, even if they spend substantially all of their time in a particular week in such activities. For example, a maintenance worker employed by a public agency who is called upon to perform fire fighting activities during an emergency would remain subject to the 240-hour limit, even if such employee spent an entire week or several weeks in a year performing public safety activities. Certain employees who work in "public safety" activities for purposes of section 7(o)(3)(A) may qualify for the partial overtime exemption in section 7(k) of the Act. (See Sec. 553.201)

(d) "Emergency response activity": The term "emergency response activity" as used in section 7(o)(3)(A) of the Act includes dispatching of emergency vehicles and personnel, rescue work and ambulance services. As is the case with "public safety" and "seasonal" activities, an employee must regularly engage in "emergency response" activities to be covered under the 480-hour limit. A city office worker who may be called upon to perform rescue work in the event of a flood or snowstorm would not be covered under the higher limit, since such emergency response activities are not a regular part of the employee's job. Certain employees who work in "emergency response" activities for purposes of section 7(o)(3)(A) may qualify for the partial overtime exemption in section 7(k) of the Act. (See Sec. 553.215.)

(e)(1) "Seasonal activity": The term "seasonal activity" includes work during periods of significantly increased demand, which are of a regular and recurring nature. In determining whether employees are considered engaged in a seasonal activity, the first consideration is whether the activity in which they are engaged is a regular and recurring aspect of the employee's work. The second consideration is whether the projected overtime hours during the period of significantly increased demand are likely to result in the accumulation during such period of more than 240 compensatory time hours (the number available under the lower cap). Such projections will normally be based on the employer's past experience with similar employment situations.

(2) Seasonal activity is not limited strictly to those operations that are very susceptible to changes in the weather. As an example, employees processing tax returns over an extended period of significantly increased demand whose overtime hours could be expected to result in the accumulation during such period of more than 240 compensatory time hours will typically qualify as engaged in a seasonal activity.

(3) While parks and recreation activity is primarily seasonal because peak demand is generally experienced in fair weather, mere periods of short but intense activity do not make an employee's job seasonal. For example, clerical employees working increased hours for several weeks on a special project or assigned to an afternoon of shoveling snow off the courthouse steps would not be considered engaged in seasonal activities, since the increased activity would not result in the accumulation during such period of more than 240 compensatory time hours. Further, persons employed in municipal auditoriums, theaters, and sports facilities that are open for specific, limited

seasons would be considered engaged in seasonal activities, while those employed in facilities that operate year round generally would not.

(4) Road crews, while not necessarily seasonal workers, may have significant periods of peak demand, for instance during the snow plowing season or road construction season. The snow plow operator/road crew employee may be able to accrue compensatory time to the higher cap, while other employees of the same department who do not have lengthy periods of peak seasonal demand would remain under the lower cap.

Section 553.25 Conditions for use of compensatory time ("reasonable period", "unduly disrupt").

(a) Section 7(o)(5) of the FLSA provides that any employee of a public agency who has accrued compensatory time and requested use of this compensatory time, shall be permitted to use such time off within a "reasonable period" after making the request, if such use does not "unduly disrupt" the operations of the agency. This provision, however, does not apply to "other compensatory time" (as defined below in Sec. 553.28), including compensatory time accrued for overtime worked prior to April 15, 1986.

(b) Compensatory time cannot be used as a means to avoid statutory overtime compensation. An employee has the right to use compensatory time earned and must not be coerced to accept more compensatory time than an employer can realistically and in good faith expect to be able to grant within a reasonable period of his or her making a request for use of such time.

(c) Reasonable period.

(1) Whether a request to use compensatory time has been granted within a "reasonable period" will be determined by considering the customary work practices within the agency based on the facts and circumstances in each case. Such practices include, but are not limited to (a) the normal schedule of work, (b) anticipated peak workloads based on past experience, (c) emergency requirements for staff and services, and (d) the availability of qualified substitute staff.

(2) The use of compensatory time in lieu of cash payment for overtime must be pursuant to some form of agreement or understanding between the employer and the employee (or the representative of the employee) reached prior to the performance of the work. (See Sec. 553.23.) To the extent that the (conditions under which an employee can take compensatory time off are contained in an agreement or understanding as defined in Sec. 553.23, the terms of such agreement or understanding will govern the meaning of "reasonable period".

(d) Unduly disrupt. When an employer receives a request for compensatory time off, it shall be honored unless to do so would be "unduly disruptive" to the agency's operations. Mere inconvenience to the employer is an insufficient basis for denial of a request for compensatory time off. (See H. Rep. 99-331, p. 23.) For an agency to turn down a request from an employee for compensatory time off requires that it should reasonably and in good faith anticipate that it would impose an unreasonable burden on the agency's ability to provide services of acceptable quality and quantity for the public during the time requested without the use of the employee's services.

Section 553.26 Cash overtime payments.

(a) Overtime compensation due under section 7 may be paid in cash at the employer's option, in lieu of providing compensatory time off under section 7(o) of the Act in any workweek or work period. The FLSA does not prohibit an employer from freely substituting cash, in whole or part, for compensatory time off; and overtime payment in cash would not affect subsequent granting of compensatory time off in future workweeks or work periods. (See Sec. 553.23(a)(2).)

(b) The principles for computing cash overtime pay are contained in 29 CFR part 778. Cash overtime compensation must be paid at a rate not less than one and one-half times the regular rate at which the employee is actually paid. (See 29 CFR 778.107.)

(c) In a workweek or work period during which an employee works hours which are overtime hours under FLSA and for which cash overtime payment will be made, and the employee also takes compensatory time off, the payment for such time off may be excluded from the regular rate of pay under section 7(e)(2) of the Act. Section 7(e)(2) provides that the regular rate shall not be deemed to include * * * payments made for occasional periods when no work is performed due to vacation, holiday, * * * or other similar cause. As explained in 29 CFR 778.218(d), the term "other similar cause" refers to payments made for periods of absence due to factors like holidays, vacations, illness, and so forth. Payments made to an employee for periods of absence due to the use of accrued compensatory time are considered to be the type of payments in this "other similar cause" category.

Section 553.27 Payments for unused compensatory time.

(a) Payments for accrued compensatory time earned after April 14, 1986, may be made at any time and shall be paid at the regular rate earned by the employee at the time the employee receives such payment.

(b) Upon termination of employment, an employee shall be paid for unused compensatory time earned after April 14, 1986, at a rate of compensation not less than--

(1) The average regular rate received by such employee during the last 3 years of the employee's employment, or

(2) The final regular rate received by such employee, whichever is higher.

(c) The phrase last 3 years of employment means the 3-year period immediately prior to termination. Where an employee's last 3 years of employment are not continuous because of a break in service, the period of employment after the break in service will be treated as new employment. However, such a break in service must have been intended to be permanent and any accrued compensatory time earned after April 14, 1986, must have been cashed out at the time of initial separation. Where the final period of employment is less than 3 years, the average rate still must be calculated based on the rate(s) in effect during such period.

(d) The term "regular rate" is defined in 29 CFR 778.108. As indicated in Sec. 778.109, the regular rate is an hourly rate, although the FLSA does not require employers to compensate employees on an hourly basis.

Section 553.28 Other compensatory time.

(a) Compensatory time which is earned and accrued by an employee for employment in excess of a nonstatutory (that is, non-FLSA) requirement is considered "other" compensatory time. The term "other" compensatory time off means hours during which an employee is not working and which are not counted as hours worked during the period when used. For example, a collective bargaining agreement may provide that compensatory time be granted to employees for hours worked in excess of 8 in a day, or for working on a scheduled day off in a nonovertime workweek. The FLSA does not require compensatory time to be granted in such situations.

(b) Compensatory time which is earned and accrued by an employee working hours which are "overtime" hours under State or local law, ordinance, or other provisions, but which are not overtime hours under section 7 of the FLSA is also considered "other" compensatory time. For example, a local law or ordinance may provide that compensatory time be granted to employees for hours worked in excess of 35 in a workweek. Under section 7(a) of the FLSA, only hours worked in excess of 40 in a workweek are overtime hours which must be compensated at one and one-half times the regular rate of pay.

(c) Similarly, compensatory time earned or accrued by an employee for employment in excess of a standard established by the personnel policy or practice of an employer, or by custom, which does not result from the FLSA provision, is another example of "other" compensatory time.

(d) The FLSA does not require that the rate at which "other" compensatory time is earned has to be at a rate of one and one-half hours for each hour of employment. The rate at which "other" compensatory time is earned may be some lesser or greater multiple of the rate or the straight-time rate itself.

(e) The requirements of section 7(o) of the FLSA, including the limitations on accrued compensatory time, do not apply to "other" compensatory time as described above.

Other Exemptions

Section 553.30 Occasional or sporadic employment-section 7(p)(2).

(a) Section 7(p)(2) of the FLSA provides that where State or local government employees, solely at their option, work occasionally or sporadically on a part-time basis for the same public agency in a different capacity from their regular employment, the hours worked in the different jobs shall not be combined for the purpose of determining overtime liability under the Act.

(b) Occasional or sporadic. (1) The term occasional or sporadic means infrequent, irregular, or occurring in scattered instances. There may be an occasional need for additional resources in the delivery of certain types of public services which is at times best met by the part-time employment of an individual who is already a public employee. Where employees freely and solely at their own option enter into such activity, the total hours worked will not be combined for purposes of determining any overtime compensation due on the regular, primary job. However, in order to prevent overtime abuse, such hours worked are to be excluded from computing overtime compensation due only where the occasional or sporadic assignments are not within the same general occupational category as the employee's regular work.

(2) In order for an employee's occasional or sporadic work on a part-time basis to qualify for exemption under section 7(p)(2), the employee's decision to work in a different capacity must be made freely and without coercion, implicit or explicit, by the employer. An employer may suggest that an employee undertake another kind of work for the same unit of government when the need for assistance arises, but the employee must be free to refuse to perform such work without sanction and without being required to explain or justify the decision.

(3) Typically, public recreation and park facilities, and stadiums or auditoriums utilize employees in occasional or sporadic work. Some of these employment activities are the taking of tickets, providing security for special events (e.g., concerts, sports events, and lectures), officiating at youth or other recreation and sports events, or engaging in food or beverage sales at special events, such as a county fair. Employment in such activity may be considered occasional or sporadic for regular employees of State or local government agencies even where the need can be anticipated because it recurs seasonally (e.g., a holiday concert at a city college, a program of scheduled sports events, or assistance by a city payroll clerk in processing returns at tax filing time). An activity does not fail to be occasional merely because it is recurring. In contrast, for example, if a parks department clerk, in addition to his or her regular job, also regularly works additional hours on a part-time basis (e.g., every week or every other week) at a public park food and beverage sales center operated by that agency, the additional work does not constitute intermittent and irregular employment and, therefore, the hours worked would be combined in computing any overtime compensation due.

(c) Different capacity.

(1) In order for employment in these occasional or sporadic activities not to be considered subject to the overtime requirements of section 7 of the FLSA, the regular government employment of the individual performing them must also be in a different capacity, i.e., it must not fall within the same general occupational category.

(2) In general, the Administrator will consider the duties and other factors contained in the definitions of the 3-digit categories of occupations in the Dictionary of Occupational Titles (except in the case of public safety employees as discussed below in section (3)), as well as all the facts and

circumstances in a particular case, in determining whether employment in a second capacity is substantially different from the regular employment.

(3) For example, if a public park employee primarily engaged in playground maintenance also from time to time cleans an evening recreation center operated by the same agency, the additional work would be considered hours worked for the same employer and subject to the Act's overtime requirements because it is not in a different capacity. This would be the case even though the work was occasional or sporadic, and, was not regularly scheduled. Public safety employees taking on any kind of security or safety function within the same local government are never considered to be employed in a different capacity.

(4) However, if a bookkeeper for a municipal park agency or a city mail clerk occasionally referees for an adult evening basketball league sponsored by the city, the hours worked as a referee would be considered to be in a different general occupational category than the primary employment and would not be counted as hours worked for overtime purposes on the regular job. A person regularly employed as a bus driver may assist in crowd control, for example, at an event such as a winter festival, and in doing so, would be deemed to be serving in a different capacity.

(5) In addition, any activity traditionally associated with teaching (e.g., coaching, career counseling, etc.) will not be considered as employment in a different capacity. However, where personnel other than teachers engage in such teaching-related activities, the work will be viewed as employment in a different capacity, provided that these activities are performed on an occasional or sporadic basis and all other requirements for this provision are met. For example, a school secretary could substitute as a coach for a basketball team or a maintenance engineer could provide instruction on auto repair on an occasional or sporadic basis.

Section 553.31 Substitution--section 7(p)(3).

(a) Section 7(p)(3) of the FLSA provides that two individuals employed in any occupation by the same public agency may agree, solely at their option and with the approval of the public agency, to substitute for one another during scheduled work hours in performance of work in the same capacity. The hours worked shall be excluded by the employer in the calculation of the hours for which the substituting employee would otherwise be entitled to overtime compensation under the Act. Where one employee substitutes for another, each employee will be credited as if he or she had worked his or her normal work schedule for that shift.

(b) The provisions of section 7(p)(3) apply only if employees' decisions to substitute for one another are made freely and without coercion, direct or implied. An employer may suggest that an employee substitute or "trade time" with another employee working in the same capacity during regularly scheduled hours, but each employee must be free to refuse to perform such work without sanction and without being required to explain or justify the decision. An employee's decision to substitute will be considered to have been made at his/her sole option when it has been made (i) without fear of reprisal or promise of reward by the employer, and (ii) exclusively for the employee's own convenience.

(c) A public agency which employs individuals who substitute or "trade time" under this subsection is not required to keep a record of the hours of the substitute work.

(d) In order to qualify under section 7(p)(3), an agreement between individuals employed by a public agency to substitute for one another at their own option must be approved by the agency. This requires that the agency be aware of the arrangement prior to the work being done, i.e., the employer must know what work is being done, by whom it is being done, and where and when it is being done. Approval is manifest when the employer is aware of the substitution and indicates approval in whatever manner is customary.

Section 553.32 Other FLSA exemptions.

(a) There are other exemptions from the minimum wage and/or overtime requirements of the FLSA which may apply to certain employees of public agencies. The following sections provide a discussion of some of the major exemptions which may be applicable. This list is not comprehensive.

(b) Section 7(k) of the Act provides a partial overtime pay exemption for public agency employees employed in fire protection or law enforcement activities (including security personnel in correctional institutions). In addition, section 13(b)(20) provides a complete overtime pay exemption for any employee of a public agency engaged in fire protection or law enforcement activities, if the public agency employs less than five employees in such activities. (See subpart C of this part.)

(c) Section 13(a)(1) of the Act provides an exemption from both the minimum wage and overtime pay requirements for any employee employed in a bona fide executive, administrative, professional, or outside sales capacity, as these terms are defined and delimited in part 541 of this title. An employee will qualify for exemption if he or she meets all of the pertinent tests relating to duties, responsibilities, and salary.

(d) Section 7(j) of the Act provides that a hospital or residential care establishment may, pursuant to a prior agreement or understanding with an employee or employees, adopt a fixed work period of 14 consecutive days for the purpose of computing overtime pay in lieu of the regular 7-day work-week. Workers employed under section 7(j) must receive not less than one and one-half times their regular rates of pay for all hours worked over 8 in any workday, and over 80 in the 14-day work period. (See Sec. 778.601 of this title.)

(e) Section 13(a)(3) of the Act provides a minimum wage and overtime pay exemption for any employee employed by an amusement or recreational establishment if (1) it does not operate for more than 7 months in any calendar year or (2) during the preceding calendar year, its average receipts for any 6 months of such year were not more than 33 1/3 percent of its average receipts for the other 6 months of such year. In order to meet the requirements of section 13(a)(3)(B), the establishment in the previous year must have received at least 75 percent of its income within 6 months. The 6 months, however, need not be 6 consecutive months. State and local governments operate parks and recreational areas to which this exemption may apply.

(f) Section 13(b)(1) of the Act provides an exemption from the overtime pay requirements for "Any employee with respect to whom the Secretary of Transportation has power to establish qualifications and maximum hours of service pursuant to the provisions of section 204 of the Motor Carrier Act, 1935." (recodified at section 3102, 49 U.S.C.). With regard to State or local governments, this overtime pay exemption may affect mass transit systems engaged in interstate commerce. This exemption is applicable to drivers, driver's helpers, loaders, and mechanics employed by a common carrier whose activities directly affect the safety of operation of motor vehicles in the transportation on the public highways of passengers or property. (See part 782 of this title.)

(g) Section 7(n) of the Act provides that, for the purpose of computing overtime pay, the hours of employment of a mass transit employee do not include the time spent in charter activities if (1) pursuant to a prior agreement the time is not to be so counted, and (2) such charter activities are not a part of the employee's regular employment.

(h) Additional overtime pay exemptions which may apply to employees of public agencies are contained in sections 13(b)(2) (employees of certain common carriers by rail), 13(b)(9) (certain employees of small market radio and television stations), and section 13(b)(12) (employees in agriculture) of the Act. Further, section 13(a)(6) of the Act provides a minimum wage and overtime pay exemption for agricultural employees who work on small farms. (See part 780 of this title.)

Record keeping

Section 553.50 Records to be kept of compensatory time.

For each employee subject to the compensatory time and compensatory time off provisions of section 7(o) of the Act, a public agency which is a State, a political subdivision of a State or an interstate governmental agency shall maintain and preserve records containing the basic information and data required by Sec. 516.2 of this title and, in addition:

(a) The number of hours of compensatory time earned pursuant to section 7(o) each workweek, or other applicable work period, by each employee at the rate of one and one-half hour for each overtime hour worked;

(b) The number of hours of such compensatory time used each workweek, or other applicable work period, by each employee;

(c) The number of hours of compensatory time compensated in cash, the total amount paid and the date of such payment; and

(d) Any collective bargaining agreement or written understanding or agreement with respect to earning and using compensatory time off. If such agreement or understanding is not in writing, a record of its existence must be kept.

Section 553.51 Records to be kept for employees paid pursuant to section 7(k).

For each employee subject to the partial overtime exemption in section 7(k) of the Act, a public agency which is a State, a political subdivision of a State, or an interstate governmental agency shall maintain and preserve records containing the information and data required by Sec. 553.50 and, in addition, make some notation on the payroll records which shows the work period for each employee and which indicates the length of that period and its starting time. If all the workers (or groups of workers) have a work period of the same length beginning at the same time on the same day, a single notation of the time of day and beginning day of the work period will suffice for these workers.

Subpart B--Volunteers

Section 553.100 General.

Section 3(e) of the Fair Labor Standards Act, as amended in 1985, provides that individuals performing volunteer services for units of State and local governments will not be regarded as "employees" under the statute. The purpose of this subpart is to define the circumstances under which individuals may perform hours of volunteer service for units of State and local governments without being considered to be their employees during such hours for purposes of the FLSA.

Section 553.101 "Volunteer" defined.

(a) An individual who performs hours of service for a public agency for civic, charitable, or humanitarian reasons, without promise, expectation or receipt of compensation for services rendered, is considered to be a volunteer during such hours. Individuals performing hours of service for such a public agency will be considered volunteers for the time so spent and not subject to sections 6, 7, and 11 of the FLSA when such hours of service are performed in accord with sections 3(e)(4) (A) and (B) of the FLSA and the guidelines in this subpart.

(b) Congress did not intend to discourage or impede volunteer activities undertaken for civic, charitable, or humanitarian purposes, but expressed its wish to prevent any manipulation or abuse of minimum wage or overtime requirements through coercion or undue pressure upon individuals to "volunteer" their services.

(c) Individuals shall be considered volunteers only where their services are offered freely and without pressure or coercion, direct or implied, from an employer.

(d) An individual shall not be considered a volunteer if the individual is otherwise employed by the same public agency to perform the same type of services as those for which the individual proposes to volunteer.

Section 553.102 Employment by the same public agency.

(a) Section 3(e)(4)(A)(ii) of the FLSA does not permit an individual to perform hours of volunteer service for a public agency when such hours involve the same type of services which the individual is employed to perform for the same public agency.

(b) Whether two agencies of the same State or local government constitute the same public agency can only be determined on a case-by-case basis. One factor that would support a conclusion that two agencies are separate is whether they are treated separately for statistical purposes in the Census of Governments issued by the Bureau of the Census, U.S. Department of Commerce.

Section 553.103 "Same type of services" defined.

(a) The 1985 Amendments provide that employees may volunteer hours of service to their public employer or agency provided "such services are not the same type of services which the individual is employed to perform for such public agency." Employees may volunteer their services in one capacity or another without contemplation of pay for services rendered. The phrase "same type of services" means similar or identical services. In general, the Administrator will consider, but not as the only criteria, the duties and other factors contained in the definitions of the 3-digit categories of occupations in the Dictionary of Occupational Titles in determining whether the volunteer activities constitute the "same type of services" as the employment activities. Equally important in such a determination will be the consideration of all the facts and circumstances in a particular case, including whether the volunteer service is closely related to the actual duties performed by or responsibilities assigned to the employee.

(b) An example of an individual performing services which constitute the "same type of services" is a nurse employed by a State hospital who proposes to volunteer to perform nursing services at a State-operated health clinic which does not qualify as a separate public agency as discussed in Sec. 553.102. Similarly, a firefighter cannot volunteer as a firefighter for the same public agency.

(c) Examples of volunteer services which do not constitute the "same type of services" include: A city police officer who volunteers as a part-time referee in a basketball league sponsored by the city; an employee of the city parks department who serves as a volunteer city firefighter; and an office employee of a city hospital or other health care institution who volunteers to spend time with a disabled or elderly person in the same institution during off duty hours as an act of charity.

Section 553.104 Private individuals who volunteer services to public agencies.

(a) Individuals who are not employed in any capacity by State or local government agencies often donate hours of service to a public agency for civic or humanitarian reasons. Such individuals are considered volunteers and not employees of such public agencies if their hours of service are provided with no promise, expectation, or receipt of compensation for the services rendered, except for reimbursement for expenses, reasonable benefits, and nominal fees, or a combination thereof, as discussed in Sec. 553.106. There are no limitations or restrictions imposed by the FLSA on the types of services which private individuals may volunteer to perform for public agencies.

(b) Examples of services which might be performed on a volunteer basis when so motivated include helping out in a sheltered workshop or providing personal services to the sick or the elderly in hospitals or nursing homes; assisting in a school library or cafeteria; or driving a school bus to carry a football team or band on a trip. Similarly, individuals may volunteer as firefighters or auxiliary police, or volunteer to perform such tasks as working with retarded or handicapped children or disadvantaged youth, helping in youth programs as camp counselors, soliciting contributions or participating in civic or charitable benefit programs and volunteering other services needed to carry out charitable or educational programs.

Section 553.105 Mutual aid agreements.

An agreement between two or more States, political subdivisions, or interstate governmental agencies for mutual aid does not change the otherwise volunteer character of services performed by employees of such agencies pursuant to said agreement. For example, where Town A and Town B have entered into a mutual aid agreement related to fire protection, a firefighter employed by Town A who also is a volunteer firefighter for Town B will not have his or her hours of volunteer service for Town B counted as part of his or her hours of employment with Town A. The mere fact that services volunteered to Town B may in some instances involve performance in Town A's geographic jurisdiction does not require that the volunteer's hours are to be counted as hours of employment with Town A.

Section 553.106 Payment of expenses, benefits, or fees.

(a) Volunteers may be paid expenses, reasonable benefits, a nominal fee, or any combination thereof, for their service without losing their status as volunteers.

(b) An individual who performs hours of service as a volunteer for a public agency may receive payment for expenses without being deemed an employee for purposes of the FLSA. A school guard does not become an employee because he or she receives a uniform allowance, or reimbursement for reasonable cleaning expenses or for wear and tear on personal clothing worn while performing hours of volunteer service. (A uniform allowance must be reasonably limited to relieving the volunteer of the cost of providing or maintaining a required uniform from personal resources.) Such individuals would not lose their volunteer status because they are reimbursed for the approximate out-of-pocket expenses incurred incidental to providing volunteer services, for example, payment for the cost of meals and transportation expenses.

(c) Individuals do not lose their status as volunteers because they are reimbursed for tuition, transportation and meal costs involved in their attending classes intended to teach them to perform efficiently the services they provide or will provide as volunteers. Likewise, the volunteer status of such individuals is not lost if they are provided books, supplies, or other materials essential to their volunteer training or reimbursement for the cost thereof.

(d) Individuals do not lose their volunteer status if they are provided reasonable benefits by a public agency for whom they perform volunteer services. Benefits would be considered reasonable, for example, when they involve inclusion of individual volunteers in group insurance plans (such as liability, health, life, disability, workers' compensation) or pension plans or "length of service" awards, commonly or traditionally provided to volunteers of State and local government agencies, which meet the additional test in paragraph (f) of this section.

(e) Individuals do not lose their volunteer status if they receive a nominal fee from a public agency. A nominal fee is not a substitute for compensation and must not be tied to productivity. However, this does not preclude the payment of a nominal amount on a "per call" or similar basis to volunteer firefighters. The following factors will be among those examined in determining whether a given amount is nominal: The distance traveled and the time and effort expended by the volunteer; whether the volunteer has agreed to be available around-the-clock or only during certain specified time periods; and whether the volunteer provides services as needed or throughout the year. An individual who volunteers to provide periodic services on a year-round basis may receive a nominal monthly or annual stipend or fee without losing volunteer status.

(f) Whether the furnishing of expenses, benefits, or fees would result in individuals' losing their status as volunteers under the FLSA can only be determined by examining the total amount of payments made (expenses, benefits, fees) in the context of the economic realities of the particular situation.

Subpart C--Fire Protection and Law Enforcement Employees of Public Agencies

General Principles

Section 553.200 Statutory provisions: section 13(b)(20).

(a) Section 13(b)(20) of the FLSA provides a complete overtime pay exemption for "any employee of a public agency who in any workweek is employed in fire protection activities or any employee of a public agency who in any workweek is employed in law enforcement activities (including security personnel in correctional institutions), if the public agency employs during the workweek less than 5 employees in fire protection or law enforcement activities, as the case may be."

(b) In determining whether a public agency qualifies for the section 13(b)(20) exemption, the fire protection and law enforcement activities are considered separately. Thus, if a public agency employs less than five employees in fire protection activities, but five or more employees in law enforcement activities (including security personnel in a correctional institution), it may claim the exemption for the fire protection employees but not for the law enforcement employees. No distinction is made between full-time and part-time employees, or between employees on duty and employees on leave status, and all such categories must be counted in determining whether the exemption applies. Individuals who are not considered "employees" for purposes of the FLSA by virtue of section 3(e) of the Act (including persons who are "volunteers" within the meaning of Sec. 553.101, and "elected officials and their appointees" within the meaning of Sec. 553.11) are not counted in determining whether the section 13(b)(20) exemption applies.

(c) The section 13(b)(20) exemption applies on a workweek basis. It is therefore possible that employees may be subject to maximum hours standard in certain workweeks, but not in others. In those workweeks in which the section 13(b)(20) exemption does not apply, the public agency is entitled to utilize the section 7(k) exemption which is explained below in Sec. 553.201.

Section 553.201 Statutory provisions: section 7(k).

(a) Section 7(k) of the Act provides a partial overtime pay exemption for fire protection and law enforcement personnel (including security personnel in correctional institutions) who are employed by public agencies on a work period basis. This section of the Act formerly permitted public agencies to pay overtime compensation to such employees in work periods of 28 consecutive days only after 216 hours of work. As further set forth in Sec. 553.230 of this part, the 216-hour standard has been replaced, pursuant to the study mandated by the statute, by 212 hours for fire protection employees and 171 hours for law enforcement employees. In the case of such employees who have a work period of at least 7 but less than 28 consecutive days, overtime compensation is required when the ratio of the number of hours worked to the number of days in the work period exceeds the ratio of 212 (or 171) hours to 28 days.

(b) As specified in Secs. 553.20 through 553.28 of subpart A, workers employed under section 7(k) may, under certain conditions, be compensated for overtime hours worked with compensatory time off rather than immediate overtime premium pay.

Section 553.202 Limitations.

The application of sections 13(b)(20) and 7(k), by their terms, is limited to public agencies, and does not apply to any private organization engaged in furnishing fire protection or law enforcement services. This is so even if the services are provided under contract with a public agency.

Exemption Requirements

Section 553.210 Fire protection activities.

(a) As used in sections 7(k) and 13(b)(20) of the Act, the term "any employee * * * in fire protection activities" refers to any employee (1) who is employed by an organized fire department or fire protection district; (2) who has been trained to the extent required by State statute or local ordinance; (3) who has the legal authority and responsibility to engage in the prevention, control or extinguishment of a fire of any type; and (4) who performs activities which are required for, and directly concerned with, the prevention, control or extinguishment of fires, including such incidental non-firefighting functions as housekeeping, equipment maintenance, lecturing, attending community fire drills and inspecting homes and schools for fire hazards. The term would include all such employees, regardless of their status as "trainee," "probationary," or "permanent," or of their particular specialty or job title (e.g., firefighter, engineer, hose or ladder operator, fire specialist, fire inspector, lieutenant, captain, inspector, fire marshal, battalion chief, deputy chief, or chief), and regardless of their assignment to support activities of the type described in paragraph (c) of this section, whether or not such assignment is for training or familiarization purposes, or for reasons of illness, injury or infirmity. The term would also include rescue and ambulance service personnel if such personnel form an integral part of the public agency's fire protection activities. See Sec. 553.215.

(b) The term "any employee in fire protection activities" also refers to employees who work for forest conservation agencies or other public agencies charged with forest fire fighting responsibilities, and who direct or engage in (1) fire spotting or lookout activities, or (2) fighting fires on the fireline or from aircraft or (3) operating tank trucks, bulldozers and tractors for the purpose of clearing fire breaks. The term includes all persons so engaged, regardless of their status as full time or part time agency employees or as temporary or casual workers employed for a particular fire or for periods of high fire danger, including those who have had no prior training. It does not include such agency employees as maintenance and office personnel who do not fight fires on a regular basis. It may include such employees during emergency situations when they are called upon to spend substantially all (i.e., 80 percent or more) of their time during the applicable work period in one or more of the activities described in paragraphs (b)(1), (2) and (3) of this section. Additionally, for those persons who actually engage in those fire protection activities, the simultaneous performance of such related functions as housekeeping, equipment maintenance, tower repairs and/or the construction of fire roads, would also be within the section 7(k) or 13(b)(20) exemption.

(c) Not included in the term "employee in fire protection activities" are the so-called "civilian" employees of a fire department, fire district, or forestry service who engage in such support activities as those performed by dispatchers, alarm operators, apparatus and equipment repair and maintenance workers, camp cooks, clerks, stenographers, etc.

Section 553.211 Law enforcement activities.

(a) As used in sections 7(k) and 13(b)(20) of the Act, the term "any employee * * * in law enforcement activities" refers to any employee (1) who is a uniformed or plainclothed member of a body of officers and subordinates who are empowered by State statute or local ordinance to enforce laws designed to maintain public peace and order and to protect both life and property from accidental or willful injury, and to prevent and detect crimes, (2) who has the power to arrest, and (3) who is presently undergoing or has undergone or will undergo on-the-job training and/or a course of instruction and study which typically includes physical training, self-defense, firearm proficiency, criminal and civil law principles, investigative and law enforcement techniques, community relations, medical aid and ethics.

(b) Employees who meet these tests are considered to be engaged in law enforcement activities regardless of their rank, or of their status as "trainee," "probationary," or "permanent," and regardless of their assignment to duties incidental to the performance of their law enforcement activities such as equipment maintenance, and lecturing, or to support activities of the type described in paragraph (g) of this section, whether or not such assignment is for training or familiarization purposes, or for reasons of illness, injury or infirmity. The term would also include rescue and ambulance service personnel if such personnel form an integral part of the public agency's law enforcement activities. See Sec. 553.215.

(c) Typically, employees engaged in law enforcement activities include city police; district or local police, sheriffs, under sheriffs or deputy sheriffs who are regularly employed and paid as such; court marshals or deputy marshals; constables and deputy constables who are regularly employed and paid as such; border control agents; state troopers and highway patrol officers. Other agency employees not specifically mentioned may, depending upon the particular facts and pertinent statutory provisions in that jurisdiction, meet the three tests described above. If so, they will also qualify as law enforcement officers. Such employees might include, for example, fish and game wardens or criminal investigative agents assigned to the office of a district attorney, an attorney general, a solicitor general or any other law enforcement agency concerned with keeping public peace and order and protecting life and property.

(d) Some of the law enforcement officers listed above, including but not limited to certain sheriffs, will not be covered by the Act if they are elected officials and if they are not subject to the civil service laws of their particular State or local jurisdiction. Section 3(e)(2)(C) of the Act excludes from its definition of "employee" elected officials and their personal staff under the conditions therein prescribed. 29 U.S.C. 203(e)(2)(C), and see Sec. 553.11. Such individuals, therefore, need not be counted in determining whether the public agency in question has less than five employees engaged in law enforcement activities for purposes of claiming the section 13(b)(20) exemption.

(e) Employees who do not meet each of the three tests described above are not engaged in "law enforcement activities" as that term is used in sections 7(k) and 13(b)(20). Employees who normally would not meet each of these tests include (1) Building inspectors (other than those defined in Sec. 553.213(a)), (2) Health inspectors, (3) Animal control personnel, (4) Sanitarians, (5) civilian traffic employees who direct vehicular and pedestrian traffic at specified intersections or other control points, (6) Civilian parking checkers who patrol assigned areas for the purpose of discovering parking violations and issuing appropriate warnings or appearance notices, (7) Wage and hour compliance officers, (8) Equal employment opportunity compliance officers, (9) Tax compliance officers, (10) Coal mining inspectors, and (11) Building guards whose primary duty is to protect the lives and property of persons within the limited area of the building.

(f) The term "any employee in law enforcement activities" also includes, by express reference, "security personnel in correctional institutions." A correctional institution is any government facility maintained as part of a penal system for the incarceration or detention of persons suspected or convicted of having breached the peace or committed some other crime. Typically, such facilities include penitentiaries, prisons, prison farms, county, city and village jails, precinct house lockups and reformatories. Employees of correctional institutions who qualify as security personnel for purposes of the section 7(k) exemption are those who have responsibility for controlling and maintaining custody of inmates and of safeguarding them from other inmates or for supervising such functions, regardless of whether their duties are performed inside the correctional institution or outside the institution (as in the case of road gangs). These employees are considered to be engaged in law enforcement activities regardless of their rank (e.g., warden, assistant warden or guard) or of their status as "trainee," "probationary," or "permanent," and regardless of their assignment to duties incidental to the performance of their law enforcement activities, or to support activities of the type described in paragraph (g) of this section, whether or not such assignment is for training or familiarization purposes or for reasons of illness, injury or infirmity.

(g) Not included in the term "employee in law enforcement activities" are the so-called "civilian" employees of law enforcement agencies or correctional institutions who engage in such support activities as those performed by dispatcher, radio operators, apparatus and equipment maintenance and repair workers, janitors, clerks and stenographers. Nor does the term include employees in correctional institutions who engage in building repair and maintenance, culinary services, teaching, or in psychological, medical and paramedical services. This is so even though such employees may, when assigned to correctional institutions, come into regular contact with the inmates in the performance of their duties.

Section 553.212 Twenty percent limitation on nonexempt work.

(a) Employees engaged in fire protection or law enforcement activities as described in Secs. 553.210 and 553.211, may also engage in some nonexempt work which is not performed as an incident to or in conjunction with their fire protection or law enforcement activities. For example, firefighters who work for forest conservation agencies may, during slack times, plant trees and perform other conservation activities unrelated to their firefighting duties. The performance of such nonexempt work will not defeat either the section 13(b)(20) or 7(k) exemptions unless it exceeds 20 percent of the total hours worked by that employee during the workweek or applicable work period. A person who spends more than 20 percent of his/her working time in nonexempt activities is not considered to be an employee engaged in fire protection or law enforcement activities for purposes of this part.

(b) Public agency fire protection and law enforcement personnel may, at their own option, undertake employment for the same employer on an occasional or sporadic and part-time basis in a different capacity from their regular employment. (See Sec. 553.30.) The performance of such work does not affect the application of the section 13(b)(20) or 7(k) exemptions with respect to the regular employment. In addition, the hours of work in the different capacity need not be counted as hours worked for overtime purposes on the regular job, nor are such hours counted in determining the 20 percent tolerance for nonexempt work discussed in paragraph (a) of this section.

Section 553.213 Public agency employees engaged in both fire protection and law enforcement activities.

(a) Some public agencies have employees (often called "public safety officers") who engage in both fire protection and law enforcement activities, depending on the agency needs at the time. This dual assignment would not defeat either the section 13(b)(20) or 7(k) exemption, provided that each of the activities performed meets the appropriate tests set forth in Secs. 553.210 and 553.211. This is so regardless of how the employee's time is divided between the two activities. However, all time spent in nonexempt activities by public safety officers within the work period, whether performed in connection with fire protection or law enforcement functions, or with neither, must be combined for purposes of the 20 percent limitation on nonexempt work discussed in Sec. 553.212.

(b) As specified in Sec. 553.230, the maximum hours standards under section 7(k) are different for employees engaged in fire protection and for employees engaged in law enforcement. For those employees who perform both fire protection and law enforcement activities, the applicable standard is the one which applies to the activity in which the employee spends the majority of work time during the work period.

Section 553.214 Trainees.

The attendance at a bona fide fire or police academy or other training facility, when required by the employing agency, constitutes engagement in activities under section 7(k) only when the employee meets all the applicable tests described in Sec. 553.210 or Sec. 553.211 (except for the power of arrest for law enforcement personnel), as the case may be. If the applicable tests are met, then basic training or advanced training is considered incidental to, and part of, the employee's fire protection or law enforcement activities.

Section 553.215 Ambulance and rescue service employees.

(a) Ambulance and rescue service employees of a public agency other than a fire protection or law enforcement agency may be treated as employees engaged in fire protection or law enforcement activities of the type contemplated by sections 7(k) and 13(b)(20) if their services are substantially related to firefighting or law enforcement activities in that (1) the ambulance and rescue service employees have received training in the rescue of fire, crime, and accident victims or firefighters or law enforcement personnel injured in the performance of their respective, duties, and (2) the ambulance and rescue service employees are regularly dispatched to fires, crime scenes, riots, natural disasters and accidents. As provided in Sec. 553.213(b), where employees perform both fire protection and law enforcement activities, the applicable standard is the one which applies to the activity in which the employee spends the majority of work time during the work period.

(b) Ambulance and rescue service employees of public agencies subject to the Act prior to the 1974 Amendments do not come within the section 7(k) or section 13(b)(20) exemptions, since it was not the purpose of those Amendments to deny the Act's protection of previously covered and nonexempt employees. This would include, for example, employees of public agencies engaged in the operation of a hospital or an institution primarily engaged in the care of the sick, the aged, the mentally ill or defective who reside on the premises of such institutions.

(c) Ambulance and rescue service employees of private organizations do not come within the section 7(k) or section 13(b)(20) exemptions even if their activities are substantially related to the fire protection and law enforcement activities performed by a public agency or their employer is under contract with a public agency to provide such services.

Section 553.216 Other exemptions.

Although the 1974 Amendments to the FLSA provided special exemptions for employees of public agencies engaged in fire protection and law enforcement activities, such workers may also be subject to other exemptions in the Act, and public agencies may claim such other applicable exemptions in lieu of sections 13(b)(20) and 7(k). For example, section 13(a)(1) provides a complete minimum wage and overtime pay exemption for any employee employed in a bona fide executive, administrative, or professional capacity, as those terms are defined and delimited in 29 CFR part 541. The section 13(a)(1) exemption can be claimed for any fire protection or law enforcement employee who meets all of the tests specified in part 541 relating to duties, responsibilities, and salary. Thus, high ranking police officials who are engaged in law enforcement activities, may also, depending on the facts, qualify for the section 13(a)(1) exemption as "executive" employees. Similarly, certain criminal investigative agents may qualify as "administrative" employees under section 13(a)(1). However, the election to take the section 13(a)(1) exemption for an employee who qualifies for it will not result in excluding that employee from the count that must be made to determine the application of the section 13(b)(20) exemption to the agency's other employees.

Tour of Duty and Compensable Hours of Work Rules

Section 553.220 "Tour of duty" defined.

(a) The term "tour of duty" is a unique concept applicable only to employees for whom the section 7(k) exemption is claimed. This term, as used in section 7(k), means the period of time during which an employee is considered to be on duty for purposes of determining compensable hours. It may be a scheduled or unscheduled period. Such periods include "shifts" assigned to employees often days in advance of the performance of the work.

Scheduled periods also include time spent in work outside the "shift" which the public agency employer assigns. For example, a police officer may be assigned to crowd control during a parade or other special event outside of his or her shift.

(b) Unscheduled periods include time spent in court by police officers, time spent handling emergency situations, and time spent working after a shift to complete an assignment. Such time must be included in the compensable tour of duty even though the specific work performed may not have been assigned in advance.

(c) The tour of duty does not include time spent working for a separate and independent employer in certain types of special details as provided in Sec. 553.227. The tour of duty does not include time spent working on an occasional or sporadic and part-time basis in a different capacity from the regular work as provided in Sec. 553.30. The tour of duty does not include time spent substituting for other employees by mutual agreement as specified in Sec. 553.31.

(d) The tour of duty does not include time spent in volunteer firefighting or law enforcement activities performed for a different jurisdiction, even where such activities take place under the terms of a mutual aid agreement in the jurisdiction in which the employee is employed. (See Sec. 553.105.)

Section 553.221 Compensable hours of work.

(a) The general rules on compensable hours of work are set forth in 29 CFR part 785 which is applicable to employees for whom the section 7(k) exemption is claimed. Special rules for sleep time (Sec. 553.222) apply to both law enforcement and firefighting employees for whom the section 7(k) exemption is claimed. Also, special rules for meal time apply in the case of firefighters (Sec. 553.223). Part 785 does not discuss the special provisions that apply to State and local government workers with respect to the treatment of substitution, special details for a separate and independent employer, early relief, and work performed on an occasional or sporadic and part-time basis, all of which are covered in this subpart.

(b) Compensable hours of work generally include all of the time during which an employee is on duty on the employer's premises or at a prescribed workplace, as well as all other time during which the employee is suffered or permitted to work for the employer. Such time includes all pre-shift and post-shift activities which are an integral part of the employee's principal activity or which are closely related to the performance of the principal activity, such as attending roll call, writing up and completing tickets or reports, and washing and re-racking fire hoses.

(c) Time spent away from the employer's premises under conditions that are so circumscribed that they restrict the employee from effectively using the time for personal pursuits also constitutes compensable hours of work. For example, where a police station must be evacuated because of an electrical failure and the employees are expected to remain in the vicinity and return to work after the emergency has passed, the entire time spent away from the premises is compensable. The employees in this example cannot use the time for their personal pursuits.

(d) An employee who is not required to remain on the employer's premises but is merely required to leave word at home or with company officials where he or she may be reached is not working while on call. Time spent at home on call may or may not be compensable depending on whether the restrictions placed on the employee preclude using the time for personal pursuits. Where, for example, a firefighter has returned home after the shift, with the understanding that he or she is expected to return to work in the event of an emergency in the night, such time spent at home is normally not compensable. On the other hand, where the conditions placed on the employee's activities are so restrictive that the employee cannot use the time effectively for personal pursuits, such time spent on call is compensable.

(e) Normal home to work travel is not compensable, even where the employee is expected to report to work at a location away from the location of the employer's premises.

(f) A police officer, who has completed his or her tour of duty and who is given a patrol car to drive home and use on personal business, is not working during the travel time even where the radio must be left on so that the officer can respond to emergency calls. Of course, the time spent in responding to such calls is compensable.

(g) The fact that employees cannot return home after work does not necessarily mean that they continue on duty after their shift. For example, firefighters working on a forest fire may be transported to a camp after their shift in order to rest and eat a meal. As a practical matter, the firefighters may be precluded from going to their homes because of the distance of the fire from their residences.

Section 553.222 Sleep time.

(a) Where a public employer elects to pay overtime compensation to firefighters and/or law enforcement personnel in accordance with section 7(a)(1) of the Act, the public agency may exclude sleep time from hours worked if all the conditions in Sec. 785.22 of this title are met.

(b) Where the employer has elected to use the section 7(k) exemption, sleep time cannot be excluded from the compensable hours of work where (1) The employee is on a tour of duty of less than 24 hours, which is the general rule applicable to all employees under Sec. 785.21, and (2) Where the employee is on a tour of duty of exactly 24 hours, which is a departure from the general rules in part 785.

(c) Sleep time can be excluded from compensable hours of work, however, in the case of police officers or firefighters who are on a tour of duty of more than 24 hours, but only if there is an expressed or implied agreement between the employer and the employees to exclude such time. In the absence of such an agreement, the sleep time is compensable. In no event shall the time excluded as sleep time exceed 8 hours in a 24-hour period. If the sleep time is interrupted by a call to duty, the interruption must be counted as hours worked. If the sleep period is interrupted to such an extent that the employee cannot get a reasonable night's sleep (which, for enforcement purposes means at least 5 hours), the entire time must be counted as hours of work.

Section 553.223 Meal time.

(a) If a public agency elects to pay overtime compensation to firefighters and law enforcement personnel in accordance with section 7(a)(1) of the Act, the public agency may exclude meal time from hours worked if all the tests in Sec. 785.19 of this title are met.

(b) If a public agency elects to use the section 7(k) exemption, the public agency may, in the case of law enforcement personnel, exclude meal time from hours worked on tours of duty of 24 hours or less, provided that the employee is completely relieved from duty during the meal period, and all the other tests in Sec. 785.19 of this title are met. On the other hand, where law enforcement personnel are required to remain on call in barracks or similar quarters, or are engaged in extended surveillance activities (e.g., "stakeouts"), they are not considered to be completely relieved from duty, and any such meal periods would be compensable.

(c) With respect to firefighters employed under section 7(k), who are confined to a duty station, the legislative history of the Act indicates Congressional intent to mandate a departure from the usual FLSA "hours of work" rules and adoption of an overtime standard keyed to the unique concept of "tour of duty" under which firefighters are employed. Where the public agency elects to use the section 7(k) exemption for firefighters, meal time cannot be excluded from the compensable hours of work where (1) the firefighter is on a tour of duty of less than 24 hours, and (2) where the firefighter is on a tour of duty of exactly 24 hours, which is a departure from the general rules in Sec. 785.22 of this title.

(d) In the case of police officers or firefighters who are on a tour of duty of more than 24 hours, meal time may be excluded from compensable hours of work provided that the tests in Secs. 785.19 and 785.22 of this title are met.

Section 553.224 "Work period" defined.

(a) As used in section 7(k), the term "work period" refers to any established and regularly recurring period of work which, under the terms of the Act and legislative history, cannot be less than 7 consecutive days nor more than 28 consecutive days. Except for this limitation, the work period can be of any length, and it need not coincide with the duty cycle or pay period or with a particular day of the week or hour of the day. Once the beginning and ending time of an employee's work period is established, however, it remains fixed regardless of how many hours are worked within the period. The beginning and ending of the work period may be changed, provided that the change is intended to be permanent and is not designed to evade the overtime compensation requirements of the Act.

(b) An employer may have one work period applicable to all employees, or different work periods for different employees or groups of employees.

Section 553.225 Early relief.

It is a common practice among employees engaged in fire protection activities to relieve employees on the previous shift prior to the scheduled starting time. Such early relief time may occur pursuant to employee agreement, either expressed or implied. This practice will not have the effect of increasing the number of compensable hours of work for employees employed under section 7(k) where it is voluntary on the part of the employees and does not result, over a period of time, in their failure to receive proper compensation for all hours actually worked. On the other hand, if the practice is required by the employer, the time involved must be added to the employee's tour of duty and treated as compensable hours of work.

Section 553.226 Training time.

(a) The general rules for determining the compensability of training time under the FLSA are set forth in Secs. 785.27 through 785.32 of this title.

(b) While time spent in attending training required by an employer is normally considered compensable hours of work, following are situations where time spent by employees of State and local governments in required training is considered to be noncompensable:

(1) Attendance outside of regular working hours at specialized or follow-up training, which is required by law for certification of public and private sector employees within a particular governmental jurisdiction (e.g., certification of public and private emergency rescue workers), does not constitute compensable hours of work for public employees within that jurisdiction and subordinate jurisdictions.

(2) Attendance outside of regular working hours at specialized or follow-up training, which is required for certification of employees of a governmental jurisdiction by law of a higher level of government (e.g., where a State or county law imposes a training obligation on city employees), does not constitute compensable hours of work.

(3) Time spent in the training described in paragraphs (b) (1) or (2) of this section is not compensable, even if all or part of the costs of the training is borne by the employer.

(c) Police officers or firefighters, who are in attendance at a police or fire academy or other training facility, are not considered to be on duty during those times when they are not in class or at a training session, if they are free to use such time for personal pursuits. Such free time is not compensable.

Section 553.227 Outside employment.

(a) Section 7(p)(1) makes special provision for fire protection and law enforcement employees of public agencies who, at their own option, perform special duty work in fire protection, law enforcement or related activities for a separate and independent employer (public or private) during their off-duty hours. The hours of work for the separate and independent employer are not combined with the hours worked for the primary public agency employer for purposes of overtime compensation.

(b) Section 7(p)(1) applies to such outside employment provided (1) The special detail work is performed solely at the employee's option, and (2) the two employers are in fact separate and independent.

(c) Whether two employers are, in fact, separate and independent can only be determined on a case-by-case basis.

(d) The primary employer may facilitate the employment or affect the conditions of employment of such employees. For example, a police department may maintain a roster of officers who wish to perform such work. The department may also select the officers for special details from a list of those wishing to participate, negotiate their pay, and retain a fee for administrative expenses. The department may require that the separate and independent employer pay the fee for such services directly to the department, and establish procedures for the officers to receive their pay for the special details through the agency's payroll system. Finally, the department may require that the officers observe their normal standards of conduct during such details and take disciplinary action against those who fail to do so.

(e) Section 7(p)(1) applies to special details even where a State law or local ordinance requires that such work be performed and that only law enforcement or fire protection employees of a public agency in the same jurisdiction perform the work. For example, a city ordinance may require the presence of city police officers at a convention center during concerts or sports events. If the officers perform such work at their own option, the hours of work need not be combined with the hours of work for their primary employer in computing overtime compensation.

(f) The principles in paragraphs (d) and (e) of this section with respect to special details of public agency fire protection and law enforcement employees under section 7(p)(1) are exceptions to the usual rules on joint employment set forth in part 791 of this title.

(g) Where an employee is directed by the public agency to perform work for a second employer, section 7(p)(1) does not apply. Thus, assignments of police officers outside of their normal work hours to perform crowd control at a parade, where the assignments are not solely at the option of the officers, would not qualify as special details subject to this exception. This would be true even if the parade organizers reimburse the public agency for providing such services.

(h) Section 7(p)(1) does not prevent a public agency from prohibiting or restricting outside employment by its employees.

Overtime Compensation Rules

Section 553.230 Maximum hours standards for work periods of 7 to 28 days--section 7(k).

(a) For those employees engaged in fire protection activities who have a work period of at least 7 but less than 28 consecutive days, no overtime compensation is required under section 7(k) until the number of hours worked exceeds the number of hours which bears the same relationship to 212 as the number of days in the work period bears to 28.

(b) For those employees engaged in law enforcement activities (including security personnel in correctional institutions) who have a work period of at least 7 but less than 28 consecutive days, no overtime compensation is required under section 7(k) until the number of hours worked exceeds the number of hours which bears the same relationship to 171 as the number of days in the work period bears to 28.

(c) The ratio of 212 hours to 28 days for employees engaged in fire protection activities is 7.57 hours per day (rounded) and the ratio of 171 hours to 28 days for employees engaged in law enforcement activities is 6.11 hours per day (rounded). Accordingly, overtime compensation (in premium pay or compensatory time) is required for all hours worked in excess of the following maximum hours standards (rounded to the nearest whole hour):

Maximum Hours Standards

Work Period	Fire Protection	Law Enforcement
28	212	171
27	204	165
26	197	159
25	189	153
24	182	147
23	174	141
22	167	134
21	159	128
20	151	122
19	144	116
18	136	110
17	129	104
16	121	98
15	114	92
14	106	86
13	98	79
12	91	73
11	83	67
10	76	61
9	68	55
8	61	49
7	53	43

Section 553.231 Compensatory time off.

(a) Law enforcement and fire protection employees who are subject to the section 7(k) exemption may receive compensatory time off in lieu of overtime pay for hours worked in excess of the maximum for their work period as set forth in Sec. 553.230. The rules for compensatory time off are set forth in Secs. 553.20 through 553.28 of this part.

(b) Section 7(k) permits public agencies to balance the hours of work over an entire work period for law enforcement and fire protection employees. For example, if a firefighter's work period is 28 consecutive days, and he or she works 80 hours in each of the first two weeks, but only 52 hours in the third week, and does not work in the fourth week, no overtime compensation (in cash wages or compensatory time) would be required since the total hours worked do not exceed 212 for the work period. If the same firefighter had a work period of only 14 days, overtime compensation or compensatory time off would be due for 54 hours (160 minus 106 hours) in the first 14 day work period.

Section 553.232 Overtime pay requirements.

If a public agency pays employees subject to section 7(k) for overtime hours worked in cash wages rather than compensatory time off, such wages must be paid at one and one-half times the employees' regular rates of pay. In addition, employees who have accrued the maximum 480 hours of compensatory time must be paid cash wages of time and one-half their regular rates of pay for overtime hours in excess of the maximum for the work period set forth in Sec. 553.230.

Section 553.233 "Regular rate" defined.

The rules for computing an employee's "regular rate", for purposes of the Act's overtime pay requirements, are set forth in part 778 of this title. These rules are applicable to employees for whom the section 7(k) exemption is claimed when overtime compensation is provided in cash wages. However, wherever the word "workweek" is used in part 778, the words "work period" should be substituted.

SECTION 778--OVERTIME COMPENSATION

Subpart A--General Considerations

Section 778.0 Introductory statement.

The Fair Labor Standards Act, as amended, hereinafter referred to as the Act, is a Federal statute of general application which establishes minimum wage, overtime pay, child labor, and equal pay requirements that apply as provided in the Act. All employees whose employment has the relationship to interstate or foreign commerce which the Act specifies are subject to the prescribed labor standards unless specifically exempted from them. Employers having such employees are required to comply with the Act's provisions in this regard unless relieved therefrom by some exemption in the Act. Such employers are also required to comply with specified recordkeeping requirements contained in part 516 of this chapter. The law authorizes the Department of Labor to investigate for compliance and, in the event of violations, to supervise the payment of unpaid wages or unpaid overtime compensation owing to any employee. The law also provides for enforcement in the courts.

Section 778.1 Purpose of interpretative bulletin.

This part 778 constitutes the official interpretation of the Department of Labor with respect to the meaning and application of the maximum hours and overtime pay requirements contained in section 7 of the Act. It is the purpose of this bulletin to make available in one place the interpretations of these provisions which will guide the Secretary of Labor and the Administrator in the performance of their duties under the Act unless and until they are otherwise directed by authoritative decisions of the courts or conclude, upon reexamination of an interpretation, that it is incorrect. These official interpretations are issued by the Administrator on the advice of the Solicitor of Labor, as authorized by the Secretary.

Section 778.2 Coverage and exemptions not discussed.

This part 778 does not deal with the general coverage of the Act or various specific exemptions provided in the statute, under which certain employees within the general coverage of the wage and hours provisions are wholly or partially excluded from the protection of the Act's minimum-wage and overtime-pay requirements. Some of these exemptions are self-executing; others call for definitions or other action by the Administrator. Regulations and interpretations relating to general coverage and specific exemptions may be found in other parts of this chapter.

Section 778.3 Interpretations made, continued, and superseded by this part.

On and after publication of this part in the Federal Register, the interpretations contained therein shall be in effect and shall remain in effect until they are modified, rescinded or withdrawn. This part supersedes and replaces the interpretations previously published in the Federal Register and Code of Federal Regulations as part 778 of this chapter. Prior opinions, rulings and interpretations and prior enforcement policies which are not inconsistent with the interpretations in this part or with the Fair Labor Standards Act as amended are continued in effect; all other opinions, rulings, interpretations, and enforcement policies on the subjects discussed in the interpretations in this part are rescinded and withdrawn. Questions on matters not fully covered by this part may be addressed to the Administrator of the Wage and Hour Division, U.S. Department of Labor, Washington, DC 20210, or to any Regional Office of the Division.

Section 778.4 Reliance on interpretations.

The interpretations of the law contained in this part 778 are official interpretations which may be relied upon as provided in section 10 of the Portal-to-Portal Act of 1947 (61 Stat. 84).

Section 778.5 Relation to other laws generally.

Various Federal, State, and local laws require the payment of minimum hourly, daily or weekly wages different from the minimum set forth in the Fair Labor Standards Act, and the payment of overtime compensation computed on bases different from those set forth in the Fair Labor Standards Act. Where such legislation is applicable and does not contravene the requirements of the Fair Labor Standards Act, nothing in the act, the regulations or the interpretations announced by the Administrator should be taken to override or nullify the provisions of these laws. Compliance with other applicable legislation does not excuse noncompliance with the Fair Labor Standards Act. Where a higher minimum wage than that set in the Fair Labor Standards Act is applicable to an employee by virtue of such other legislation, the regular rate of the employee, as the term is used in the Fair

Labor Standards Act, cannot be lower than such applicable minimum, for the words "regular rate at which he is employed" as used in section 7 must be construed to mean the regular rate at which he is lawfully employed.

Subpart B--The Overtime Pay Requirements
Introductory

Section 778.100 The maximum-hours provisions.

Section 7(a) of the Act deals with maximum hours and overtime compensation for employees who are within the general coverage of the Act and are not specifically exempt from its overtime pay requirements. It prescribes the maximum weekly hours of work permitted for the employment of such employees in any workweek without extra compensation for overtime, and a general overtime rate of pay not less than one and one-half times the employee's regular rate which the employee must receive for all hours worked in any workweek in excess of the applicable maximum hours. The employment by an employer of an employee in any work subject to the Act in any workweek brings these provisions into operation. The employer is prohibited from employing the employee in excess of the prescribed maximum hours in such workweek without paying him the required extra compensation for the overtime hours worked at a rate meeting the statutory requirement.

Section 778.101 Maximum nonovertime hours.

As a general standard, section 7(a) of the Act provides 40 hours as the maximum number that an employee subject to its provisions may work for an employer in any workweek without receiving additional compensation at not less than the statutory rate for overtime. Hours worked in excess of the statutory maximum in any workweek are overtime hours under the statute; a workweek no longer than the prescribed maximum is a nonovertime workweek under the Act, to which the pay requirements of section 6 (minimum wage and equal pay) but not those of section 7(a) are applicable.

Section 778.102 Application of overtime provisions generally.

Since there is no absolute limitation in the Act (apart from the child labor provisions and regulations thereunder) on the number of hours that an employee may work in any workweek, he may work as many hours a week as he and his employer see fit, so long as the required overtime compensation is paid him for hours worked in excess of the maximum workweek prescribed by section 7(a). The Act does not generally require, however, that an employee be paid overtime compensation for hours in excess of eight per day, or for work on Saturdays, Sundays, holidays or regular days of rest. If no more than the maximum number of hours prescribed in the Act are actually worked in the workweek, overtime compensation pursuant to section 7(a) need not be paid. Nothing in the Act, however, will relieve an employer of any obligation he may have assumed by contract or of any obligation imposed by other Federal or State law to limit overtime hours of work or to pay premium rates for work in excess of a daily standard or for work on

Saturdays, Sundays, holidays, or other periods outside of or in excess of the normal or regular workweek or workday. (The effect of making such payments is discussed in Secs. 778.201 through 778.207 and 778.219.)

Section 778.103 The workweek as the basis for applying section 7(a).

If in any workweek an employee is covered by the Act and is not exempt from its overtime pay requirements, the employer must total all the hours worked by the employee for him in that workweek (even though two or more unrelated job assignments may have been performed), and pay overtime compensation for each hour worked in excess of the maximum hours applicable under section 7(a) of the Act. In the case of an employee employed jointly by two or more employers (see part 791 of this chapter), all hours worked by the employee for such employers during the workweek must be totaled in determining the number of hours to be compensated in accordance with section 7(a). The principles for determining what hours are hours worked within the meaning of the Act are discussed in part 785 of this chapter.

Section 778.104 Each workweek stands alone.

The Act takes a single workweek as its standard and does not permit averaging of hours over 2 or more weeks. Thus, if an employee works 30 hours one week and 50 hours the next, he must receive overtime compensation for the overtime hours worked beyond the applicable maximum in the second week, even though the average number of hours worked in the 2 weeks is 40. This is true regardless of whether the employee works on a standard or swing-shift schedule and regardless of whether he is paid on a daily, weekly, biweekly, monthly or other basis. The rule is also applicable to pieceworkers and employees paid on a commission basis. It is therefore necessary to determine the hours worked and the compensation earned by pieceworkers and commission employees on a weekly basis.

Section 778.105 Determining the workweek.

An employee's workweek is a fixed and regularly recurring period of 168 hours--seven consecutive 24-hour periods. It need not coincide with the calendar week but may begin on any day and at any hour of the day. For purposes of computing pay due under the Fair Labor Standards Act, a single workweek may be established for a plant or other establishment as a whole or different workweeks may be established for different employees or groups of employees. Once the beginning time of an employee's workweek is established, it remains fixed regardless of the schedule of hours worked by him. The beginning of the workweek may be changed if the change is intended to be permanent and is not designed to evade the overtime requirements of the Act. The proper method of computing overtime pay in a period in which a change in the time of commencement of the workweek is made, is discussed in Secs. 778.301 and 778.302.

Section 778.106 Time of payment.

There is no requirement in the Act that overtime compensation be paid weekly. The general rule is that overtime compensation earned in a particular workweek must be paid on the regular pay day for the period in which such workweek ends. When the correct amount of overtime compensation cannot be determined until some time after the regular pay period, however, the requirements of the Act will be satisfied if the employer pays the excess overtime compensation as soon after the regular pay period as is practicable. Payment may not be delayed for a period longer than is reasonably necessary for the employer to compute and arrange for payment of the amount due and in no event may payment be delayed beyond the next payday after such computation can be made. Where retroactive wage increases are made, retroactive overtime compensation is due at the time the increase is paid, as discussed in Sec. 778.303. For a discussion of overtime payments due because of increases by way of bonuses, see Sec. 778.209.

Principles for Computing Overtime Pay Based on the "Regular Rate"

Section 778.107 General standard for overtime pay.

The general overtime pay standard in section 7(a) requires that overtime must be compensated at a rate not less than one and one-half times the regular rate at which the employee is actually employed. The regular rate of pay at which the employee is employed may in no event be less than the statutory minimum. (The statutory minimum is the specified minimum wage applicable under section 6 of the Act, except in the case of workers specially provided for in section 14 and workers in Puerto Rico, the Virgin Islands, and American Samoa who are covered by wage orders issued pursuant to section 8 of the Act.) If the employee's regular rate of pay is higher than the statutory minimum, his overtime compensation must be computed at a rate not less than one and one-half times such higher rate. Under certain conditions prescribed in section 7 (f), (g), and (j), the Act provides limited exceptions to the application of the general standard of section 7(a) for computing overtime pay based on the regular rate. With respect to these, see Secs. 778.400 through 778.421 and 778.601 and part 548 of this chapter. The Act also provides, in section 7(b), (i), (k) and (m) and in section 13, certain partial and total exemptions from the application of section 7(a) to certain employees and under certain conditions. Regulations and interpretations concerning these exemptions are outside the scope of this part 778 and reference should be made to other applicable parts of this chapter.

Section 778.108 The "regular rate".

The "regular rate" of pay under the Act cannot be left to a declaration by the parties as to what is to be treated as the regular rate for an employee; it must be drawn from what happens under the employment contract (*Bay Ridge Operating Co. v. Aaron*, 334 U.S. 446). The Supreme Court has described it as the hourly rate actually paid the employee for the normal, nonovertime workweek for which he is employed--an "actual fact" (*Walling v. Younger-man-Reynolds Hardwood Co.*, 325 U.S. 419). Section 7(e) of the Act requires inclusion in the regular rate of "all remuneration for employment paid to, or on behalf of, the employee" except payments specifically excluded by paragraphs (1) through (7) of that subsection. (These seven types of payments, which are set forth in Sec. 778.200 and discussed in Secs. 778.201

through 778.224, are hereafter referred to as "statutory exclusions.") As stated by the Supreme Court in the *Youngerman-Reynolds* case cited above: "Once the parties have decided upon the amount of wages and the mode of payment the determination of the regular rate becomes a matter of mathematical computation, the result of which is unaffected by any designation of a contrary 'regular rate' in the wage contracts."

Section 778.109 The regular rate is an hourly rate.

The "regular rate" under the Act is a rate per hour. The Act does not require employers to compensate employees on an hourly rate basis; their earnings may be determined on a piece-rate, salary, commission, or other basis, but in such case the overtime compensation due to employees must be computed on the basis of the hourly rate derived therefrom and, therefore, it is necessary to compute the regular hourly rate of such employees during each workweek, with certain statutory exceptions discussed in Secs. 778.400 through 778.421. The regular hourly rate of pay of an employee is determined by dividing his total remuneration for employment (except statutory exclusions) in any workweek by the total number of hours actually worked by him in that workweek for which such compensation was paid. The following sections give some examples of the proper method of determining the regular rate of pay in particular instances: (The maximum hours standard used in these examples is 40 hours in a workweek).

Section 778.110 Hourly rate employee.

(a) Earnings at hourly rate exclusively. If the employee is employed solely on the basis of a single hourly rate, the hourly rate is his regular rate. For his overtime work he must be paid, in addition to his straight time hourly earnings, a sum determined by multiplying one-half the hourly rate by the number of hours worked in excess of 40 in the week. Thus a $6 hourly rate will bring, for an employee who works 46 hours, a total weekly wage of $294 (46 hours at $6 plus 6 at $3). In other words, the employee is entitled to be paid an amount equal to $6 an hour for 40 hours and $9 an hour for the 6 hours of overtime, or a total of $294.

(b) Hourly rate and bonus. If the employee receives, in addition to is earnings at the hourly rate, a production bonus of $9.20, the regular hourly rate of pay is $6.20 an hour (46 hours at $6 yields $276; the addition of the $9.20 bonus makes a total of $285.20; this total divided by 46 hours yields a rate of $6.20). The employee is then entitled to be paid a total wage of $303.80 for 46 hours (46 hours at $6.20 plus 6 hours at $3.10, or 40 hours at $6.20 plus 6 hours at $9.30).

Section.778.113 Salaried employees--general.

(a) Weekly salary. If the employee is employed solely on a weekly salary basis, his regular hourly rate of pay, on which time and a half must be paid, is computed by dividing the salary by the number of hours which the salary is intended to compensate. If an employee is hired at a salary of $182.70 and if it is understood that this salary is compensation for a regular workweek of 35 hours, the employee's regular rate of pay is $182.70 divided by 35 hours, or $5.22 an hour, and when he works overtime he is entitled to receive $5.22 for each of the first 40 hours and $7.83 (one and one-half times $5.22) for each hour thereafter. If an employee is hired at a salary of $220.80 for a 40-hour week his regular rate is $5.52 an hour.

(b) Salary for periods other than workweek. Where the salary covers a period longer than a workweek, such as a month, it must be reduced to its workweek equivalent. A monthly salary is subject to translation to its equivalent weekly wage by multiplying by 12 (the number of months) and dividing by 52 (the number of weeks). A semimonthly salary is translated into its equivalent weekly wage by multiplying by 24 and dividing by 52. Once the weekly wage is arrived at, the regular hourly rate of pay will be calculated as indicated above. The regular rate of an employee who is paid a regular monthly salary of $1,040, or a regular semimonthly salary of $520 for 40 hours a week, is thus found to be $6 per hour. Under regulations of the Administrator, pursuant to the authority given to him in section 7(g)(3) of the Act, the parties may provide that the regular rates shall be determined by dividing the monthly salary by the number of working days in the month and then by the number of hours of the normal or regular workday. Of course, the resultant rate in such a case must not be less than the statutory minimum wage.

Section 778.114 Fixed salary for fluctuating hours.

(a) An employee employed on a salary basis may have hours of work which fluctuate from week to week and the salary may be paid him pursuant to an understanding with his employer that he will receive such fixed amount as straight time pay for whatever hours he is called upon to work in a workweek, whether few or many. Where there is a clear mutual understanding of the parties that the fixed salary is compensation (apart from overtime premiums) for the hours worked each workweek, whatever their number, rather than for working 40 hours or some other fixed weekly work period, such a salary arrangement is permitted by the Act if the amount of the salary is sufficient to provide compensation to the employee at a rate not less than the applicable minimum wage rate for every hour worked in those workweeks in which the number of hours he works is greatest, and if he receives extra compensation, in addition to such salary, for all overtime hours worked at a rate not less than one-half his regular rate of pay. Since the salary in such a situation is intended to compensate the employee at straight time rates for whatever hours are worked in the workweek, the regular rate of the employee will vary from week to week and is determined by dividing the number of hours worked in the workweek into the amount of the salary to obtain the applicable hourly rate for the week. Payment for overtime hours at one-half such rate in addition to the salary satisfies the overtime pay requirement because such hours have already been compensated at the straight time regular rate, under the salary arrangement.

(b) The application of the principles above stated may be illustrated by the case of an employee whose hours of work do not customarily follow a regular schedule but vary from week to week, whose overtime work is never in excess of 50 hours in a workweek, and whose salary of $250 a week is paid with the understanding that it constitutes his compensation, except for overtime premiums, for whatever hours are worked in the workweek. If during the course of 4 weeks this employee works 40, 44, 50, and 48 hours, his regular hourly rate of pay in each of these weeks is approximately $6.25, $5.68, $5, and $5.21, respectively. Since the employee has already received straight-time compensation on a salary basis for all hours worked, only additional half-time pay is due. For the first week the employee is entitled to be paid $250; for the second week $261.36 ($250 plus 4 hours at $2.84, or 40 hours at $5.68 plus 4 hours at $8.52); for the third week $275 ($250 plus 10 hours at $2.50, or 40 hours at $5 plus 10 hours at $7.50); for the fourth week approximately $270.88 ($250 plus 8 hours at $2.61 or 40 hours at $5.21 plus 8 hours at $7.82).

(c) The "fluctuating workweek" method of overtime payment may not be used unless the salary is sufficiently large to assure that no workweek will be worked in which the employee's average hourly earnings from the salary fall below the minimum hourly wage rate applicable under the Act, and unless the employee clearly understands that the salary covers whatever hours the job may demand in a particular workweek and the employer pays the salary even though the workweek is one in which a full schedule of hours is not worked. Typically, such salaries are paid to employees who do not customarily work a regular schedule of hours and are in amounts agreed on by the parties as adequate straight-time compensation for long workweeks as well as short ones, under the circumstances of the employment as a whole. Where all the legal prerequisites for use of the "fluctuating workweek" method of overtime payment are present, the Act, in requiring that "not less than" the prescribed premium of 50 percent for overtime hours worked be paid, does not prohibit paying more. On the other hand, where all the facts indicate that an employee is being paid for his overtime hours at a rate no greater than that which he receives for nonovertime hours, compliance with the Act cannot be rested on any application of the fluctuating workweek overtime formula.

Section 778.115 Employees working at two or more rates.

Where an employee in a single workweek works at two or more different types of work for which different nonovertime rates of pay (of not less than the applicable minimum wage) have been established, his regular rate for that week is the weighted average of such rates. That is, his total earnings (except statutory exclusions) are computed to include his compensation during the workweek from all such rates, and are then divided by the total number of hours worked at all jobs. Certain statutory exceptions permitting alternative methods of computing overtime pay in such cases are discussed in Secs. 778.400 and 778.415 through 778.421.

Section 778.116 Payments other than cash.

Where payments are made to employees in the form of goods or facilities which are regarded as part of wages, the reasonable cost to the employer or the fair value of such goods or of furnishing such facilities must be included in the regular rate. (See part 531 of this chapter for a discussion as to the inclusion of goods and facilities in wages and the method of determining reasonable cost.) Where, for example, an employer furnishes lodging to his employees in addition to cash wages the reasonable cost or the fair value of the lodging (per week) must be added to the cash wages before the regular rate is determined.

Subpart C--Payments That May Be Excluded From the "Regular Rate"

The Statutory Provisions

Section 778.200 Provisions governing inclusion, exclusion, and crediting of particular payments.

(a) Section 7(e). This subsection of the Act provides as follows:

As used in this section the regular rate at which an employee is employed shall be deemed to include all remuneration for employment paid to, or on behalf of, the employee, but shall not be deemed to include:

(1) Sums paid as gifts; payments in the nature of gifts made at Christmas time or on other special occasions, as a reward for service, the amounts of which are not measured by or dependent on hours worked, production, or efficiency; [discussed in Sec. 778.212].

(2) Payments made for occasional periods when no work is performed due to vacation, holiday, illness, failure of the employer to provide sufficient work, or other similar cause; reasonable payments for traveling expenses, or other expenses, incurred by an employee in the furtherance of his employer's interests and properly reimbursable by the employer; and other similar payments to an employee which are not made as compensation for his hours of employment.

(3) Sums paid in recognition of services performed during a given period if either, (a) both the fact that payment is to be made and the amount of the payment are determined at the sole discretion of the employer at or near the end of the period and not pursuant to any prior contract, agreement, or promise causing the employee to expect such payments regularly; or (b) the payments are made pursuant to a bona fide profit-sharing plan or trust or bona fide thrift or savings plan, meeting the requirements of the Secretary of Labor set forth in appropriate regulations which he shall issue, having due regard among other relevant factors, to the extent to which the amounts paid to the employee are determined without regard to hours of work, production, or efficiency; or (c) the payments are talent fees (as such talent fees are defined and delimited by regulations of the Secretary) paid to performers, including announcers, on radio and television programs; [discussed in Secs. 778.208 through 778.215 and 778.225].

(4) Contributions irrevocably made by an employer to a trustee or third person pursuant to a bona fide plan for providing old-age, retirement, life, accident, or health insurance or similar benefits for employees; [discussed in Secs. 778.214 and 778.215].

(5) Extra compensation provided by a premium rate paid for certain hours worked by the employee in any day or workweek because such hours are hours worked in excess of eight in a day or in excess of the maximum

workweek applicable to such employee under subsection (a) or in excess of the employee's normal working hours or regular working hours, as the case may be; [discussed in Secs. 778.201 and 778.202].

(6) Extra compensation provided by a premium rate paid for work by the employee on Saturdays, Sundays, holidays, or regular days of rest, or on the sixth or seventh day of the workweek, where such premium rate is not less than one and one-half times the rate established in good faith for like work performed in nonovertime hours on other days; or [discussed in Secs. 778.203, 778.205, and 778.206].

(7) Extra compensation provided by a premium rate paid to the employee, in pursuance of an applicable employment contract or collective bargaining agreement, for work outside of the hours established in good faith by the contract or agreement as the basic, normal, or regular workday (not exceeding eight hours) or workweek (not exceeding the maximum workweek applicable to such employee under subsection (a)), where such premium rate is not less than one and one-half times the rate established in good faith by the contract or agreement for like work performed during such workday or workweek; [discussed in Secs. 778.201 and 778.206].

(b) Section 7(h). This subsection of the Act provides as follows:

Extra compensation paid as described in paragraphs (5), (6), and (7) of subsection (e) shall be creditable toward overtime compensation payable pursuant to this section.

(c) Only the statutory exclusions are authorized. It is important to determine the scope of these exclusions, since all remuneration for employment paid to employees which does not fall within one of these seven exclusionary clauses must be added into the total compensation received by the employee before his regular hourly rate of pay is determined.

Extra Compensation Paid for Overtime

Section 778.201 Overtime premiums--general.

(a) Certain premium payments made by employers for work in excess of or outside of specified daily or weekly standard work periods or on certain special days are regarded as overtime premiums. In such case, the extra compensation provided by the premium rates need not be included in the employee's regular rate of pay for the purpose of computing overtime compensation due under section 7(a) of the Act. Moreover, under section 7(h) this extra compensation may be credited toward the overtime payments required by the Act.

(b) The three types of extra premium payments which may thus be treated as overtime premiums for purposes of the Act are outlined in section 7(e) (5), (6), and (7) of the Act as set forth in Sec. 778.200(a). These are discussed in detail in the sections following.

(c) Section 7(h) of the Act specifically states that the extra compensation provided by these three types of payments may be credited toward overtime compensation due under section 7(a) for work in excess of the applicable maximum hours standard. No other types of remuneration for employment may be so credited.

Section 778.202 Premium pay for hours in excess of a daily or weekly standard.

(a) Hours in excess of 8 per day or statutory weekly standard. Many employment contracts provide for the payment of overtime compensation for hours worked in excess of 8 per day or 40 per week. Under some contracts such overtime compensation is fixed at one and one-half times the base rate; under others the overtime rate may be greater or less than one and one-half times the base rate. If the payment of such contract overtime compensation is in fact contingent upon the employee's having worked in excess of 8 hours in a day or in excess of the number of hours in the workweek specified in section 7(a) of the Act as the weekly maximum, the extra premium compensation paid for the excess hours is excludable from the regular rate under section 7(e)(5) and may be credited toward statutory overtime payments pursuant to section 7(h) of the Act. In applying these rules to situations where it is the custom to pay employees for hours during which no work is performed due to vacation, holiday, illness, failure of the employer to provide sufficient work, or other similar cause, as these terms are explained in Secs. 778.216 to 778.224, it is permissible (but not required) to count these hours as hours worked in determining the amount of overtime premium pay, due for hours in excess of 8 per day or the applicable maximum hours standard, which may be excluded from the regular rate and credited toward the statutory overtime compensation.

(b) Hours in excess of normal or regular working hours. Similarly, where the employee's normal or regular daily or weekly working hours are greater or less than 8 hours and 40 hours respectively and his contract provides for the payment of premium rates for work in excess of such normal or regular hours of work for the day or week (such as 7 in a day or 35 in a week) the extra compensation provided by such premium rates, paid for excessive hours, is a true overtime premium to be excluded from the regular rate and it may be credited toward overtime compensation due under the Act.

(c) Premiums for excessive daily hours. If an employee whose maximum hours standard is 40 hours is hired at the rate of $5.75 an hour and receives, as overtime compensation under his contract, $6.25 per hour for each hour actually worked in excess of 8 per day (or in excess of his normal or regular daily working hours), his employer may exclude the premium portion of the overtime rate from the employee's regular rate and credit the total of the extra 50-cent payments thus made for daily overtime hours against the overtime compensation which is due under the statute for hours in excess of 40 in that workweek. If the same contract further provided for the payment of $6.75 for hours in excess of 12 per day, the extra $1 payments could likewise be credited toward overtime compensation due under the Act. To qualify as overtime premiums under section 7(e)(5), the daily overtime premium payments must be made for hours in excess of 8 hours per day or the employee's normal or regular working hours. If the normal workday is artificially divided into a "straight time" period to which one rate is assigned, followed by a so-called "overtime" period for which a higher "rate" is specified, the arrangement will be regarded as a device to contravene the statutory purposes and the premiums will be considered part of the regular rate. For a fuller discussion of this problem, see Sec. 778.501.

(d) Hours in excess of other statutory standard. Where payment at premium rates for hours worked in excess of a specified daily or weekly standard is made pursuant to the requirements of another applicable statute, the extra compensation provided by such premium rates will be regarded as a true overtime premium.

(e) Premium pay for sixth or seventh day worked. Under section 7(e)(6) and 7(h), extra premium compensation paid pursuant to contract or statute for work on the sixth or seventh day worked in the workweek is regarded in the same light as premiums paid for work in excess of the applicable maximum hours standard or the employee's normal or regular workweek.

Section 778.203 Premium pay for work on Saturdays, Sundays, and other "special days".

Under section 7(e)(6) and 7(h) of the Act, extra compensation provided by a Premium rate of at least time and one-half which is paid for work on Saturdays, Sundays, holidays, or regular days of rest or on the sixth or seventh day of the workweek (hereinafter referred to as "special days") may be treated as an overtime premium for the purposes of the Act. If the premium rate is less than time and one-half, the extra compensation provided by such rate must be included in determining the employee's regular rate of pay and cannot be credited toward statutory overtime due, unless it qualifies as an overtime premium under section 7(e)(5).

(a) "Special days" rate must be at least time and one-half to qualify as overtime premium: The premium rate must be at least "one and one-half times the rate established in good faith for like work performed in nonovertime hours on other days." Where an employee is hired on the basis of a salary for a fixed workweek or at a single hourly rate of pay, the rate paid for work on "special days" must be at least time and one-half his regular hourly rate in order to qualify under section 7(e)(6). If the employee is a pieceworker or if he works at more than one job for which different hourly or piece rates have been established and these are bona fide rates applicable to the work when performed during nonovertime hours, the extra compensation provided by a premium rate of at least one and one-half times either (1) the bona fide rate applicable to the type of job the employee performs on the "special days", or (2) the average hourly earnings in the week in question, will qualify as an overtime premium under this section. (For a fuller discussion of computation on the average rate, see Sec. 778.111; on the rate applicable to the job, see Secs. 778.415 through 778.421; on the "established" rate, see Sec. 778.400.)

(b) Bona fide base rate required. The statute authorizes such premiums paid for work on "special days" to be treated as overtime premiums only if they are actually based on a "rate established in good faith for like work performed in nonovertime hours on other days." This phrase is used for the purpose of distinguishing the bona fide employment standards contemplated

394

by section 7(e)(6) from fictitious schemes and artificial or evasive devices as discussed in Subpart F of this part. Clearly, a rate which yields the employee less than time and one-half the minimum rate prescribed by the Act would not be a rate established in good faith.

(c) Work on the specified "special days": To qualify as an overtime premium under section 7(e)(6), the extra compensation must be paid for work on the specified days. The term "holiday" is read in its ordinary usage to refer to those days customarily observed in the community in celebration of some historical or religious occasion. A day of rest arbitrarily granted to employees because of lack of work is not a "holiday" within the meaning of this section, nor is it a "regular day of rest." The term "regular day of rest" means a day on which the employee in accordance with his regular prearranged schedule is not expected to report for work. In some instances the "regular day of rest" occurs on the same day or days each week for a particular employee; in other cases, pursuant to a swing shift schedule, the schedule day of rest rotates in a definite pattern, such as 6 days work followed by 2 days of rest. In either case the extra compensation provided by a premium rate for work on such scheduled days of rest (if such rate is at least one and one-half times the bona fide rate established for like work during nonovertime hours on other days) may be treated as an overtime premium and thus need not be included in computing the employee's regular rate of pay and may be credited toward overtime payments due under the Act.

(d) Payment of premiums for work performed on the "special day": To qualify as an overtime premium under section 7(e)(6), the premium must be paid because work is performed on the days specified and not for some other reason which would not qualify the premium as an overtime premium under section 7(e)(5), (6), or (7). (For examples distinguishing pay for work on a holiday from idle holiday pay, see Sec. 778.219.) Thus a premium rate paid to an employee only when he received less than 24 hours' notice that he is required to report for work on his regular day of rest is not a premium paid for work on one of the specified days; it is a premium imposed as a penalty upon the employer for failure to give adequate notice to compensate the employee for the inconvenience of disarranging his private life. The extra compensation is not an overtime premium. It is part of his regular rate of pay unless such extra compensation is paid the employee on infrequent and sporadic occasions so as to qualify for exclusion under section 7(e)(2) in which event it need not be included in computing his regular rate of pay, as explained in Sec. 778.222.

Section 778.204 "Clock pattern" premium pay.

(a) Overtime premiums under section 7(e)(7). Where a collective bargaining agreement or other applicable employment contract in good faith establishes certain hours of the day as the basic, normal, or regular workday (not exceeding 8 hours) or workweek (not exceeding the maximum hours standard applicable under section 7(a)) and provides for the payment of a premium rate for work outside such hours, the extra compensation provided by such premium rate will be treated as an overtime premium if the premium rate is not less than one and one-half times the rate established in good faith by the contract or agreement for like work performed during the basic, normal or regular workday or workweek.

(b) Premiums for hours outside established working hours. To qualify as an overtime premium under section 7(e)(7) the premium must be paid because the work was performed during hours "outside of the hours established * * * as the basic * * * workday or workweek" and not for some other reason. Thus, if the basic workday is established in good faith as the hours from 8 a.m. to 5 p.m. a premium of time and one-half paid for hours between 5 p.m. and 8 a.m. would qualify as an overtime premium. However, where the contract does not provide for the payment of a premium except for work between midnight and 6 a.m. the premium would not qualify under this section since it is not a premium paid for work outside the established workday but only for certain special hours outside the established workday, in most instances because they are undesirable hours. Similarly, where payments of premium rates for work are made after 5 p.m. only if the employee has not had a meal period or rest period, they are not regarded as overtime premiums; they are premiums paid because of undesirable working conditions.

(c) Payment in pursuance of agreement. Premiums of the type which section 7(e)(7) authorizes to be treated as overtime premiums must be paid "in pursuance of an applicable employment contract or collective bargaining agreement," and the rates of pay and the daily and weekly work periods referred to must be established in good faith by such contract or agreement. Although as a general rule a collective bargaining agreement is a formal agreement which has been reduced to writing, an employment contract for purposes of section 7(e)(7) may be either written or oral. Where there is a written employment contract and the practices of the parties differ from its provisions, it must be determined whether the practices of the parties have modified the contract. If the practices of the parties have modified the written provisions of the contract, the provisions of the contract as modified by the practices of the parties will be controlling in determining whether the requirements of section 7(e)(7) are satisfied. The determination as to the existence of the requisite provisions in an applicable oral employment contract will necessarily be based on all the facts, including those showing the terms of the oral contract and the actual employment and pay practices thereunder.

Section 778.205 Premiums for weekend and holiday work--example.

The application of section 7(e)(6) may be illustrated by the following example: Suppose an agreement of employment calls for the payment of $7.50 an hour for all hours worked on a holiday or on Sunday in the operation of machines by operators whose maximum hours standard is 40 hours and who are paid a bona fide hourly rate of $5 for like work performed during nonovertime hours on other days. Suppose further that the workweek of such an employee begins at 12:01 a.m. Sunday, and in a particular week he works a schedule of 8 hours on Sunday and on each day from Monday through Saturday, making a total of 56 hours worked in the workweek. Tuesday is a holiday. The payment of $320 to which the employee is entitled under the employment agreement will satisfy the requirements of the Act since the employer may properly exclude from the regular rate the extra $20 paid for work on Sunday and the extra $20 paid for holiday work and credit himself with such amount against the statutory overtime premium required to be paid for the 16 hours worked over 40.

Section 778.206 Premiums for work outside basic workday or workweek--examples.

The effect of section 7(e)(7) where "clock pattern" premiums are paid may be illustrated by reference to provisions typical of the applicable collective bargaining agreements traditionally in effect between employers and employees in the longshore and stevedoring industries. These agreements specify straight time rates applicable during the hours established in good faith under the agreement as the basic, normal, or regular workday and workweek. Under one such agreement, for example, such workday and workweek are established as the first 6 hours of work, exclusive of mealtime, each day, Monday through Friday, between the hours of 8 a.m. and 5 p.m. Under another typical agreement, such workday and workweek are established as the hours between 8 a.m. and 12 noon and between 1 p.m. and 5 p.m., Monday through Friday. Work outside such workday and workweek is paid for at premium rates not less than one and one-half times the bona fide straight-time rates applicable to like work when performed during the basic, normal, or regular workday or workweek. The extra compensation provided by such premium rates will be excluded in computing the regular rate at which the employees so paid are employed and may be credited toward overtime compensation due under the Act. For example, if an employee is paid $5 an hour under such an agreement for handling general cargo during the basic, normal, or regular workday and $7.50 per hour for like work outside of such workday, the extra $2.50 will be excluded from the regular rate and may be credited to overtime pay due under the Act. Similarly, if the straight time rate established in good faith by the contract should be higher because of handling dangerous or obnoxious cargo, recognition of skill differentials, or similar reasons, so as to be $7.50 an hour during the hours established as the basic or normal or regular workday or workweek, and a premium rate of $11.25 an hour is paid for the same work performed during other hours of the day or week, the extra $3.75 may be excluded from the regular rate of pay and may be credited toward overtime pay due under the Act. Similar principles are applicable where agreements following this general pattern exist in other industries.

Section 778.207 Other types of contract premium pay distinguished.

(a) Overtime premiums are those defined by the statute. The various types of contract premium rates which provide extra compensation qualifying as overtime premiums to be excluded from the regular rate (under section 7(e) (5), (6), and (7) and credited toward statutory overtime pay requirements (under section 7(h)) have been described in Secs. 778.201 through 778.206. The plain wording of the statute makes it clear that extra compensation provided by premium rates other than those described cannot be treated as overtime premiums. Wherever such other premiums are paid, they must be included in the employee's regular rate before statutory overtime compensation is computed; no part of such premiums may be credited toward statutory overtime pay.

(b) Nonovertime premiums. The Act requires the inclusion in the regular rate of such extra premiums as nightshift differentials (whether they take the form of a percent of the base rate or an addition of so many cents per hour) and premiums paid for hazardous, arduous or dirty work. It also requires inclusion of any extra compensation which is paid as an incentive for the rapid performance of work, and since any extra compensation in order to qualify as an overtime premium must be provided by a premium rate per hour, except in the special case of pieceworkers as discussed in Sec. 778.418, lump sum premiums which are paid without regard to the number of hours worked are not overtime premiums and must be included in the regular rate. For example, where an employer pays 8 hours' pay for a particular job whether it is performed in 8 hours or in less time, the extra premium of 2 hours' pay received by an employee who completes the job in 6 hours must be included in his regular rate. Similarly, where an employer pays for 8 hours at premium rates for a job performed during the overtime hours whether it is completed in 8 hours or less, no part of the premium paid qualifies as overtime premium under sections 7(e) (5), (6), or (7). (For a further discussion of this and related problems, see Secs. 778.308 to 778.314.)

Payments not for Hours Worked

Section 778.216 The provisions of section 7(e)(2) of the Act.

Section 7(e)(2) of the Act provides that the term "regular rate" shall not be deemed to include "payments made for occasional periods when no work is performed due to vacation, holiday, illness, failure of the employer to provide sufficient work, or other similar cause; reasonable payments for traveling expenses, or other expenses, incurred by an employee in the furtherance of his employer's interests and properly reimbursable by the employer; and other similar payments to an employee which are not made as compensation for his hours of employment * * *." However, since such payments are not made as compensation for the employee's hours worked in any workweek, no part of such payments can be credited toward overtime compensation due under the Act.

Section 778.217 Reimbursement for expenses.

(a) General rule. Where an employee incurs expenses on his employer's behalf or where he is required to expend sums solely by reason of action taken for the convenience of his employer, section 7(e)(2) is applicable to reimbursement for such expenses. Payments made by the employer to cover such expenses are not included in the employee's regular rate (if the amount of the reimbursement reasonably approximates the expenses incurred). Such payment is not compensation for services rendered by the employees during any hours worked in the workweek.

(b) Illustrations. Payment by way of reimbursement for the following types of expenses will not be regarded as part of the employee's regular rate:

(1) The actual amount expended by an employee in purchasing supplies, tools, materials, or equipment on behalf of his employer.

(2) The actual or reasonably approximate amount expended by an employee in purchasing, laundering or repairing uniforms or special clothing which his employer requires him to wear.

(3) The actual or reasonably approximate amount expended by an employee, who is traveling "over the road" on his employer's business, for transportation (whether by private car or common carrier) and living expenses away from home, other travel expenses, such as taxicab fares, incurred while traveling on the employer's business.

(4) "Supper money", a reasonable amount given to an employee, who ordinarily works the day shift and can ordinarily return home for supper, to cover the cost of supper when he is requested by his employer to continue work during the evening hours.

(5) The actual or reasonably approximate amount expended by an employee as temporary excess home-to-work travel expenses incurred (i) because the employer has moved the plant to another town before the employee has had an opportunity to find living quarters at the new location or (ii) because the employee, on a particular occasion, is required to report for work at a place other than his regular workplace. The foregoing list is intended to be illustrative rather than exhaustive.

(c) *Payments excluding expenses.* It should be noted that only the actual or reasonably approximate amount of the expense is excludable from the regular rate. If the amount paid as "reimbursement" is disproportionately large, the excess amount will be included in the regular rate.

(d) *Payments for expenses personal to the employee.* The expenses for which reimbursement is made must in order to merit exclusion from the regular rate under this section, be expenses incurred by the employee on the employer's behalf or for his benefit or convenience. If the employer reimburses the employee for expenses normally incurred by the employee for his own benefit, he is, of course, increasing the employee's regular rate thereby. An employee normally incurs expenses in traveling to and from work, buying lunch, paying rent, and the like. If the employer reimburses him for these normal everyday expenses, the payment is not excluded from the regular rate as "reimbursement" for expenses. Whether the employer "reimburses" the employee for such expenses or furnishes the facilities (such as free lunches or free housing), the amount paid to the employee (or the reasonable cost to the employer or fair value where facilities are furnished) enters into the regular rate of pay as discussed in Sec. 778.116. See also Sec. 531.37(b) of this chapter.

Section 778.220 "Show-up" or "reporting" pay.

(a) *Applicable principles.* Under some employment agreements, an employee may be paid a minimum of a specified number of hours' pay at the applicable straight time or overtime rate on infrequent and sporadic occasions when, after reporting to work at his scheduled starting time on a regular workday or on another day on which he has been scheduled to work, he is not provided with the expected amount of work. The amounts that may be paid under such an agreement over and above what the employee would receive if paid at his customary rate only for the number of hours worked are paid to compensate the employee for the time wasted by him in reporting for work and to prevent undue loss of pay resulting from the employer's failure to provide expected work during regular hours. One of the primary purposes of such an arrangement is to discourage employers from calling their employees in to work for only a fraction of a day when they might get full-time work elsewhere. Pay arrangements of this kind are commonly referred to as "show-up" or "reporting" pay. Under the principles and subject to the conditions set forth in subpart B of this part and Secs. 778.201 through 778.207, that portion of such payment which represents compensation at the applicable rates for the straight time or overtime hours actually worked, if any, during such period may be credited as straight time or overtime compensation, as the case may be, in computing overtime compensation due under the Act. The amount by which the specified number of hours' pay exceeds such compensation for the hours actually worked is considered as a payment that is not made for hours worked. As such, it may be excluded from the computation of the employee's regular rate and cannot be credited toward statutory overtime compensation due him.

(b) Application illustrated. To illustrate, assume that an employee entitled to overtime pay after 40 hours a week whose workweek begins on Monday and who is paid $5 an hour reports for work on Monday according to schedule and is sent home after being given only 2 hours of work. He then works 8 hours each day on Tuesday through Saturday, inclusive, making a total of 42 hours for the week. The employment agreement covering the employees in the plant, who normally work 8 hours a day, Monday through Friday, provides that an employee reporting for scheduled work on any day will receive a minimum of 4 hours' work or pay. The employee thus receives not only the $10 earned in the 2 hours of work on Monday but an extra 2 hours' "show-up" pay, or $10 by reason of this agreement. However, since this $10 in "show-up" pay is not regarded as compensation for hours worked, the employee's regular rate remains $5 and the overtime requirements of the Act are satisfied if he receives, in addition to the $210 straight-time pay for 42 hours and the $10 "show-up" payment, the sum of $5 as extra compensation for the 2 hours of overtime work on Saturday.

Section 778.221 "Call-back" pay.

(a) General. In the interest of simplicity and uniformity, the principles discussed in Sec. 778.220 are applied also with respect to typical minimum "call-back" or "call-out" payments made pursuant to employment agreements. Typically, such minimum payments consist of a specified number of hours' pay at the applicable straight time or overtime rates which an employee receives on infrequent and sporadic occasions when, after his scheduled hours of work have ended and without prearrangement, he responds to a call from his employer to perform extra work.

(b) Application illustrated. The application of these principles to call-back payments may be illustrated as follows: An employment agreement provides a minimum of 3 hours' pay at time and one-half for any employee called back to work outside his scheduled hours. The employees covered by the agreement, who are entitled to overtime pay after 40 hours a week, normally work 8 hours each day, Monday through Friday, inclusive, in a workweek beginning on Monday, and are paid overtime compensation at time and one-half for all hours worked in excess of 8 in any day or 40 in any workweek. Assume that an employee covered by this agreement and paid at the rate of $5 an hour works 1 hour overtime or a total of 9 hours on Monday, and works 8 hours each on Tuesday through Friday, inclusive. After he has gone home on Friday evening he is called back to perform an emergency job. His hours worked on the call total 2 hours and he receives 3 hours' pay at time and one-half, or $22.50, under the call-back provision, in addition to $200 for working his regular schedule and $7.50 for overtime worked on Monday evening. In computing overtime compensation due this employee under the Act, the 43 actual hours (not 44) are counted as working time during the week. In addition to $215 pay at the $5 rate for all these hours, he has received under the agreement a premium of $2.50 for the 1 overtime hour on Monday and of $5 for the 2 hours of overtime work on the call, plus an extra sum of $7.50 paid by reason of the provision for minimum call-back pay. For purposes of the Act, the extra premiums paid for actual hours of overtime work on Monday and on the Friday call (a total of $7.50) may be excluded as true overtime premiums in computing his regular rate for the week and may be credited toward compensation due under the Act, but the extra $7.50 received under the call-back provision is not regarded as paid for hours worked; therefore, it may be excluded from the regular rate, but it cannot be credited toward overtime compensation due under the Act. The regular rate of the employee, therefore, remains $5, and he has received an overtime premium of $2.50 an hour for 3 overtime hours of work. This satisfies the requirements of section 7 of the Act. The same would be true, of course, if in the foregoing example, the employee was called back outside his scheduled hours for the 2-hour emergency job on another night of the week or on Saturday or Sunday, instead of on Friday night.

Section 778.222 Other payments similar to "call-back" pay.

The principles discussed in Secs. 778.220 and 778.221 are also applied with respect to certain types of extra payments which are similar to call-back pay, such as: (a) Extra payments made to employees, on infrequent and sporadic occasions, for failure to give the employee sufficient notice to report for work on regular days of rest or during hours outside of his regular work schedule; and (b) extra payments made, on infrequent and sporadic occasions, solely because the employee has been called back to work before the expiration of a specified number of hours between shifts or tours of duty, sometimes referred to as a "rest period" The extra payment, over and above the employee's earnings for the hours actually worked at his applicable rate (straight time or overtime, as the case may be), is considered as a payment that is not made for hours worked.

Section 778.223 Pay for non-productive hours distinguished.

Under the Act an employee must be compensated for all hours worked. As a general rule the term "hours worked" will include: (a) All time during which an employee is required to be on duty or to be on the employer's premises or at a prescribed workplace and (b) all time during which an employee is suffered or permitted to work whether or not he is required to do so. Thus, working time is not limited to the hours spent in active productive labor, but includes time given by the employee to the employer even though part of the time may be spent in idleness. Some of the hours spent by employees, under certain circumstances, in such activities as waiting for work, remaining "on call", traveling on the employer's business or to and from workplaces, and in meal periods and rest periods are regarded as working time and some are not. The governing principles are discussed in part 785 of this chapter (interpretative bulletin on "hours worked") and part 790 of this chapter (statement of effect of Portal-to-Portal Act of 1947). To the extent that these hours are regarded as working time, payment made as compensation for these hours obviously cannot be characterized as "payments not for hours worked." Such compensation is treated in the same manner as compensation for any other working time and is, of course, included in the regular rate of pay. Where payment is ostensibly made as compensation for such of these hours as are not regarded as working time under the Act, the payment is nevertheless included in the regular rate of pay unless it qualifies for exclusion from the regular rate as one of a type of "payments made for occasional periods when no work is performed due to * * * failure of the employer to provide sufficient work, or other similar cause" as discussed in Sec. 778.218 or is excludable on some other basis under section 7(e)(2). For example, an employment contract may provide that employees who are assigned to take calls for specific periods will receive a payment of $5 for each 8-hour period during which they are "on call" in addition to pay at their regular (or overtime) rate for hours actually spent in making calls. If the employees who are thus on call are not confined to their homes or to any particular place, but may come and go as they please, provided that they leave word where they may be reached, the hours spent "on call" are not considered as hours worked. Although the payment received by such employees for such "on call" time is, therefore, not allocable to any specific hours of work, it is clearly paid as compensation for performing a duty involved in the employee's job and is not of a type excludable under section 7(e)(2). The payment must therefore be included in the employee's regular rate in the same manner as any payment for services, such as an attendance bonus, which is not related to any specific hours of work.

Section 778.224 "Other similar payments".

(a) General. The preceding sections have enumerated and discussed the basic types of payments for which exclusion from the regular rate is specifically provided under section 7(e)(2) because they are not made as compensation for hours of work. Section 7(e) (2) also authorizes exclusion from the regular rate of "other similar payments to an employee which are not made as compensation for his hours of employment." Since a variety of miscellaneous payments are paid by an employer to an employee under peculiar circumstances, it was not considered feasible to attempt to list them. They must, however, be "similar" in character to the payments specifically described in section 7(e)(2). It is clear that the clause was not intended to permit the exclusion from the regular rate of payments such as bonuses or the furnishing of facilities like board and lodging which, though not directly attributable to any particular hours of work are, nevertheless, clearly understood to be compensation for services.

(b) Examples of other excludable payments. A few examples may serve to illustrate some of the types of payments intended to be excluded as "other similar payments":

(1) Sums paid to an employee for the rental of his truck or car.

(2) Loans or advances made by the employer to the employee.

(3) The cost to the employer of conveniences furnished to the employee such as parking space, restrooms, lockers, on-the-job medical care and recreational facilities.

Subpart D--Special Problems
Change in the Beginning of the Workweek

Section 778.301 Overlapping when change of workweek is made.

As stated in Sec. 778.105, the beginning of the workweek may be changed for an employee or for a group of employees if the change is intended to be permanent and is not designed to evade the overtime requirements of the Act. A change in the workweek necessarily results in a situation in which one or more hours or days fall in both the "old" workweek as previously constituted and the "new" workweek. Thus, if the workweek in the plant commenced at 7 a.m. on Monday and it is now proposed to begin the workweek at 7 a.m. on Sunday, the hours worked from 7 a.m. Sunday to 7 a.m. Monday will constitute both the last hours of the old workweek and the first hours of the newly established workweek.

Section 778.302 Computation of overtime due for overlapping workweeks.

(a) General rule. When the beginning of the workweek is changed, if the hours which fall within both "old" and "new" workweeks as explained in Sec. 778.301 are hours in which the employee does no work, his statutory compensation for each workweek is, of course, determinable in precisely the same manner as it would be if no overlap existed. If, on the other hand, some of the employee's working time falls within hours which are included in both workweeks, the Department of Labor, as an enforcement policy, will assume that the overtime requirements of section 7 of the Act have been satisfied if computation is made as follows:

(1) Assume first that the overlapping hours are to be counted as hours worked only in the "old" workweek and not in the new; compute straight time and overtime compensation due for each of the 2 workweeks on this basis and total the two sums.

403

(2) Assume now that the overlapping hours are to be counted as hours worked only in the new workweek and not in the old, and complete the total computation accordingly.

(3) Pay the employee an amount not less than the greater of the amounts computed by methods (1) and (2).

(b) Application of rule illustrated. Suppose that, in the example given in Sec. 778.301, the employee, who receives $5 an hour and is subject to overtime pay after 40 hours a week, worked 5 hours on Sunday, March 7, 1965. Suppose also that his last "old" workweek commenced at 7 a.m. on Monday, March 1, and he worked 40 hours March 1 through March 5 so that for the workweek ending March 7 he would be owed straight time and overtime compensation for 45 hours. The proposal is to commence the "new" workweek at 7 a.m. on March 7. If in the "new" workweek of Sunday, March 7, through Saturday, March 13, the employee worked a total of 40 hours, including the 5 hours worked on Sunday, it is obvious that the allocation of the Sunday hours to the old workweek will result in higher total compensation to the employee for the 13-day period. He should, therefore, be paid $237.50 (40 x $5+5 x $7.50) for the period of March 1 through March 7, and $175 (35 x $5) for the period of March 8 through March 13.

(c) Nonstatutory obligations unaffected. The fact that this method of compensation is permissible under the Fair Labor Standards Act when the beginning of the workweek is changed will not alter any obligation the employer may have under his employment contract to pay a greater amount of overtime compensation for the period in question.

Additional Pay for Past Period

Section 778.303 Retroactive pay increases.

Where a retroactive pay increase is awarded to employees as a result of collective bargaining or otherwise, it operates to increase the regular rate of pay of the employees for the period of its retroactivity. Thus, if an employee is awarded a retroactive increase of 10 cents per hour, he is owed, under the Act, a retroactive increase of 15 cents for each overtime hour he has worked during the period, no matter what the agreement of the parties may be. A retroactive pay increase in the form of a lump sum for a particular period must be prorated back over the hours of the period to which it is allocable to determine the resultant increases in the regular rate, in precisely the same manner as a lump sum bonus. For a discussion of the method of allocating bonuses based on employment in a prior period to the workweeks covered by the bonus payment, see Sec. 778.209.

How Deductions Affect the Regular Rate

Section 778.304 Amounts deducted from cash wages--general.

(a) The word "deduction" is often loosely used to cover reductions in pay resulting from several causes:

(1) Deductions to cover the cost to the employer of furnishing "board, lodging or other facilities," within the meaning of section 3(m) of the Act.

(2) Deductions for other items such as tools and uniforms which are not regarded as "facilities."

(3) Deductions authorized by the employee (such as union dues) or required by law (such as taxes and garnishments).

(4) Reductions in a fixed salary paid for a fixed workweek in weeks in which the employee fails to work the full schedule.

(5) Deductions for disciplinary reasons.

(b) In general, where such deductions are made, the employee's regular rate is the same as it would have been if the occasion for the deduction had not arisen. Also, as explained in part 531 of this chapter, the requirements of the Act place certain limitations on the making of some of the above deductions.

Section 778.305 Computation where particular types of deductions are made.

The regular rate of pay of an employee whose earnings are subject to deductions of the types described in paragraphs (a)(1), (2), and (3) of Sec. 778.304 is determined by dividing his total compensation (except statutory exclusions) before deductions by the total hours worked in the workweek. (See also Secs. 531.36--531.40 of this chapter.)

Section 778.306 Salary reductions in short workweeks.

(a) The reductions in pay described in Sec. 778.304(a)(4) are not, properly speaking, "deductions" at all. If an employee is compensated at a fixed salary for a fixed workweek and if this salary is reduced by the amount of the average hourly earnings for each hour lost by the employee in a short workweek, the employee is, for all practical purposes, employed at an hourly rate of pay. This hourly rate is the quotient of the fixed salary divided by the fixed number of hours it is intended to compensate. If an employee is hired at a fixed salary of $200 for a 40-hour week, his hourly rate is $5. When he works only 36 hours he is therefore entitled to $180. The employer makes a "deduction" of $20 from his salary to achieve this result. The regular hourly rate is not altered.

(b) When an employee is paid a fixed salary for a workweek of variable hours (or a guarantee of pay under the provisions of section 7(f) of the Act, as discussed in Secs. 778.402 through 778.414), the understanding is that the salary or guarantee is due the employee in short workweeks as well as in longer ones and "deductions" of this type are not made. Therefore, in cases where the understanding of the parties is not clearly shown as to whether a fixed salary is intended to cover a fixed or a variable workweek the practice of making "deductions" from the salary for hours not worked in short weeks will be considered strong, if not conclusive, evidence that the salary covers a fixed workweek.

Section 778.307 Disciplinary deductions.

Where deductions as described in Sec. 778.304(a)(5) are made for disciplinary reasons, the regular rate of an employee is computed before deductions are made, as in the case of deductions of the types in paragraphs (a) (1), (2), and (3) of Sec. 778.304. Thus where disciplinary deductions are made from a piece-worker's earnings, the earnings at piece rates must be totaled and divided by the total hours worked to determine the regular rate before the deduction is applied. In no event may such deductions (or deductions of the type described in Sec. 778.304(a)(2)) reduce the earnings to an average below the applicable minimum wage or cut into any part of the overtime compensation due the employee. For a full discussion of the limits placed on such deductions, see part 531 of this chapter. The principles set forth therein with relation to deductions have no application, however, to situations involving refusal or failure to pay the full amount of wages due. See part 531 of this chapter; also Sec. 778.306. It should be noted that although an employer may penalize an employee for lateness subject to the limitations stated above by deducting a half hour's straight time pay from his wages, for example, for each half hour, or fraction thereof of his lateness, the employer must still count as hours worked all the time actually worked by the employee in determining the amount of overtime compensation due for the workweek.

Effect of Failure To Count or Pay for Certain Working Hours

Section 778.315 Payment for all hours worked in overtime workweek is required.

In determining the number of hours for which overtime compensation is due, all hours worked (see Sec. 778.223) by an employee for an employer in a particular workweek must be counted. Overtime compensation, at a rate not less than one and one-half times the regular rate of pay, must be paid for each hour worked in the workweek in excess of the applicable maximum hours standard. This extra compensation for the excess hours of overtime work under the Act cannot be said to have been paid to an employee unless all the straight time compensation due him for the nonovertime hours under his contract (express or implied) or under any applicable statute has been paid.

Section 778.316 Agreements or practices in conflict with statutory requirements are ineffective.

While it is permissible for an employer and an employee to agree upon different base rates of pay for different types of work, it is settled under the Act that where a rate has been agreed upon as applicable to a particular type of work the parties cannot lawfully agree that the rate for that work shall be lower merely because the work is performed during the statutory overtime hours, or during a week in which statutory overtime is worked. Since a lower rate cannot lawfully be set for overtime hours it is obvious that the parties cannot lawfully agree that the working time will not be paid for at all. An agreement that only the first 8 hours of work on any days or only the hours worked between certain fixed hours of the day or only the first 40 hours of any week will be counted as working time will clearly fail of its evasive purpose. An announcement by the employer that no overtime work will be permitted, or that overtime work will not be compensated unless authorized in advance, will not impair the employee's right to compensation for work which he is actually suffered or permitted to perform.

Section 778.317 Agreements not to pay for certain nonovertime hours.

An agreement not to compensate employees for certain nonovertime hours stands on no better footing since it would have the same effect of diminishing the employee's total overtime compensation. An agreement, for example, to pay an employee whose maximum hours standard for the particular workweek is 40 hours, $5 an hour for the first 35 hours, nothing for the hours between 35 and 40 and $7.50 an hour for the hours in excess of 40 would not meet the overtime requirements of the Act. Under the principles set forth in Sec. 778.315, the employee would have to be paid $25 for the 5 hours worked between 35 and 40 before any sums ostensibly paid for overtime could be credited toward overtime compensation due under the Act. Unless the employee is first paid $5 for each nonovertime hour worked, the $7.50 per hour payment purportedly for overtime hours is not in fact an overtime payment.

Section 778.318 Productive and nonproductive hours of work.

(a) Failure to pay for nonproductive time worked. Some agreements provide for payment only for the hours spent in productive work; the work hours spent in waiting time, time spent in travel on the employer's behalf or similar nonproductive time are not made compensable and in some cases are neither counted nor compensated. Payment pursuant to such an agreement will not comply with the Act; such nonproductive working hours must be counted and paid for.

(b) Compensation payable for nonproductive hours worked. The parties may agree to compensate nonproductive hours worked at a rate (at least the minimum) which is lower than the rate applicable to productive work. In such a case, the regular rate is the weighted average of the two rates, as discussed in Sec. 778.115 and the employee whose maximum hours standard is 40 hours is owed compensation at his regular rate for all of the first 40 hours and at a rate not less than one and one-half times this rate for all hours in excess of 40. (See Sec. 778.415 for the alternative method of computing overtime pay on the applicable rate.) In the absence of any agreement setting a different rate for nonproductive hours, the employee would be owed compensation at the regular hourly rate set for productive work for all hours up to 40 and at a rate at least one and one-half times that rate for hours in excess of 40.

(c) Compensation attributable to both productive and nonproductive hours. The situation described in paragraph (a) of this section is to be distinguished from one in which such nonproductive hours are properly counted as working time but no special hourly rate is assigned to such hours because it is understood by the parties that the other compensation received by the employee is intended to cover pay for such hours. For example, while it is not proper for an employer to agree with his pieceworkers that the hours spent in down-time (waiting for work) will not be paid for or will be neither paid for nor counted, it is permissible for the parties to agree that the pay the employees will earn at piece rates is intended to compensate them for all hours worked, the productive as well as the nonproductive hours. If this is the agreement of the parties, the regular rate of the pieceworker will be the rate determined by dividing the total piecework earnings by the total hours worked (both productive and nonproductive) in the workweek. Extra compensation (one-half the rate as so determined) would, of course, be due for each hour worked in excess of the applicable maximum hours standard.

Effect of Paying for But Not Counting Certain Hours

Section 778.319 Paying for but not counting hours worked.

In some contracts provision is made for payment for certain hours, which constitute working time under the Act, coupled with a provision that these hours will not be counted as working time. Such a provision is a nullity. If the hours in question are hours worked, they must be counted as such in determining whether more than the applicable maximum hours have been worked in the workweek. If more hours have been worked, the employee must be paid overtime compensation at not less than one and one-half times his regular rate for all overtime hours. A provision that certain hours will be compensated only at straight time rates is likewise invalid. If the hours are actually hours worked in excess of the applicable maximum hours standard, extra half-time compensation will be due regardless of any agreement to the contrary.

Section 778.320 Hours that would not be hours worked if not paid for.

In some cases an agreement provides for compensation for hours spent in certain types of activities which would not be regarded as working time under the Act if no compensation were provided. Preliminary and postliminary activities and time spent in eating meals between working hours fall in this category. The agreement of the parties to provide compensation for such hours may or may not convert them into hours worked, depending on whether or not it appears from all the pertinent facts that the parties have agreed to treat such time as hours worked. Except for certain activity governed by the Portal-to-Portal Act (see paragraph (b) of this section), the agreement of the parties will be respected, if reasonable.

(a) Parties have agreed to treat time as hours worked. Where the parties have reasonably agreed to include as hours worked time devoted to activities of the type described above, payments for such hours will not have the mathematical effect of increasing or decreasing the regular rate of an employee if the hours are compensated at the same rate as other working hours. The requirements of section 7(a) of the Act will be considered to be met where overtime compensation at one and one-half times such rate is paid for the hours so compensated in the workweek which are in excess of the statutory maximum.

(b) Parties have agreed not to treat time as hours worked. Under the principles set forth in Sec. 778.319, where the payments are made for time spent in an activity which, if compensable under contract, custom, or practice, is required to be counted as hours worked under the Act by virtue of Section 4 of the Portal-to-Portal Act of 1947 (see parts 785 and 790 of this chapter), no agreement by the parties to exclude such compensable time from hours worked would be valid. On the other hand, in the case of time spent in activity which would not be hours worked under the Act if not compensated and would not become hours worked under the Portal-to-Portal Act even if made compensable by contract, custom, or practice, the parties may reasonably agree that the time will not be counted as hours worked. Activities of this type include eating meals between working hours. Where it appears from all the pertinent facts that the parties have agreed to exclude such activities from hours worked, payments for such time will be regarded as qualifying for exclusion from the regular rate under the provisions of section 7(e)(2), as explained in Secs. 778.216 to 778.224. The payments for such hours cannot, of course, qualify as overtime premiums creditable toward overtime compensation under section 7(h) of the Act.

Subpart F--Pay Plans Which Circumvent the Act

Section 778.500 Artificial regular rates.

Devices To Evade the Overtime Requirements

(a) Since the term regular rate is defined to include all remuneration for employment (except statutory exclusions) whether derived from hourly rates, piece rates, production bonuses or other sources, the overtime provisions of the act cannot be avoided by setting an artificially low hourly rate upon which overtime pay is to be based and making up the additional compensation due to employees by other means. The established hourly rate is the regular rate to an employee only if the hourly earnings are the sole source of his compensation. Payment for overtime on the basis of an artificial "regular" rate will not result in compliance with the overtime provisions of the Act.

(b) It may be helpful to describe a few schemes that have been attempted and to indicate the pitfalls inherent in the adoption of such schemes. The device of the varying rate which decreases as the length of the workweek increases has already been discussed in Secs. 778.321 through 778.329. It might be well, however, to re-emphasize that the hourly rate paid for the identical work during the hours in excess of the applicable maximum hours standard cannot be lower than the rate paid for the non-overtime hours nor can the hourly rate vary from week to week inversely with the length of the workweek. It has been pointed out that, except in limited situations under contracts which qualify under section 7(f), it is not possible for an employer lawfully to agree with his employees that they will receive the same total sum, comprising both straight time and overtime compensation, in all weeks without regard to the number of overtime hours (if any) worked in any workweek. The result cannot be achieved by the payment of a fixed salary or by the payment of a lump sum for overtime or by any other method or device.

(c) Where the employee is hired at a low hourly rate supplemented by facilities furnished by the employer, bonuses (other than those excluded under section 7(e)), commissions, pay ostensibly (but not actually) made for idle hours, or the like, his regular rate is not the hourly rate but is the rate determined by dividing his total compensation from all these sources in any workweek by the number of hours worked in the week. Payment of overtime compensation based on the hourly rate alone in such a situation would not meet the overtime requirements of the Act.

(d) One scheme to evade the full penalty of the Act was that of setting an arbitrary low hourly rate upon which overtime compensation at time and one-half would be computed for all hours worked in excess of the applicable maximum hours standard; coupled with this arrangement was a guarantee that if the employee's straight time and overtime compensation, based on this rate, fell short, in any week, of the compensation that would be due on a piece-rate basis of x cents per piece, the employee would be paid on the piece-rate basis instead. The hourly rate was set so low that it never (or seldom) was operative. This scheme was found by the Supreme Court to be violative of the overtime provisions of the Act in the case of *Walling v. Youngerman-Reynolds Hardwood Co.*, 325 U.S. 427. The regular rate of the employee involved was found to be the quotient of total piece-rate earnings paid in any week divided by the total hours worked in such week.

(e) The scheme is no better if the employer agrees to pay straight time and overtime compensation on the arbitrary hourly rates and to make up the difference between this total sum and the piece-rate total in the form of a bonus to each employee. (For further discussion of the refinements of this plan, see Secs. 778.502 and 778.503.)

SECTION 785--HOURS WORKED

Subpart A--General Considerations

Section 785.1 Introductory statement.

Section 6 of the Fair Labor Standards Act of 1938 (29 U.S.C. 206) requires that each employee, not specifically exempted, who is engaged in commerce, or in the production of goods for commerce, or who is employed in an enterprise engaged in commerce, or in the production of goods for commerce receive a specified minimum wage. Section 7 of the Act (29 U.S.C. 207) provides that persons may not be employed for more than a stated number of hours a week without receiving at least one and one-half times their regular rate of pay for the overtime hours. The amount of money an employee should receive cannot be determined without knowing the number of hours worked. This part discusses the principles involved in determining what constitutes working time. It also seeks to apply these principles to situations that frequently arise. It cannot include every possible situation. No inference should be drawn from the fact that a subject or an illustration is omitted. If doubt arises inquiries should be sent to the Administrator of the Wage and Hour Division, U.S. Department of Labor, Washington, DC 20210, or to any area or Regional Office of the Division.

Excerpts From Regulations Under The FLSA

Section 785.2 Decisions on interpretations; use of interpretations.

The ultimate decisions on interpretations of the act are made by the courts. The Administrator must determine in the first instance the positions he will take in the enforcement of the Act. The regulations in this part seek to inform the public of such positions. It should thus provide a "practical guide for employers and employees as to how the office representing the public interest in its enforcement will seek to apply it." (*Skidmore v. Swift*, 323 U.S. 134, 138 (1944).)

Section 785.3 Period of effectiveness of interpretations.

These interpretations will remain in effect until they are rescinded, modified or withdrawn. This will be done when and if the Administrator concludes upon reexamination, or in the light of judicial decision, that a particular interpretation, ruling or enforcement policy is incorrect or unwarranted. All other rulings, interpretations or enforcement policies inconsistent with any portion of this part are superseded by it. The Portal-to-Portal Bulletin (part 790 of this chapter) is still in effect except insofar as it may not be consistent with any portion hereof. The applicable statutory provisions are set forth in Sec. 785.50.

Subpart B--Principles for Determination of Hours Worked

Section 785.5 General requirements of sections 6 and 7 of the Fair Labor Standards Act.

Section 6 requires the payment of a minimum wage by an employer to his employees who are subject to the Act. Section 7 prohibits their employment for more than a specified number of hours per week without proper overtime compensation.

Section 785.6 Definition of "employ" and partial definition of "hours worked".

By statutory definition the term "employ" includes (section 3(g)) "to suffer or permit to work." The act, however, contains no definition of "work". Section 3(o) of the Fair Labor Standards Act contains a partial definition of "hours worked" in the form of a limited exception for clothes-changing and wash-up time.

Section 785.7 Judicial construction.

The United States Supreme Court originally stated that employees subject to the act must be paid for all time spent in "physical or mental exertion (whether burdensome or not) controlled or required by the employer and pursued necessarily and primarily for the benefit of the employer of his business." (*Tennessee Coal, Iron & Railroad Co. v. Muscoda Local No. 123*, 321 U. S. 590 (1944)) Subsequently, the Court ruled that there need be no exertion at all and that all hours are hours worked which the employee is required to give his employer, that "an employer, if he chooses, may hire a man to do nothing, or to do nothing but wait for something to happen. Refraining from other activity often is a factor of instant readiness to serve,

411

and idleness plays a part in all employments in a stand-by capacity. Readiness to serve may be hired, quite as much as service itself, and time spent lying in wait for threats to the safety of the employer's property may be treated by the parties as a benefit to the employer." (*Armour & Co. v. Wantock*, 323 U.S. 126 (1944); *Skidmore v. Swift*, 323 U.S. 134 (1944)) The workweek ordinarily includes "all the time during which an employee is necessarily required to be on the employer's premises, on duty or at a prescribed work place". (Anderson v. Mt. Clemens Pottery Co., 328 U.S. 680 (1946)) The Portal-to-Portal Act did not change the rule except to provide an exception for preliminary and postliminary activities. See Sec. 785.34.

Section 785.8 Effect of custom, contract, or agreement.

The principles are applicable, even though there may be a custom, contract, or agreement not to pay for the time so spent with special statutory exceptions discussed in Secs. 785.9 and 785.26.

Section 785.9 Statutory exemptions.

(a) The Portal-to-Portal Act. The Portal-to-Portal Act (secs. 1-13, 61 Stat. 84-89, 29 U.S.C. 251-262) eliminates from working time certain travel and walking time and other similar "preliminary" and "postliminary" activities performed "prior" or "subsequent" to the "workday" that are not made compensable by contract, custom, or practice. It should be noted that "preliminary" activities do not include "principal" activities. See Secs. 790.6 to 790.8 of this chapter. Section 4 of the Portal-to-Portal Act does not affect the computation of hours worked within the "workday". "Workday" in general, means the period between "the time on any particular workday at which such employee commences (his) principal activity or activities" and "the time on any particular workday at which he ceases such principal activity or activities." The "workday" may thus be longer than the employee's scheduled shift, hours, tour of duty, or time on the production line. Also, its duration may vary from day to day depending upon when the employee commences or ceases his "principal" activities. With respect to time spent in any "preliminary" or "postliminary" activity compensable by contract, custom, or practice, the Portal-to-Portal Act requires that such time must also be counted for purposes of the Fair Labor Standards Act. There are, however, limitations on this requirement. The "preliminary" or "postliminary" activity in question must be engaged in during the portion of the day with respect to which it is made compensable by the contract, custom, or practice. Also, only the amount of time allowed by the contract or under the custom or practice is required to be counted. If, for example, the time allowed is 15 minutes but the activity takes 25 minutes, the time to be added to other working time would be limited to 15 minutes. (*Galvin v. National Biscuit Co.*, 82 F. Supp. 535 (S.D.N.Y. 1949) appeal dismissed, 177 F. 2d 963 (C.A. 2, 1949))

(b) Section 3(o) of the Fair Labor Standards Act. Section 3(o) gives statutory effect, as explained in Sec. 785.26, to the exclusion from measured working time of certain clothes-changing and washing time at the beginning or the end of the workday by the parties to collective bargaining agreements.

Excerpts From Regulations Under The FLSA

Subpart C--Application of Principles
Employees "Suffered or Permitted" to Work

Section 785.11 General.

Work not requested but suffered or permitted is work time. For example, an employee may voluntarily continue to work at the end of the shift. He may be a pieceworker, he may desire to finish an assigned task or he may wish to correct errors, paste work tickets, prepare time reports or other records. The reason is immaterial. The employer knows or has reason to believe that he is continuing to work and the time is working time. (*Handler v. Thrasher*, 191, F. 2d 120 (C.A. 10, 1951); *Republican Publishing Co. v. American Newspaper Guild*, 172 F. 2d 943 (C.A. 1, 1949; *Kappler v. Republic Pictures Corp.*, 59 F. Supp. 112 (S.D. Iowa 1945), aff'd 151 F. 2d 543 (C.A. 8, 1945); 327 U.S. 757 (1946); *Hogue v. National Automotive Parts Ass'n.* 87 F. Supp. 816 (E.D. Mich. 1949); *Barker v. Georgia Power & Light Co.*, 2 W.H. Cases 486; 5 CCH Labor Cases, para. 61,095 (M.D. Ga. 1942); *Steger v. Beard & Stone Electric Co.*, Inc., 1 W.H. Cases 593; 4 Labor Cases 60,643 (N.D. Texas, 1941))

Section 785.12 Work performed away from the premises or job site.

The rule is also applicable to work performed away from the premises or the job site, or even at home. If the employer knows or has reason to believe that the work is being performed, he must count the time as hours worked.

Section 785.13 Duty of management.

In all such cases it is the duty of the management to exercise its control and see that the work is not performed if it does not want it to be performed. It cannot sit back and accept the benefits without compensating for them. The mere promulgation of a rule against such work is not enough. Management has the power to enforce the rule and must make every effort to do so.

Waiting Time

Section 785.14 General.

Whether waiting time is time worked under the Act depends upon particular circumstances. The determination involves "scrutiny and construction of the agreements between particular parties, appraisal of their practical construction of the working agreement by conduct, consideration of the nature of the service, and its relation to the waiting time, and all of the circumstances. Facts may show that the employee was engaged to wait or they may show that he waited to be engaged." (*Skidmore v. Swift*, 323 U.S. 134 (1944)) Such questions "must be determined in accordance with common sense and the general concept of work or employment." (*Central Mo. Tel. Co. v. Conwell*, 170 F. 2d 641 (C.A. 8, 1948))

Section 785.15 On duty.

A stenographer who reads a book while waiting for dictation, a messenger who works a crossword puzzle while awaiting assignments, fireman who

413

plays checkers while waiting for alarms and a factory worker who talks to his fellow employees while waiting for machinery to be repaired are all working during their periods of inactivity. The rule also applies to employees who work away from the plant. For example, a repair man is working while he waits for his employer's customer to get the premises in readiness. The time is worktime even though the employee is allowed to leave the premises or the job site during such periods of inactivity. The periods during which these occur are unpredictable. They are usually of short duration. In either event the employee is unable to use the time effectively for his own purposes. It belongs to and is controlled by the employer. In all of these cases waiting is an integral part of the job. The employee is engaged to wait.

Section 785.16 Off duty.

(a) General. Periods during which an employee is completely relieved from duty and which are long enough to enable him to use the time effectively for his own purposes are not hours worked. He is not completely relieved from duty and cannot use the time effectively for his own purposes unless he is definitely told in advance that he may leave the job and that he will not have to commence work until a definitely specified hour has arrived. Whether the time is long enough to enable him to use the time effectively for his own purposes depends upon all of the facts and circumstances of the case.

(b) Truck drivers; specific examples. A truck driver who has to wait at or near the job site for goods to be loaded is working during the loading period. If the driver reaches his destination and while awaiting the return trip is required to take care of his employer's property, he is also working while waiting. In both cases the employee is engaged to wait. Waiting is an integral part of the job. On the other hand, for example, if the truck driver is sent from Washington, DC to New York City, leaving at 6 a.m. and arriving at 12 noon, and is completely and specifically relieved from all duty until 6 p.m. when he again goes on duty for the return trip the idle time is not working time. He is waiting to be engaged.

Section 785.17 On-call time.

An employee who is required to remain on call on the employer's premises or so close thereto that he cannot use the time effectively for his own purposes is working while "on call". An employee who is not required to remain on the employer's premises but is merely required to leave word at his home or with company officials where he may be reached is not working while on call.

Rest and Meal Periods

Section 785.18 Rest.

Rest periods of short duration, running from 5 minutes to about 20 minutes, are common in industry. They promote the efficiency of the employee and are customarily paid for as working time. They must be counted as hours worked. Compensable time of rest periods may not be offset against other working time such as compensable waiting time or on-call time.

Section 785.19 Meal.

(a) Bona fide meal periods. Bona fide meal periods are not worktime. Bona fide meal periods do not include coffee breaks or time for snacks. These are rest periods. The employee must be completely relieved from duty for the purposes of eating regular meals. Ordinarily 30 minutes or more is long enough for a bona fide meal period. A shorter period may be long enough under special conditions. The employee is not relieved if he is required to perform any duties, whether active or inactive, while eating. For example, an office employee who is required to eat at his desk or a factory worker who is required to be at his machine is working while eating.

(b) Where no permission to leave premises. It is not necessary that an employee be permitted to leave the premises if he is otherwise completely freed from duties during the meal period.

Sleeping Time and Certain Other Activities

Section 785.20 General.

Under certain conditions an employee is considered to be working even though some of his time is spent in sleeping or in certain other activities.

Section 785.21 Less than 24-hour duty.

An employee who is required to be on duty for less than 24 hours is working even though he is permitted to sleep or engage in other personal activities when not busy. A telephone operator, for example, who is required to be on duty for specified hours is working even though she is permitted to sleep when not busy answering calls. It makes no difference that she is furnished facilities for sleeping. Her time is given to her employer. She is required to be on duty and the time is worktime.

Section 785.22 Duty of 24 hours or more.

(a) General. Where an employee is required to be on duty for 24 hours or more, the employer and the employee may agree to exclude bona fide meal periods and a bona fide regularly scheduled sleeping period of not more than 8 hours from hours worked, provided adequate sleeping facilities are furnished by the employer and the employee can usually enjoy an uninterrupted night's sleep. If sleeping period is of more than 8 hours, only 8 hours will be credited. Where no expressed or implied agreement to the contrary is present, the 8 hours of sleeping time and lunch periods constitute hours worked.

(b) Interruptions of sleep. If the sleeping period is interrupted by a call to duty, the interruption must be counted as hours worked. If the period is interrupted to such an extent that the employee cannot get a reasonable night's sleep, the entire period must be counted. For enforcement purposes, the Divisions have adopted the rule that if the employee cannot get at least 5 hours' sleep during the scheduled period the entire time is working time.

Section 785.23 Employees residing on employer's premises or working at home.

An employee who resides on his employer's premises on a permanent basis or for extended periods of time is not considered as working all the time he is on the premises. Ordinarily, he may engage in normal private pursuits and thus have enough time for eating, sleeping, entertaining, and other periods of complete freedom from all duties when he may leave the premises for purposes of his own. It is, of course, difficult to determine the exact hours worked under these circumstances and any reasonable agreement of the parties which takes into consideration all of the pertinent facts will be accepted. This rule would apply, for example, to the pumper of a stripper well who resides on the premises of his employer and also to a telephone operator who has the switchboard in her own home.

Preparatory and Concluding Activities

Section 785.24 Principles noted in Portal-to-Portal Bulletin.

In November, 1947, the Administrator issued the Portal-to-Portal Bulletin (part 790 of this chapter). In dealing with this subject, Sec. 790.8 (b) and (c) of this chapter said:

(b) The term "principal activities" includes all activities which are an integral part of a principal activity. Two examples of what is meant by an integral part of a principal activity are found in the report of the Judiciary Committee of the Senate on the Portal-to-Portal bill. They are the following:

(1) In connection with the operation of a lathe, an employee will frequently, at the commencement of his workday, oil, grease, or clean his machine, or install a new cutting tool. Such activities are an integral part of the principal activity, and are included within such term.

(2) In the case of a garment worker in a textile mill, who is required to report 30 minutes before other employees report to commence their principal activities, and who during such 30 minutes distributes clothing or parts of clothing at the workbenches of other employees and gets machines in readiness for operation by other employees, such activities are among the principal activities of such employee.

Such preparatory activities, which the Administrator has always regarded as work and as compensable under the Fair Labor Standards Act, remain so under the Portal Act, regardless of contrary custom or contract.

(c) Among the activities included as an integral part of a principal activity are those closely related activities which are indispensable to its performance. If an employee in a chemical plant, for example, cannot perform his principal activities without putting on certain clothes, changing clothes on the employer's premises at the beginning and end of the workday would be an integral part of the employee's principal activity. On the other hand, if changing clothes is merely a convenience to the employee and not directly related to his principal activities, it would be considered as a "preliminary" or "postliminary" activity rather than a principal part of the activity. However, activities such as checking in and out and waiting in line to do so would not ordinarily be regarded as integral parts of the principal activity or activities.

Section 785.25 Illustrative U.S. Supreme Court decisions.

These principles have guided the Administrator in the enforcement of the Act. Two cases decided by the U.S. Supreme Court further illustrate the types of activities which are considered an integral part of the employees' jobs. In one, employees changed their clothes and took showers in a battery plant where the manufacturing process involved the extensive use of caustic and toxic materials. (*Steiner v. Mitchell*, 350 U.S. 247 (1956).) In another case, knifemen in a meatpacking plant sharpened their knives before and after their scheduled workday (*Mitchell v. King Packing Co.*, 350 U.S. 260 (1956)). In both cases the Supreme Court held that these activities are an integral and indispensable part of the employees' principal activities.

Section 785.26 Section 3(o) of the Fair Labor Standards Act.

Section 3(o) of the Act provides an exception to the general rule for employees under collective bargaining agreements. This section provides for the exclusion from hours worked of time spent by an employee in changing clothes or washing at the beginning or end of each workday which was excluded from measured working time during the week involved by the express terms of or by custom or practice under a bona fide collective-bargaining agreement applicable to the particular employee. During any week in which such clothes-changing or washing time was not so excluded, it must be counted as hours worked if the changing of clothes or washing is indispensable to the performance of the employee's work or is required by law or by the rules of the employer. The same would be true if the changing of clothes or washing was a preliminary or postliminary activity compensable by contract, custom, or practice as provided by section 4 of the Portal-to-Portal Act, and as discussed in Sec. 785.9 and part 790 of this chapter.

Lectures, Meetings and Training Programs

Section 785.27 General.

Attendance at lectures, meetings, training programs and similar activities need not be counted as working time if the following four criteria are met:

(a) Attendance is outside of the employee's regular working hours;

(b) Attendance is in fact voluntary;

(c) The course, lecture, or meeting is not directly related to the

employee's job; and

(d) The employee does not perform any productive work during such attendance.

Section 785.28 Involuntary attendance.

Attendance is not voluntary, of course, if it is required by the employer. It is not voluntary in fact if the employee is given to understand or led to believe that his present working conditions or the continuance of his employment would be adversely affected by nonattendance.

Section 785.29 Training directly related to employee's job.

The training is directly related to the employee's job if it is designed to make the employee handle his job more effectively as distinguished from training him for another job, or to a new or additional skill. For example, a stenographer who is given a course in stenography is engaged in an activity to make her a better stenographer. Time spent in such a course given by the employer or under his auspices is hours worked. However, if the stenographer takes a course in bookkeeping, it may not be directly related to her job. Thus, the time she spends voluntarily in taking such a bookkeeping course, outside of regular working hours, need not be counted as working time. Where a training course is instituted for the bona fide purpose of preparing for advancement through upgrading the employee to a higher skill, and is not intended to make the employee more efficient in his present job, the training is not considered directly related to the employee's job even though the course incidentally improves his skill in doing his regular work.

Section 785.30 Independent training.

Of course, if an employee on his own initiative attends an independent school, college or independent trade school after hours, the time is not hours worked for his employer even if the courses are related to his job.

Section 785.31 Special situations.

There are some special situations where the time spent in attending lectures, training sessions and courses of instruction is not regarded as hours worked. For example, an employer may establish for the benefit of his employees a program of instruction which corresponds to courses offered by independent bona fide institutions of learning. Voluntary attendance by an employee at such courses outside of working hours would not be hours worked even if they are directly related to his job, or paid for by the employer.

Section 785.32 Apprenticeship training.

As an enforcement policy, time spent in an organized program of related, supplemental instruction by employees working under bona fide apprenticeship programs may be excluded from working time if the following criteria are met:

(a) The apprentice is employed under a written apprenticeship agreement or program which substantially meets the fundamental standards of the Bureau of Apprenticeship and Training of the U.S. Department of Labor; and

(b) Such time does not involve productive work or performance of the apprentice's regular duties. If the above criteria are met the time spent in such related supplemental training shall not be counted as hours worked unless the written agreement specifically provides that it is hours worked. The mere payment or agreement to pay for time spent in related instruction does not constitute an agreement that such time is hours worked.

Traveltime

Section 785.33 General.

The principles which apply in determining whether or not time spent in travel is working time depend upon the kind of travel involved. The subject is discussed in Secs. 785.35 to 785.41, which are preceded by a brief discussion in Sec. 785.34 of the Portal-to-Portal Act as it applies to traveltime.

Section 785.34 Effect of section 4 of the Portal-to-Portal Act.

The Portal Act provides in section 4(a) that except as provided in subsection (b) no employer shall be liable for the failure to pay the minimum wage or overtime compensation for time spent in "walking, riding, or traveling to and from the actual place of performance of the principal activity or activities which such employee is employed to perform either prior to the time on any particular workday at which such employee commences, or subsequent to the time on any particular workday at which he ceases, such principal activity or activities." Subsection (b) provides that the employer shall not be relieved from liability if the activity is compensable by express contract or by custom or practice not inconsistent with an express contract. Thus traveltime at the commencement or cessation of the workday which was originally considered as working time under the Fair Labor Standards Act (such as underground travel in mines or walking from time clock to work-bench) need not be counted as working time unless it is compensable by contract, custom or practice. If compensable by express contract or by custom or practice not inconsistent with an express contract, such traveltime must be counted in computing hours worked. However, ordinary travel from home to work (see Sec. 785.35) need not be counted as hours worked even if the employer agrees to pay for it.

Section 785.35 Home to work; ordinary situation.

An employee who travels from home before his regular workday and returns to his home at the end of the workday is engaged in ordinary home to work travel which is a normal incident of employment. This is true whether he works at a fixed location or at different job sites. Normal travel from home to work is not worktime.

Section 785.36 Home to work in emergency situations.

There may be instances when travel from home to work is overtime. For example, if an employee who has gone home after completing his day's work is subsequently called out at night to travel a substantial distance to perform an emergency job for one of his employer's customers all time spent on such travel is working time. The Divisions are taking no position on whether travel to the job and back home by an employee who receives an emergency call outside of his regular hours to report back to his regular place of business to do a job is working time.

Section 785.37 Home to work on special one-day assignment in another city.

A problem arises when an employee who regularly works at a fixed location in one city is given a special 1-day work assignment in another city. For example, an employee who works in Washington, DC, with regular working hours from 9 a.m. to 5 p.m. may be given a special assignment in New York City, with instructions to leave Washington at 8 a.m. He arrives in New York at 12 noon, ready for work. The special assignment is completed at 3 p.m., and the employee arrives back in Washington at 7 p.m. Such travel cannot be regarded as ordinary home-to-work travel occasioned merely by the fact of employment. It was performed for the employer's benefit and at his special request to meet the needs of the particular and unusual assignment. It would thus qualify as an integral part of the "principal" activity which the employee was hired to perform on the workday in question; it is like travel involved in an emergency call (described in Sec. 785.36), or like travel that is all in the day's work (see Sec. 785.38). All the time involved, however, need not be counted. Since, except for the special assignment, the employee would have had to report to his regular work site, the travel between his home and the railroad depot may be deducted, it being in the "home-to-work" category. Also, of course, the usual meal time would be deductible.

Section 785.38 Travel that is all in the day's work.

Time spent by an employee in travel as part of his principal activity, such as travel from job site to job site during the workday, must be counted as hours worked. Where an employee is required to report at a meeting place to receive instructions or to perform other work there, or to pick up and to carry tools, the travel from the designated place to the work place is part of the day's work, and must be counted as hours worked regardless of contract, custom, or practice. If an employee normally finishes his work on the premises at 5 p.m. and is sent to another job which he finishes at 8 p.m. and is required to return to his employer's premises arriving at 9 p.m., all of the time is working time. However, if the employee goes home instead of returning to his employer's premises, the travel after 8 p.m. is home-to-work travel and is not hours worked.

Section 785.39 Travel away from home community.

Travel that keeps an employee away from home overnight is travel away from home. Travel away from home is clearly worktime when it cuts across the employee's workday. The employee is simply substituting travel for other duties. The time is not only hours worked on regular working days during normal working hours but also during the corresponding hours on nonworking days. Thus, if an employee regularly works from 9 a.m. to 5 p.m. from Monday through Friday the travel time during these hours is worktime on Saturday and Sunday as well as on the other days. Regular meal period time is not counted. As an enforcement policy the Divisions will not consider as worktime that time spent in travel away from home outside of regular working hours as a passenger on an airplane, train, boat, bus, or automobile.

Section 785.40 When private automobile is used in travel away from home community.

If an employee is offered public transportation but requests permission to drive his car instead, the employer may count as hours worked either the time spent driving the car or the time he would have had to count as hours worked during working hours if the employee had used the public conveyance.

Section 785.41 Work performed while traveling.

Any work which an employee is required to perform while traveling must, of course, be counted as hours worked. An employee who drives a truck, bus, automobile, boat or airplane, or an employee who is required to ride therein as an assistant or helper, is working while riding, except during bona fide meal periods or when he is permitted to sleep in adequate facilities furnished by the employer.

Adjusting Grievances, Medical Attention, Civic and Charitable Work, and Suggestion Systems

Section 785.42 Adjusting grievances.

Time spent in adjusting grievances between an employer and employees during the time the employees are required to be on the premises is hours worked, but in the event a bona fide union is involved the counting of such time will, as a matter of enforcement policy, be left to the process of collective bargaining or to the custom or practice under the collective bargaining agreement.

Section 785.43 Medical attention.

Time spent by an employee in waiting for and receiving medical attention on the premises or at the direction of the employer during the employee's normal working hours on days when he is working constitutes hours worked.

Section 785.44 Civic and charitable work.

Time spent in work for public or charitable purposes at the employer's request, or under his direction or control, or while the employee is required to be on the premises, is working time. However, time spent voluntarily in such activities outside of the employee's normal working hours is not hours worked.

Section 785.45 Suggestion systems.

Generally, time spent by employees outside of their regular working hours in developing suggestions under a general suggestion system is not working time, but if employees are permitted to work on suggestions during regular working hours the time spent must be counted as hours worked. Where an employee is assigned to work on the development of a suggestion, the time is considered hours worked.

421

REGULATIONS UNDER THE PORTAL-TO-PORTAL ACT.

Section 790.1 - Introductory statement.

(a) The Portal-to-Portal Act of 1947 was approved May 4, 1947. It contains provisions which, in certain circumstances, affect the rights and liabilities of employees and employers with regard to alleged underpayments of minimum or overtime wages under the provisions of the Fair Labor Standards Act of 1938, the Walsh-Healey Public Contracts Act, and the Bacon-Davis Act. The Portal Act also establishes time limitations for the bringing of certain actions under these three Acts, limits the jurisdiction of the courts with respect to certain claims, and in other respects affects employee suits and proceedings under these Acts.

(b) It is the purpose of this part to outline and explain the major provisions of the Portal Act as they affect the application to employers and employees of the provisions of the Fair Labor Standards Act. The effect of the Portal Act in relation to the Walsh-Healey Act and the Bacon-Davis Act is not within the scope of this part, and is not discussed herein. Many of the provisions of the Portal Act do not apply to claims or liabilities arising out of activities engaged in after the enactment of the Act. These provisions are not discussed at length in this part, because the primary purpose of this part is to indicate the effect of the Portal Act upon the future administration and enforcement of the Fair Labor Standards Act, with which the Administrator of the Wage and Hour Division is charged under the law. The discussion of the Portal Act in this part is therefore directed principally to those provisions that have to do with the application of the Fair Labor Standards Act on or after May 14, 1947.

(c) The correctness of an interpretation of the Portal Act, like the correctness of an interpretation of the Fair Labor Standards Act, can be determined finally and authoritatively only by the courts. It is necessary, however, for the Administrator to reach informed conclusions as to the meaning of the law in order to enable him to carry out his statutory duties of administration and enforcement. It would seem desirable also that he makes these conclusions known to persons affected by the law. Accordingly, as in the case of the interpretative bulletins previously issued on various provisions of the Fair Labor Standards Act, the interpretations set forth herein are intended to indicate the construction of the law which the Administration believes to be correct and which will guide him in the performance of his administrative duties under the Fair Labor Standards Act, unless and until he is directed otherwise by authoritative rulings of the courts or concludes, upon reexamination of an interpretation, that it is incorrect. As the Supreme Court has pointed out, such interpretations provide a practical guide to employers and employees as to how the office representing the public interest in enforcement of the law will seek to apply it. As has been the case in the past with respect to other interpretative bulletins, the Administrator will receive and consider statements suggesting change of any interpretation contained in this part.

Section 790.2 - Interrelationship of the two acts.

(a) The effect on the Fair Labor Standards Act of the various provisions of the Portal Act must necessarily be determined by viewing the two acts as interrelated parts of the entire statutory scheme for the establishment of basic fair labor standards. The Portal Act contemplates that employers will be relieved, in certain circumstances, from liabilities or punishments to which they might otherwise be subject under the Fair Labor Standards Act. But the act makes no express change in the national policy, declared by Congress in section 2 of the Fair Labor Standards Act, of eliminating labor conditions "detrimental to the maintenance of the minimum standard of living necessary for health, efficiency, and general well-being of workers." The legislative history indicates that the Portal Act was not intended to change this general policy. The Congressional declaration of policy in section 1 of the Portal Act is explicitly directed to the meeting of the existing emergency and the correction, both retroactively and prospectively, of existing evils referred to therein. Sponsors of the legislation in both Houses of Congress asserted that it "in no way repeals the minimum wage requirements and the overtime compensation requirements of the Fair Labor Standards Act" that it "protects the legitimate claims" under that Act, and that one of the objectives of the sponsors was to "preserve to the worker the rights he has gained under the Fair Labor Standards Act." It would therefore appear that the Congress did not intend by the Portal Act to change the general rule that the remedial provisions of the Fair Labor Standards Act are to be given a liberal interpretation and exemptions therefrom are to be narrowly construed and limited to those who can meet the burden of showing that they come "plainly and unmistakably within (the) terms and spirit" of such an exemption.

(b) It is clear from the legislative history of the Portal Act that the major provisions of the Fair Labor Standards Act remain in full force and effect, although the application of some of them is affected in certain respects by the 1947 Act. The provisions of the Portal Act do not directly affect the provisions of section 15(a)(1) of the Fair Labor Standards Act banning shipments in interstate commerce of "hot" goods produced by employees not paid in accordance with the Act's requirements, or the provisions of section 11(c) requiring employers to keep records in accordance with the regulations prescribed by the Administrator. The Portal Act does not affect in any way the provision in section 15(a)(3) banning discrimination against employees who assert their rights under the Fair Labor Standards Act, or the provisions of section 12(a) of the Act banning from interstate commerce goods produced in establishments in or about which oppressive child labor is employed. The effect of the Portal Act in relation to the minimum and overtime wage requirements of the Fair Labor Standards Act is considered in this part in connection with the discussion of specific provisions of the 1947 Act.

Section 790.3 - Provisions of the statute.

Section 4 of the Portal Act, which relates to so-called "portal-to-portal" activities engaged in by employees on or after May 14, 1947, provides as follows:

(a) Except as provided in subsection (b), no employer shall be subject to any liability or punishment under the Fair Labor Standards Act of 1938, as amended, * * * on account of the failure of such employer to pay an employee minimum wages, or to pay an employee overtime compensation, for or on account of any of the following activities of such employee engaged in on or after the date of the enactment of this Act:

(1) Walking, riding, or traveling to and from the actual place of performance of the principal activity or activities which such employee is employed to perform, and

(2) Activities which are preliminary to or postliminary to said principal activity or activities which occur either prior to the time on any particular workday at which such employee commences, or subsequent to the time on any particular workday at which he ceases, such principal activity or activities.

(b) Notwithstanding the provisions of subsection (a) which relieve an employer from liability and punishment with respect to an activity, the employer shall not be so relieved if such activity is compensable by either:

(1) An express provision of a written or nonwritten contract in effect, at the time of such activity, between such employee, his agent, or collective-bargaining representative and his employer; or

(2) A custom or practice in effect, at the time of such activity, at the establishment or other place where such employee is employed, covering such activity, not inconsistent with a written or nonwritten contract, in effect at the time of such activity, between such employee, his agent, or collective-bargaining representative and his employer.

(c) For the purpose of subsection (b), an activity shall be considered as compensable under such contract provision or such custom or practice only when it is engaged in during the portion of the day with respect to which it is so made compensable.

(d) In the application of the minimum wage and overtime compensation provisions of the Fair Labor Standards Act of 1938, as amended, * * * in determining the time for which an employer employs an employee with respect to walking, riding, traveling, or other preliminary or postliminary activities described in subsection (a) of this section, there shall be counted all that time, but only that time, during which the employee engages in any such activity which is compensable within the meaning of subsections (b) and (c) of this section.

Section 790.4 - Liability of employer; effect of contract, custom, or practice.

(a) Section 4 of the Portal Act, quoted above, applies to situations where an employee, on or after May 14, 1974, has engaged in activities of the kind described in this section and has not been paid for or on account of these activities in accordance with the statutory standards established by the Fair Labor Standards Act. Where, in these circumstances such activities are not compensable by contract, custom, or practice as described in section 4, this section relieves the employer from certain liabilities or punishments to which he might otherwise be subject under the provisions of the Fair Labor Standards Act. The primary Congressional objectives in enacting section 4 of the Portal Act, as disclosed by the statutory language and legislative history were:

(1) To minimize uncertainty as to the liabilities of employers which it was felt might arise in the future if the compensability under the Fair Labor Standards Act of such preliminary or postliminary activities should continue to be tested solely by existing criteria for determining compensable worktime, independently of contract, custom, or practice; and

(2) To leave in effect, with respect to the workday proper, the interpretations by the courts and the Administrator of the requirements of the Fair Labor Standards Act with regard to the compensability of activities and time to be included in computing hours worked.

(b) Under section 4 of the Portal Act, an employer who fails to pay an employee minimum wages or overtime compensation for or on account of activities engaged in by such employee is relieved from liability or punishment therefore if, and only if, such activities meet the following three tests:

(1) They constitute "walking, riding, or traveling" of the kind described in the statute, or other activities "preliminary" or "postliminary" to the "principal activity or activities" which the employee is employed to perform; and

(2) They take place before or after the performance of all the employee's "principal activities" in the workday; and

(3) They are not compensable, during the portion of the day when they are engaged in, by virtue of any contract, custom, or practice of the kind described in the statute.

(c) It will be observed that section 4 of the Portal Act relieves an employer of liability or punishment only with respect to activities of the kind described, which have not been made compensable by a contract or by a custom or practice (not inconsistent with a contract) at the place of employment, in effect at the time the activities are performed. The statute states that "the employer shall not be so relieved" if such activities are so compensable; it does not matter in such a situation that they are so-called "portal-to-portal" activities.

Accordingly, an employer who fails to take such activities into account in paying compensation to an employee who is subject to the Fair Labor Standards Act is not protected from liability or punishment in either of the following situations.

(1) Where, at the time such activities are performed there is a contract, whether written or not, in effect between the employer and the employee (or the employee's agent or collective-bargaining representative), and by an express provision of this contract the activities are to be paid for; or

(2) Where, at the time such activities are performed, there is in effect at the place of employment a custom or practice to pay for such activities, and this custom or practice is not inconsistent with any applicable contract between such parties.

In applying these principles, it should be kept in mind that under the provisions of section 4(c) of the Portal-to-Portal Act, "preliminary" or "postliminary" activities which take place outside the workday "before the morning whistle" or "after the evening whistle" are, for purposes of the statute, not to be considered compensable by a contract, custom or practice if such contract, custom or practice makes them compensable only during some other portion of the day.

Section 790.5 - Effect of Portal-to-Portal Act on determination of hours worked.

(a) In the application of the minimum wage and overtime compensation provisions of the Fair Labor Standards Act to activities of employees on or after May 14, 1947, the determination of hours worked is affected by the Portal Act only to the extent stated in section 4(d). This section requires that: * * * in determining the time for which an employer employs an employee with respect to walking, riding, traveling or other preliminary or postliminary activities described (in section 4(a)) there shall be counted all that time, but only that time, during which the employee engages in any such activity which is compensable (under contract, custom, or practice within the meaning of section 4 (b), (c)).

(b) The operation of section 4(d) may be illustrated by the common situation of underground miners who spend time in traveling between the portal of the mine and the working face at the beginning and end of each workday. Before enactment of the Portal Act, time thus spent constituted hours worked. Under the law as changed by the Portal Act, if there is a contract between the employer and the miners calling for payment for all or a part of this travel, or if there is a custom or practice to the same effect of the kind described in section 4, the employer is still required to count as hours worked, for purposes of the Fair Labor Standards Act, all of the time spent in the travel which is so made compensable. But if there is no such contract, custom, or practice, such time will be excluded in computing worktime for purposes of the Act. And under the provisions of section 4(c) of the Portal Act, if a contract, custom, or practice of the kind described makes such travel compensable only during the portion of the day before the miners arrive at the working face and not during the portion of the day when they return from the working face to the portal of the mine, the only time spent in such travel which the employer is required to count as hours worked will be the time spent in traveling from the portal to the working face at the beginning of the workday.

Section 790.6 - Periods within the "workday" unaffected.

(a) Section 4 of the Portal Act does not affect the computation of hours worked within the "workday" proper, roughly described as the period "from whistle to whistle," and its provisions have nothing to do with the compensability under the Fair Labor Standards Act of any activities engaged in by an employee during that period. Under the provisions of section 4, one of the conditions that must be present before "preliminary" or "postliminary" activities are excluded from hours worked is that they "occur either prior to the time on any particular workday at which the employee commences, or subsequent to the time on any particular workday at which he ceases" the principal activity or activities which he is employed to perform. Accordingly, to the extent that activities engaged in by an employee occur after the employee commences to perform the first principal activity on a particular workday and before he ceases the performance of the last principal activity on a particular workday, the provisions of that section have no application. Periods of time between the commencement of the employee's first principal activity and the completion of his last principal activity on any workday must be included in the computation of hours worked to the same extent as would be required if the Portal Act had not been enacted. The principles for determining hours worked within the "workday" proper will continue to be those established under the Fair Labor Standards Act without reference to the Portal Act, which is concerned with this question only as it relates to time spent outside the "workday" in activities of the kind described in section 4.

(b) "Workday" as used in the Portal Act means, in general, the period between the commencement and completion on the same workday of an employee's principal activity or activities. It includes all time within that period whether or not the employee engages in work throughout all of that period. For example, a rest period or a lunch period is part of the "workday," and section 4 of the Portal Act therefore plays no part in determining whether such a period, under the particular circumstances presented, is or is not compensable, or whether it should be included in the computation of hours worked. If an employee is required to report at the actual place of perform-ance of his principal activity at a certain specific time, his "workday" commences at the time he reports there for work in accordance with the employer's requirement, even though through a cause beyond the employee's control, he is not able to commence performance of his productive activities until a later time. In such a situation the time spent waiting for work would be part of the workday, and section 4 of the Portal Act would not affect its inclusion in hours worked for purposes of the Fair Labor Standards Act.

Section 790.7 - "Preliminary" and "postliminary" activities.

(a) Since section 4 of the Portal Act applies only to situations where employees engage in "preliminary" or "postliminary" activities outside the workday proper, it is necessary to consider what activities fall within this description. The fact that an employee devotes some of his time to an activity of this type is, however, not a sufficient reason for disregarding the time devoted to such activity in computing hours worked. If such time would otherwise be counted as time worked under the Fair Labor Standards Act, section 4 may not change the situation. Whether such time must be counted or may be disregarded, and whether the relief from liability or punishment afforded by section 4 of the Portal Act is available to the employer in such a situation will depend on the compensability of the activity under contract, custom, or practice within the meaning of that section. On the other hand, the criteria described in the Portal Act have no bearing on the compensability or the status as worktime under the Fair Labor Standards Act of activities that are not "preliminary" or "postliminary" activities outside the workday. And even where there is a contract, custom, or practice to pay for time spent in such a "preliminary" or "postliminary" activity, section 4(d) of the Portal Act does not make such time hours worked under the Fair Labor Standards Act, if it would not be so counted under the latter Act alone.

(b) The words "preliminary activity" mean an activity engaged in by an employee before the commencement of his "principal" activity or activities, and the words "postliminary activity" means an activity engaged in by an employee after the completion of his "principal" activity or activities. No categorical list of "preliminary" and "postliminary" activities except those named in the Act can be made, since activities which under one set of circumstances may be "preliminary" or "postliminary" activities, may under other conditions be "principal" activities. The following "preliminary" or "postliminary" activities are expressly mentioned in the Act: "Walking, riding, or traveling to or from the actual place of performance of the principal activity or activities which (the) employee is employed to perform."

(c) The statutory language and the legislative history indicate that the "walking, riding or traveling" to which section 4(a) refers is that which occurs, whether on or off the employer's premises, in the course of an employee's ordinary daily trips between his home or lodging and the actual place where he does what he is employed to do. It does not, however, include travel from the place of performance of one principal activity to the place of performance of another, nor does it include travel during the employee's regular working hours. For example, travel by a repairman from one place where he performs repair work to another such place, or travel by a messenger delivering messages, is not the kind of "walking, riding or traveling" described in section 4(a). Also, where an employee travels outside his regular working hours at the direction and on the business of his employer, the travel would not ordinarily be "walking, riding, or traveling" of the type referred to in section 4(a). One example would be a traveling employee whose duties require him to travel from town to town outside his regular working hours; another would be an employee who has gone home after completing his day's work but is subsequently called out at night to travel a substantial distance and perform an emergency job for one of his employer's customers. In situations such as these, where an employee's travel is not of the kind to which section 4(a) of the Portal Act refers, the question whether the travel time is to be counted as worktime under the Fair Labor Standards Act will continue to be determined by principles established under this Act, without reference to the Portal Act.

(d) An employee who walks, rides or otherwise travels while performing active duties is not engaged in the activities described in section 4(a). An illustration of such travel would be the carrying by a logger of a portable power saw or other heavy equipment (as distinguished from ordinary hand tools) on his trip into the woods to the cutting area. In such a situation, the walking, riding, or traveling is not segregable from the simultaneous performance of his assigned work (the carrying of the equipment, etc.) and it does not constitute travel "to and from the actual place of performance" of the principal activities he is employed to perform.

(e) The report of the Senate Committee on the Judiciary (p. 47) describes the travel affected by the statute as "walking, riding, or traveling to and from the actual place of performance of the principal activity or activities within the employer's plant, mine, building, or other place of employment, irrespective of whether such walking, riding, or traveling occur on or off the premises of the employer or before or after the employee has checked in or out." The phrase, "actual place of performance," as used in section 4(a), thus emphasizes that the ordinary travel at the beginning and end of the workday to which this section relates includes the employee's travel on the employer's premises until he reaches his workbench or other place where he commences the performance of the principal activity or activities, and the return travel from that place at the end of the workday. However where an employee performs his principal activity at various places (common examples would be a telephone lineman, a "trouble-shooter" in a manufacturing plant, a meter reader, or an exterminator) the travel between those places is not travel of the nature described in this section, and the Portal Act has not significance in determining whether the travel time should be counted as time worked.

(f) Examples of walking, riding, or traveling which may be performed outside the workday and would normally be considered "preliminary" or "postliminary" activities are (1) walking or riding by an employee between the plant gate and the employee's lathe, workbench or other actual place of performance of his principal activity or activities; (2) riding on buses between a town and an outlying mine or factory where the employee is employed; and (3) riding on buses or trains from a logging camp to a particular site at which the logging operations are actually being conducted.

(g) Other types of activities which may be performed outside the workday and, when performed under the conditions normally present, would be considered "preliminary" or "postliminary" activities, include checking in and out and waiting in line to do so, changing clothes, washing up or showering, and waiting in line to receive pay checks.

(h) As indicated above, an activity which is a "preliminary" or "postliminary" activity under one set of circumstances may be a principal activity under other conditions. This may be illustrated by the following example: Waiting before the time established for the commencement of work would be regarded as a preliminary activity when the employee voluntarily arrives at his place of employment earlier than he is either required or expected to arrive. Where, however, an employee is required by his employer to report at a particular hour at his workbench or other place where he performs his principal activity, if the employee is there at that hour ready and willing to work but for some reason beyond his control there is no work for him to perform until some time has elapsed, waiting for work would be an integral part of the employee's principal activities. The difference in the two situations is that in the second the employee was engaged to wait while in the first the employee waited to be engaged.

Section 790.8 - "Principal" activities.

(a) An employer's liabilities and obligations under the Fair Labor Standards Act with respect to the "principal" activities his employees are employed to perform are not changed in any way by section 4 of the Portal Act, and time devoted to such activities must be taken into account in computing hours worked to the same extent as it would if the Portal Act had not been enacted. But before it can be determined whether an activity is "preliminary or postliminary to (the) principal activity or activities" which the employee is employed to perform, it is generally necessary to determine what are such "principal" activities.

The use by Congress of the plural form "activities" in the statute makes it clear that in order for an activity to be a "principal" activity, it need not be predominant in some way over all other activities engaged in by the employee in performing his job; rather, an employee may, for purposes of the Portal-to-Portal Act be engaged in several "principal" activities during the workday. The "principal" activities referred to in the statute are activities which the employee is "employed to perform"; they do not include noncompensable "walking, riding, or traveling" of the type referred to in section 4 of the Act. Several guides to determine what constitute "principal activities" was suggested in the legislative debates. One of the members of the conference committee stated to the House of Representatives that "the realities of industrial life," rather than arbitrary standards, "are intended to be applied in defining the term 'principal activity or activities,'" and that these words should "be interpreted with due regard to generally established compensation practices in the particular industry and trade." The legislative history further indicates that Congress intended the words "principal activities" to be construed liberally in the light of the foregoing principles to include any work of consequence performed for an employer, no matter when the work is performed.

(b) The term "principal activities" includes all activities which are an integral part of a principal activity. Two examples of what is meant by an integral part of a principal activity are found in the Report of the Judiciary Committee of the Senate on the Portal-to-Portal Act. They are the following:

(1) In connection with the operation of a lathe an employee will frequently at the commencement of his workday oil, grease or clean his machine, or install a new cutting tool. Such activities are an integral part of the principal activity, and are included within such term.

(2) In the case of a garment worker in a textile mill, who is required to report 30 minutes before other employees report to commence their principal activities, and who during such 30 minutes distributes clothing or parts of clothing at the work-benches of other employees and gets machines in readiness for operation by other employees, such activities are among the principal activities of such employee. Such preparatory activities, which the Administrator has always regarded as work and as compensable under the Fair Labor Standards Act, remain so under the Portal Act, regardless of contrary custom or contract.

(c) Among the activities included as an integral part of a principal activity are those closely related activities which are indispensable to its performance. If an employee in a chemical plant, for example, cannot perform his principal activities without putting on certain clothes, changing clothes on the employer's premises at the beginning and end of the workday would be an integral part of the employee's principal activity. On the other hand, if changing clothes is merely a convenience to the employee and not directly related to his principal activities, it would be considered as a "preliminary" or "postliminary" activity rather than a principal part of the activity. However, activities such as checking in and out and waiting in line to do so would not ordinarily be regarded as integral parts of the principal activity or activities.

Section 790.9 - "Compensable * * * by an express provision of a written or nonwritten contract."

(a) Where an employee engages in a "preliminary" or "postliminary" activity of the kind described in section 4(a) of the Portal Act and this activity is "compensable * * * by an express provision of a written or nonwritten contract" applicable to the employment, section 4 does not operate to relieve the employer of liability or punishment under the Fair Labor Standards Act with respect to such activity, and does not relieve the employer of any obligation he would otherwise have under that Act to include time spent in such activity in computing hours worked.

(b) The word "compensable," is used in subsections (b), (c), and (d) of section 4 without qualification.(70) It is apparent from these provisions that "compensable" as used in the statute, means compensable in any amount.

(c) The phrase "compensable by an express provision of a written or non- written contract" in section 4(b) of the Portal Act offers no difficulty where a written contract states that compensation shall be paid for the specific activities in question, naming them in explicit terms or identifying them through any appropriate language. Such a provision clearly falls within the statutory description. The existence or nonexistence of an express provision making an activity compensable is more difficult to determine in the case of a nonwritten contract since there may well be conflicting recollections as to the exact terms of the agreement. The words "compensable by an express provision" indicate that both the intent of the parties to contract with respect to the activity in question and their intent to provide compensation for the employee's performance of the activity must satisfactorily appear from the express terms of the agreement.

(d) An activity of an employee is not "compensable by * * * a written or nonwritten contract" within the meaning of section 4(b) of the Portal Act unless the contract making the activity compensable is one "between such employee, his agent, or collective-bargaining representative and his employer." Thus, a provision in a contract between a government agency and the employer, relating to compensation of the contractor's employees, would not in itself establish the compensability by "contract" of an activity, for purposes of section 4.

Section 790.10 - "Compensable * * * by a custom or practice."

(a) A "preliminary" or "postliminary" activity of the type described in section 4(a) of the Portal Act may be "compensable" within the meaning of section 4(b), by a custom or practice as well as by a contract. If it is so compensable, the relief afforded by section 4 is not available to the employer with respect to such activity, and section 4(d) does not operate to exclude the time spent in such activity from hours worked under the Fair Labor Standards Act. Accordingly, in the event that no "express provision of a written or nonwritten contract" makes compensable the activity in question, it is necessary to determine whether the activity is made compensable by a custom or practice, not inconsistent with such a contract, in effect at the establishment or other place where the employee was employed. The same is true with respect to the activities referred to in section 2 of the Portal Act in an action or proceeding relating to activities performed before May 14, 1947. See Senate Report, p. 45. See also Section 790.23.

(b) The meaning of the word "compensable" is the same, for purposes of the statute, whether a contract or a custom or practice is involved.

(c) The phrase, "custom or practice," is one which, in common meaning, is rather broad in scope. The meaning of these words as used in the Portal Act is not stated in the statute; it must be ascertained from their context and from other available evidence of the Congressional intent, with such aid as may be had from the many judicial decisions interpreting the words "custom" and "practice" as used in other connections. Although the legislative history casts little light on the precise limits of these terms, it is believed that the Congressional reference to contract, custom or practice was a deliberate use of non-technical words which are commonly understood and broad enough to cover every normal situation under which an employee works for an employer for compensation. Accordingly, "custom" and "practice," as used in section 4(b) of the Portal Act, may be said to be descriptive generally of those situations where an employer, without being compelled to do so by an express provision of a contract, has paid employees for certain activities performed. One of the sponsors of the legislation in the House of Representatives indicated that the intention was not only "to protect every collective bargaining agreement about these activities" but "to protect the agreement between one workman and his employer" and "every practice or custom which we assume must have entered into the minds of the people when they made the contract."

(d) The words, "custom or practice," as used in the Portal Act, do not refer to industry custom or the habits of the community which are familiar to the people; these words are qualified by the phrase "in effect * * * at the establishment or other place where such employee was employed." The compensability of an activity under custom or practice, for purposes of this Act, is tested by the custom or the practice at the "particular place of business," "plant," "mine," "factory," "forest," etc.

(e) "The custom or practice" by which compensability of an activity is tested under the statute is one "covering such activity." Thus, a custom or practice to pay for washing up in the plant after the end of the workday, for example, would not necessarily establish the compensability of walking time thereafter from the washroom in the plant to the plant gate. It is enough, however, if there is a custom or practice covering "such activity"; there is no provision, as there is with regard to contracts, that the custom or practice be one "between such employee, his agent, or collective-bargaining representative, and his employer."

(f) Another qualification of the "custom or practice" referred to in the statute is that it be "not inconsistent with a written or non-written contract" of the kind mentioned therein. If the contract is silent on the question of compensability of the activity, a custom or practice to pay for it would not be inconsistent with the contract. However, the intent of the provision is that a custom or practice which is inconsistent with the terms of any such contract shall not be taken into account in determining whether such an activity is compensable.

Section 790.11 - Contract, custom or practice in effect "at the time of such activity."

The "contract," "custom" or "practice" on which the compensability of the activities referred to in section 4 of the Portal Act may be based, is a contract, custom or practice in effect "at the time of such activity." Thus, the compensability of such an activity, and its inclusion in computation of hours worked, is not determinable by a custom or practice which had been terminated before the activity was engaged in or was adopted some time after the activity was performed. This phrase would also seem to permit recognition of changes in customs, practices and agreements which reflect changes in labor-management relations or policies.

Section 790.12 - "Portion of the day."

A "preliminary" or "postliminary" activity of the kind referred to in section 4 of the Portal Act is compensable under a contract, custom, or practice within the meaning of that section "only when it is engaged in during the portion of the day with respect to which it is so made compensable." This provision in no way affects the compensability of activities performed within the workday proper or the computation of hours worked within such workday for purposes of the Fair Labor Standards Act; the provision is applicable only to walking, riding, traveling or other "preliminary" or "postliminary" activities of the kind described in section 4(a) of the Portal Act, which are engaged in outside the workday, during the portions of the day before performance of the first principal activity and after performance of the last principal activity of the employee. The scope of section 4(c) is narrower in this respect than that of section 2(b), which is couched in identical language. Cf. Conference Report, pp. 9, 10; pp. 12, 13. See also 790.23.

Defense of Good Faith Reliance on Administrative Regulations, etc.

Section 790.13 - General nature of defense.

(a) Under the provisions of sections 9 and 10 of the Portal Act, an employer has a defense against liability or punishment in any action or proceeding brought against him for failure to comply with the minimum wage and overtime provisions of the Fair Labor Standards Act, where the employer pleads and proves that "the act or omission complained of was in good faith in conformity with and in reliance on any administrative regulation, order, ruling, approval, or interpretation" or "any administrative practice or enforcement policy * * * with respect to the class of employers to which he belonged." In order to provide a defense with respect to acts or omissions occurring on or after May 14, 1947 (the effective date of the Portal Act), the regulation, order, ruling, approval, interpretation, administrative practice or enforcement policy relied upon and conformed with must be that of the "Administrator of the Wage and Hour Division of the Department of Labor," and a regulation, order, ruling, approval, or interpretation of the Administrator may be relied on only if it is in writing. But where the acts or omissions complained of occurred before May 14, 1947, the employer may show that they were in good faith in conformity with and in reliance on "any" (written or nonwritten) administrative regulation, order, ruling, or interpretation of "any agency of the United States," or any administrative practice or enforcement policy of "any such agency" with respect to the class of employers to which he belonged. In all cases, however, the act or omission complained of must be both "in conformity with" and "in reliance on" the administrative regulation, order, ruling, approval, interpretation, practice, or enforcement policy, as the case may be, and such conformance and reliance and such act or omission must be "in good faith." The relief from liability or punishment provided by sections 9 and 10 of the Portal Act is limited by the statute to employers who both plead and prove all the requirements of the defense. The requirements of the statute as to pleading and proof emphasize the continuing recognition by Congress of the remedial nature of the Fair Labor Standards Act and of the need for safeguarding the protection which Congress intended it to afford employees. See 790.2; of. statements of Senator Wiley, 93 Cong. Rec. 4270; Senator Donnell, 93 Cong. Rec. 4452, and Representative Walter, 93 Cong. Rec. 4388, 4389.

(b) The distinctions mentioned in paragraph (a) of this section, depending on whether the acts or omissions complained of occurred before or after May 14, 1947, may be illustrated as follows: Assume that an employer, on commencing performance of a contract with X Federal Agency extending from January 1, 1947 to January 1, 1948, received an opinion from the agency that employees working under the contract were not covered by the Fair Labor Standards Act. Assume further that the employer may be said to have relied in good faith upon this opinion and therefore did not compensate such employees during the period of the contract in accordance with the provisions of the Act. After completion of the contract on January 1, 1948, the employees, who have learned that they are probably covered by the Act, bring suit against their employer for unpaid overtime compensation which they claim is due them. If the court finds that the employees were performing work subject to the Act, they can recover for the period commencing May 14, 1947, even though the employer pleads and proves that his failure to pay overtime was in good faith in conformity with and in reliance on the opinion of X Agency, because for that period the defense would, under section 10 of the Portal Act, have to be based upon written administrative regulation, order, ruling, approval, or interpretation, or an administrative practice or enforcement policy of the Administrator of the Wage and Hour Division. The defense would, however, be good for the period from January 1, 1947 to May 14, 1947, and the employer would be freed from liability for that period under the provisions of section 9 of the statute.

Section 790.14 - "In conformity with."

(a) The "good faith" defense is not available to an employer unless the acts or omissions complained of were "in conformity with" the regulation, order, ruling, approval, interpretation, administrative practice or enforcement policy upon which he relied. This is true even though the employer errone- ously believes he conformed with it and in good faith relied upon it; actual conformity is necessary.

(b) An example of an employer not acting "in conformity with" an ad- ministrative regulation, order, ruling, approval, practice, or enforcement policy is a situation where an employer receives a letter from the Administra- tor of the Wage and Hour Division, stating that if certain specified circum- stances and facts regarding the work performed by the employer's employees exist, the employees are, in his opinion, exempt from provisions of the Fair Labor Standards Act. One of these hypothetical circumstances upon which the opinion was based does not exist regarding these employees, but the employer, erroneously assuming that this circumstance is irrelevant, relies upon the Administrator's ruling and fails to compensate the employees in accordance with the Act. Since he did not act "in conformity" with that opinion, he has no defense under section 9 or 10 of the Portal Act.

(c) As a further example of the requirement of conformity, reference is made to the illustration given in 790.13(b), where an employer, who had a contract with the X Federal Agency covering the period from January 1, 1947 to January 1, 1948, received an opinion from the agency that employees working on the contract were not covered by the Fair Labor Standards Act. Assume (1) that the X Agency's opinion was confined solely and exclusively to activities performed under the particular contract held by the employer with the agency and made no general statement regarding the status under the Act of the employer's employees while performing other work; and (2) that the employer, erroneously believing the reasoning used in the agency's opinion also applied to other and different work performed by his employees, did not compensate them for such different work, relying upon that opinion. As previously pointed out, the opinion from the X Agency, if relied on and conformed with in good faith by the employer, would form the basis of a "good faith" defense for the period prior to May 14, 1947, insofar as the work performed by the employees on this particular contract with that agency was concerned. The opinion would not, however, furnish the employer a defense regarding any other activities of a different nature performed by his employees, because it was not an opinion concerning such activities, and insofar as those activities are concerned, the employer could not act "in conformity" with it.

Section 790.15 - "Good faith."

(a) One of the most important requirements of sections 9 and 10 is proof by the employer that the act or omission complained of and his conformance with and reliance upon an administrative regulation, order, ruling, approval, interpretation, practice or enforcement policy, were in good faith. The legislative history of the Portal Act makes it clear that the employer's "good faith" is not to be determined merely from the actual state of his mind.

Statements made in the House and Senate indicate that "good faith" also depends upon an objective test - whether the employer, in acting or omitting to act as he did, and in relying upon the regulation, order, ruling, approval, interpretation, administrative practice or enforcement policy, acted as a reasonably prudent man would have acted under the same or similar circumstances. "Good faith" requires that the employer have honesty of intention and no knowledge of circumstances which ought to put him upon inquiry.

(b) Some situations illustrating the application of the principles stated in paragraph (a) of this section may be mentioned. Assume that a ruling from the Administrator, stating positively that the Fair Labor Standards Act does not apply to certain employees, is received by an employer in response to a request which fully described the duties of the employees and the circumstances surrounding their employment. It is clear that the employer's employment of such employees in such duties and under such circumstances in reliance on the Administrator's ruling, without compensating them in accordance with the Act, would be in good faith so long as the ruling remained unrevoked and the employer had no notice of any facts or circumstances which would lead a reasonably prudent man to make further inquiry as to whether the employees came within the Act's provisions. Assume, however, that the Administrator's ruling was expressly based on certain court decisions holding that employees so engaged in commerce or in the production of goods for commerce, and that the employer subsequently learned from his attorney that a higher court had reversed these decisions or had cast doubt on their correctness by holding employees similarly situated to be engaged in an occupation necessary to the production of goods for interstate commerce. Assume further that the employer, after learning of this, made no further inquiry but continued to pay the employees without regard to the requirements of the Act in reliance on the Administrator's earlier ruling. In such a situation, if the employees later brought an action against the employer, the court might determine that they were entitled to the benefits of the Act and might decide that the employer, after learning of the decision of the higher court, knew facts which would put a reasonably prudent man upon inquiry and therefore had not provided his good faith in relying upon the Administrator's ruling after receiving this advice.

(c) In order to illustrate further the test of "good faith," suppose that the X Federal Agency published a general bulletin regarding manufacturing, which contained the erroneous statement that all foremen are exempt under the Fair Labor Standards Act as employed in a "bona fide executive * * * capacity." Suppose also that an employer knowing that the Administrator of the Wage and Hour Division is charged with the duties of administering the Fair Labor Standards Act and of defining the phrase "bona fide executive * * * capacity" in that Act, nevertheless relied upon the above bulletin without inquiring further and, in conformity with this advice, failed to compensate his nonexempt foremen in accordance with the overtime provisions of the Fair Labor Standards Act for work subject to that Act, performed before May 14, 1947. If the employer had inquired of the Administrator or had consulted the Code of Federal Regulations, he would have found that his foremen were not exempt. In a subsequent action brought by employees under section 16(b) of the Fair Labor Standards Act, the court may decide that the employer knew facts which ought to have put him as a reasonable man upon further inquiry, and, consequently, that he did not rely "in good faith" within the meaning of section 9, upon the bulletin published by the X Agency.

(d) Insofar as the period prior to May 14, 1947, is concerned, the employer may have received an interpretation from an agency which conflicted with an interpretation of the Administrator of the Wage and Hour Division of which he was also aware. If the employer chose to reply upon the interpretation of the other agency, which interpretation worked to his advantage, considerable weight may well be given to the fact that the employer ignored the interpretation of the agency charged with the administration of the Fair Labor Standards Act and chose instead to rely upon the interpretation of an outside agency. Under these circumstances "the question could properly be considered as to whether it was a good faith reliance or whether the employer was simply choosing a course which was most favorable to him." This problem will not arise in regard to any acts or omissions by the employer occurring on or after May 14, 1947, because section 10 provides that the employer, insofar as the Fair Labor Standards Act is concerned, may rely only upon regulations, orders, rulings, approvals, interpretations, administrative practices and enforcement policies of the Administrator of the Wage and Hour Division.

Section 790.16 - "In reliance on."

(a) In addition to acting (or omitting to act) in good faith and in conformity with an administrative regulation, order, ruling, approval, interpretation, enforcement policy or practice, the employer must also prove that he actually relied upon it.

(b) Assume, for example, that an employer failed to pay his employees in accordance with the overtime provisions of the Fair Labor Standards Act. After an employee suit has been brought against him, another employer calls his attention to a letter that had been written by the Administrator of the Wage and Hour Division, in which the opinion was expressed that employees of the type employed by the defendant were exempt from the overtime provisions of the Fair Labor Standards Act. The defendant had no previous knowledge of this letter. In the pending employee suit, the court may decide that the opinion of the Administrator was erroneous and that the plaintiffs should have been paid in accordance with the overtime provisions of the Fair Labor Standards Act. Since the employer had no knowledge of the administrator's interpretation at the time of his violations, his failure to comply with the overtime provisions could not have been "in reliance on" that interpretation; consequently, he has no defense under section 9 or section 10 of the Portal Act.

Section 790.17 - "Administrative regulation, order, ruling, approval, or interpretation."

(a) Administrative regulations, orders, rulings, approvals, and interpretations are all grouped together in sections 9 and 10, with no distinction being made in regard to their function under the "good faith" defense. Accordingly,

THE FLSA – A USER'S MANUAL (THIRD EDITION)

no useful purpose would be served by an attempt to precisely define and distinguish each term from the others, especially since some of these terms are often employed interchangeably as having the same meaning.

(b) The terms "regulation" and "order" are variously used to connote the great variety of authoritative rules issued pursuant to statute by an administrative agency, which have the binding effect of law, unless set aside upon judicial review as arbitrary, capricious, an abuse of discretion, or otherwise not in accordance with law.

(c) The term "interpretation" has been used to describe a statement "ordinarily of an advisory character, indicating merely the agency's present belief concerning the meaning of applicable statutory language." This would include bulletins, releases, and other statements issued by an agency which indicate its interpretation of the provisions of a statute.

(d) The term "ruling" commonly refers to an interpretation made by an agency "as a consequence of individual requests for rulings upon particular questions." Opinion letters of an agency expressing opinions as to the application of the law to particular facts presented by specific inquiries fall within this description.

(e) The term "approval" includes the granting of licenses, permits, certificates or other forms of permission by an agency, pursuant to statutory authority.

(f) The terms "administrative regulation order, ruling, approval, or interpretation" connote affirmative action on the part of an agency. A failure to act or a failure to reply to an inquiry on the part of an administrative agency is not a "regulation, order, ruling, approval, or interpretation" within the meaning of sections 9 and 10. Thus, suppose that an employer writes a letter to the Administrator of the Wage and Hour Division, setting forth the facts concerning his business. He goes on to state in his letter that he believes his employees are not covered by the Fair Labor Standards Act, and that unless he hears to the contrary from the Administrator, he will not pay them in accordance with its provisions. When the employer does not receive a reply to his letter within what he regards as a reasonable time, he assumes that the Administrator agrees with his (the employer's) interpretation of the Act and he acts accordingly. The employer's reliance under such circumstances is not a reliance upon an administrative regulation, order, ruling, approval or interpretation, within the meaning of sections 9 and 10.

(g) The affirmative action taken by the agency must be one which actually results in a "regulation, order, ruling, approval, or interpretation." If for example, the agency declines to express an opinion as to the application of the law in a particular fact situation, the agency is refraining from interpreting the law rather than giving an interpretation.

(h) An employer does not have a defense under these two sections unless the regulation, order, ruling, approval, or interpretation, upon which he relies, is in effect and operation at the time of his reliance. To the extent that it has been rescinded, modified, or determined by judicial authority to be invalid, it is no longer a "regulation, order, ruling, approval, or interpretation," and, consequently, an employer's subsequent reliance upon it offers him no defense under section 9 and 10. On the other hand, the last sentence in section 9 and in section 10 expressly provides that where the employer's good faith reliance on a regulation, order, ruling, approval or interpretation occurs before it is rescinded, modified, or determined by judicial authority to be invalid, his claim of a "good faith" defense for such earlier period is not defeated by the subsequent rescission or modification or by the subsequent determination of invalidity.

(i) To illustrate these principles, assume that the Administrator of the Wage and Hour Division, in reply to an inquiry received from a particular employer, sends him a letter, in which the opinion is expressed that employees performing a particular type of work are not covered by the Fair Labor Standards Act. The employer relied upon the Administrator's letter and did not pay his employees who were engaged in such work, in accordance with the provisions of the Fair Labor Standards Act. Several months later the Administrator issues a general statement, published in the Federal Register and given general distribution, that recent court decisions have persuaded him that the class of employees referred to above are within the coverage of the Fair Labor Standards Act. Accordingly, the statement continues, the Administrator hereby rescinds all his previous interpretations and rulings to the contrary. The employer who had received the Administrator's letter, not learning of the Administrator's subsequent published statement rescinding his contrary interpretations, continued to rely upon the Administrator's letter after the effective date of the published statement. Under these circumstances, the employer would, from the date he received the Administrator's letter to the effective date of the published statement rescinding the position expressed in the letter, have a defense under section 9 or 10, assuming he relied upon and conformed with that letter in good faith. However, in spite of the fact that this employer did not receive actual notice of the subsequent published statement, he has no defense for his reliance upon the letter during the period after the effective date of the public statement, because the letter, having been rescinded, was no longer an "administrative * * * ruling * * * or interpretation" within the meaning of sections 9 and 10. The fact that an employer has no defense under section 9 or 10 of the Portal Act in the situation stated in the text would not, of course, preclude a court from finding that he acted in good faith having reasonable grounds to believe he was not in violation of the law. In such event, section 11 of the Act would permit the court to reduce or eliminate the employer's liability for liquidated damages in an employee suit. See 790.22.

Section 790.18 - "Administrative practice or enforcement policy."

(a) The terms "administrative practice or enforcement policy" refer to courses of conduct or policies which an agency has determined to follow in the administration and enforcement of a statute, either generally, or with respect to specific classes of situations. Administrative practices and enforcement policies may be set forth in statements addressed by the agency to the public. Although they may be, and frequently are, based upon decisions or views which the agency has set forth in its regulations, orders, rulings, approvals, or interpretations, nevertheless administrative practices and enforcement policies differ from these forms of agency action in that such practices or policies are not limited to matters concerned with the meaning or legal effect of the statutes administered by the agency and may be based wholly or in part on other considerations.

(b) To illustrate this distinction, suppose the Administrator of the Wage and Hour Division issues a general statement indicating that in his opinion a certain class of employees come within a specified exemption from provisions of the Fair Labor Standards Act in any workweek when they do not engage in a substantial amount of nonexempt work. Such a statement is an "interpretation" within the meaning of sections 9 and 10 of the Portal Act. Assume that at the same time, the Administrator states that for purposes of enforcement, until further notice such an employee will be considered as engaged in a substantial amount of nonexempt work in any workweek when he spends in excess of a specified percentage of his time in such nonexempt work. This latter type of statement announces an "administrative practice or enforcement policy" within the meaning of sections 9 and 10 of the Portal Act.

(c) An administrative practice or enforcement policy may, under certain circumstances be at variance with the agency's current interpretation of the law. For example, suppose the Administrator announces that as a result of court decisions he has changed his view as to coverage of a certain class of employees under the Fair Labor Standards Act. However, he may at the same time announce that in order to give affected employers an opportunity to make the adjustments necessary for compliance with the changed interpretation, the Wage and Hour Division will not commence to enforce the Act on the basis of the new interpretation until the expiration of a specified period.

(d) In the statement of the managers on the part of the House, accompanying the report of the Conference Committee on the Portal-to-Portal Act, it is indicated (page 16) that under sections 9 and 10 "an employer will be relieved from liability, in an action by an employee, because of reliance in good faith on an administrative practice or enforcement policy only (1) where such practice or policy was based on the ground that an act or omission was not a violation of the (Fair Labor Standards) Act, or (2) where a practice or policy of not enforcing the Act with respect to acts or omissions led the employer to believe in good faith that such acts or omissions were not violations of the Act."

(e) The statement explaining the Conference Committee Report goes on to say, "However, the employer will be relieved from criminal proceedings or injunctions brought by the United States, not only in the cases described in the preceding paragraph, but also where the practice or policy was such as to lead him in good faith to believe that he would not be proceeded against by the United States."

(f) The statement explaining the Conference Committee Report gives the following illustrations of the above rules: An employer will not be relieved from liability under the Fair Labor Standards Act of 1938 to his employees (in an action by them) for the period December 26, 1946, to March 1, 1947, if he is not exempt under the "Area of Production" regulations published in the Federal Register of December 25, 1946, notwithstanding the press release issued by the Administrator of the Wage and Hour Division of the Department of Labor, in which he stated that he would not enforce the Fair Labor Standards Act of 1938 on account of acts or omissions occurring prior to March 1, 1947. On the other hand, he will, by reason of the enforcement policy set forth in such press releases, have a good defense to a criminal proceeding or injunction brought by the United States based on an act or omission prior to March 1, 1947.

(g) It is to be noted that, under the language of sections 9 and 10, an employer has a defense for good faith reliance on an administrative practice or an enforcement policy only when such practice or policy is "with respect to the class of employers to which he belonged." Thus where an enforcement policy has been announced pertaining to laundries and linen-supply companies serving industrial or commercial establishments the operator of an establishment furnishing window-washing service to industrial and commercial concerns, who relied upon that policy in regard to his employees, has no defense under sections 9 and 10. The enforcement policy upon which he claimed reliance did not pertain to "the class of employers to which he belonged."

(h) Administrative practices and enforcement policies, similar to administrative regulations, orders, rulings, approvals and interpretations required affirmative action by an administrative agency. This should not be construed as meaning that an agency may not have administrative practices or policies to refrain from taking certain action as well as practices or policies contemplating positive acts of some kind. But before it can be determined that an agency actually has a practice or policy to refrain from acting, there must be evidence of its adoption by the agency through some affirmative action establishing it as the practice or policy of the agency. Suppose, for example, that shoe factories in a particular area were not investigated by Wage and Hour Division inspectors operating in the area. This fact would not establish the existence of a practice or policy of the Administrator to treat the employees of such establishments, for enforcement purposes, as not subject to the provisions of the Fair Labor Standards Act, in the absence of proof of some affirmative action by the Administrator adopting such a practice or policy. A failure to inspect might be due to any one of a number of different reasons. It might, for instance, be due entirely to the fact that the inspectors' time was fully occupied in inspections of other industries in the area.

(i) It was pointed out above that sections 9 and 10 do not offer a defense to the employer who relies upon a regulation, order, ruling, approval or interpretation which at the time of his reliance has been rescinded, modified or determined by judicial authority to be invalid. The same is true regarding administrative practices and enforcement policies. However, a plea of a "good faith" defense is not defeated by the fact that after the employer's reliance, the practice or policy is rescinded, modified, or declared invalid.

Section 790.19 - "Agency of the United States."

(a) In order to provide a defense under section 9 or section 10 of the Portal Act, the regulation, order, ruling, approval, interpretation, administrative practice or enforcement policy relied upon and conformed with must be that of an "agency of the United States." Insofar as acts or omissions occurring on or after May 14, 1947 are concerned, it must be that of the "agency of the United States specified in" section 10(b), which, in the case of the Fair Labor Standards Act, is "the Administrator of the Wage and House Division of the Department of Labor." However, with respect to acts or omissions occurring prior to May 14, 1947, section 9 of the Act permits the employer to show that he relied upon and conformed with a regulation, order, ruling, approval, interpretation, administrative practice or enforcement policy of "any agency of the United States."

(b) The Portal Act contains no comprehensive definition of "agency" as used in sections 9 and 10, but an indication of the meaning intended by Congress may be found in section 10. In that section, where the "agency" whose regulation, order, ruling, approval, interpretation, administrative practice or enforcement policy may be relied on is confined to "the agency of the United States" specified in the section, the Act expressly limits the meaning of the term to the official or officials actually vested with final authority under the statutes involved. Similarly, the definitions of "agency" in other Federal statutes indicate that the term has customarily been restricted in its usage by Congress to the persons vested under the statutes with the real power to act for the Government - those who actually have the power to act as (rather than merely for) the highest administrative authority of the Government establishment. Furthermore, it appears from the statement of the managers on the part of the House accompanying the Conference Committee Report, that the term "agency" as appearing in the Portal Act was employed in this sense. As there stated (p. 16), the regulations, orders, ruling, approvals, interpretations, administrative practices and enforcement policies relied upon and conformed with "must be those of an 'agency' and not of an individual officer or employee of the agency. Thus, if inspector A tells the employer that the agency interpretation is that the employer is not subject to the (Fair Labor Standards) Act, the employer is not relieved from liability, despite his reliance in good faith on such interpretations, unless it is in fact the interpretation of the agency." Similarly, the Chairman of the Senate Judiciary Committee, in explaining the conference agreement to the Senate, made the following statement concerning the "good faith" defense. "It will be noted that the relief from liability must be based on a ruling of a Federal agency, and not a minor official thereof. I, therefore, feel that the legitimate interest of labor will be adequately protected under such a provision, since the agency will exercise due care in the issuance of any such ruling."

(c) Accordingly, the defense provided by sections 9 and 10 of the Portal Act is restricted to those situations where the employer can show that the regulation, order, ruling, approval, interpretation, administrative practice or enforcement policy with which he conformed and on which he relied in good faith was actually that of the authority vested with power to issue or adopt regulations, orders, rulings, approvals, interpretations, administrative practices or enforcement policies of a final nature as the official act or policy of the agency. Statements made by other officials or employees are not regulations, orders, rulings, approvals, interpretations, administrative practices or enforcement policies of the agency within the meaning of sections 9 and 10.

Restrictions and Limitations on Employee Suits

Section 790.20 - Right of employees to sue; restrictions on representative actions.

Section 16(b) of the Fair Labor Standards Act, as amended by section 5 of the Portal Act, no longer permits an employee or employees to designate an agent or representative (other than a member of the affected group) to maintain, an action for and in behalf of all employees similarly situated. Collective actions brought by an employee or employees (a real party in interest) for and in behalf of himself or themselves and other employees similarly situated may still be brought in accordance with the provisions of section 16(b). With respect to these actions, the amendment provides that no employee shall be a party plaintiff to any such action unless he gives his consent in writing to become such a party and such consent is filed in the court in which such action is brought. The amendment is expressly limited to actions which are commenced on or after the date of enactment of the Portal Act. Representative actions which were pending on May 14, 1947 are not affected by this amendment. However, under sections 6 and 8 of the Portal Act, a collective or representative action commenced prior to such date will be barred as to an individual claimant who was not specifically named as a party plaintiff to the action on or before September 11, 1947, if his written consent to become such a party is not filed with the court within a prescribed period.

Section 790.21 - Time for bringing employee suits.

(a) The Portal Act provides a statute of limitations fixing the time limits within which actions by employees under section 16(b) of the Fair Labor Standards Act may be commenced, as follows:

(1) Actions to enforce causes of action accruing on or after May 14, 1947, two years. (2) Actions to enforce causes of action accruing before May 14, 1947, two years or period prescribed by applicable State statute of limitations, whichever is shorter. These are maximum periods for bringing such actions, measured from the time the employee's cause of action accrues to the time his action is commenced.

(b) The courts have held that a cause of action under the Fair Labor Standards Act for unpaid minimum wages or unpaid overtime compensation and for liquidated damages "accrues" when the employer fails to pay the required compensation for any workweek at the regular payday for the period in which the workweek ends. The Portal Act provides that an action to enforce such a cause of action shall be considered to be "commenced": (1) In individual actions, on the date the complaint is filed; (2) In collective or class actions, as to an individual claimant.

(i) On the date the complaint is filed, if he is specifically named therein as a party plaintiff and his written consent to become such is filed with the court on that date, or (ii) On the subsequent date when his written consent to become a party plaintiff is filed in the court, if it was not so filed when the complaint was filed or if he was not then named therein as a party plaintiff.

(c) The statute of limitations in the Portal Act is silent as to whether or not the running of the two-year period of limitations may be suspended for any cause. In this connection, attention is directed to section 205 of the Soldiers' and Sailors' Civil Relief Act of 1940, (136) as amended, which provides that the period of military service shall not be included in the period limited by law for the bringing of an action or proceeding, whether the cause of action shall have accrued prior to or during the period of such service.

Section 790.22 - Discretion of court as to assessment of liquidated damages.

(a) Section 11 of the Portal Act provides that in any action brought under the Fair Labor Standards Act to recover unpaid minimum wages, unpaid overtime, compensation, or liquidated damages, the court may, subject to prescribed conditions, in its sound discretion award no liquidated damages or award any amount of such damages not to exceed the amount specified in section 16 (b) of the Fair Labor Standards Act.

(b) The conditions prescribed as prerequisites to such an exercise of discretion by the court are two: (1) The employers must show to the satisfaction of the court that the act or omission giving rise to such action was in good faith; and (2) he must show also, to the satisfaction of the court, that he had reasonable grounds for believing that his act or omission was not a violation of the Fair Labor Standards Act. If these conditions are met by the employer against whom the suit is brought, the court is permitted, but not required, in its sound discretion to reduce or eliminate the liquidated damages which would otherwise be required in any judgment against the employer. This may be done in any action brought under section 16(b) of the Fair Labor Standards Act, regardless of whether the action was instituted prior to or on or after May 14, 1947, and regardless of when the employee activities on which it is based were engaged in. If, however, the employer does not show to the satisfaction of the court that he has met the two conditions mentioned above, the court is given no discretion by the statute, and it continues to be the duty of the court to award liquidated damages.

(c) What constitutes good faith on the part of an employer and whether he had reasonable grounds for believing that his act or omission was not a violation of the Fair Labor Standards Act are mixed questions of fact and law, which should be determined by objective tests. Where an employer makes the required showing, it is for the court to determine in its sound discretion what would be just according to the law on the facts shown.

(d) Section 11 of the Portal Act does not change the provisions of section 16(b) of the Fair Labor Standards Act under which attorney's fees and court costs are recoverable when judgment is awarded to the plaintiff.

CHAPTER THIRTEEN
GLOSSARY OF CITATION FORMS

Throughout this book, a variety of citations to published authorities have been used. To assist you locating these authorities, the following glossary provides the full names of publications which have been referred to:

Abbreviation	Full Name
A.	Atlantic Reporter (West)
A.2d	Atlantic Reporter 2nd Series (West)
A.L.R.	Atlantic Law Reporter
C.F.R.	Code of Federal Regulations
Cl.Ct.	Claims Court Reporter
Ct.Cl.	Court of Claims Reporter
F.	Federal Reporter
F.2d	Federal Reporter 2nd Series
F.3d	Federal Reporter Third Series
F.Supp.	Federal Supplement
Fed.Cl.	Federal Claims Reporter
Fed. Reg.	Federal Register
N.E.	Northeast Reporter (West)
N.E.2d	Northeast Reporter 2nd Series (West)
N.W.	Northwest Reporter (West)
N.W.2d	Northwest Reporter 2nd Series (West)
P.	Pacific Reporter (West)
P.2d	Pacific Reporter 2nd Series (West)
So.	Southern Reporter (West)

So.2d	Southern Reporter 2nd Series
S.Ct.	Supreme Court Reporter
S.E.	Southeast Reporter (West)
S.E.2d	Southeast Reporter 2nd Series (West)
U.S.	United States Reporter
U.S.C.	Unites States Code
U.S.C.A.	United States Code Annotated
WH Cases	Wage and Hour Cases
WH Cases2d	Wage and Hour Cases 2d Series

INDEX

A

Accrual Limitations
   Compensatory time off, 149, 357
Administrative Employees, 217, 234, 306, 325
   Definition of, 234, 306
   Duties of, 236
Ahern v. State of New York, 236, 250
Aiken v. City of Memphis, 144, 157, 167
Alden v. Maine, 8, 13, 281, 283, 295
Alex v. City of Chicago, 206, 214
Allen v. United States, 92, 138
Ambulance and Rescue
   Personnel, 374
Amendments To The FLSA
   1947 Amendment, 263, 271, 443
   1961 Amendment, 3
   1966 Amendment, 3, 4, 15, 318, 352
   1972 Amendment, 352
   1974 Amendment, 4, 23, 169, 170, 352, 375
   1985 Amendment, 7, 103, 105, 108, 109, 153, 159, 274, 275, 351, 352, 356, 367
Amos v. City of Winston-Salem, 233, 245, 248
Anderson v. County of Kershaw, 58, 77
Artistic Professions, 342
Attorney Fees, 267

Auer v. Robbins, 8, 13, 33, 37, 220, 221, 222, 225, 233, 243, 247

B

Baker v. City of Pomona, 89
Bankston v. State of Illinois, 243, 261, 284, 286, 288
Beebe v. United States, 11, 86, 135, 136, 211
Berry v. County of Sonoma, 93, 94, 138
Blackie v. State of Maine, 273, 291
Brennan v. New Jersey, 147, 165
Briefing Periods, 50, 177
   7(k) exemption, 53
   Inclusion in hours worked, 85
Brock v. City of Cincinnati, 114, 144
Brooklyn Savings Bank v. O'Neal, 279, 293
Burgess v. Catawba County, 58, 77, 135, 136, 167, 208, 215, 286
Bus And Streetcar Employees, 25

C

Callback Pay, 400
   Inclusion in regular rate, 65
Canine Officers, 112
   Physical fitness programs, 127
   Premium pay, 115